ANXIETY DISORDERS IN ADULTS

GUIDEBOOKS IN CLINICAL PSYCHOLOGY

Series Editors

Larry E. Beutler
John F. Clarkin

Guidelines for the Systematic Treatment
of the Depressed Patient
Larry E. Beutler, John F. Clarkin, and Bruce Bongar

Anxiety Disorders in Adults:
An Evidence-Based Approach to Psychological Treatment
Peter D. McLean and Sheila R. Woody

Anxiety Disorders
in Adults

AN EVIDENCE-BASED APPROACH
TO PSYCHOLOGICAL TREATMENT

Peter D. McLean
Sheila R. Woody

OXFORD
UNIVERSITY PRESS

2001

OXFORD

UNIVERSITY PRESS

Oxford New York

Athens   Auckland   Bangkok   Bogotá   Buenos Aires   Calcutta
Cape Town   Chennai   Dar es Salaam   Delhi   Florence   Hong Kong   Istanbul
Karachi   Kuala Lumpur   Madrid   Melbourne   Mexico City   Mumbai
Nairobi   Paris   São Paulo   Shanghai   Singapore   Taipei   Tokyo   Toronto   Warsaw

and associated companies in

Berlin   Ibadan

Copyright © 2001 Oxford University Press, Inc.

Published by Oxford University Press, Inc.,
198 Madison Avenue, New York, New York 10016

Oxford is a registered trademark of Oxford University Press.

Library of Congress Cataloging-in-Publication Data
McLean, Peter D.
  Anxiety disorders in adults : an evidence-based approach to psychological treatment /
Peter D. McLean and Sheila R. Woody.
    p. cm.—(Guidebooks in clinical psychology)
  Includes bibliographical references and index.
  ISBN 0-19-511625-9
    1. Anxiety—Treatment.   I. Woody, Sheila R.   II. Title.   III. Series.
  RC531.M365 2000
  616.85′223—dc21   00-020809

9 8 7 6 5 4 3 2 1

Printed in the United States of America
on acid-free paper

Preface

This book aims to help bridge the gap between academics and clinicians. We have found it challenging to provide information that will please both groups. Our aim has been to provide scientific information to clinicians in a format that is accessible and relevant to everyday clinical concerns. Accordingly, we have declined to include many details of issues that are important to understanding psychosocial interventions, such as why therapy works or how the interpersonal process of therapy unfolds. Although some practitioners may find that we have included more academic information than they typically read, at each step we considered whether a given line of research had practical relevance for conducting treatment or evaluating outcomes.

The book begins with a discussion of recent events that shape the push toward evidence-based practice. In the first chapter, we outline a model of the modern scientist-practitioner that we believe better suits the demands of clinical practice today. This model describes an educated, eclectic, empirical style of therapy in which the practitioner is scientific by virtue of consuming and applying the results of empirical research—particularly research on therapy outcome. In those cases where extant research does not address the client's problem, or where a first-line treatment has failed, the clinician uses an eclectic approach relying on careful measurement of progress. In this way, the practitioner approaches therapy from a scientific perspective (with a skeptical attitude) without the expectation that a contribution to the scientific literature will result.

In chapter 2, we discuss some of the basic theoretical background in how anxiety has been conceptualized. Diagnostic classification systems have become much more elaborated and reliable in recent decades, but they inherently assume a categorical model of anxiety, whereby people with anxiety disorders are categorically different from those without a disorder. Obviously, everyone experiences anxiety at some point in their lives, so some theorists have argued that anxiety should be considered dimensionally. While this argument may seem at first to be an academic debate, most clients with anxiety disorders hold some erroneous views about the nature of anxiety, and these mistaken ideas can make it difficult to cope. Thus, the chapter on the nature of anxiety outlines several perspectives on the psychology of anxiety, including information on the behavioral, cognitive, and physiological components of anxiety.

In chapters 3 through 8, we separately discuss the most common anxiety disorders: specific phobia, social phobia, panic disorder and agoraphobia, obsessive-compulsive disorder, posttraumatic stress disorder, and generalized anxiety disorder. The emphasis in each disorder chapter is on phenomenology, assessment, and treatment outcome. Each chapter begins with a thorough overview of what is known about the psychopathology of the disorder and a discussion of various theoretical conceptualizations of the disorder. For those approaches that have been scientifically tested (usually in randomized controlled trials), we then carefully outline the mechanics of how to conduct the treatment and assess the progress of treatment. Where more detailed treatment manuals are available, we include information on how to obtain them for clinicians who are completely new to these treatment approaches.

Evaluating and improving quality of care is a theme that runs throughout the book. In the chapters focused on specific disorders, we have included copies of assessment tools useful in evaluating outcomes of treatment for anxiety disorders where possible. In the case of copyrighted instruments that we find to be particularly useful, we have also provided information on how to contact the publishers to purchase the measures. The final chapter is devoted to concrete steps to maximize quality of care, beginning with a discussion of the construct of quality as it applies to mental health care. Although the examples we use are focused on anxiety disorders, we aimed to provide guidance for monitoring quality of care that is independent of the type of population served. The chapter is primarily appropriate for those interested in applying outcomes-measurement at a local level like a group practice.

We do recognize that rigorously controlled clinical trials have some decided limitations in the degree to which they can be applied to practice, and some of these issues are discussed in chapter 1. Nevertheless, this book is based on the assumption that such trials are the best way currently available for ascertaining whether a given treatment produced changes observed in the client. Our recommendations for assessment are based on a second assumption, that psychotherapy should produce changes that are observable to the client, the clinician, and to a skeptical third party. The treatments we review in this volume have been demonstrated to produce such changes in university-based studies, and we endeavor to provide clinicians with the tools to ascertain whether they are also observing comparable changes in the practice setting. While many medications have also demonstrated good outcomes in well-controlled research, the focus of this book is on psychosocial interventions. In order to devote as much space as possible to the details of conducting these interventions, we have elected to mention medications only in passing, primarily where their use impacts on the practice of psycho-therapy.

As with any large project, we would not have been able to complete this book without the assistance of others. We particularly thank Becky Miller, who was an essential behind-the-scenes word-processing partner. Without support from our universities, collaborating from opposite ends of the conti-nent would have been impossible. We thank Yale University for a generous sabbatical year and the Psychiatry Department at University of British Co-lumbia for office space and administrative support during an extended visit.

Vancouver, British Columbia   P. D. M.
New Haven, Connecticut   S. R. W.
June 2000

Contents

ANXIETY DISORDERS IN ADULTS

1 _Evidence-Based Practice_

Several different models of the scientist-practitioner concept have emerged since the beginning of the Boulder model movement in the 1940s. Some constructions of the model have turned out to be unfeasible for the average practitioner because few have the time to fit formal research into a large caseload. At times, the concept of a scientist-practitioner has seemed like a model to which many aspire, but which few have successfully implemented. The idea of the scientist-practitioner has been disparaged as a model whose time has passed and has even been declared dead (Barlow, Hayes, & Nelson, 1984). In the past decade, however, spiraling health care costs around the world have sparked a reexamination of funding priorities. No one wants to pay for interventions that do not work, regardless of the type of problem. This emphasis on accountability encouraged practitioners to begin thinking about documenting the quality of care they administer, the outcomes of treatment, and the cost of helping (or failing to help) the client. These trends are by no means limited to psychological problems. Clinical practice guidelines have begun to appear across all areas of medicine in response to health services research showing significant variations in practice patterns and costs after adjusting for differences in the types of patients typically seen in different practice settings. Organizations that represent psychologists, psychiatrists, and health care policy analysts have also been concerned with educating practitioners and the public about treatments that have been demonstrated to work.

By attending to research that seeks to establish what treatments work for what problems and under what conditions, practitioners can effectively be scientist-practitioners without engaging in the conduct of scientific studies. Where research fails to inform the practitioner about what intervention to choose, careful measurement of the client's progress serves as a guide. In this chapter, recent developments in the scientist-practitioner movement will be reviewed, taking into special account the eclecticism that is increasingly

3

adopted by practitioners. We will discuss limitations in the applicability of scientific findings to the everyday practice of psychology, along with some of the strengths of applying manualized treatments. This contemporary perspective on the scientist-practitioner model sets the stage for later chapters in which we provide information about the results of treatment outcome studies as well as tips on how to proceed with assessment of progress during therapy. Finally, because many readers will no doubt be involved in writing treatment guidelines at the local level, we recommend some components of good guidelines to facilitate this process.

RECENT DEVELOPMENTS IN THE SCIENTIST-PRACTITIONER MOVEMENT

Which Treatments Work?

In the early 1980s, the Quality Assurance Project was begun in Australia. This ambitious project aimed to develop treatment outlines for specific emotional disorders, beginning with two common problems, depression and agoraphobia. The panel responsible for developing these outlines used three avenues for identifying which treatments work: research findings, community standards of practice, and expert opinion (Quality Assurance Project, 1982a). First, project members conducted meta-analyses of the treatment outcome literature, but their work did not stop at the library. They mounted a comprehensive survey of nearly 17% of practicing Australian psychiatrists to ascertain commonly used, but uncommonly studied, interventions. These practitioners completed questionnaires about treatment strategies they would initiate on the basis of a set of written clinical vignettes. Finally, separate panels of experts were convened to make recommendations on treatments that work for depression and agoraphobia. The members of the panel were nominated by their peers in academia, private practice, and the public sector. These three separate sources of information, formal research reports, practitioners in the field, and experts from diverse settings, were incorporated into a set of guidelines for approaching the treatment of depression and agoraphobia. These and later guidelines were directed toward practicing psychiatrists and were published in the *Australian and New Zealand Journal of Psychiatry*.

Reading through these guidelines, the difficulties of incorporating information from these separate sources becomes clear. For example, in the outline for treatment of agoraphobia (Quality Assurance Project, 1982b), meta-analyses of clinical trials revealed that the strongest consistent effects across studies were obtained with a combination of antidepressant medication and graded *in vivo* exposure. The committee noted that while results of exposure treatment were clearly robust, studies examining antidepressants needed more replication at the time the report was written. When the committee then examined community practice standards (in their survey of practicing psychiatrists), they found that the hypothetical treatment plans offered by survey respondents reflected the current state of research. Practitioners recommended essentially the same treatment plan that researchers supported. Although a number of other treatment approaches were frequently included in the hypothetical treatment plans, graded exposure was consistently listed in the top three, whether in response to a general question about treatment of agoraphobia or in response to specific vignettes for which treatment plans were to be designed. This concordance between research findings and typical practice standards allowed members of the Quality Assurance Project to present a coherent set of recommendations, which are more fully reflected in chapter 5 of this volume. The outline for treatment of obsessive-compulsive disorder (OCD) did not enjoy such happy agreement between researchers and practitioners (Quality Assurance Project, 1985), and as a result, the treatment outline fails to leave the reader with a coherent plan of action for approaching the treatment of OCD.

In the United States, the issue of health care became a hot topic in the 1992 presidential election. Once elected, President and Mrs. Clinton mounted a major attempt to reform systems of health care delivery and payment. Although many psychological interventions had good scientific evidence of efficacy, there was widespread ignorance of this evidence among the public and legislators. Division 12 (Clinical Psychology) of the American Psychological Association, under the leadership of David Barlow, appointed a Task Force to identify and publicize treatments that were known to work for specific problems. The Task Force, initially chaired by Dianne Chambless, first established relatively conservative criteria by which treatments were evaluated and classified as "well-established" or "probably efficacious," depending on the quality of scientific support each treatment had received (Task Force on Promotion and Dissemination of Psychological Procedures, 1993). The resulting lists of "empirically-validated treatments" provide examples of treatments in which the members of the Task Force have fairly strong confidence. While the lists continue to be revised and extended (Chambless, 1996; Chambless et al., 1998), many effective treatments are probably not yet included because they have not been sufficiently studied to meet the standard of proof required by the Task Force. These standards will be discussed in more detail below.

Aren't All Treatments Equally Effective?

Unlike the Quality Assurance Project described above, the Division 12 Task Force on Psychological Interventions did not perform meta-analyses of the treatment outcome literature. Each treatment was carefully examined, including all available studies in support (or in contradiction) of the treatment's efficacy. In well-publicized meta-analyses, earlier researchers had concluded that all psychotherapies were equally effective, but these earlier studies were based on treatments and samples that were not as well-defined as those available by the 1990s. If we assume for a moment that some approaches are specifically helpful for some problems (and not so helpful for other problems), then we can see that failing to carefully define a sample of clients would lead to an erroneous conclusion that all treatments are equally effective. In effect, a heterogeneous sample hides genuine differences as to which treatments are more effective for which problems. Thus, one criterion by which the Task Force selected studies was a well-defined sample. While most studies used diagnoses based on various editions of the Diagnostic and Statistical Manual (DSM), some problems examined by the Task Force were well-defined without being official diagnoses, such as binge-eating or coping with stressful life events.

In addition to including clients with a clearly specified problem, the Task Force criteria required the intervention to be well specified, so that properly trained independent clinicians would be able to deliver the same treatment. If we were to compare studies that involved treatments that were only loosely outlined, so that study therapists were largely free to use their own discretion, then it would be very difficult to find differences between the treatments, even if they differed greatly in philosophy. In practical terms, specifying the treatment usually means documenting the procedures of the treatment in a manual, from which therapists in the study are trained and supervised.

Finally, not all studies are designed equally well, so it is necessary to choose studies that have used a convincing experimental design with appropriate controls before drawing conclusions about which treatments work. Simply demonstrating that clients changed for the better during the treatment is not sufficient, because this pre-post measurement design does not conclusively rule out alternative explanations for client improvement (aside from the treatment). For example, depression is known to have an episodic course, with cycles of exacerbation and remission. A study that simply demonstrated that clients were less depressed after treatment with Therapy A would not rule out the possibility that simple passage of time would have produced the same results as Therapy A.

Therefore, as further assurance that a given treatment was specifically responsible for observed changes in clients' problems, the Task Force required that the treatment be shown to be superior to some alternative: a waitlist controlling for the passage of time and effects of assessment or a psychological placebo. Studies with a sufficiently large sample size were also included if the treatment under investigation proved to be *as effective* as another treatment that the Task Force had already judged to be effective. There were also provisions for establishing confidence in a treatment on the basis of a series of single case experimental designs.

As mentioned above, these criteria were purposefully conservative. Treatments that fail to meet the criteria for inclusion on the list are not necessarily *in*effective, because they may not have been adequately tested. Nevertheless, the Task Force lists do provide examples of therapies that have been sufficiently tested to be considered well-established or probably efficacious for treatment of specific problems. Certainly cognitive-behavioral interventions are most well-represented, because they have been investigated with research designs that fit the Task Force criteria. However, other interventions are also featured prominently, including interpersonal therapy for depression and for bulimia, hypnosis as an adjunct to cognitive-behavioral therapy (CBT) for obesity, insight-oriented marital therapy, and reminiscence therapy for depressed geriatric clients. Presently, the most recent Task Force report can be obtained from the Society for a Science of Clinical Psychology website at http://www.sscp.psych.ndsu.nodak.edu. Because research on anxiety disorders has flourished in recent years, there are many examples of treatments for anxiety that the Task Force judged to be efficacious, and almost all of these are cognitive-behavioral in approach. Most of the treatments described in this book appear on the Task Force lists.

Treatment Guidelines

Due to an increasing perception that patients sometimes receive inappropriate health and mental health care, along with rising concern over the health and economic consequences of such inappropriate care, treatment guidelines are now being widely developed in the United States and elsewhere (Smith & Hamilton, 1994). Guidelines have been issued by managed care organizations, teams of practitioners, professional associations such as the American Psychiatric Association, and governmental bodies like the Agency for Health Care Policy and Research (AHCPR). Such guidelines tend to rely on scientific findings as a basis for recommending treatment strategies, but they also recognize the role of the provider in tailoring interventions to each individual client. The AHCPR guideline for treatment of depression (Depression Guideline Panel, 1993) explicitly recommends treatments that have been studied in randomized controlled trials as first-line interventions, particularly if one approach is chosen as the sole treatment.

There are compelling reasons to extend this advice to treatment of anxiety disorders. As highlighted in the report from the NIMH-sponsored Consensus Development Conference on Panic (Wolfe & Maser, 1994), the nature of the therapeutic relationship makes it unlikely that a client will feel comfortable seeking additional or alternative treatment, due to feelings of loyalty to the therapist. Thus, if the clinician has misplaced confidence in one form of psychotherapy, the client may not be able to obtain a more effective treatment. The Panic Consensus Statement goes on to caution that failure to provide an empirically supported treatment, when one exists, may constitute malpractice in some states, as legislation has been proposed that recognizes treatment guidelines as standards of care. By starting with an empirically supported treatment, if one exists, and carefully monitoring outcomes to guide the course of treatment, clinicians can be confident that they are providing the highest quality of care.

Clinical guidelines have been developed by many agencies, both public and private, and these guidelines vary greatly in quality. Because psychologists have expertise in methodology for evaluating assessment and treatment strategies, the American Psychological Association formed its own Task Force to develop a template to promote comprehensiveness and consistency in various guidelines. The report from this Task Force was approved by the APA Council of Representatives in February of 1995 (Task Force on Psychological Intervention Guidelines, 1995). See Barlow and Barlow (1995) for an accessible and helpful overview of the template. The template provides a type of road map for those groups who wish to formulate practice guidelines. Although the template recommends the same reliance on the research literature for identifying efficacious treatments as the one we have outlined, the template also recommends considering the feasibility and applicability of research findings in each local setting.

The need for such a template is evident even when examining such thorough treatment guidelines as those established by the Quality Assurance Project in Australia. Comparing the various guidelines for different disorders produced by members of this project reveals differences in the type and amount of direction offered to clinicians. For example, the guideline on agoraphobia carefully outlines recommendations for the therapist, such as the importance of establishing a good working alliance or the utility of involving significant others to prevent disruptions to the family system that might otherwise be caused by dramatic changes in the client's behavior. This guideline even estimates the amount of therapist time required for each phase of assessment and specific treatment. The other guidelines on anxiety disorders are not quite as thorough or direct in their recommendations to clinicians.

Managed Care

These days, most conversations with clinicians about practice issues in places like the United States seem to turn rather quickly to the topic of managed care. Experimenting with different ways of containing health care costs while delivering good quality care has become a worldwide trend. Even practitioners in countries with well-established national health care systems such as Canada have found themselves dealing with capitated plans, preapproval of treatment, and other administrative hurdles. Worrisome stories of limited access to care abound among clinicians, but the managed care movement can also have some positive benefit for our field by encouraging clinicians to be accountable for the effectiveness of their interventions, thereby winning increasing public support.

In days past, insurance plans routinely picked up the tab for psychotherapy with few, if any, checks and balances to assure independent judgment that treatment was actually needed or useful for the client. While most clinicians undoubtedly had the best intentions, this system of reimbursement created an incentive for continued therapy—because the clinician's income depended on it! Nowadays, the clinician may be permitted a very limited number of sessions in which to help the client. Thus, today's mental health care professional needs to be skilled in empirically supported interventions, so that these approaches can be considered as possible components of a brief treatment plan. With only a few sessions to work with, the therapist is pressured to first try interventions that have demonstrated efficacy.

As with all businesses, the "bottom line" drives privately owned health care provider organizations. Some unscrupulous outfits may aim to increase profits by simply cutting costs—perhaps including costs legitimately associated with provision of necessary services. This strategy may be summed up by "what is cheapest is best" (Pincus, 1994), and clinicians may be caught in a conflict between this philosophy and their professional ethics to provide good care. As fully capitated plans become more common, managed care organizations are beginning to recognize that inappropriately limiting treatment may save dollars for one department (for example, behavioral health), but will inevitably cost another department (for example, primary care) because the patient's problem was not resolved. In this system of health care coverage, the managed care organization has a financial incentive to encourage clinicians to choose interventions that are likely to be inexpensive *and* effective as first-line treatment. As managed care organizations become more adept at collecting data on quality and outcomes of care, treatment standards and guidelines hopefully will more fully reflect "best practices" (Pallack, 1995).

THE EDUCATED ECLECTIC EMPIRICIST

More and more mental health professionals identify their theoretical orientation as eclectic, but it is not clear whether this is a positive development. Some skeptical observers have argued that eclecticism results in therapists who know a little about a lot of different approaches, so that the result is casually planned treatment that is poorly justified by research or theory (Fonagy & Target, 1996). And it is certainly true that the scientific community offers little help to the practicing clinician who wishes to fashion a treatment plan composed of a little of this and a little of that, as most clinical trials use relatively pure (and intensive) forms of a single treatment. There will never be enough resources to do clinical trials comparing all possible permutations of treatment plans for all types of clients who seek help. Even large and expensive studies, while important in establishing treatments that are effective in general, fail to provide sufficient guidance to the individual clinician formulating a treatment plan for a specific client who may have multiple problems.

The word "eclectic" does not have to connote a lack of thorough knowledge or a haphazard approach to treatment planning. A clinician who embraces this label may also be one who eschews rigid adherence to any one theoretical orientation, be that psychodynamic, cognitive-behavioral, family systems, or any other. If solid theoretical orientation does not ground this modern eclectic clinician, then what principles guide assessment and treatment planning? Scientifically sound practice calls for an *educated eclectic empiricist*. This elaboration on the concept of eclectic practice involves a clinician who uses a system of checks and balances between the scientific literature (*educated*), a variety of tested interventions (*eclectic*), and sound measurement (*empiricist*). This approach requires the clinician to stay informed about recent developments in treatment research and to seek supervised training in new innovations with promising research support. We wrote this book in an effort to help with that process by providing a combination of information about scientific findings along with details about how to conduct treatments that have empirical support for treatment of anxiety disorders.

In the best-researched areas of psychopathology, there are often several empirically supported treatments to choose from, and the clinician should first rely on available research findings that guide patient-treatment matching. However, sometimes there is conflicting research, or there may be no research on the pattern of problems a specific client brings to therapy. Clinicians are often left to their own creativity (with assistance from theoretical understanding of psychopathology, human development, and sociology) to devise a treatment plan. Regular measurement using reliable and valid instruments provides the eclectic clinician with the means for more confidently deciding when to maintain an ongoing intervention and when to switch to a new approach. Evidence-based practice, then, rests on three interlocking components: knowledge of the scientific findings, effective transfer of technology from science to practice, and sound measurement of client progress. Each of these three components will be discussed in turn.

Scientific Literature

Clinicians have been taking a beating in the psychological press in the last few years. There have been numerous articles (e.g., Wilson, 1996) that have attempted to debunk myths involving the value of clinical judgment and clinical experience. Popular books, such as *House of Cards* by Robyn Dawes (1994) and *We've Had a Hundred Years of Psychotherapy and the World's Getting Worse* by Hillman and Ventura (1993), have blasted clinicians by painting them as ignorant of important principles of psychology and ineffective in alleviating emotional distress. It would be easy to become defensive in the face of the critical (and sometimes hostile) tone taken by some of these writers, but it is just as important to recognize the limitations of conventional clinical wisdom as it is to be aware of the shortcomings of current scientific methods. The useful point these writers make is that human beings cannot be relied upon to make unbiased judgments, even when we try.

Cognitive biases outside of our awareness influence our judgments, with well-documented processes such as the fundamental attribution error, judgment heuristics, and the confirmatory bias. Many examples are available from the research literature to document the influence of these cognitive biases on clinician judgment. For example, studies have demonstrated that criterion-based diagnoses and those based on our clinical judgment do not correspond very well (McFall, Murburg, Smith, & Jensen, 1991; Morey & Ochoa, 1989). Garb (1994) concludes that clinically based diagnoses seem to be based on the representativeness heuristic, in which the clinician makes a judgment by deciding whether an individual is representative of a category. Chapman and Chapman (1967) concluded that clinicians make personality judgments about clients on the basis of illusory correlations, which are examples of the availability heuristic. The availability heuristic involves making judgments that are influenced by the ease with which examples can be remembered. Thus, a highly salient client behavior may be seen by the clinician as more widely characteristic of the client. Clinical judgment can also be influenced by anchoring heuristics, in which clinicians rely more on initial impressions than on information presented later. For example, Garb outlines evidence that clinicians frequently are influenced by prior diagnoses that a client may carry (a labeling bias), even when they believe they are not influenced by this information.

When people initially learn about the results obtained in Stanley Milgram's famous experiments on obedience (Milgram, 1974), most balk at the idea that they probably would have behaved in a similar way if they had been subjects in the experiment. The majority of Milgram's participants delivered what they believed were dangerous levels of electric shock to another person out of obedience to the experimenter. In a similar vein, most clinicians would like to believe that our training and years of experience prevent us from falling into the types of cognitive errors studied by social psychologists. "Other clinicians might make those errors," the thinking goes, "but my judgment feels sound to me."

In fact, confidence in one's judgments is no indication of their validity. As Garb (1994) reviews, when making predictions about which clients would remain in treatment, which children in a classroom were receiving psychological services, or expected behavior patterns of a normal subject, clinicians' judgments were overconfident. On the other hand, when using Halstead-Reitan neuropsychological test battery results to classify patients, clinicians were *underconfident*, meaning that they classified patients more reliably by using test results than they believed they did. There is no shame in the fallibility of clinical judgment, because cognitive biases arise through no personal faults and probably cannot be transcended so long as one remains human! The real shame is in failing to acknowledge our limitations in making judgments and in failing to take steps to use actuarial and statistical data to make clinical decisions when possible.

A documented example of the value of empirical predictors over clinician judgment is offered in a patient-treatment matching study (Kadden, Cooney,

Getter, & Litt, 1989). This study identified three patient factors identified in previous research as having prognostic significance in alcoholism. Patients being discharged from an inpatient alcohol dependence unit were assigned to one of two aftercare treatments: behavioral coping skills or interactional therapy. The authors predicted that patient characteristics would interact with treatment type in determining the number of abstinent days each patient achieved.

In a subset of their sample, researchers asked primary therapists from the inpatient treatment to make a recommendation about which aftercare treatment would most likely benefit their patient. By chance, 18 of these patients had been assigned to the recommended treatment, and 15 had been assigned to the nonrecommended treatment. By the end of aftercare, the mean number of heavy drinking days in the last 6 months was 11.2 for patients who had received the recommended treatment. Although the difference was not statistically significant, patients who received the treatment their primary therapist did *not* recommend were doing even better, with an average of only 5.3 heavy drinking days. These results are humbling for those of us who make such recommendations, and they certainly highlight the need for more patient-treatment matching research.

Clinicians have not been standing still for all this criticism of clinical wisdom! Numerous articles have appeared that sharply criticize the kinds of clinical information that contemporary researchers fail to consider. Research findings, as dull as they may sometimes be, are born out of the scientific method, which seeks to construct experiments to limit the effects of human judgment errors on conclusions about cause and effect. While much information may be left out of each individual study, there is no denying the powerful advances that have been made in various basic and applied fields by implementing the basic rule of manipulating only one variable at a time. Educating oneself about clinical research, and using that information to guide assessment and treatment planning, is one way to increase the validity of clinical decision making.

Arguably, the most important scientific findings for clinical practice are treatment outcome studies. There are many different types of treatment studies, ranging from a single case report to a large multicenter effort that may enroll hundreds of clients. Some studies simply aim to report on a strategy that was used with a particularly interesting client, with apparent good results. Other studies apply more controls to boost confidence that the treatment was the critical factor in helping the client to feel better. After a treatment is demonstrated to benefit clients with a given problem, still more research is done because these treatments are likely to have multiple components. In an effort to make treatment more efficient and cost-effective, researchers attempt to dismantle these multiple components, searching for the essential effective ingredients of the intervention. These different types of studies may be published in as many as 20 different journals; each tells a different piece of the story about effective treatment; some may yield conflicting results. Even the most highly specialized practicing clinician has difficulty keeping up with all these lines of research; the generalist would seem doomed.

Despite all the criticisms and drawbacks of treatment guidelines, lists of empirically supported treatments, and manualized therapy, their educational value for both practicing clinicians and the lay public is considerable if these tools are carefully developed. Guidelines are ideally prepared by teams of individuals who thoroughly review the literature in a search for all available treatment studies focusing on a given problem. These teams inevitably run into conflicting evidence, gaps in information, and controversy about how to weigh different studies using different methodologies. Ideally, consistent decision rules are adopted, and the result is a document that guides clinicians as far as current science will take us. Admittedly, this process stops far short of the full information a practitioner needs, but these tools can provide a shortcut for the busy clinician to keep abreast of current research. Certainly many of the studies upon which a guideline is based will be flawed, and there are also many effective treatments that will not be included in such guidelines because they have yet to be adequately tested. Scientific findings do not have to be the complete guide to clinical procedures, because the educated eclectic empiricist has other tools for evidence-based practice, such as outcomes measurement.

Transfer of Technology

Most contemporary treatment outcome studies use written manuals to train research therapists to implement interventions reliably. These manuals vary considerably in their degree of detail. Some simply outline a general philosophy about the approaches that are considered to be consistent with the intervention. Others are extremely structured, with instructions for what therapists should do in session-by-session detail, including recommendations therapists should make for between-session activities. Manuals with a mid-range degree of detail might specify therapist behaviors in the early sessions and then outline a general approach for later sessions. Some of these manuals have been published; others may be available from the authors for a small photocopying charge. Recent listings of available manuals for some well-established treatments have been published (Sanderson & Woody, 1995; Woody & Sanderson, 1998), including some training centers where professionals can obtain supervised experience implementing these treatments. (This listing of manuals can also be found on the website for the Society for a Science of Clinical Psychology, listed earlier in this chapter.)

Treatment manuals provide details of the treatment that was implemented in research trials. As such, they offer promise for efficient ways of transferring technology developed in the laboratory into community settings where most people are treated. Use of manuals to train psychotherapists has been shown to reduce between-therapist variability in outcome. In essence, using a manual ensures more consistent outcome across different clients treated by each therapist. Especially for those therapists who had less formal supervision prior to the training, use of a manual to train experienced psychotherapists to perform a short-form version of dynamic therapy has resulted in better client outcomes (Henry, 1991, cited in Moras, 1993).

Treatments in the Real World

When facing an individual client in the therapy room, how should clinicians go about adapting treatment protocols? How is the clinician to decide which modifications to the manual, if any, are required? Many treatment protocols written for research provide little help for the clinician faced with a challenging differential diagnosis or a client with multiple problems that seem to be functionally related. Another factor to consider may be the need to tailor a treatment plan for a client with chronic problems who frequently returns to the clinic with relapses. The episodic model of treatment, in which treatment occurs in brief episodes over the life span of a client with chronic problems, is not typically addressed in treatment manuals written for randomized controlled trials.

Therapists in the community may also need to negotiate treatment goals with the client, particularly with those clients who have multiple problems. Some problems may worry the therapist more than they concern the client, particularly problems that are commonly minimized by clients, such as eating disorders or substance abuse. In other situations, the client may have one problem for which there is a well-established treatment, but this problem is not the primary complaint. For example, a woman was referred to one of our clinics by her family physician for treatment of panic disorder with agoraphobia. The woman's fear was intense enough that she had changed job assignments several times to avoid frightening situations such as elevators or rooms full of co-workers. Despite her intense anxiety (for which there are readily available empirically supported treatments), this woman was even more disturbed by her relationship with her long-term boyfriend. He frequently criticized her mistakes and repeatedly broke off the relationship. The couple usually reunited a few days later, after the client had experienced harrowing anxiety that occasionally resulted in brief hospitalizations. These problems were clearly intertwined, and we struggled in our treatment team with how to prioritize her problems for a sensible treatment plan.

In the end, the therapist decided to begin with relaxation training, then to proceed with an exposure-based treatment to help her with the agoraphobic avoidance. The reasoning was twofold. First, the therapist anticipated that the client might feel more independent of her boyfriend if she felt more free to go places or socialize without him. Second, the therapist felt confident in the research literature supporting the treatment for agoraphobia, but he was less confident in his ability to help her make changes in her relationship without her boyfriend's participation in treatment. Although she consented to the treatment plan, the client clearly had her own treatment plan in mind. She grudgingly complied with in-session exposure but did not comply very well with homework exposure. Although she was happy to see progress with her avoidance, she repeatedly let the therapist know that she really wanted to be working more directly on her relationship issue, which the therapist agreed to do after meeting some of the agoraphobia-related treatment goals.

Although this treatment had a moderately good outcome, this is an example of a client who essentially was offered a nonpreferred treatment plan. This probably is not uncommon in research settings, as conducting a randomized controlled trial requires some randomization! There is some evidence that matching a treatment plan to the client's preferences might have an impact on outcome, although the mechanism for this advantage is unclear. One interesting analogue study looked at this question with snake-fearful participants (Devine & Fernald, 1973). Before therapy, each participant viewed four videotapes of therapists using specific methods of treatment: systematic desensitization, an encounter approach, rational-emotive therapy, and participant modeling. Participants stated a preference for which treatment they wished to receive. Then they were randomly assigned to their preferred treatment, a nonpreferred treatment, or a random treatment. The therapies were all reasonably effective in this sample, but participants receiving their preferred treatment showed less fear of snakes at posttest than those receiving a random or nonpreferred mode of treatment.

Client preference is one way to choose a treatment plan for a given client, but there are clearly others. Many investigators have attempted to identify client factors, such as personality, attributional style, or social functioning, that facilitate success in different therapies. Researchers in the treatment of alcoholism have been perhaps the most dedicated to pursuing this issue in recent years (Mattson, 1995). Even in other specialty areas, the therapist is often faced with choices between several effective treatments that use very different approaches to achieve the same goals. Would certain types of clients benefit more from Therapy A, while others more often succeed in Therapy B? Should the therapist choose a treatment that uses strategies that complement the client's strengths, or one that uses techniques that might provide the client with skills in areas that are currently weak? In a cost-conscious health care environment, the therapist is under pressure to try to initially implement a treatment that has the highest chance of working.

Some evidence suggests it may be better to play on a client's strengths by choosing a treatment that is compatible with the client's personality and cognitive style. As one example, Liberman (1978) reported a study that examined the relationship between locus of control and attribution for success in treatment. In this study, some clients were encouraged to attribute symptom improvement to their own efforts in complying with treatment. Those clients with a primarily internal locus of control had superior outcomes in this condition. In another condition, however, clients were led to believe that a pill placebo was responsible for observed improvement. In this case, the clients with a primarily external locus of control showed better outcomes. These results suggest that when the attribution for improvement matched the client's general world view, the client was able to make better use of the treatment. In the area of anxiety disorders, some investigators have recommended that therapists use a client's primary response profile (cognitive, behavioral, or physiological) as a guide to treatment matching (Menzies, 1996).

Although patient-treatment matching is an appealing concept, the research is difficult to do because clients can be categorized in so many different ways. Combinations of different factors, like attributional style as it interacts with response profile, may impact on optimal treatment matching. At this point, research is still underway, and it is probably too soon to offer general practical recommendations about patient-treatment matching. There is reason to stay tuned to the research literature on this point, however, because implicit judgments that therapists make about clients can influence recommendations. Applying research results in the formulation of treatment plans will help to reduce the effect of the types of implicit biases discussed earlier and will facilitate evidence-based practice.

Fidelity and Competence

Treatment manuals written for research therapy may need modification when they are applied in clinic settings, but there obviously is a limit to how much the treatment can be altered and yet still be considered the same therapy. Treatment guidelines urge clinicians to choose therapies with demonstrated empirical support as first-line interventions. How important is it, really, to maintain treatment fidelity when implementing these strategies in the clinic? Though this question is only beginning to draw research attention, several interesting studies have addressed this point.

In one study done in Germany, 120 phobic clients (78% had agoraphobia) were treated in one of three conditions designed to test the value of individually tailoring a treatment plan (Schulte, Kunzel, Pepping, & Schulte-Bahrenberg, 1992). In the first condition, therapists who were trained in behavior therapy, and supervised by experienced therapists, provided individualized therapy to their clients. Therapists were permitted to use all methods commonly employed in CBT approaches, and the number of sessions was also individualized (to a maximum of 36 sessions). In the second condition, therapists were asked to adhere to a 5-page manual describing exposure treatment plus a version of cognitive restructuring. Treatment length was predetermined at 25 sessions.

Finally, a third group received a "yoked" treatment. Clients in this group were treated with a treatment plan that had been individualized and implemented with a specific client in the individualized group. Essentially, a treatment was individualized to one client but applied to another (i.e., clients received someone else's treatment). In this way, the methods were comparable between a client in the third group and the matched client in the individualized group, but for the "yoked" client, the treatment plan was constructed without any knowledge about the client. Many of the therapists treated clients in more than one condition. Contrary to the investigators' expectations, tailoring the treatment to suit the individual client did not lead to better results than the standardized treatment. In fact, clients in the manualized therapy obtained better outcomes, despite the fact that the therapists were equally experienced. Clients in each group were comparably severe, and there were equivalent numbers of dropouts from each group. Fidelity ratings by therapists and supervisors indicated near-perfect adherence to the manual. Schulte et al. (1992) point out that the results may only be valid for a homogeneous group of clients with phobias. Similar results have been found in a sample of clients with obsessive-compulsive disorder (Emmelkamp, Bouman, & Blaauw, 1994), in which there were no differences between standardized and individualized treatment, despite the greater variety of procedures used by the individualized therapists.

Neil Jacobson and his colleagues (Jacobson et al., 1989) conducted a similar study, in which distressed couples were treated with social learning-based marital therapy. In this study, all therapists participated in both the manualized version and the individually tailored version of the treatment. However, unlike in the Schulte et al. (1992) study, these therapists were constrained from engaging in any intervention that did not appear in the standardized manual, although they were not required to use all the interventions. Strategies could also be implemented in any order that therapists thought appropriate. There were no differences between the two versions of the therapy at posttest. At 6 months follow-up, a few couples in the research-structured treatment had relapsed. However, there were also several couples in that group who continued to improve during the follow-up period, which was not true for the group who had received individualized treatment. The similarities between the two treatment conditions prevent strong conclusions about the effects of deviation from a treatment manual. On the other hand, if the results can be generalized to other treatments, the results imply that simply rearranging the order of techniques and leaving out procedures that seem not to be appropriate for a given client will not rob a treatment of its power.

Use of treatment manuals does appear to reduce therapist variance, but it does not eliminate individual differences between therapists (Luborsky, McLellan, Woody, O'Brien, & Auerbach, 1985). Simply following the treatment guideline or manual is not sufficient; skill is also important. An example used by Sanderson (1997) illustrates this point by making an analogy to surgeons. A given surgical technique may be effective when implemented appropriately, but different skill levels of surgeons (and different patient factors) may affect outcome. As Sanderson argues, this phenomenon does not take away from the effectiveness of the surgery, but instead puts the emphasis on proper training to maximize successful implementation of the procedure.

Without wanting to stretch this analogy too far, with surgeons it is clear that procedural adherence is but one component of competence, and several parallels can be drawn to psychological practice. Components of the surgical procedure may be applied with more or less skill, resulting in outcome differences. For example, one may close an incision with such skill that little trace of scar remains, which would most likely improve patient satisfaction even if there were no direct medical consequences. Likewise, a psychological procedure, say psychoeducation about the nature of the anxiety response, can be performed with such skill that the client feels as though all the therapist's comments are personalized for that client, even though the therapist has relayed the same information to dozens of clients. Alternatively, the same information can be presented in such a way that the client feels that s/he is receiving "drive-thru" therapy. While the content of both applications of the procedure may technically represent high adherence, the skill level (and therapeutic alliance) of the former is likely to be much higher.

Another important aspect of skillful practice is handling of unexpected events during treatment; such emergent situations are typically not addressed by procedural guidelines. This undoubtedly arises frequently in a surgeon's practice. Patients may be on medications or have comorbid medical conditions that complicate the surgical plan; they may be obese or elderly; in the midst of surgery for one problem, another is surprisingly discovered. The skill with which surgeons handle these unexpected developments no doubt contributes to the success of the procedure. Likewise, therapist skill and professional judgment will continue to be important aspects of evidence-based practice even as treatment guidelines and manuals become more widely disseminated. The therapist implementing a manualized treatment needs skill to respond to the changing emotional needs of the client while implementing specific psychological procedures. In addition, there are common factors of good psychotherapy that appear to transcend specific psychological procedures. These common factors appear in many cases to be necessary (though not always sufficient) for effective treatment; these factors probably require as much therapist skill as specified techniques.

Common Factors

If there is one issue on which clinicians and scientists come to agreement, it is that a positive working relationship is essential to the conduct of successful psychotherapy—of whatever orientation. The research literature is thoroughly summarized in an ambitious meta-analysis of the impact of diverse process measures on outcome conducted by Orlinsky, Grawe, and Parks (1994). After examining 132 research reports, they concluded that therapeutic alliance has a significant positive association with outcome in 66% of these studies. Only one study reported a negative association between alliance and outcome. These findings seem to be robust regardless of whether the alliance is measured from the perspective of the therapist, the client, or an objective observer.

Therapeutic alliance is a comprehensive concept, so the working relationship has been broadly divided into bond and task components for better specification. The social-emotional bond between therapist and client encompasses communication style and mutual affect—the quality of personal rapport. The instrumental aspect of therapeutic work includes collaboration on treatment goals and mutual coordination of therapeutic tasks—the quality of teamwork between therapist and client. Research on aspects of the therapeutic bond has often demonstrated that mutual respect and liking between the participants in the therapy process is related to positive outcome. Evidence of the impact of bond on outcome is perhaps strongest for continuation in therapy. Poor alliance in terms of bond-related factors can contribute to premature termination. For example, Kokotovic and Tracey (1987) reported that client satisfaction and perceptions of therapist trustworthiness and expertness were related to clients' failure to return to the clinic for scheduled appointments following intake in a university counseling center. Another study reported that clients who dropped out early had reported poor bond-related alliance at the initial screening interview (Mohl, Martinez, Ticknor, Huang, & Cordell, 1991). Clients who terminated prematurely liked the clinician less, felt less liked and respected by the clinician, and experienced a weaker helping alliance than clients who remained in treatment.

Specific components of the instrumental work involved in therapy have also been highlighted as probably effective in contributing to good treatment outcome. Some of the tasks that cut across theoretical orientations include providing an explanation for the problem and a rationale for treatment, instilling hope through encouraging feedback to the client, and provision of coping skills. In most forms of treatment, as Wilson (1996) points out, clinicians supplement these coping skills by helping clients make a commitment to change despite inevitable ambivalence and setbacks in the process. Currently available treatment manuals often fail to instruct clinicians in relevant relationship-building or general interviewing skills (Moras, 1993), although some do provide tips on fostering a collaborative relationship (Beck, Rush, Shaw, & Emery, 1979). As treatment guidelines and manualized treatments become more popular, future generations of manuals will hopefully strengthen their instruction on common factors in the application of specific interventions.

In summary, scientific findings are a helpful foundation on which to base evidence-based practice. Transferring the psychological interventions, or technology, developed in clinical laboratories is probably most efficiently begun with treatment manuals. However, as we have seen, these manuals uniformly fall short of being cookbooks for good practice—one cannot simply pick up a manual, follow the directions, and expect good treatment outcome. A skillful therapist adheres to the manual as appropriate, making adjustments for individual clients and clinic settings, all in the context of a respectful and collaborative relationship that fosters the client's ability and willingness to change. As current manifestations of treatment guidelines and manuals admittedly fail to adequately convey the complexities of actual clinical practice, the educated eclectic empiricist requires a third guidepost for evidence-based practice. That guidepost is outcomes measurement.

Measurement of Client Progress

At their best, clinical guidelines and protocols offer a statement about which interventions are most likely to be beneficial to the average client with a particular problem, usually a DSM diagnosis, that relies heavily on research results. However, research often stops far short of the information needed to make sound clinical decisions. For example, studying clinical problems that are not DSM diagnoses has become extremely difficult because researchers cannot secure funding for these projects. In most cases, the use of DSM diagnoses in research has improved the reliability of diagnostic assessment, reducing error variance and improving internal validity. However, as Goldfried and Wolfe (1996) point out, even problems that are relatively well-defined, such as lack of assertiveness, cannot be adequately studied if the DSM is the sole definition of psychological problems. This obviously limits the degree to which clinicians can rely on research results to guide their work when building assertiveness skills for clients with problems like agoraphobia, social phobia, or depression.

Reliance on DSM categories is just one of the facets of treatment outcome research that limits the applicability of research to clinical practice. Investigators typically exercise considerable control over sample selection (e.g., excluding clients with certain comorbid disorders) and delivery of the intervention (e.g., frequent supervision and adherence meetings). In initial efforts to determine the benefits of a given psychological intervention, these procedures are essential to ensure that the intervention is given the best chance of success by reducing variance due to factors associated with heterogeneous clients, settings, or therapist style. As a result, efficacy studies demonstrate the probability of benefit to individuals in a defined population from a technology applied for a given problem under *ideal* conditions of use (Brook & Lohr, 1985). Because the conditions in a treatment study are tightly controlled where possible, the results demonstrate the potential of a given intervention, rather than its actual effects when applied in a decidedly uncontrolled community-based practice. Such well-controlled studies may provide overly optimistic assessments of course of treatment (including expected duration of treatment), patient outcomes, and economic benefits of treatment delivery. In other words, establishing the efficacy of a treatment does not necessarily establish that the treatment is efficient or practical. Differences between randomized controlled trials and clinical practice are even more poignant when one recalls that treatment outcome researchers examine average effects for groups of clients, whereas the individual clinician is interested in treatment planning and prognostication for a single client.

Few clients resemble the "average" client, so clinicians must constantly monitor client progress to make sure that the recommended treatment is indeed being effective. This ongoing measurement is just as essential when applying a well-established treatment as it is when treating a client whose problems have been poorly researched, because not all clients improve with even the best-researched approaches. The assessment plan must include at least some measures that are administered periodically during the course of treatment, to guide necessary changes in the treatment plan in the event the client is not improving as expected. Measures that specifically apply to the client's problem will probably be more useful than global measures (Nelson-Gray, 1996). Throughout this book, we will provide recommendations of specific measures useful for repeated efficient measurement of problems associated with anxiety disorders.

Implementing a consistent system of outcomes measurement can also improve quality of care in a group practice or multidisciplinary clinic setting. Fonagy and Target (1996) used the term *clinical audit* to describe this type of accountability. In addition to shaping treatment and discharge plans, a clinical audit can help practice managers to identify gaps in skills or training among staff members. The prospect of clinical audits may be threatening to many staff members because of concerns about job security. However, responsibly conveyed information from clinical audits can help clinicians to base their plans for continuing education on an objective assessment of their areas of weakness, thus working to ameliorate these deficiencies, improving quality of care and treatment outcomes.

Formulating a plan for assessment is an essential part of a treatment plan, but one that is often ignored. Most frequently, treatment plans include behavioral objectives or goals, as well as planned interventions to help the client reach these objectives. Ideally, the treatment plan includes a timetable for administering specific assessments, and an explicit statement of how the results of those assessments relate to the treatment goals. In addition, it is helpful if the clinician is able to set specific criteria for termination. How much progress on each goal is expected before stopping treatment? After how many sessions of nonimprovement on a given goal does the clinician consider shifting strategies or providers? In a paper designed to assist clinicians who are considering developing an outcomes-management database, Clement—himself a full-time practitioner—outlined some specific considerations for treatment planning including explicit suggestions for database design (Clement, 1996).

When a first-line treatment fails, or research fails to clearly point to an empirically supported treatment, having a reliable and valid system of outcomes measurement can help the practitioner maintain accountability in psychotherapy. Therapists must resort to a hypothesis-testing approach at that point, and using data from the client about whether progress is being made helps to minimize the effects of the therapist judgment biases discussed earlier. Failure to respond to empirically supported treatments might be a criterion to transfer the client to a doctoral-level consultant or specialist if treatment is being done in a multidisciplinary team setting (Wilson, 1996).

To conclude, evidence-based practice provides a practical way for individual clinicians to be scientist-practitioners. By basing treatment plans on scientific findings where possible and taking advantage of the well-specified psychological procedures offered in treatment manuals, the practitioner is a consumer of science as it applies to practice. Because clinical guidelines will never provide all the information a clinician needs for effective practice, the final component of evidence-based practice is regular measurement of client progress. Reliable and valid measurement is perhaps the most efficient and relevant way that clinicians can bring the scientific method to bear on practice. The best treatment guidelines incorporate recommendations for clinicians at each of the three levels, outlining relevant research findings, specifying psychological interventions, and describing useful assessment procedures. In the next section, we will discuss components of clinical guidelines in more detail.

COMPONENTS OF GOOD GUIDELINES

One of the most common concerns that clinicians express about the proliferation of treatment guidelines is that guidelines will hamstring good therapists and limit their ability to make solid clinical decisions. Certainly, poorly constructed guidelines (or guidelines written for the sole purpose of containing costs) have this potential, which is one reason the APA Task Force on Psychological Intervention Guidelines set out to disseminate a template for guidelines that are developed for the benefit of clients. We include a discussion of the issues here as a guide to clinicians who may be developing treatment guidelines for their own organizations.

Well-constructed guidelines have several features that aim to maximize quality of care and capitalize on the wisdom and experience of practicing clinicians. One example has been the proposal that treatment guidelines be built upon what especially effective therapists actually *do* in practice (Chambless, 1996). This would involve identifying particularly effective therapists and codifying their behaviors so that other clinicians might replicate these interventions. Although some work has been done to identify especially effective therapists in the context of research therapy (Blatt, Sanislow, Zuroff, & Pilkonis, 1996), at present this suggestion remains an unrealized ideal. The Quality Assurance Project discussed earlier did include practicing psychiatrists' views on appropriate treatment planning, but these were based on the psychiatrists' responses to written clinical vignettes. The psychiatrists stated which treatments they would recommend in each case, and they noted which treatment they would consider to be critical. This is obviously very different from studying what clinicians actually do.

In the absence of sufficient resources to codify the practices of particularly effective clinicians, committees constructing guidelines should nonetheless include clinicians in the process. Clinician input will help to ensure that implicit community standards of practice are incorporated into the guideline. In addition, practitioners are more likely to embrace clinical guidelines if they participate in their development. In this way, treatment guidelines can be a forum in which clinicians educate each other about useful interventions. Good guidelines should maximize therapist choice among potentially effective treatments. The APA Template for Developing Guidelines also recommends that proposed guidelines be widely distributed to providers (and consumers if possible) before the guidelines are adopted. This provides an avenue by which affected practitioners can offer comments even if they were not personally involved in the development committee.

Some of the concern that practitioners have about treatment guidelines may stem from a misconception of what good guidelines (the ones constructed with client welfare in mind) actually are. Treatment guidelines are necessarily somewhat flexible, because they are written to be applicable to a wide variety of clients. True, most current guidelines are disorder-based, but clients are all remarkably unique, despite shared disorders. Thoughtful guidelines take into account how different interventions may need to be tailored on the basis of the cultural background, gender, or developmental level of the client. Guidelines do not specify what the therapist will do during each session, but they may point the clinician to a treatment manual that recommends such structured interventions.

Some policymakers have referred to highly structured clinical management plans that organize and sequence interventions as *clinical pathways*. These and treatment manuals differ from guidelines in that both are implemented after the clinician has already decided to use a particular type of treatment. *Clinical guidelines* assist the clinician in choosing a treatment plan by organizing information relevant to these decisions. This book is designed to assist in that process. Both clinical pathways and treatment manuals are protocols detailing a set procedure for the intervention. However, clinical pathways, unlike treatment manuals, are developed locally and take into account the infrastructure of the setting in which care is being delivered. An example of a clinical pathway might be the procedures that clinicians are to follow in the event that ongoing child abuse is suspected. An organization might specify what steps clinicians are to take (e.g., whom to notify, via telephone or letter) and in what order. Local laws and governmental structures would obviously influence the details of this clinical pathway. Treatment manuals, in contrast, are typically developed during the research process of testing the efficacy of an intervention and do not make accommodations for idiosyncrasies in the local setting.

Standards of Proof

Throughout this chapter, we have expressed clear support for the use of scientific evidence to guide clinical decision making. In the abstract, this view sounds easy to apply, and it seems to make sense. However, the criteria established by Task Forces and other groups for considering a treatment to be empirically supported are not uncontroversial. Spirited debates can occur when scientists gather to write a definition of what constitutes sufficient scientific evidence of effective treatment. To make matters more complicated, scientists are not the only ones with opinions about which treatments work! Some might argue that science provides an objective indication of proof that a treatment works, but critics could generate plenty of examples where scientists' biases and implicit theories influence their standards of proof toward supporting a favored viewpoint or rejecting an unfavored one.

Those who believe themselves to be immune to this type of bias should test themselves with the example of the X Test provided by Beutler and Davison (1995). The tale of the X Test outlines various types of evidence of the utility of a "mystery" test, and the reader is invited to form an opinion about the advisability of using this test in assessment, treatment planning, and graduate education curricula. When the name of the test is later revealed, readers may be tempted to suddenly change their opinion, revealing the shifting sands of standards of proof. In addition to this allegorical example, Beutler and Davison make a strong case for including consensually adopted nonempirical methods of evaluating the utility of a treatment or assessment procedures. For example, a treatment that has strong empirical evidence but poor face validity (i.e., does not look good or make logical sense) is unlikely to be accepted by clinicians or clients. On the other hand, a treatment that has secure consensual validity (i.e., everybody "knows" it works), such as Alcoholics Anonymous, would be extremely controversial to omit from a treatment guideline even in the absence of empirical support.

As more behavioral health provider organizations move to a multidisciplinary approach, clinicians with less professional education or training may more often be involved in primary care, with doctoral level practitioners reserved for more complicated cases. If this trend becomes popular, treatment guidelines will also need to incorporate specifications for triage. Under what conditions should clients be referred to master's-level providers within the clinic? What factors would indicate a consultation with or transfer to a supervisor-level provider? What different guidelines might be offered for the care of clients with treatment-resistant problems, who might require longer term assistance from mental health professionals? In order to be maximally useful to the clinicians who use them, treatment guidelines need to outline thoughtful responses to these questions and others that arise in the clinic setting. Results from research trials are unlikely to be very helpful on these thorny issues, but frank and open exchange of ideas among different concerned professionals (and consumers) may illuminate a path.

SUMMARY

In this chapter, we have presented the underlying philosophy that guides our recommendations for the treatment of specific anxiety disorders that will be presented in the chapters of this book. We introduced the concept of an educated eclectic empiricist for scientifically sound practice that maintains accountability for efficient provision of psychological services. To reiterate, the educated eclectic empiricist relies on three guideposts for assessment and treatment. Results from well-controlled scientific studies, when they are available to address the client's specific problem, form the foundation for a treatment plan. Techniques for assessment and treatment drawn from these studies and adapted by knowledgeable clinicians for local settings and particular clients then provide the specifics of the treatment plan. Finally, careful measurement of relevant domains of client functioning guide the clinician in making decisions about altering or terminating the treatment. Well-constructed treatment guidelines can provide a convenient synopsis of recent empirical findings as well as establish community standards for practice. Guidelines constructed with the welfare of the client in mind can be useful for stimulating peer supervision among clinicians and for educating the public about psychological interventions that work.

In the next chapter, we will provide background on the nature of anxiety, reviewing what is known about anxiety in a general sense, before moving on in later chapters to discuss the assessment and treatment of specific anxiety disorders. The next chapter is primarily focused on the phenomenon of anxiety, with particular focus on mechanisms that have been found to mediate anxiety, including cognitive, behavioral, and biological factors.

2 The Nature of Anxiety

As a primary emotion, anxiety has long been viewed as an adaptive means of preparing for threat and danger. Charles Darwin (1872/1965) argued that the fundamental qualities of fear reactions are determined by natural selection. Freud (1933) considered fear and anxiety to be universally experienced as aversive and distinct from other negative emotional states. Anthropologists and epidemiologists have since verified the universality of anxiety as a human experience. Although people from all cultures have been observed to experience anxiety, there are great individual differences in which stimuli have the power to evoke anxiety and in the intensity of the anxiety response. Why does a given situation or object provoke strong anxiety in some individuals while causing little concern in others? Are individual differences in anxiety caused by our unique past histories with specific stressors, or are they the result of temperament or biology?

In this chapter, we explore the extent of current knowledge on the general nature of anxiety. We begin with a discussion of categorical and dimensional views of anxiety, including issues of diagnosis, subtyping, and comorbidity. Recent work in experimental psychopathology has uncovered many clues regarding mechanisms underlying normal and pathological anxiety. For example, researchers have identified a type of negative affect that is common to anxiety states and depression, which appears to support a dimensional view of anxiety across different disorders. At the same time, researchers have discovered cognitive factors that distinguish different anxiety syndromes, a result that seems to support a categorical view of anxiety disorders as distinct entities. We will review these findings as well as a hierarchical model of anxiety that incorporates information from both perspectives. Finally, several areas of recent research have direct bearing on how we understand anxiety across the disorders. We will discuss results from research examining distinct components of the anxiety response: behavior, cognition, and physiology. After discussing these various constituents of the anxiety experience, the chapter will end with some of our thoughts on the implications for diagnosis and treatment planning.

THE NATURE OF ANXIETY: CATEGORICAL AND DIMENSIONAL VIEWS

Researchers, clinicians, and philosophers have engaged in lengthy debate about the nature of psychopathology, particularly when it comes to experiences so universally human as anxiety. With a phenomenon that everyone experiences at some point, and with such obvious survival implications in the presence of genuine threat, many observers have concluded that the difference between adaptive and pathological anxiety is simply one of degree. Proponents of this dimensional view of anxiety sometimes scoff at attempts to categorize specific anxiety disorders, pointing to notable similarities across the disorders. On the other hand, specialists who work closely with clients seeking treatment for anxiety are impressed with the clustering of symptoms into readily identifiable syndromes. They point to differences between the syndromes, such as different rates of familial transmission, as evidence of distinct disorders.

Regardless of how one sees the philosophical issue, there are distinct advantages to the categorical approach. Assuming the classification system is reliable, meaning that different clinicians interviewing the same client would arrive at the same diagnosis, then the categories provide a shorthand language for communication between professionals. In addition, if effective treatments vary depending on diagnosis, then this categorization obviously gives the clinician a head start on formulating a treatment plan. As we will discuss later, however, there are limitations to the categorical view. The value of categorizing a client depends on how prototypical the client's problems are; atypical presentations may force the clinician to rely on case formulation that transcends diagnostic categories. We will discuss some of these factors when we turn to considering the dimensional view. First, we will review the categorical perspective on anxiety.

The Categorical Perspective: Diagnoses

The specific features of both the stimulus and response involved in pathological anxiety differ across categories of anxiety disorder. Differences in anxiety levels include whether the response is reliably cued by a stimulus or is spontaneously experienced and whether the anxiety is typically managed by avoiding the stimulus or by using rituals or safety behaviors as protection from harm. Feared stimuli differ in their content, and in whether they are internal (i.e., bodily sensations or thoughts) or external stimuli. Diagnostic systems are naturally products of cultural interpretation, and determining when an anxiety response is severe enough to be pathological can be ambiguous. For example, one client we saw had many serious medical problems, including recent surgeries for a spinal problem and cancer. Her generalized anxiety and worry seemed understandable under the circumstances, but by the time she was seen for treatment of anxiety, she had been free of medical treatments for a full year. Determining a cutoff for a pathological level of anxiety under such stressful circumstances is arbitrary. Most common anxiety symptoms are considered to be clinically significant when they interfere with everyday functioning, but there are times when a client's functioning does not appear to be terribly impaired. These clients have adapted their lifestyle to accommodate the symptoms, which can nevertheless remain troublesome.

Depending on the rationale behind the classification system, experts propose a variety of different specific anxiety disorders. The American Psychiatric Association's revised third edition of the Diagnostic and Statistical Manual of Mental Disorders (American Psychiatric Association, 1987) classified eight anxiety disorders with three others reserved for children and adolescents. The current edition of this manual, DSM-IV (American Psychiatric Association, 1994), contains twelve categories as well as separation anxiety disorder, in the case of children. It includes acute stress disorder as a completely new disorder category that had not been represented in any form in prior editions. The European approach to the classification of mental disorders (WHO, 1992) and its counterpart, the American DSM series, have evolved increasingly similar criteria for classifying anxiety disorders. The World Health Organization and a former agency of the United States (the Alcohol, Drug Abuse, and Mental Health Administration) have collaborated on the Composite International Diagnostic Interview that combines these two sets of diagnostic criteria in a diagnostic interview that will likely prove helpful in international studies. In this volume we address the six most common anxiety disorders, all of which have extensive research available to guide treatment decision making. Although each disorder is thoroughly described in its own chapter, including differential diagnosis considerations, we will briefly introduce the diagnoses here.

Distinctions Between Diagnostic Categories

The main feature of *panic disorder* is obviously uncued or unexpected panic attacks, which consist of intense anxiety with a sudden and often unexpected onset. The intense anxiety usually declines within a few minutes, but it may sometimes be hours before the individual feels that she has returned to a normal state. During the panic attack, there are usually numerous bodily signs of anxiety, including racing heart, shortness of breath, sweating, or trembling. Most clients also experience thoughts of catastrophic medical emergencies or embarrassment. During an attack, clients often strongly believe these terrible events will occur (or are occurring), and some clients repeatedly rush to the hospital emergency department, convinced they are having a heart attack. Between attacks, clients report feeling relatively normal, but most describe a constant fear of future attacks. As a result of this constant fear, many clients with panic disorder also experience generalized anxiety, and many develop at least some degree of agoraphobia. The basis of agoraphobia is anxiety about being unable to escape or seek assistance in the event of a panic attack. As a result of this fear, clients with agoraphobia avoid situations in which it might be difficult to get help or embarrassing to suddenly flee. Agoraphobia can range from extremely mild (e.g., feeling "trapped" in the barber's chair, but not avoiding) to complete avoidance (e.g., housebound except when accompanied by a trusted companion). Panic disorder and agoraphobia are more fully described in chapter 5.

Unlike panic attacks, which may occur at any time and seemingly without warning, the occurrence of an anxiety response in *specific phobia* is relatively predictable and is situationally bound. Confrontation of the dreaded object or situation, or even the anticipation of doing so, invariably evokes an immediate intense anxiety response. Despite the fact that the client recognizes that the fear is either excessive or unreasonable (note that phobic children may lack this insight), he nevertheless remains terrified of the stimulus and experiences anxiety in its presence or in anticipation of being in its presence. The nearer the client comes to the stimulus, the more intense the fear response, assuming there is no opportunity to avoid or escape. Functional impairment ranges from none (e.g., terror of air travel, without a real need to fly) to considerable (e.g., fear of bridges when one lives in Stockholm). Clients are often able to minimize their experience of the fear by avoiding, but some stimuli simply cannot be avoided. Because the stimulus is often predictable and relatively easy to control (in contrast to social situations, for instance), researchers have often studied specific phobia as an exemplar of pathological fear. The next chapter of this volume outlines what we have learned from these studies and discusses treatment approaches for specific phobias.

In *social phobia*, the pattern of phobic anxiety is similar to specific phobia in that anxiety is provoked by identifiable external factors, namely social interactions. At its core, social phobia involves a fear of negative evaluation from others, and interactions with other people provoke the phobic response. In this sense, the features of social phobia also resemble panic disorder, because the client cannot always control or predict when a social interaction will spontaneously occur. Thus, the individual with social phobia often has more generalized anxiety than the person with specific phobia, because other people may start a conversation with the client at any moment! Social phobia often involves intense discomfort in a wide range of routine social situations. The intensity of the response is often related to specific features of one's potential social partners. For example, a client's anxiety may be proportional to the potential for novelty (e.g., a party with strangers), authority status (e.g., bank manager), or embarrassment in a given social situation. On the other hand, some clients experience social anxiety only in circumscribed situations. These individuals can feel socially competent and at ease in routine social situations, with family members, for example, but they experience extreme anxiety in highly specific situations (e.g., public speaking or urinating in public washrooms). In either case, clients with social phobia describe irrational beliefs about social situations and exhibit a range of avoidance behaviors.

Clients with *obsessive compulsive disorder* (OCD) engage in thoughts or actions designed to neutralize anxiety produced by intrusive thoughts that are repetitive, unwanted, and disturbing. Themes of obsessions and compulsions vary, but the most common involve rituals of washing or checking. OCD can be a crippling disorder, as clients often feel large parts of their lives have been surrendered to unwanted thoughts and rituals. As will be seen in chapter 6, those who suffer from OCD mostly recognize that their responses are excessive or illogical, but during times of intense anxiety, this insight can be elusive. Some clients try to avoid situations that trigger obsessions or compulsions. Avoidance is not always convenient, however, as these situations can involve everyday activities like dressing, bathing, or driving. An intrusive image or impulse (e.g., hitting one's child) often sparks a negative appraisal (e.g., "I'm an unfit father") and catastrophic predictions about potential consequences (e.g., "I could lose control, kill my son, and be charged with manslaughter"). Rituals that function to reduce this terrible anxiety can be overt (such as checking to be sure that the knives are still tucked in the kitchen drawer) or covert (such as silently repeating words of repentance). Clients often attempt to resist both obsessive thoughts and neutralizing rituals, but many find that efforts at resistance simply increase anxiety. As with panic disorder, the interpretation of the significance of internal events escalates anxiety. With panic disorder, the internal event is most often a perceived sign of anxiety, such as increased heart rate. In OCD, the internal event is usually a thought, impulse, or image. However, unique to OCD, rituals serve to temporarily relieve anxiety, usually by "undoing" the unwanted thought. The ritual may bear a logical relationship to the obsession (like washing when feeling contaminated), but many times there is no logical connection (such as tapping a specified number of times after an intrusive thought).

The cardinal feature of *generalized anxiety disorder* (GAD) is persistent, uncontrollable worry accompanied by chronic symptoms of anxious arousal (e.g., muscle tension, hypervigilance, irritability, and insomnia). The worry is often focused on one's own welfare and the current and future well-being of loved ones. While the content reflects the type of routine worries that many people have, including finances, family relationships, and school or job performance, the process is somewhat different. As discussed in chapter 7, worry as experienced in GAD is difficult or impossible to control. Clients are unable to turn their minds to other things, and worrisome thoughts preoccupy them. Suppressing the worry only makes things worse. A generalized feeling of anxiety commonly occurs within other anxiety disorders as well, but the feature of uncontrollable worry (about things other than the specific content of other anxiety disorders) distinguishes the separate diagnosis of GAD.

Posttraumatic stress disorder (PTSD) has features of several other anxiety disorders. Like specific phobia, the anxiety associated with this disorder is primarily bound to an evocative stimulus. Clients with PTSD report that stimuli connected with the traumatic event, including images, smells, sounds, memories, or internal bodily states, have the power to evoke an intense anxiety response. Similar to the case with OCD, clients with PTSD experience intrusive thoughts relevant to their fear, and these thoughts can have disturbing implications to the client (e.g., "It was my fault"). A primary requirement for a diagnosis of PTSD is exposure to a situation involving the threat of serious injury or death, in which the individual's reaction was one of extreme distress or horror. Certainly, not everyone who experiences such a terrible event develops PTSD, and there are undoubtedly areas of overlap between an expected response to trauma and the pathological reaction known as PTSD. Following the event, traumatized persons experience a characteristic and sustained pattern of anxious arousal, intrusive recollection of the traumatic event, and avoidance of things and places that remind them of the trauma. Clients with PTSD suffer these after-effects of the trauma long after the expected recovery period. In chapter 8, we discuss this unique disorder in more detail.

Diagnostic Subtypes

Not only has each edition of the DSM described a greater number of anxiety disorders, but also the practice of diagnostic subtyping has become more common. With the publication of DSM-IV, most anxiety disorders include descriptions of subtypes. In some cases, these subtypes will undoubtedly turn out to be useful discriminations. For example, researchers have begun to reveal important differences between blood/injury phobia, a type of specific phobia, and other subtypes. Blood/injury phobia appears to have a stronger genetic loading than other specific phobias; its prevalence, characteristics, and age of onset are different, and treatments targeted specifically for this subtype of phobia have been developed. Likewise, researchers have observed different physiological response profiles between clients with generalized versus circumscribed social phobias. More detailed issues regarding subtypes of each disorder will be discussed within the disorder-specific chapters of the book.

Prevalence of Disorders

Techniques for estimating the prevalence of emotional disorders in the population are constantly being refined. In current studies, researchers personally interview thousands of randomly selected citizens, to determine the current or lifetime presence of various disorders. With each population study, as the methodology has become more sophisticated, estimated prevalence rates have increased. Before the interview methods were developed, estimates of the prevalence of "anxiety neuroses" were inferred on the basis of clinical visits to specialists' offices. For example, clients visiting a cardiologist for heart symptoms but who were found to have no organic disease might be followed and assumed to have an anxiety disorder (Wheeler, White, & Reed, 1950). Population prevalence was estimated from the prevalence of these types of complaints in routine medical practice. Clearly, these estimates would be very specific, depending on the type of specialist's office. Comprehensive estimates across anxiety diagnostic categories were difficult to make until the arrival of large-scale population studies.

A landmark epidemiological study of psychiatric disorder in North America was conducted in the 1980s. The Epidemiologic Catchment Area (ECA) Study involved structured diagnostic interviews with some 20,000 respondents in five communities. Estimates for lifetime prevalence of specific anxiety disorders (DSM-III criteria) were high, ranging from 10% to 25% of the population (Bourdon et al., 1988; Robins et al., 1984). In contrast, an epidemiological survey of a Canadian city found lifetime prevalence rates for any anxiety disorder to be 11% (Bland, Orn, & Newman, 1988). Discrepancies in survey findings between ECA sites are thought to reflect variation in interviewer instructions, and discrepancies between American and Canadian estimates are attributed to methods used to standardize prevalence rates. A decade later, Kessler et al. (1994) reported the results of another national population survey in the United States. This study, known as the National Comorbidity Survey, represented a methodological advance because structured interviews were conducted with a national probability sample, which attempts to capture respondents from all strata of society. In this survey, which used DSM-III-R criteria, lifetime prevalence for any anxiety disorder was 25% (31% for women, and 19% for men). Lifetime prevalence for individual anxiety disorder categories ranged from 4% for panic disorder to 13% for social phobia.

The National Comorbidity Study (Kessler et al., 1994) yielded several additional findings of interest. Generally, highest prevalence rates were reported for young adults, 25 to 34 years old, with prevalence diminishing for each successively older age group. In keeping with earlier studies, women are over-represented among those identified with anxiety disorders in the National Comorbidity Study. In all reported anxiety diagnostic groups, for both 12-month and lifetime prevalence estimates, women had twice the prevalence rates of men, except in the case of social phobia, where there were three women for every two men. Race was not a factor in prevalence rates. Comorbidity was commonplace; 56% of respondents who had a history of at least one psychiatric disorder also qualified for at least one additional disorder. The comorbidity, or overlap between disorders, was particularly evident within anxiety disorders. Consistent with previous epidemiological surveys, the National Comorbidity Study also found that only a minority of those with a psychiatric disorder had ever sought professional treatment. These epidemiological studies provide evidence that anxiety disorders are more prevalent than we previously thought, and that the various anxiety disorders commonly occur together.

Dimensional Perspectives on Anxiety

While construing anxiety in terms of diagnostic categories lends convenience in characterizing a given client's problems and represents a good starting point, there are limits to the utility of a diagnosis alone. Diagnoses, like other methods of categorizing "types" of people, can involve elements of stereotyping in which we as observers fail to note exceptions to the rules by which we have classified someone. (We discussed some common judgment biases that may influence clinical decisions in the previous chapter.) Each client presents with a complex set of responses. To the extent that a given client deviates from the prototypical, it is helpful to know something about the nature of anxiety apart from diagnostic categories. Often clients seek treatment for anxiety that is not severe enough to warrant an official diagnosis but that is nevertheless troublesome. Some clients seem to fall between the diagnostic cracks within the anxiety disorders, or defy categorization altogether. In other cases, treatment might not be working and it may be useful to speculate about why the intervention may be failing. For these and other reasons, conceptualizing clients' problems dimensionally, as well as categorically, bears advantage.

There are two perspectives to a discussion of the dimensional nature of anxiety. The first perspective is delineating normal from pathological levels of anxiety. There is often no objective delineation of the magnitude, as every person experiences at least some anxiety at some time, and most anxious clients are relaxed some of the time. The second dimensional perspective on anxiety involves common elements across categories within the anxiety disorders, which may lead to common treatment procedures. Anxiety itself appears to vary along several dimensions, including an anxious arousal dimension and a dimension of control, ranging from relative self-control to a feeling of helplessness (Barlow, 1985). A clinician may address anxious arousal with a single procedure despite different diagnostic categories. For example, progressive muscle relaxation may have a role wherever muscular tension is found, whether the case is conceptualized as specific phobia, GAD, or some other anxiety disorder. Similarly, regardless of diagnostic category, anxious clients vary in the degree of perceived control they experience over both their symptoms and the feared consequences of their symptoms. The therapist often expends considerable therapeutic effort helping to reinstate the perception of self-control and self-efficacy, no matter which anxiety disorder is being treated.

One of the difficulties in thinking about anxiety from a dimensional perspective is language. Some of the concepts of anxiety are in such common use in everyday language that their meaning can become confused. Take the example of "stress" and "anxiety," two words that lay people often use interchangeably. In early work on the nature of anxiety, Spielberger (1971) noted this problem of confusing the stimulus with the response. In this case, stress is seen as the objective stimulus. Anxiety pertains to the subjective emotional response to the stressor. This emotional response is based on the individual's *perception* of threat, rather than a linear reaction to the *objective* threat value of the stressor itself (Lazarus, 1996; Spielberger, 1972a). We see this most clearly in the anxiety disorders, in which the client responds to her ideas about a stimulus rather than necessarily attending to the objective features of the stimulus.

Another language problem in the study of anxiety involves a failure to distinguish between transitory anxiety states and personality-based individual differences in anxiety proneness (Spielberger, 1972a; Spielberger, 1972b), known as state and trait anxiety. Trait anxiety refers to characteristic (i.e., personality) response tendencies, while state anxiety usually describes current anxiety levels. Implicit in Spielberger's configuration of anxiety is the interaction of these factors. Hence an individual's anxiety symptoms at any moment are the result of an interaction between the *objective* threat posed by a local set of circumstances and *perception* of that threat as filtered through one's relatively enduring tendency to respond anxiously.

In our earlier brief consideration of several anxiety disorder diagnoses, we observed considerable variation across categories in the cues that produce anxiety, the intensity of the response, and the characteristic response to the fear-provoking stimulus. However, apart from simple content, the process of pathological anxious responding can also have striking similarities across categories. Looking beneath the surface, we can see that while two disorders appear to be very different, similar processes are nonetheless occurring. For example, panic disorder and specific phobia appear to be worlds apart at first glance. One involves a fear of clearly definable objects or situations (e.g., an animal), whereas with the other, a client seems to be at the mercy of unpredictable and uncontrollable attacks that come from out of the blue. If we focus on the similarities between anxiety disorders, on the other hand, we begin to search for *cues* that provoke anxiety and to question the function of avoidance. Examining panic from this perspective, we uncover predictable cues that provoke the panic response, and the attack no longer appears to arise so inexplicably. We also note that panic attacks can occur in almost all of the anxiety disorders. As another example, careful observation reveals that fear of negative social evaluation is not limited to social phobia. Rather, shame and fear of public humiliation play a role in most anxiety disorders. Understanding the nature of anxiety and the social implications of a client's specific fears can help clinicians tailor more effective treatment plans for individual clients. Appreciating some of the commonly observed characteristics associated with all anxiety disorders can also help clinicians to measure progress during treatment on diverse areas of concern to each client.

One implication of a dimensional perspective on anxiety is that it is natural for the boundaries between diagnostic categories to have quite a bit of overlap. Examining consecutive admissions to a specialty clinic for treatment of anxiety disorders, Barlow (1985) has observed high rates of comorbidity. Using a structured diagnostic interview, the Anxiety Disorders Interview Schedule (DiNardo, O'Brien, Barlow, Waddell, & Blanchard, 1983), clinicians assigned primary and secondary diagnoses on the basis of severity and functional interference. Secondary anxiety disorder diagnoses were assigned for 88% of clients diagnosed with primary panic disorder and *all* clients with primary OCD. Clients with other primary anxiety disorder diagnoses also received frequent secondary diagnoses: agoraphobia (51%), social phobia (47%), simple phobia (57%), and GAD (83%). One interpretation of these figures is that anticipatory anxiety and panic have dimensional features that underlie all the diagnostic categories, potentially inflating the perception of overlap (Barlow, DiNardo, Vermilyea, Vermilyea, & Blanchard, 1986).

Cross-cultural influences on the experience and expression of anxiety can also be viewed within a dimensional context. While the biological processes involved within any individual's anxiety response may be stable across cultures, there is overwhelming evidence that cultural context determines interpretation of distress. Culture formats the "natural history" of anxiety disorders in terms of age of onset, course, social distribution, and consequences for the lives of sufferers (Friedman, 1977; Good & Kleinman, 1985). Thus, distress stemming from threats to safety, health, social or occupational stability, fertility, dream experiences, or other sources, is interpreted and shaped by cultural influences, resulting in considerable symptom variation in anxiety across cultures.

Cross-cultural research has been limited by methodological problems. For example, psychometric instruments developed in western Europe, the United States, or Canada are often carefully translated for use in host study nations. These questionnaires assume similar qualities of anxiety symptoms across cultures. However, this assumption may not be valid. Similarly, cross-cultural studies of diagnostic categories have been limited by the 'importation' of translated disorder criteria, based on symptom profiles validated in another culture. Simply translating diagnostic categories into another language without revalidating the categories as they pertain to the different culture may not be appropriate. Such practices may have the effect of under- or overestimating the local prevalence of anxiety disorders. For instance, in many countries, anxiety symptoms are often expressed in the form of socially sanctioned somatic symptoms. Neurasthenia, meaning "neurological weakness," is a disorder conceptualized in several Asian nations. Neurasthenia is similar to Western descriptions of somatic symptoms of depression, anxiety, and somatoform disorder, combined with some culture-specific complaints. The current trend toward using culture-specific symptom vocabularies in epidemiological research should prove helpful in estimating international prevalence rates.

Cultural relativity in the meaning and expression of the experience of anxiety poses challenges for practitioners. Especially in urban areas of most Western countries, immigration patterns have rendered clinical practice multicultural. To keep up with changes in their client populations, many practitioners now participate in study groups provided by community agencies. Where available, these study groups provide expert consultants who are well versed in cultural interpretations of illness, specifically designed for health professionals.

Hierarchical Models of Anxiety: A Compromise Between Categories and Dimensions

As we have just seen, there are compelling reasons to consider anxiety, even in its pathological extremes, from a dimensional perspective. Yet, there are also clear indications that anxiety disorders are meaningful categories into which symptom clusters can be divided. Recent research has spawned a hierarchical model of anxiety, which simultaneously captures many of the similarities and differences between these views. In this hierarchical model, a nonspecific personality style is viewed as an overarching (dimensional) factor. At a secondary level in the model are specific anxiety disorders. All share the commonalities of the higher order factor, yet they are meaningful categories with specific dimensions associated with anxiety and depression in adults (Clark, Beck, & Stewart, 1990) and children (Lonigan, Carey, & Finch, 1994). Increasing evidence points to the personality factor as a marker for vulnerability for the development of anxiety disorders. Although the word used by various theorists to describe this temperament varies, including neuroticism (Eysenck, 1967) or behavioral inhibition (Kagan, 1994), research has demonstrated that the overlap among these constructs is more impressive than the distinctions between them (Zinbarg & Barlow, 1996).

This hierarchical model of anxiety, with an overall factor of anxious personality and subordinate factors of distinct disorders, grew out of research to understand the relationship between anxiety and depression. Researchers had been unable to decide whether anxiety and depression were distinct syndromes or part of the same phenomenon. Symptom scales of anxiety and depression have always been very highly correlated, meaning that someone who is high on a measure of anxiety is also likely to show high levels of depression. Factor analytic studies, which use large numbers of respondents to try to understand how various traits are related, revealed a general distress factor, which was dubbed *negative affectivity* (Watson, Clark, &

Carey, 1988). Negative affectivity, which describes a general emotional malaise, seemed to be related to both anxiety and depressive disorders. Negative affectivity has come to be seen as the state version of the trait neuroticism. Where neuroticism is seen as a relatively enduring personality characteristic, negative affectivity is expected to only be apparent during a clinical episode.

Historically, theorists from Freud forward have tried to explain the observation that some individuals become disproportionately anxious in response to relatively minor circumstances that would cause other people to experience little, if any, anxiety. This anxiety proneness has been described as neuroticism (Eysenck, 1968) and as trait anxiety (Spielberger, 1972a). Longitudinal studies, in which researchers monitor individuals over the course of years, have revealed links between neuroticism and the development of anxiety disorders (Andrews, 1996a). If neuroticism manifests as negative affectivity during clinical episodes, then treatment efforts to reduce neuroticism may in turn reduce vulnerability for future episodes (Andrews, 1996b). Jang, Livesley, and Vernon (1996) studied 357 Canadian and 900 German twin pairs (Jang, McCrae, Angleitner, Riemann, & Livesley, in press) to track genetic factors influencing neuroticism. They found the magnitude of heritability for neuroticism to be in the 40–50% range and the type of genes involved to be the same. Presumably the remaining variance (50–60%) accounting for neuroticism can be attributed to environmental or learned factors, which may be able to be altered.

Of particular interest in the hierarchical model of anxiety is the nature of the lower order factors and their ability to distinguish between the anxiety disorders. Based on a combination of self-report questionnaires and a semi-structured clinical interview, Zinbarg and Barlow (1996) found that anxiety-disordered clients clearly had more negative affectivity than individuals with no mental disorder. More impressive, however, was a set of six lower order factors (e.g., social anxiety, fear of fear, generalized dysphoria) that differentiated eight specific diagnostic groups (six anxiety disorder groups, depression, and a no mental disorder group).

COMPONENTS OF THE ANXIETY RESPONSE

Clearly, many psychological factors mediate the various dimensions of anxiety. In this section, we briefly review a number of mechanisms that play a role in the maintenance of anxiety. An appreciation of these mechanisms is essential for both therapists and clients, as they are features of anxiety that transcend diagnosis and even pathology. Understanding these features of anxiety can guide therapists to creatively apply treatment strategies addressing each client's idiosyncrasies. In addition, helping clients to understand the components of the anxiety response can provide them with a basis for being less afraid of their own anxiety. Throughout this book, we will discuss the features of the anxiety response in terms of three main components: behavior, cognition, and physiology. These three components are characteristics of all levels of anxiety, which is, at some level, a normal and adaptive response. Behaviors such as avoidance or escape have obvious survival benefit in the face of true danger. Cognitive features like hypervigilance can provide an early detection system for recognizing threatening situations. Physiological responses involve preparing the organism for defensive strategies such as fighting or fleeing, both of which create strong metabolic demands.

Behavioral Response

The two most obvious behavioral manifestations of fear and anxiety in humans are avoidance and escape. Both may be conceptualized as coping strategies. Escape involves fleeing the scene when one is confronted with a feared stimulus. For example, as a child, one of us (SRW) saved a mouse from the jaws of a cat and proudly took it home. When Mom saw the mouse, she immediately ran out the back door in fear and disgust! This is a simple example of escape, although it quickly turned to avoidance, as the mouse was forcibly repatriated to the outdoors. Escape usually occurs when a person or animal is surprised by the presence of a feared stimulus, and fleeing is a method of seeking safety. Clients will also escape when they are surprised by the intensity of their fear. Another behavioral response to being surprised by a feared stimulus can be freezing, or becoming motionless.

Many people choose a simple coping action in advance of being confronted with a fear-provoking situation: avoidance. On the face of it, avoiding the feared stimulus seems like a good idea. After all, unpleasant feelings of fear can be avoided altogether by simply refusing to engage with the stimulus. Avoidance of flying in airplanes, for example, saves the individual from days or weeks of anxious apprehension in advance of a flight. In fact, simply deciding to avoid a specific flight can relieve anxious apprehension immediately. Herein lies the danger: the reduction in anxiety that occurs as a result of the decision to avoid *reinforces* that behavior, making it more likely that the person will avoid the next time. Greater avoidance can ensue, eventually interfering with functioning. Perhaps because avoidance of frightening situations is so functional and natural, its role in the maintenance of fear is often not obvious to clients.

Theoretical accounts of avoidance behavior have evolved considerably since the Miller-Mowrer theory of conditioned avoidance (Rachman, 1984). This theory holds that avoidance of threatening situations provides a feeling of relief, which rewards or reinforces the avoidance behavior. Although this theory was very influential in early behavior therapy, some writers have raised questions about the details of the theory (Rachman, 1984). For example, avoidance often continues long after the threatening stimulus has been removed. Gray (1987) refers to a study in which dogs received a single shock preceded by a warning signal. Later, when the dogs were placed in the same experimental situation, they continued to run to safety (escape) when cued by the warning signal for over 200 trials, despite never experiencing shock again. A human example of this persistent avoidance can be observed in driving phobias brought about by a car accident.

Other phenomena that have proved difficult for the Miller-Mowrer theory are avoidance in the absence of fear and the wide variability in strength of avoidance over time. Clinicians who have treated clients with agoraphobia are familiar with the latter phenomenon. On good days, these clients are able to attempt challenging situations such as a crowded grocery store. The same client may be unable to attempt even a deserted store on a bad day. In a search for theoretical answers to these questions, Rachman (1984) identified six contending theories, each attempting to overcome problems in the Miller-Mowrer theory. Interested readers can compare these theories: Beck's cognitive theory (Beck, 1974), Lang's bioinformational theory (Lang, 1968), Eysenck's revised neobehavioristic theory (Eysenck, 1982), Bandura's self-efficacy theory (Bandura, 1977), and Rachman's theory of emotional processing of fear (Rachman, 1980). A shared theme among these models of avoidance is the inclusion of a wide range of complex influences on avoidance behavior, including anxiety sensitivity, personality or temperament, cues indicating safety, and information processing biases.

Cognitive Phenomena

Cognitive Content

Aaron T. Beck, the innovator of cognitive theory of depression over thirty years ago, has since expanded this theory to explain other emotional disorders (1996). In this schematic model, frightening stimuli activate cognitive schemata, which are heuristics for organizing information in memory. When a particular schema is activated, a set of expectations and beliefs are also primed. Thus, schemata related to a frightening situation are believed to influence motivation, affect, and behavior. Schemata related to emotional disorders are believed to consist of characteristic ideas and beliefs, which give rise to dysfunctional interpretations and predictions of future events. Automatic thoughts are believed to spring from the activation of these schemata. Research has shown that the content of automatic thoughts varies predictably between nonclient and client samples. Even more impressive, the content of these thoughts can distinguish anxious clients from depressed clients, which is important given the high degree of overlap in questionnaire measurement of these problems. Anxious clients tend to endorse automatic thoughts related to harm and danger, whereas clients with depression more commonly report thoughts of loss and failure (Clark, Beck, & Brown, 1989).

Clinicians and researchers alike have noted characteristic *dysfunctional beliefs* associated with specific anxiety disorders. The characteristic cognitive content is perhaps most notable in panic disorder, in which clients believe that bodily sensations are signs of impending physical catastrophes or medical emergencies. Characteristic beliefs can also be observed in most of the other anxiety disorders. The nature of these beliefs will be elaborated in following chapters. These dysfunctional beliefs can be distinct from one disorder to the next, yet all are threatening in tone. Keeping in mind that the anxious person is hypervigilant to early warning signs of danger, a relationship between these threatening ideas and their exacerbation in arousal becomes clear. In fact, researchers have identified numerous ways that cognitive processing, including perception, attention, and memory, is subject to systematic bias related to anxiety disorders (see Eysenck & Mogg, 1992 for review). Clients' beliefs and assumptions confer meaning upon events, often outside of their awareness, resulting in the inference of personal danger or threat.

Overprediction of Fear

When clients predict how afraid they think they will be when they confront their feared situation, this estimate often turns out to have been inflated. That is, when actually confronting the situation, many clients are not as afraid as they had anticipated they would be. This overprediction of fear is a cognitive bias that strongly and systematically increases the expectation of fear and adversity in a threatening situation, thereby increasing anticipatory anxiety and the likelihood of avoidance. Surprisingly, past experiences with overestimating fear may not help clients more accurately predict fear levels in the future. Unless clients systematically track and reconcile predictions versus outcomes of fearful situations, the overprediction of fear may go undetected. Frightening predictions, such as the occurrence of a panic attack, that turn out not to occur, may be attributed to luck.

Rachman (1994) concluded that fearful individuals routinely overpredict both the probability of aversive consequences in fear-provoking situations and the amount of fear they expect to experience. Unexpected aversive experiences like panic attacks make a disproportionate contribution to this prediction bias, as clients show a hearty overprediction of fear in the wake of one of these experiences. Laboratory studies have shown that a single, unpredicted fear experience (e.g., a sharp pain lasting 1–2 seconds) sharply increases the likelihood of future overpredictions (Davey, 1989). This phenomenon may be related to clinical findings in the pediatric literature on acquisition of dental phobias, which highlights the role of unexpected dental pain in the acquisition of phobias of dental treatment. Contributing to the overprediction of fear, clients appear to ignore safety information in formulating estimates of fear.

In an interesting study, Telch, Valentiner, and Bolte (1994) asked claustrophobic clients to complete a claustrophobic challenge. This challenge involved remaining in a long narrow chamber with the door closed. To investigate the role of safety cues in clients' estimates of fear, researchers compared two variants on the claustrophobic challenge. These variants involved clients being asked to stay in a chamber that was either near or far from an exit door (i.e., for escape to safety). Anticipated distance from the exit did not impact on the predicted fear ratings in the claustrophobic situation. However, once in the challenge situation, claustrophobics who were nearer to the door felt less anxiety than did those who were far from the exit. These results indicated that proximity to the exit influenced clients' actual experiences of fear, but the clients did not take this factor into account in making advance estimates of how afraid they would be in the challenge situation. Clearly, the irrational levels of fear seen in anxiety disorders are not based on a full appraisal of the circumstances. This type of research helps us to understand the bases of irrational fear, and we are thereby better able to help clients reduce their fear.

As long as fear is relatively predictable, repeated exposure to the frightening situation is expected to gradually reduce both the predicted levels of fear and the actual experience of fear. However, unexpected (underpredicted) fear during an encounter with the frightening stimulus can sharply increase anticipatory anxiety, and hence avoidance. Thus, it may be helpful to inform anxious clients about the probability that they will experience some intense anxiety during initial stages of exposure-based treatments. In this way, the potential negative effects of unexpected fear reactions may be avoided (Cox & Swinson, 1994). Similarly, the findings on safety signals suggest that clinicians should encourage clients to appropriately attend to safety resources in frightening situations. If clients overestimate safety signals, meaning that they fail to attend to the relative lack of escape options in a given situation, then they may underpredict fear. The chief danger in underprediction of fear is that clients may experience an unexpected intense anxiety reaction, which sets the stage for prolonged overprediction of fear (and greater future avoidance). On the other hand, if clients ignore the presence of safety resources when anticipating a frightening situation, they may overpredict the intensity of their fear reaction, which makes entering the situation even more challenging.

Memory bias favoring negative information, or *selective recall*, has been demonstrated repeatedly in the case of depressed clients (see Blaney, 1986 for review), and theoretically plays a role in anxiety disorders (Beck, Emery, & Greenberg, 1985; Bower, 1981). However, research on this topic has been mixed, and at present, no firm conclusions can be drawn about the role of memory bias (see Eysenck & Mogg, 1992 for review). We would have expected that anxious clients would show a memory advantage for highly threatening material. Clients with social phobia, for instance, would be expected to selectively remember moments in an interaction that were interpreted as failure, forgetting those moments that seemed to go well. The conflicting evidence may reflect inadequacies in laboratory procedures for assessing recall of threatening material. Compared to personally relevant recollections, Eysenck and Mogg (1992) suggest that memories created and tested in the laboratory may not be very powerful.

To test this possibility, Burke and Mathews (1992) assessed autobiographical memory in clients with generalized anxiety disorder and normal controls. First, research participants were asked to associate any personal memory with specified neutral words. Those with GAD subsequently recalled more nervous, rather than pleasant, memories when compared to participants in the control group. Next, the two groups were asked to associate both anxious and nonanxious personal memories, each to neutral words that were provided. Upon recall evaluation, GAD subjects recalled relatively more anxiety-evoking memories, and did so more quickly, compared to control subjects. From this evidence, it appears that clinically anxious clients are prone to selectively recall personally threatening or anxious events more readily than other memories.

A different sort of selective memory impairment appears to be induced by benzodiazepines (Barbee, 1993). Significant proportions of anxious clients are using benzodiazepine medication when they present for psychological treatment. These drugs do not impair the recollection of previously learned information. Rather, memory deficits produced by these drugs are selective and involve problems in transferring new information into long-term memory. These effects are more evident at higher doses, and they may impair learning during psychological treatments for anxiety disorders. For example, Wilhelm and Roth (1997) gave flight phobics either 1 mg of alprazolam or a placebo (double blind) 1 hour before a flight. While the alprazolam reduced self-reported anxiety and symptoms more than placebo, it induced an increase in heart rate, as assessed by ambulatory physiological recording. On a second flight a week later, taken without medication, those who had received alprazolam just before the first flight reported more anxiety during the second flight, experienced further increases in heart rate, and were more likely to have a panic attack compared to their first flight. These results warn than alprazolam can influence learning in complex ways that may compromise exposure-based treatment.

Attentional Bias

Another type of distortion in information processing that is characteristic of pathological anxiety is attentional bias. This involves an active process of highlighting threat-related information. In the routine stream of sensory information, many of these cues would otherwise be quickly ignored. By making the client more aware of cues regarding potential threat, attentional bias has the effect of increasing the rate at which the client responds with anxiety in situations that do not truly represent danger. As an example, clients with a phobia of flying who nevertheless manage to fly are usually hypervigilant for minor variations in aircraft movement and sounds. Once observed, the client attempts to evaluate these movements and sounds in terms of their threat potential. Because these movements and sounds are associated with normal aircraft operation, yet still provoke intense anxiety, attentional bias has led to a false alarm, and unnecessary discomfort for the client. This type of information processing is sufficiently routine that the bias can become automatic, involuntary, and unconscious (McNally, 1995).

Experimental psychopathologists have used a variety of experimental tasks to detect attentional bias. These tasks often measure the time required for processing emotional versus neutral information. Typically, anxious subjects can be differentiated from nonanxious subjects in these studies, as anxious subjects routinely demonstrate an interference effect when processing threat-related information. This selective interference effect suggests that individuals with pathological levels of anxiety are distracted by threatening information even when such information is irrelevant to the task at hand. Such findings have been interpreted as indicating that the attentional bias in anxious individuals occurs very quickly—prior to awareness of the stimulus (Mathews & MacLeod, 1986). As might be expected, exactly which external threat cues evoke an attentional bias is specific to the anxiety disorder involved (for review, see Logan & Goetsch, 1993). For example, Tata, Leibowitz, Prunty, Cameron, and Pickering (1996) have demonstrated that clients with OCD are hypervigilant for contamination-related words in comparison to a highly anxious normal control group.

Anxiety Sensitivity

Clinicians have long noted that some clients are better able to tolerate the sensations of anxiety than others are. Anxiety sensitivity describes individual differences in fear of the manifestations of anxiety (Reiss & McNally, 1985). In contrast, neuroticism is a somewhat broader concept than anxiety sensitivity, although they overlap. The construct of anxiety sensitivity highlights fear of anxiety and implicates beliefs about the consequences of experiencing anxiety as the source of this fear. For example, an individual with high anxiety sensitivity may worry about physical sensations associated with intense emotions.

The Anxiety Sensitivity Index (Reiss, Peterson, Gursky, & McNally, 1986) is a self-report measure of anxiety sensitivity that assesses concerns about potential consequences of anxiety. An example of an item on the ASI is, "When I notice that my heart is beating rapidly, I worry that I might be having a heart attack." Much research is available to support the validity of this dispositional variable. Anxiety sensitivity has demonstrated stability over extended periods and an ability to predict future panic attacks. High ASI scores have predicted the frequency and intensity of panic attacks 3 years later, and people who scored high on the ASI were 5 times more likely to experience panic attacks over the period of 3 years compared to those with low ASI scores (Maller & Reiss, 1992).

In summary, anxiety sensitivity is a construct that describes a relatively stable characteristic of fear of anxiety symptoms. Anxiety sensitivity is believed to represent a personal vulnerability that mediates anxiety. From a practical point of view, anxiety sensitivity, as assessed by the ASI, can be identified as a risk factor for panic attacks, which are commonly experienced across anxiety disorders. There is some clinical evidence that treatment can diminish anxiety sensitivity, presumably by altering beliefs about the consequences of anxiety symptoms.

Biological and Physiological Components

A detailed understanding of the physiological components of the anxiety response may not be necessary for clinicians using psychological interventions. Nevertheless, having some basic knowledge about the biology of the autonomic nervous system is helpful. Many clients who experience chronic anxiety are curious about the role of physiology in their anxiety, and quite a few have fears about the physiological impact of anxiety. In this section, we will briefly discuss changes in the autonomic nervous system that occur during times of alarm or more chronic stress. Interested readers may wish to pursue a more detailed study of the biological basis of anxiety. LeDoux (1995) and Davis (1992) both provide reviews of the neural bases of emotion, especially the central role of the amygdala in appraisal of danger as well as the learning and extinction of fear. Gray (1987) offers a book-length examination of the psychology of fear and stress, with detailed explanations of the experimental basis for physiological theories of anxiety.

The autonomic nervous system is divided into two branches, the sympathetic and parasympathetic nervous systems. The sympathetic nervous system is associated with arousal, and the parasympathetic system is in charge of slowing things down. In the brain, the hypothalamus is a main controller of the autonomic nervous system and the endocrine system. The hypothalamus is also closely involved in the regulation of all kinds of emotional behavior. The adrenal gland is an important endocrine component of the sympathetic nervous system. Neurochemicals released by the adrenal gland (under the coordination of the hypothalamus through the pituitary) influence changes in bodily organs including the sense organs, bladder, blood vessels, and major organs like the heart, lungs, and gastrointestinal system. The sympathetic nervous system is primarily responsible for the rapid alarm response that brings near-instantaneous arousal known as the "fight or flight" response.

When a swift response to immediate danger is required, the hypothalamus (having been "warned" by the sense organs) stimulates the adrenal gland to secrete epinephrine (adrenaline) and norepinephrine (noradrenaline). These chemicals travel through the bloodstream to various organs, preparing each system to enable the body to take strong and immediate action. For example, the heart rate increases in rate and strength, which moves oxygen around the body more quickly, enabling the muscles to work better. There is increased respiration and dilation of the bronchi in the lungs, again increasing the amount of oxygen available in the bloodstream. The liver releases stored sugars, and the spleen releases red blood cells to carry oxygen, both of which help power the muscles. The body prepares to defend against injury by increasing blood stores of coagulant (facilitating clotting) and lymphocytes, which are cells that assist in repairing damaged tissues. Obviously this is a dramatic system, and in the case of a real emergency, the body is well prepared for the metabolically demanding tasks of fighting or fleeing.

During a situation where real danger is present, the hypothalamus uses corticotropin-releasing hormone (CRH) to signal the alarm to the pituitary, which goes on to influence the adrenal gland as described above. However, in the 1980s, CRH was synthesized in the laboratory, so researchers began to experiment with the conditions that might lead to the release of CRH by the hypothalamus. In particular, researchers were interested in responses to conditioned stimuli—those that are not in themselves threatening but which have become associated (conditioned) with aversive outcomes. Hellhammer and his colleagues (1992) have noted that CRH activation in humans occurs during situations involving unpredictability, lack of control, or novelty. They suggest that CRH activation can become learned and triggered by feelings of unpredictability and lack of control. This type of research highlights the interactive relationship between psychological and biological components of anxiety.

During more prolonged stress, the adrenal gland secretes other hormones, including glucocorticoids. These neurochemicals (such as corticosterone, hydrocortisone, and cortisol) act to provide usable energy to the body, as well as maintain the continued ability to mobilize oxygen for action. Nonsugars are transformed into sugars, and sugar deposits in the liver increase. In addition, the reactions of the blood vessels are facilitated. However, the glucocorticoids may also reduce resistance to infection, inhibit inflammation (which is involved in tissue repair), and influence the development of gastrointestinal ulcers and stores of body fat. Continued high levels of stress seem to decrease thyroid activity, which slows down metabolism and body growth, and suppress reproductive functioning in both women and men. The mechanisms for these "side effects" of chronic stress are not well understood.

The hypothalamus, discussed above, is only one of several structures in the limbic system that is involved in basic emotions. The hippocampus, septum, amygdala, and cingulum are also involved, as is the locus ceruleus, which enervates much of the limbic system. Although we often think of anxiety and fear as excitatory, because they involve arousal, inhibition is just as important to the total equation because a failure of inhibition produces a net result of arousal. As an example, benzodiazepines are a class of medications that have been observed to *activate* a specific receptor, closely coupled to the GABA (γ-aminobutyrate) receptor. GABA is an inhibitory transmitter, so when benzodiazepines increase the action of GABA, the net result is inhibition of attention, arousal, interest, and response to novel stimuli. Barbiturates appear to have the same effect at another receptor closely tied to GABA sites.

An interesting example of the interface between psychology and biology in anxiety has developed recently, as investigators have begun to examine changes in brain chemistry following behavior therapy. Baxter et al. (1992) used positron emission tomography (PET scan) to measure rates of glucose metabolism in the caudate nuclei of clients diagnosed with OCD. Before treatment, glucose is metabolized at a higher rate in these brain regions for clients with OCD than for those without OCD. Interestingly, Gray (1987) speculates the caudate nucleus may be involved in the relationship between the septo-hippocampal system (discussed above) and motor behavior, which is obviously an important feature in obsessive-compulsive rituals. Baxter et al. found both drug and behavioral treatments produced brain changes related to treatment response. Clients whose OCD symptoms improved during drug or behavioral treatment showed moderated glucose metabolism in the caudate nucleus when compared to untreated OCD clients. These results have been replicated (Schwartz, Stoessel, Baxter, Martin, & Phelps, 1996) in OCD clients treated with behavior therapy, and there is some indication that the effects extend to brain areas beyond the caudate nucleus.

IMPLICATIONS FOR DIAGNOSIS AND TREATMENT PLANNING

While there are some clear areas of distinction between different anxiety disorders, there are also many areas of overlap. These areas of overlap can be seen especially clearly when one considers the basic features of the anxiety response, in terms of behavior, physiology, and the cognitive or experiential component. Specific psychological interventions have been developed to address each component of anxiety, including cognitive restructuring, *in vivo* exposure, and progressive muscle relaxation. Many of these procedures have also been incorporated into "brand name" treatments targeted toward specific anxiety disorders. However, some suggest that treatment may be more effective when key features of an anxiety disorder are specifically addressed (Andrews, Crino, Hunt, Lampe, & Page, 1994). This implies that not only should the clinician attend to the issue of differential diagnosis, but also to the idiosyncratic manifestations of a particular disorder for a given client. Some clients may have a predominantly physiological response, where others may be less physically anxious but more affectively or cognitively anxious. It is clear that cognitions, expectations, memory, attention, and avoidance, as well as biological and cultural influences, play important roles in the regulation of anxiety. Throughout the chapters on specific disorders, we note where research results provide guidance to the therapist regarding specific treatment approaches that appear to be especially effective with particular client profiles.

SUMMARY

In this chapter we considered the nature of anxiety and how it is experienced, conceptualized, and described. The dimensional and categorical approaches to the assessment of anxiety are both important, and they offer distinct clinical information. Using both perspectives captures the unique and common characteristics across anxiety disorders and milder forms of anxiety states (i.e., the wide range of subclinical anxiety). The hierarchical model developed by careful study of symptoms among patient and nonpatient populations serves as a useful way to understand the relationship between neurotic vulnerability and specific anxiety disorder groupings. We included this information as well as a brief review of the psychological and biological components involved in anxiety as they are often useful in helping clients interpret their experiences and understand biopsychological interactions, thereby helping to remove the mystery, fear, and uncertainty associated with the experience of intense anxiety. In the next chapter we begin our review of evidence-based assessment and treatment approaches for the most common anxiety disorders, starting with specific phobia.

3 Specific Fears and Phobias

In the last chapter, we discussed the nature of anxiety in general, including some theories about how fear and anxiety operate. Much of what we know about fear is based on studies of simple phobias and common subclinical fears. Early work on behavioral treatments began with specific phobias and agoraphobia, and experiments on conditioning theories have often used specific phobias as a model from which to work. Reflecting this tradition, this chapter will include additional information on basic fears as well as focusing on the assessment and treatment of specific phobias. Conceptually, the information in this chapter provides an informational and theoretical base from which we will expand into more complex anxiety disorders in later chapters. Specific phobias will be considered within a three-systems perspective, including behavioral, physiological, and cognitive components of the fear response. Unique features of some of the specific phobias will be discussed, and empirically supported treatment procedures will be described.

Surveys of the general population reveal that many people have strong fears of various things, including death, specific animals or insects, heights, air travel, public speaking, surgery or other medical procedures, and storms. The usual phobias seen in a clinic are more narrow and include claustrophobia, blood/injury or dental phobia, and small animal phobias (Barlow, 1988). Clients do not typically present for treatment with a specific phobia as their main or only complaint. Phobics who do seek treatment more often have multiple phobias or phobias that are complicated by panic disorder (Chapman, Fyer, Mannuzza, & Klein, 1993). Occasionally, clients seek treatment for a single specific phobia, particularly if the content of the phobia has begun to interfere with day-to-day functioning, although this may be 20 or more years after the phobia began (Öst, 1987a). For example, we might see someone with a fear of snakes who has just taken up an outdoor hobby or sport. Individuals with blood and injury or dental phobias can be significantly impaired in their ability to seek health care; when this problem becomes more urgent, psychological treatment may be sought. More typical in the clinic setting is the client whose other anxiety problems are primary, but for whom the specific phobia adds significant additional disruption.

Normative patterns of intense fears change throughout the life span. Children between the ages of 2 and 4 commonly develop fears of animals, but most become less fearful as they mature (Marks, 1987). Children are also frequently afraid of ghosts, darkness, dogs, and becoming ill or injured (Bauer, 1976; Strauss & Last, 1993). These intense fears are equally common among younger boys and girls, but by adolescence girls are more likely to report fears than boys, and this sex difference continues through adulthood (Fredrikson, Annas, Fischer, & Wik, 1996). What children are afraid of also changes over time, with fears centered on school and social relationships becoming more common by sixth grade. It is not clear to what extent these intense fears among children represent clinically significant problems, as few studies have addressed this question.

In the late stages of life, it appears that the patterns of intense fears undergo more change, as older adults tend to report feeling less afraid of animals, especially spiders, than younger adults. However, fear of other things, such as lightning, heights, and air travel, appears to rise among older adults (Fredrikson et al., 1996). After a fall, it is not uncommon for elderly persons to become frightened of further falls (Isaacs, 1978), clutching objects in an effort to obtain physical support. Because of the risks associated with falls in the elderly, many of these fears can be reality-based. Despite these changing patterns of fears, Agras, Sylvester, and Oliveau (1969) reported generally lower levels of common fears in older adults. This pattern is also reflected in the prevalence rates of phobic disorders, which appear to be lower among older adults, but this may also be a cohort effect related to the social climate characteristic of different generations (Kramer, German, Anthony, Von Korff, & Skinner, 1985).

Turning from common intense fears to actual clinical phobias, we see that most specific phobias typically begin in childhood, which is not surprising, given the frequency with which young children have intense focal fears. Claustrophobia is one exception to the childhood-onset rule, with the average onset being in the late teens (Öst, 1987a). While most children grow out of these fears, some individuals do not, but it is not yet clear what distinguishes those people who remain afraid of things like snakes or dogs. One possibility is certainly that those who gain experience and exposure to the feared object become less afraid; those persons whose avoidant style or overprotective parents prevent such exposure may retain the fear. Personal tolerance for anxiety may also play a role, so that those who are more sensitive to anxiety sensations may be more likely to use avoidance as a coping strategy, thereby obtaining less experience with the feared object.

What is the prevalence of specific phobias? Different studies of prevalence in community samples report widely differing figures, in large part due to differences in measurement methods and the time period in question. Weissman (1985) reported 1.4% of the population met criteria for current specific phobia, but estimates as high as 11.3% have been given for lifetime prevalence of specific phobia (Magee, Eaton, Wittchen, McGonagle, & Kessler, 1996). The National Comorbidity Survey, described in the previous chapter, reported that only 30% of respondents meeting criteria for specific phobia had sought professional help for the problem (Magee et al., 1996). However, this figure might be an overestimate because it does not control for other diagnoses that might have been the primary motivation for seeking treatment.

THREE SYSTEMS OF ANXIETY

Anxiety is a complex emotion consisting of features from multiple response systems: behavior, physiology, and cognition. Responses from these systems interact through internal (neural and hormonal) channels and through their reciprocal influence on the environment. Take the example of a person with a dog phobia who is walking down a quiet street when she sees a dog in a yard just ahead. Her initial response may be an intense reaction in all three systems: she may have a frightening image of a dog attack (cognition); her rate of heartbeat and breathing will probably increase (physiological arousal); she may stop, frozen in her tracks (behavior). It is easy to imagine how any one of these systems might impact on the other. The image of an aggressive, snarling, snapping dog would probably quicken her breathing and, in turn, increase the likelihood she will avoid going near the dog.

Although these channels are related and influence one another, they are each mediated by different factors and can be surprisingly independent. Returning to our example of the dog phobic, while her autonomic arousal is very high, her behavior may not "match" with this high arousal level; she may continue walking down the street rather than avoiding the dog. Perhaps some other motivation, such as rushing to catch a bus, impels her to proceed despite feeling afraid. Cognitive factors may also influence her to behave incongruously with her fear. For example, she may notice a fence around the yard with the dog and consciously weigh the risks of walking past. If she knows a dog lives on a certain block, she may avoid walking past even in the absence of autonomic arousal.

This situation, when the different response systems of anxiety are not in parallel, has been termed *desynchrony* by Rachman and Hodgson (1974). Because we cannot measure fear, but can only infer it from measures of cognition, affect, autonomic arousal, and behavior, desynchrony presents some problems in defining anxiety. How does an assessor determine how anxious a client really is? When has anxiety declined enough to be regarded as a clinically significant reduction? If the client reports feeling anxious but is not objectively aroused, is the client "really" anxious?

As a case example of striking desynchrony, one of us once treated a man with severe and longstanding obsessive-compulsive disorder. At the time of initial evaluation he was nearly housebound due to his fears and avoidance. He was afraid of contracting cancer by contamination, and his avoidance was so entrenched that he had sections of the house blocked off to prevent contaminants from spreading. His wife and children were required to undergo elaborate decontamination procedures whenever they had ventured outside. During an early exposure session, a "contaminated" hat was presented to him, and the therapist asked him to hold the hat, rubbing it over his hands, clothing, and head. He sobbed and trembled during this procedure, obviously in great distress. At the time, he was wearing electrodes connected to a polygraph machine, which recorded his psychophysiological responses. On the polygraph, there was no sign of arousal! On none of the measures (e.g., heart rate, respiration) did he show an elevation above baseline. Yet any observer would have been convinced that this man was experiencing intense distress.

This same phenomenon has been observed repeatedly in laboratories around the world. There is some indication that intense emotions are usually associated with greater concordance of these response channels than milder emotions, but this is not always the case. The client we just discussed is a good example, and people who display courageous behavior under threatening circumstances are another. Rachman's discussion of fear and courage displayed by World War II servicemen details several interesting examples (Rachman, 1990). In the case of these servicemen (e.g., airplane pilots, gunners, and navigators), not only was there intense emotional arousal, but also the demands of the situation were high. In the case of high demand, laboratory studies have demonstrated that desynchrony often occurs—usually the individual performs what is demanded despite experiencing fear. In low-demand situations, where the option of avoiding is more permissible, there may be more concordance between response systems, as people feel more free to avoid when anxious.

The power of social demand, or pressure to perform, can be a tool for the therapist to utilize in helping clients to engage in exposure-based treatments (described later). While the therapist carefully chooses each step of exposure to match the client's expected ability at that moment in treatment, the process is probably facilitated by the expression of confident, clear expectations that the client will approach the feared stimulus. Often, the professional status of the therapist as an expert helper will contribute to the social demand that urges a client to engage in exposure. Sometimes, however, the therapist must make the encouragement or pressure more explicit. Such encouragement may include reminding the client of the rationale for the treatment plan or insisting that the client engage in some type of exposure during each session, even if it means taking a small step backward to repeat work done in the last session. These techniques can help a client who has high anxiety and high avoidance; in this case, creating desynchrony by stopping the avoidance will be the first step toward resolution of the phobia.

Although the general idea of three systems of responding is a simple one, specific issues are raised within each system. Over the next few pages, some of these issues will be discussed as they relate to specific phobias. While the different response systems are discussed separately, it is important to remember that they are intimately related. Cognitions can affect degree of physiological response as well as the likelihood of avoidance or escape, and these in turn impact on the beliefs that a person will have about the feared situation.

Behavioral Component

The interference with one's lifestyle that is a consequence of avoidance is one of the primary reasons clients seek treatment for a specific phobia. If avoiding the feared stimulus is relatively easy and causes no impediments to reaching life's important goals, there is usually little distress about having a specific fear. An example of this is the common fear of heights. Many people have lifestyles that do not require going in high places. However, a change in life's habits, such as being offered a new job in a skyscraper, may provide the impetus for seeking treatment. As an example, one of our clients was very afraid of enclosed places and had been able to avoid them relatively easily. However, she was transferred to a new job in a building where she had to descend to a sub-basement to punch the time clock every morning and then go to the fourth floor to do her job. To avoid using the elevator, she had been using the stairs for this twice-daily trip, but she felt self-conscious in front of her co-workers, who all rode the elevator together to clock in and clock out. Her embarrassment prompted her to seek treatment for the claustrophobia.

Women more commonly avoid fear-provoking situations than men do. Whether men and women typically *fear* the same things has been the subject of some controversy, with a number of studies devoted to extensive surveys of the types of situations or objects people fear. As some of the most feared items in some studies (e.g., fear of being punished by God) are not included in the surveys of other studies, it is hard to really say with certainty "what people fear the most." Women often report more intense fears overall than men (Fredrikson et al., 1996), and women are more avoidant than are men when confronted with a fear-provoking stimulus such as a snake. Even when men and women are matched for how scared they say they are, once confronted with an actual snake, women are more avoidant, look more anxious, and report feeling more fear (Speltz & Bernstein, 1976; Woody & Chambless, 1989, April). This difference in fearful behavior shows up again in prevalence rates for phobias; community studies show that women outnumber men with specific phobias 2:1 (Bourdon et al., 1988; Magee et al., 1996).

Why are women over-represented among phobics? One theory blames sociocultural factors (Chambless, 1987). The traditional masculine sex role involves bravery and prizes assertive, instrumental behavior. Developing boys who display fear may be encouraged to confront their fears; they are almost certainly teased for avoiding or running away. The expectations for girls are different. While fearful behavior may not be actively encouraged, it is certainly tolerated to a greater extent than among boys. Thus, girls may feel less pressure to perform fearlessly, which constitutes a low-demand situation. As discussed above, this circumstance is more likely to be associated with avoidant behavior in the face of fear than a high-demand situation such as the one boys are likely to be facing. If this theory is accurate, social pressure creates a high level of demand for boys and men to behave as though they are not afraid, even when they are. As Chambless (1987) hypothesizes, this active, instrumental behavior may be prophylactic against potential phobias; exposure to feared stimuli may prevent incipient phobias from developing.

Physiological Component

In thinking of fear as a fight-or-flight defensive response to threat, it is clear that the body has high metabolic (energy) requirements for either fighting or fleeing. Some of the earliest research recording physiological responses of emotion revealed intense responses associated with fear (Ax, 1953). As discussed in chapter 2, the sympathetic nervous system is activated when people are confronted with a frightening stimulus (Fredrikson, 1981; Hare & Bleving, 1976), thus mobilizing resources for the strong physical acts of fighting or fleeing. This activation is evident in various bodily systems: skin conductance increases (indicating sweating), breathing and heart rate increase, and there are more peaks in measures of muscle tension. These responses are not characteristic of the usual "squeamish" type of fear, such as most people might experience upon seeing a spider in the kitchen. Rather, this type of reaction is reserved for situations in which extreme danger is perceived; even phobic people do not show this response when they are confronted by an equivalent stimulus that they do not fear (e.g., seeing a spider when one is afraid of snakes).

Given this intense physiological response, one might expect that blocking the major physiological signs of anxiety would eliminate the phobic response. Several approaches have been tried: biofeedback and medication. Biofeedback was only marginally successful at reducing the tachycardia (rapid heartbeat) that occurs during contact with a phobic stimulus, and it had no beneficial effect on other psychophysiological signs of anxiety or on self-reported anxiety (Nunes & Marks, 1975; Nunes & Marks, 1976). Medications, specifically beta-blockers, consistently eliminate the tachycardia associated with exposure to the phobic object. Phobics who have taken a beta-blocker prior to coming in contact with the phobic stimulus do not experience an elevation in heart rate. However, several studies have just as consistently shown that this effect is not accompanied by lower anxiety or a greater willingness to approach the stimulus (Bernadt, Silverstone, & Singleton, 1980; Campos, Solyom, & Koelink, 1984; Gaind, Suri, & Thompson, 1975). This discrepancy obviously limits the utility of this approach for treating specific phobia.

Cognitive Component

On the surface, cognitive activity in specific phobia would seem to be about the phobic stimulus—whether and how the stimulus might pose a danger. "The elevator cable could snap, and then we will fall 20 floors!" "Lightning might strike the house and burn it down." Surprisingly, when clients with specific phobias are asked about their cognitions, much of the content relates to the consequences of experiencing intense anxiety. In one study, 91% of animal phobics were afraid of *panicking* when confronted with the animal they feared (McNally & Steketee, 1985). In a sample of diverse types of specific phobias, most respondents expressed at least a 40% degree of belief in ideas related to fear of physical consequences of anxiety—similar to those observed in anxiety sensitivity or panic disorder (Thorpe & Salkovskis, 1995). The most common cognitions endorsed in the Thorpe and Salkovskis study were "I will make a fool of myself," "I will feel faint," "I will lose control," "I will be unable to escape," and "I will feel trapped." In that study, phobics only indicated having these thoughts in the context of being in contact (in the same room) with the phobic stimulus.

Cognition in specific phobia goes beyond fear of the consequences of anxiety. As we might expect, many instances of distorted thinking are tied directly to the phobic stimulus. Rachman and Cuk (1992) relate several interesting clinical anecdotes of patients with anxiety disorders who experience what appear to be distortions in their *perception* of feared stimuli. In the case of a snake that is perceived to be longer than it actually is or to dart more quickly than it really does, distortions or misperceptions are easy to understand. Some of the patients discussed by Rachman and Cuk went further, however, with misperceptions of roads and bridges that appeared to tilt dangerously as the patient approached.

In a more systematic study of perceptual distortion among snake-fearful college students, Taylor and Rachman (1994) found that bias in estimating properties of the stimulus contributed to anxiety during an opportunity to touch a snake. Distortions in the properties of the stimulus also led students to overpredict the amount of fear they would experience if they were to approach the snake. Taylor and Rachman suggested that global stimulus biases (e.g., estimate of overall dangerousness) were more influential than perceptual errors about specific features of the stimulus (e.g., length, activity level).

Predictions about terrible things that could happen if one engages with the phobic stimulus may also play a role in anticipatory anxiety and avoidance. Some clients have vivid and terrifying imagery of catastrophes like plane crashes, car accidents, drowning, or suffocating. A key component of the fear response is narrowing of attention, an adaptive feature that enables one to detect threat. Attention is drawn to these terrifying images as though rehearsing for catastrophe. Clearly, these ideas and images heighten anxiety about the feared situation and increase the probability of avoidance.

ARE ALL SPECIFIC PHOBIAS CREATED EQUAL?

Thus far, we have been discussing specific phobias as though they were interchangeable. While some phobias appear to be quite similar in phenomenology, such as fears of spiders and snakes, several of the specific phobias have unique characteristics that require mention. For example, Öst (1987a) sees claustrophobia as distinct from other specific phobias, potentially being descriptively and functionally equivalent to agoraphobia, with claustrophobics simply having a more restricted pattern of avoidance. The major specific phobias that require special consideration are phobias of blood/injury/injection and of having dental work performed.

Blood/Injury Phobia

In the previous chapter, we discussed the typical physiological response when a phobic person confronts a feared stimulus: marked increase in heart rate, respiration, skin conductance, and blood pressure. Blood and injury (B/I) phobia is associated with an unusual and sometimes dramatic physiological response—a vasovagal response. Studies of blood phobics and blood donors who faint have revealed a diphasic response, with an initial increase in heart rate and blood pressure (the typical sympathetic response), followed by a precipitous drop in blood pressure and heart rate. This reaction may be accompanied by nausea, without fear of vomiting (Marks, 1987). Many B/I phobics actually faint, something that does not occur as a phobic response to other stimuli (see sidebar 3-1 for a case illustration).

Öst, Sterner, and Lindahl (1984) provided a fascinating account of a group of B/I phobics who were asked to watch a gruesome video of thoracic surgery. Participants were permitted to turn off the video when it got to be too intense. During the baseline (before they knew the video was coming), there was a stable physiological pattern. During the few minutes in which participants listened to instructions about the video, heart rate and blood pressure rose markedly. Then blood pressure and heart rate began to *decrease*, consistently reaching their lowest point about 4 minutes after the participant had turned off the video. Five participants who fainted or came closest to fainting were examined in more detail. Some participants experienced a gradual decline in heart rate and blood pressure for a few minutes and then a dramatic drop, which was often followed by the participant turn-

CASE DESCRIPTION

Jeanine was a 35-year-old bus driver. Her job involved long days of driving tourists from her base city to a casino in a neighboring state, waiting a few hours, and then driving them back. Since her childhood, Jeanine had been afraid of blood and gruesome stimuli, and she coped with this fear by avoiding television programs, movies, and visiting friends in the hospital. She had occasionally fainted when exposed to stimuli related to blood. One day shortly before she sought treatment, a passenger was telling a gruesome story in the seat behind her, and she fainted. Fortunately, she had been stopped at a traffic light and there was no accident. Her union intervened to prevent the bus company from firing her, and she was ordered to seek behavior therapy for the blood/injury phobia in order to return to work.

Her fear was relatively circumscribed, typically occurring in response to auditory stimuli. She was able to appropriately handle her children's injuries without feeling faint or anxious, and she did not avoid medical procedures (although she was very healthy). Treatment first began with instructing Jeanine in muscle tension techniques. Several strategies were required before Jeanine felt that she could tense her quadriceps as fully as her arms.

After a session of instruction in muscle tension (and home practice), the therapist described an imaginal scene involving a car accident with several injured passengers. Jeanine's job was to apply the muscle tension as she began to feel her body responding to the scene. This first exposure session was very challenging for Jeanine. Soon after the therapist started describing the scene, Jeanine's face became ashen and she said that she felt nauseated and faint. Her anxiety was 80 on the SUDS scale. The therapist encouraged her to continue tensing her muscles, and Jeanine was able to avoid fainting. Although this session was difficult, her success gave Jeanine confidence that she would be able to prevent fainting in the future.

Jeanine was seen three more times. During session 3, Jeanine accompanied her therapist to a blood drive, where she first watched her therapist give blood and then donated blood herself. For session 4, the therapist asked a friend who works in an emergency room to audiotape vivid descriptions of horrible injuries he had seen. By the last session, Jeanine had obtained a graphic video of heart surgery, which she and the therapist watched in the session. Between sessions, Jeanine was able to ask her friends to describe childhood injuries and surgeries. In addition, she purposely looked for bloody television programs rather than avoiding such content as she had in the past. In all these cases, Jeanine applied muscle tension. By the end of treatment, Jeanine felt confident in her ability to handle any stimulus related to blood or injury, and her anxiety level during contact with such stimuli was 10–20.

ing off the video. In one individual, heart rate dropped as low as 28 beats per minute. Öst et al. observed frequent periods of asystole (when the heart stops contracting) in almost all participants, varying from 2 to 9 seconds.

Many people are squeamish at the sight of blood. Marks (1987) notes that various species of mammals become alarmed at the sight of an injured or dead member of their own species. Marks further points out that the diphasic cardiovascular response also occurs in people without B/I phobia, but the difference is one of degree. Clearly, this characteristic has implications for treatment of B/I phobia. Some specific treatment procedures have been developed, which will be discussed later in the chapter. However, even if the treatment approach is in vivo or imaginal exposure, Barlow (1988) recommends having the client lie down during initial exposure sessions to prevent injury in the event that the client does faint.

A final aspect of B/I phobia distinguishing it from other specific phobias is the strong familial component. As reviewed by Marks (1987), the majority of patients with B/I phobia report having family members with a blood phobia, a much higher rate than with other types of phobia. Marks suggests that the intense bradycardia (marked slowing of heart rate) described above may be the key to the genetic component of B/I phobia. If the tendency to faint in the presence of blood is genetically mediated, then this dramatic and frightening physiological response may lead to the development of a phobia. However, it is important to note that these hypotheses are based on family studies, not twin studies, which provide better evidence of genetic linkage. The only twin studies of anxiety disorders that we are aware of (Kendler, Neale, Kessler, Heath, & Eaves, 1992; Torgersen, 1983) did not specifically examine B/I phobias.

Dental Phobia

Many adults delay dental visits or avoid preventative care, but 5% or fewer have dental phobia (Marks, 1987). As with all types of phobia, in the case of dental fears, the clinician must evaluate the *specific* aspect of dental care that the client fears. Individuals who are afraid of dental visits are commonly concerned with anticipated pain, which can itself be exacerbated by anxiety. However, there are other less obvious fears related to dental visits, such as being trapped, becoming infected with HIV, or retching. Wilks (1993) described the case of a man whose hypersensitive gag reflex precluded dental work. Detailed assessment revealed that the man could swallow only with his teeth tightly clenched together, which he had been unaware of doing. He further acknowledged a pronounced aversion to rubber gloves, instruments, or tubes. Wilks reports treating this man with an approach that involved focused relaxation while swallowing, which reduced the gag reflex and allowed gradual exposure to dental tools.

Other fears associated with dental work can be fears of choking, of asphyxiation, or fears that needles or drills will break or that instruments or debris will be dropped down the patient's throat. These fears can often be reduced through provision of accurate information about dental procedures (de Jongh et al., 1995). We have even used videotapes of individuals comfortably undergoing dental work in order to provide the patient with a good view of what happens during dental examinations and treatment. In a one-session treatment study, de Jongh et al. described a cognitive intervention that included corrective information about the specific procedure the patient was facing, along with therapist assistance in using this information to question evidence for negative cognitions associated with the patient's specific fear. This personalized information targeted to patients' specific fears reduced the frequency and believability of frightening dental cognitions more than general dental information on hygiene and dental treatment. Reductions in dental anxiety were maintained through 1-year follow-up.

THEORIES OF ETIOLOGY AND MAINTENANCE

Conditioning Theory

Over the last 30 years, learning theory accounts of specific phobias have become the dominant theory. Briefly, phobias are regarded as conditioned responses. Fear of a neutral stimulus is attributed to a co-occurrence of the stimulus with an aversive incident at some point in the client's history. Examples of inherently aversive incidents include pain, threat of abandonment, or spontaneous panic attack. The fear stemming from the aversive incident is presumed to generalize beyond the original fearful stimulus to include the neutral (now phobic) stimulus as well. Presumably, the aversive stimulus could be an external or an internal event (Rescorla, 1988). This process is probably most easily understood using the example of conditioned taste aversion. Many people have had the experience of becoming sick soon after eating a meal, whether because of food poisoning or a virus. Not uncommonly, the specific food continues to evoke nausea or disgust long after the illness is over.

This process, whereby people become afraid of something once it has been paired with an aversive event, has been demonstrated many times in laboratories. Thus, it is clear that phobias *can* be initiated in this way. However, whether real life phobias are *typically* due to a conditioning process is more difficult to say. Only a minority of clients with specific phobia actually recall a traumatic onset of their phobia (McNally & Steketee, 1985; Öst & Hugdahl, 1981). On the other hand, the onset of specific phobias, particularly the animal phobias, may be so early in life that people are unable to recall the triggering event. There are some indications that phobias can follow aversive events in real life, particularly for nonanimal phobias that begin in adulthood. For example, 38% of a group of 55 survivors of automobile accidents subsequently developed a driving phobia (Kuch, Cox, Evans, & Shulman, 1994). In addition, a primary basis of choking and dental phobias is a previous frightening experience such as actually choking on food or having a painful dental visit (Greenberg, Stern, & Weilburg, 1988; Moore, Brodsgaard, & Birn, 1991).

Several modifications to conditioning theory have been proposed through the years. One of the most relevant for clinical practice has been Mowrer's (1960) two-stage theory. In the first stage, which we have just discussed, a neutral stimulus is paired with an aversive one. The fear associated with the aversive stimulus becomes attached to the neutral stimulus, and a phobia is born. In Mowrer's second stage, the person learns that the uncomfortable fear response can be diminished if he or she simply avoids the phobic stimulus. As discussed in the previous chapter, the subsequent reduction in arousal reinforces avoidance, which may then become habitual. The process of conditioning is helped along if the person has had little experience with the neutral stimulus. For example, people who have been around dogs all their lives are much less likely to become afraid of dogs after a traumatic encounter with a dog than someone who has had little experience with them (Doogan & Thomas, 1992).

Rachman (1977) has proposed additional pathways to acquisition of fear. In addition to the conditioning route just described, he proposed that some phobias are acquired through cultural means, by experiencing vicarious conditioning or hearing frightening information. Experiments suggest that phobias can be acquired through these indirect means (Mineka, Davidson, Cook, & Keir, 1984; Öst & Hugdahl, 1981). An example of vicarious conditioning might be witnessing a boating accident and subsequently becoming afraid of being on boats or near deep water. Acquiring fears through information would include hearing frightening warnings from family members about the dangers of the neutral stimulus. This phenomenon is readily observed in those clients with a phobia of flying who have never taken an airplane trip.

Intrapsychic Theories

Briefly, the classic psychoanalytic formulation of phobias, as described by Goisman (1983), involves an anxiety-provoking impulse, often sexual, that is repressed because it is too threatening to be acknowledged. The impulse and its associated anxiety are displaced onto a symbolically or temporally associated object. Generalization may occur, incorporating similar objects. Because confronting the object would involve confronting the threatening impulse, the stimulus is avoided. In this account, neurotic anxiety arises purely internally. The formation of a phobic symptom is seen as an attempt to "bind" the anxiety so that it can masquerade as a realistic external fear, and hence be avoided (Compton, 1992). The key to these accounts of the development of phobias is in the intrapsychic source of anxiety, and it is here that different writers diverge in their view of the specific impulse being defended against.

Psychoanalytic theory lacks a coherent explanation of focal phobias, possibly due to the often arbitrary interpretations of the specific symptoms (Snaith, 1968). Compton (1992) points to three writers who target the "discovery of the genital difference" as the precipitating event for childhood phobias. Snaith attributes claustrophobia or fear of being alone to a defensive reaction against the temptation to masturbate. The agoraphobic fear of "going shopping" is taken to indicate a wish to take mother's place beside father (Snaith, 1968). These types of explanations leave no avenue to verify their accuracy, and different writers often disagree on the basis of the same information. For example, Freud's explanation for Little Hans' horse phobia was based in Oedipal rivalry for his mother, but Lief (1968) argues that the boy's phobia was based on fear of punishment for masturbation.

In contrast to the radical psychoanalytic position, contemporary psychodynamic viewpoints emphasize the personal meaning of the stimulus, and thus have closer associations with learning theory—especially formulations that encompass cognitive components along with behavioral ones. Salzman's (1968) account takes the aggressive/sexual impulse theory of the psychoanalysts and expands it to include any potential threat to the patient's capacity for self-control. The humiliating and threatening consequences of losing control lead to attendant fears of public display of inadequacy and imperfection. The phobia is seen as a "ritual of inaction" (avoidance) designed to exert control over the threat of unmasking one's inadequacies. Recall that the most common fears endorsed by clients with specific phobia are fears of the consequences of panic, among them losing control and public humiliation. Those who argue that the success of treatment for simple phobia is due to restoring a sense of self-efficacy (Williams, Turner, & Peer, 1985) or changing core beliefs about the consequences of experiencing anxiety (Thorpe & Salkovskis, 1995) do not seem to be too far from Salzman's formulation.

Other similarities between Salzman's (1968) psychodynamic ideas on phobias and contemporary cognitive behavioral theories include the mechanism of generalization. Learning theory points to stimulus similarity as the main mechanism for generalization; fear responses are more likely to generalize to related stimuli if they share many characteristics with the original phobic stimulus. For example, going to visit a friend in the hospital is likely to arouse fear for a blood phobic, as hospitals are filled with stimuli likely to have been encountered during injections or blood draws. Visiting the same friend in a college dormitory is unlikely to provoke the fear response, as dormitories share few stimulus characteristics with doctors' offices. Perhaps in recognition of the laboratory work done by behavioral psychopathologists who were his contemporaries, Salzman's viewpoint on generalization is consistent with this account. However, Salzman went one step further, proposing that generalization can also be driven by the symbolic meaning of the stimulus. As an example, he points to "feeling trapped," which might underlie fear and avoidance of a number of specific situations, such as elevators, having one's hair cut, or wearing heavy clothing or a seatbelt. Similarly, a contemporary cognitive behavioral therapist, hearing this constellation of feared stimuli, would probably ask about the feared consequences of these situations, in an attempt to understand the symbolic meaning that ties these stimuli together in one parsimonious case conceptualization.

These similarities between different theoretical formulations of fears and phobias demonstrate that clinicians from diverse backgrounds may form a common language to approach effective treatments for anxiety disorders. Specific phobias were among the first disorders to be treated with newly developed behavioral methods in the 1950s (Wolpe, 1958), presumably because these problems are relatively well defined and circumscribed. Recently, as psychotherapy researchers from nonbehavioral backgrounds are developing new methods for investigating efficacy, some are likewise turning to specific phobia as an initial problem for testing their methods. For example, Johnson and Smith (1997) developed a manualized version of the empty-chair technique as an initial step in testing the efficacy of Gestalt therapy for specific phobias. Although there appear to be areas of overlap in theoretical formulations of specific phobia, there is probably much less overlap in terms of the specific procedures recommended by developers of behavioral and psychodynamic treatment approaches.

Concern about symptom substitution constitutes one basis for the marked difference in treatment approaches between the intrapsychic and behavioral camps. As described above, the nature of intrapsychic conflicts are most often seen as developmental, aggressive, or sexual. If the underlying conflict is not addressed, traditional lore warns that the phobia will return or another symptom will be substituted to continue expressing the conflict. Arguing against the occurrence of symptom substitution are scores of studies successfully using behavioral approaches to treat clients with a diverse range of anxiety-based disorders. Behaviorists point to these studies as evidence that the overt symptom can be safely and effectively treated without risk of new problems developing. On the other hand, behavioral approaches do not always work! Oftentimes, patients experience improvement in their functioning but are unable to completely rid themselves of the phobia. Plus, as Blanchard and Hersen (1976) pointed out, there are persistent anecdotal indications of the occurrence of symptom substitution. How are these seeming contradictions to be resolved?

First, it is clear that symptom substitution is not a necessary side effect of problem-focused treatment, because numerous clinical studies have documented good outcomes with most clients participating in behavioral treatment. If we point to well-maintained positive outcomes as evidence that symptom substitution does not occur, how are we to understand clients who fail to improve in treatments like systematic desensitization or progressive muscle relaxation? One theory proposes that state-dependent learning and memory may facilitate or impair the client's ability to learn new responses to a given stimulus (Bodden, 1991). Bodden argues that unconscious origins of a phobia lie not in intrapsychic conflict, but in inaccessible memories of the emotional and environmental stimuli associated with the original development of the phobic response. Bodden describes an uncontrolled study with two cases in which hypnosis was used as an adjunct to behavioral methods to facilitate recall of the phobia's origins.

For some neurotic problems, symptom substitution does seem to occur, although not with phobias. Blanchard and Hersen (1976) distinguished between avoidance-based problems, which are maintained primarily by the anxiety-reduction of avoidance or escape, and hysterical and conversion problems, which are maintained by secondary gain. In this second type of neurotic behavior, Blanchard and Hersen—speaking from a strictly behavioral perspective—expected symptom return or substitution if the symptom were to be removed without changing the environment or teaching the patient more adaptive ways of meeting the goals of the secondary gain. In support of their view, they presented four cases of conversion disorders treated behaviorally in which symptom substitution was evident.

Despite our inability to proclaim 100% success rates for treating specific phobia, there are several treatment approaches that show very good outcomes. Because of their documented success, these approaches are recommended as first-line treatments for specific phobia. In the remainder of this chapter, specific assessment and treatment approaches with scientific support will be described.

ASSESSMENT PROCEDURES

Differential Diagnosis

When a client seeks treatment for a specific phobia, differential diagnosis may not be a complicated issue. Because the fear is so circumscribed, clients are generally very clear on the parameters of their fear. Often, a thorough interview will reveal most of the necessary information about the feared stimulus, the fear response itself, the extent of avoidance, and feared consequences. Sometimes complications will arise, particularly around the issue of panic attacks, which can occur in the context of most anxiety disorders. Thus, the presence of panic attacks does not automatically signal that the case should be treated as panic disorder. See chapter 5 in this volume for a complete description of panic attacks and panic disorder.

Specific phobia is distinguished from panic disorder primarily by the observation that the panic attacks are *cued* in simple phobia. Cued panic attacks occur exclusively in the context of a feared stimulus, with no history of occurring spontaneously, or coming from "out of the blue." A possible exception to this rule may be a phobia that develops in conjunction with a single unexpected panic attack. All subsequent attacks would be cued by the presence of the phobic stimulus. For example, the client might panic when suddenly confronted with the feared stimulus, such as encountering a tunnel while driving. Even the anticipation of encountering the stimulus may be frightening enough to provoke a panic attack. Nevertheless, a cued panic attack always occurs in response to a feared stimulus, whether that stimulus is presented in reality, in fantasy, pictorially, or in anticipation of a future event.

The feared stimulus itself often provides a clue as to which differential diagnostic questions will arise. In the case of commonly observed fears of animals, so long as the clinician establishes that an intense fear response occurs specifically in relation to exposure to the animal or insect, there is usually little debate about diagnosis. In contrast, several prevalent specific phobias are also commonly observed as part of the cluster of feared situations in agoraphobia, including claustrophobia and fears of heights, air travel, and driving. When a patient presents with one of these fears, and there is no evidence of a history of spontaneous panic attacks, then the case probably should be treated as a specific phobia. Differential diagnosis is more complicated when the patient routinely has panic attacks in one of these feared situations. In this case, feared consequences will provide cues for how to conceptualize the problem. What is the patient afraid will happen when he encounters one of these situations? If the client primarily fears having a panic attack or some physical catastrophe, such as a heart attack, fainting, or suffocating, then the case is probably best approached as panic disorder. On the other hand, if the client primarily fears some feature of the stimulus, such as the airplane free-falling from its flight path, then it is probably best conceptualized as specific phobia.

While there may seem to be little reason to request a medical evaluation for a straightforward spider phobia, there are numerous physical disorders that produce symptoms that mimic anxiety and panic attacks. Thus, it is always a good idea to ascertain that anxious clients have been medically evaluated to rule out organic causes for their symptoms. Finally, as with other more obviously complicated problems, it is useful to assess other factors, such as caffeine or other stimulant use, benzodiazepine use, or relationship discord that may impact on the phobia. What appears to be a straightforward phobia may also be complicated by intolerance of anxiety, but this will often become apparent soon after exposure-based treatment has begun.

Measurement of Progress

Pressure on clinicians to be accountable for quality of care and to rapidly produce good outcomes has heightened the need for measurement of progress. Cost-effective measures of treatment progress are essential in formulating treatment plans that are responsive to the rate and pattern of improvement. Some behavioral health care organizations have begun to implement their own outcomes monitoring systems, but these systems may address global functioning without being sufficiently sensitive to change on specific problems. Assessment of the severity of specific phobias can often be aided by the use of fear inventories, but these inventories may fail to address important aspects of a particular client's phobia. In this case, several methods of idiographic assessment used in laboratory studies can be adapted for use in the clinic.

Fear Inventories

A widely used measure is the *Fear Questionnaire* (Marks & Mathews, 1979). This one page measure has three phobic subscales: Agoraphobia, Social Phobia, and Blood/Injury Phobia. The subscales can be combined for a Total Phobia score. Each item is rated on a 0–8 scale indicating degree to which the respondent is "troubled by" or avoids the item. There is also an idiographic single item asking respondents to list the "main phobia you want treated" and rate its severity. Finally, a single item assesses clients' perceptions of the global state of their phobic symptoms. The brevity of the Fear Questionnaire makes it a useful tool in the clinical setting, assuming the scale addresses the client's particular problem area. The Fear Questionnaire is reprinted in Appendix A. The questionnaire yields several scores: (a) main target phobia, (b) global phobia, (c) total phobia, and (d) specific subscales. The Main Phobia is simply the first question ("main phobia you want treated"). The Global Phobia is a single item representing degree of distress and avoidance (the last item on the scale). The subscales on this measure are easy to calculate by adding the scores in the boxes aligned with the "Ag," "BI," and "Soc" (for agoraphobia, blood/injury, and social, respectively) scoring key after question 17. These subscales (items 2–16) sum to the Total Phobia score. Good test-retest reliabilities have been reported for each of these scores (Marks & Mathews, 1979; Michelson & Mavissakalian, 1983).

In addition to these widely used broad-based measures of phobia, specific questionnaires have been constructed to assess fear and fear-related beliefs regarding common phobias (Klorman, Weerts, Hastings, Melamed, & Lang, 1974). Because they are so specific, many of these measures might not be worth the trouble of obtaining them for a clinician who rarely sees animal phobias. Nonetheless, they are instructive for the types of information they elicit about feared stimuli. The scales themselves may even be useful as low-level stimuli for early stages of exposure therapy with very severe phobics. For instance, several measures on fears of spiders have been constructed.

Two examples are the *Fear of Spiders Questionnaire* (Szymanski & O'Donohue, 1995) and the *Spider Phobia Beliefs Questionnaire* (Arntz, Lavy, van den Berg, & van Rijsoort, 1993). The Fear of Spiders Questionnaire obtains the client's own report of avoidant behavior and fear of harm.

Items include "If I came across a spider now, I would get help from someone to remove it," "If I saw a spider now, I would feel very panicky," and "I now think a lot about spiders." The Spider Phobia Beliefs Questionnaire evaluates the client's ideas about likely spider behavior, as well as the client's likely response upon encountering a spider. Items referring to the spider's behavior include belief that the spider "will bite me," "senses that I'm anxious," "will crawl into my clothes," and "is never alone; there are always more of them." Items referring to the client's likely response include predictions that the client will "have a heart attack," "get nightmares of creepy spiders," and "be unable to think rationally."

Idiographic Assessment

There are a number of ways to objectively evaluate severity of phobia over the course of treatment without using standardized questionnaires. The most obvious are measures involving observable indications of functioning that can be tracked over time. For example, Ball and Otto (1994) described three cases of choking phobia which were characterized by fears of swallowing. An important measure they used to track functional improvement was weight gain, as each patient had been avoiding eating due to fear of choking on food. Likewise, for clients who have B/I or dental phobias, a critical measure of functioning is the degree to which they begin to seek appropriate medical or dental care. As another example, a client with a height phobia seen at one of our clinics was afraid of driving across a particularly high bridge, which unfortunately was situated between her home and her workplace. In order to avoid driving across this bridge, she drove an hour out of the way in each direction to take another bridge that was not as high. Throughout her treatment, we monitored the number of unnecessary trips she made each week as an indicator of treatment progress. Such signs of functional improvement are inexpensive to monitor and relate directly to the client's problems.

For this particular client with the difficulty crossing bridges, we also asked her to record her degree of anxiety during each driving trip. This is typically done using a scale called the *Subjective Units of Distress Scale* (SUDS), which is a 0–100 scale used by the client to monitor and communicate subjective anxiety levels. On this scale, 0 represents no anxiety, a state that is extremely relaxed and not a usual part of everyday experience for most active people. On the other end, 100 represents the most anxiety the client can imagine experiencing. Usually clients are able to begin using the scale proficiently with just this amount of introduction, although the scale sometimes does feel artificial at first to those who are not accustomed to using it.

Asking the patient to communicate level of anxiety with a number provides a common language and a metric enabling the therapist to obtain a quick appreciation for how anxious the patient is feeling. Each client probably uses the scale in a slightly different way, and the therapist should be alert to gross miscommunication about the scale at the outset. For example, a client who initially responds with 0 when asked how anxious he currently is feeling might revise his estimate if the therapist gently asks him if he can imagine being more relaxed than he is right now. While we use a 0–100 scale, others prefer a 0–10 or 0–8 scale; whatever metric the therapist feels comfortable using is fine.

In preparation for exposure-based methods of treatment, which will be described in detail below, the clinician should prepare a list of feared stimuli, along with SUDS ratings. This list, or *hierarchy*, should include features of the stimulus that have particular meaning for a given client. (See sidebar 3-2 for more about constructing a hierarchy.) Stimuli that are peripheral to the phobic object would be included on the hierarchy, although they may have lower fear ratings associated with them. As the therapist and client begin to do exposure with the stimuli on the hierarchy, improvements may generalize to other stimuli on the hierarchy. By repeatedly asking for SUDS ratings of each item on the hierarchy, the therapist has an easy measure of progress that folds into treatment planning.

As an example, a case reported in the literature of a young man with a balloon phobia included fears of other loud sudden noises (Houlihan, Schwartz, Miltenberger, & Heuton, 1993). Besides balloons themselves, the man was intensely afraid of noises related to bursting balloons, fireworks, guns, and backfiring cars. As a result of the probability of encountering balloons in certain situations, the man avoided social settings like dances, birthday parties, athletic events, and weddings. All of these situations would be listed on his fear hierarchy. The top item on this man's hierarchy (at an anxiety level of 100) was being in a treatment room with 100 large balloons in it. Other items on the hierarchy included being in smaller rooms with fewer balloons, as well as popping balloons. Houlihan et al. used the man's ratings of anxiety and confidence in his ability to cope with each item on the hierarchy as an indication of progress during therapy and at a follow-up meeting.

Another widely used idiographic assessment in phobia research has been the *behavioral avoidance test*. The primary advantage of this test is that it involves direct observation of the client's behavior as s/he is given an opportunity to interact with the feared stimulus. This is useful because it allows the clinician to evaluate the client's coping behavior and tolerance for anxiety. As self-reported fear and avoidance do not always go hand-in-hand, this direct measure of avoidance is useful in addition to the hierarchy ratings. The primary obstacle to conducting the behavioral avoidance test is arranging for access to the stimulus, such as obtaining a snake or spider or gaining permission to use an elevator in a tall building. After the therapist arranges for access to the stimulus (necessary for exposure-based treatment), the behavioral avoidance test is only one more step. Sidebar 3-3 provides some ideas for how to obtain these stimuli.

BUILDING A HIERARCHY

As the clinician conducts an interview assessing features of feared stimuli, she or he can make a rough hierarchy as the client reveals situations that are "very frightening" and those that are only "a little scary." By jotting down these items as they are spontaneously mentioned by the client, the beginnings of a hierarchy are formed. Before beginning exposure-based treatment, these notes should be transformed into a formal hierarchy of feared stimuli by asking more specific questions. Assigning numbers to the fear levels (SUDS—see text) helps the therapist and client communicate more precisely. In addition, building the hierarchy fills in details about the cues that provoke fear. For example:

T: Let's review the things that are frightening for you. You mentioned that driving on highways is the biggest problem for you. Is there a specific freeway that scares you more than others?

C: Yes, Highway 71 is the worst. People really drive fast on that one, and there always seems to be some sort of construction, so the lanes are often changed, and there are those awful concrete barriers. Plus, I hear about accidents on 71 nearly every day on the radio.

T: Let's use a 0–100 scale to indicate how anxious you feel about driving in each of these different situations. We'll use this scale often in our work together. On this scale, 100 is the most anxiety you can imagine experiencing. Zero would be the most relaxed you can imagine being, perhaps like lounging in a warm spot while vacationing. Using that scale, how anxious would you feel if you were to drive on Highway 71?

C: It depends on what part of 71. Going north from town is less crowded, except on holiday weekends and Fridays during the summer, but going south is always awful.

T: OK, let's start with going south. How anxious would that make you?

C: On that 0–100 scale? 100, definitely. I get nervous just thinking about it.

T: (makes note) All right. And how about going north from town on a Friday in the summer?

C: Another 100. It is pretty bad on Fridays, too.

T: (makes note) And what about going north from town on a regular weeknight?

C: Those are still really scary . . . 100.

T: So going north on a weeknight is as bad as going south?

C: No, I guess not. I'll say 95.

(continued)

Sidebar 3.2 (*continued*)

> T: OK, let's talk about some of the other driving you're afraid of. We want to add those situations to our list. Now, how about Handelman Parkway, which is a less crowded road?
>
> C: Yes, that road still has four lanes, but it is not as busy. That would be about an 85 or 90.
>
> T: (makes note) What about driving across different bridges in the area? Are some more frightening for you than others?

This therapist has begun the process of constructing a formal hierarchy. Notice that she used the clues that the client gave her about anxiety-provoking cues, namely a busy road with changing traffic patterns. As she works her way through her informal list of stimuli, she continues asking about these cues, assessing how they contribute to different anxiety levels. At this early stage in her interview, she has only high-fear items on the hierarchy (SUDS ≥ 85). As her assessment continues, she will ask about different combinations of cues within the situation that moderate anxiety. Optimally, the hierarchy should have a wide range of anxiety levels on it, including items that are only moderately anxiety-provoking (e.g., SUDS $= 40$) and those that are very intense, with many items in between.

In this example, this therapist might ask about whether there are differences in anxiety depending on whether the client is driving at night vs. in daylight, on rainy vs. dry roads, or in a car with vs. without modern safety features like anti-lock brakes or airbags. Other parameters might include whether the client has passengers, an automotive club card, or a cell phone in the car. Using this process, the therapist obtains information about the specific anxiety-provoking cues within the broad situation of "driving" for this client. As a general rule of thumb, a good hierarchy has a minimum of 10 items. When the hierarchy is complete, the therapist has a clear guide for proceeding with exposure-based treatment. Items on the hierarchy should periodically be reevaluated, because anxiety levels will shift during treatment as improvements on one item generalize to other items.

The behavioral avoidance test involves setting up a situation in which the client is provided with an opportunity to approach ever nearer to a phobic stimulus at or near the top of the hierarchy. Usually, the test is scored for both avoidance and anxiety (SUDS). Avoidance is designated by a number reflecting the point at which the client terminates the test by refusing to go further. An example of the avoidance scoring, a snake behavioral avoidance test from Gauthier and Ladouceur (1981), is shown in table 3.1. In this study, participants were asked to enter a large room with a glass cage containing a live boa constrictor (5 feet long). The top of the cage had a wire screen covering. Higher scores indicate a greater degree of avoidance of the

OBTAINING PHOBIC STIMULI

Obtaining the stimuli necessary for exposure treatment of animal phobias can be challenging. Specialty pet stores are good places to start. Such stores will often have snakes, spiders, and a variety of rodents. Garter snakes will be relatively inexpensive, but larger snakes such as boa constrictors and rat snakes obviously cost more. If an animal is borrowed or purchased, be sure to get detailed instructions on its care. It is often possible to make advance arrangements whereby the pet store will buy back the snake or spider when you are finished with it. Some stores may even allow you to conduct exposure inside the store, although it is best to choose a time when the store is relatively empty. Similar arrangements can often be made with zookeepers or children's museums. Another source for spiders, rodents, or harmless snakes is elementary schools, where science teachers often have animals in the classroom. It may be possible to arrange for a series of after-school visits, or the animal may be borrowed for several weeks during a recess.

At the beginning of treatment, simply using photos or film clips (perhaps from television episodes of nature programs) may be a good place to start exposure. Also, walking around in places the client fears may harbor the animal (e.g., basements, grassy areas) can be useful as exposure. Realistic toys may also be useful in the early stages. Finally, remember to use the client as a source for some of these creatures. If the phobia involves crickets, for instance, and there are many crickets around the client's home, it may be possible to have a family member collect some crickets in a jar and bring them to the office.

As a final tip, it may be advantageous to handle the animal in advance of the session to work through any natural apprehension about touching an unfamiliar animal. This will allow the therapist to act as a calm, confident model in the exposure session.

snake. To assist in scoring the first few steps of the behavioral avoidance test, the floor may be marked with masking tape to indicate specified distances from the cage (e.g., 16 feet, 11 feet, 7 feet).

There is nothing sacred about the distances used or the scoring; the point is to develop an observable test of avoidance that can be repeated. Even with a stimulus such as heights, the same test can apply. For example, the stimulus for testing might be a fire escape on a building near the therapist's office. Each floor the client climbs on the fire escape might represent a step in the behavioral avoidance test. If the test were to be used for gaining information about severity of avoidance and tolerance of anxiety before commencing with exposure treatment, then any fear-producing stimulus from the client's hierarchy would be appropriate. On the other hand, if the test is

Table 3.1 Sample Scoring for a Behavioral Avoidance Test With a Snake

BAT Score	Client's Behavior
20	Standing 16 feet from the cage
19	Standing 11 feet from the cage
18	Standing 7 feet from the cage
17	Standing 4 feet from the cage
16	Standing 2 feet from the cage
15	Standing 1 foot from the cage
14	Looking down at the snake through the top screen
13	Placing hand against the glass of cage nearest the snake
12	Lifting top screen of cage a couple of inches
11	Removing top screen altogether
10	Looking down at snake with top screen removed
9	Putting a pointer into cage
8	Touching snake with the pointer
7	Putting a gloved hand into cage
6	Touching snake briefly with gloved hand
5	Putting a bare hand into cage
4	Touching snake briefly with bare hand
3	Petting snake with bare hand
2	Lifting or moving any part of snake with whole hand
1	Picking up snake with both hands

Adapted with permission from J. Gauthier, & R. Ladouceur (1981). The influence of self-efficacy reports on performance. *Behavior Therapy, 12*, 438.

to be repeated over time, as a measure of the progress of treatment, then the test stimulus should be reserved for that purpose. In this way, the behavioral avoidance test represents a check on the degree to which the client is able to approach unfamiliar instances of the feared stimulus.

Because the behavioral avoidance test is very sensitive to changes in test conditions (such as feeling safer with the therapist or having stronger verbal pressure to complete the test), repetitions of the test should carefully replicate the conditions of the initial test. It may be useful to have a colleague or assistant conduct the behavioral avoidance test for this reason. The client may even be asked to conduct the test on his own, as a homework assignment. Phobic clients are typically very honest about how well they were able to approach the feared situation. When interpreting the results of the test, the clinician should remember that it is not unusual for anxiety ratings to remain steady or even temporarily increase if the client stops avoiding. Less avoidance and lower anxiety are signs of progress, but the client may not improve in these two response domains at the same rate.

Physiological monitoring can also be conducted as a part of the behavioral avoidance test. As discussed earlier, physiological arousal is an important part of the fear response, and it does not necessarily correspond to self-reports of anxiety or avoidance. Many clinicians are apprehensive about using physiological monitoring, and it is true that the cost and complexity of equipment for monitoring physiological responding varies enormously. However, the clinician does not need to become a psychophysicist in order to monitor the basic heart rate response. Inexpensive equipment designed for monitoring heart rate during exercise is widely available from sporting goods stores or catalogues. Some models look like a wristwatch; others gently grasp the earlobe or index finger. As the reliability of these instruments can vary almost as much as their prices, it is important to test whether the heart rate stays relatively stable during periods of rest or continuous exercise. If so, then one has more faith in the results when the instrument is used during assessment of phobic response. Clinicians who wish to monitor blood pressure or skin conductance in addition to heart rate must be prepared to invest a bit more money and time in the instruments.

TREATMENT PROCEDURES

Clinicians from most disciplines and theoretical orientations are in agreement that successful treatment for simple phobia requires exposure to the feared stimulus. Because of the specificity of simple phobia, structured treatment based on a hierarchy of intensity of fear is readily conducted. Although a number of different variations on exposure-based treatment have been developed, there seems to be no particular advantage for one type of exposure over another (Barlow, 1988). In the following pages, treatment procedures for exposure will be outlined, including participant modeling (also called guided mastery), flooding, systematic desensitization, implosive therapy, imaginal exposure, and applied tension. Exposure to the feared stimulus is clearly the key to the success of these treatments, and choosing among the specific methods is often a matter of what style the therapist and client prefer. At times, logistic considerations may also influence the means by which exposure is accomplished. For example, in vivo treatment of phobias of air travel may be difficult (although not impossible) to arrange.

Participant Modeling or Guided Mastery

Albert Bandura developed participant modeling in the late 1960s as an outgrowth of his ideas on self-efficacy. His thinking was that the key to the success of exposure treatment was in helping the client to become more confident about her or his ability to actually engage with the feared stimulus. As with all exposure treatments, the therapist first conducts a thorough assessment and builds a hierarchy of feared situations (see sidebar 3-2). In order to help the client feel more confident, the therapist first engages with the stimulus (modeling) and then encourages the client to follow in the same manner. Within each step of the formal hierarchy, the therapist can also construct a series of mini-hierarchies. These mini-hierarchies are detailed steps involved in approaching a single feared stimulus, much like the behavioral avoidance test described in table 3.1.

With the client observing, the therapist engages in the first step of the mini-hierarchy and subsequently invites the client to do exactly the same thing. For example, the therapist working with an acrophobic client might begin with a hierarchy item "fire escape." The therapist would initially proceed through the steps of approaching the fire escape, including climbing from the ground to the first floor landing on a fire escape, walking around on the landing, looking over the edge while holding the railing, and finally looking over the edge without touching the railing. The clinician would then ask if the client feels up to replicating the therapist's behavior.

If the client feels too afraid to simply repeat the steps after the therapist modeled them, then the therapist can offer a number of strategies to help the client feel more confident about engaging in this step of the exposure. First, the therapist might break down the task into smaller, more manageable steps. For example, the client might first attempt to climb halfway up the first flight of stairs and return to the ground. The second attempt might involve climbing to the same spot (halfway up) and staying there for 2–3 minutes. The basic idea is to collaborate with the client to plan a sequence of exposure tasks that is challenging without being overwhelming. Verbal encouragement from the therapist also helps the client to celebrate mastering each step.

At times, the patient may still be too afraid to proceed along an exposure mini-hierarchy without further intervention from the clinician, even when the steps are very progressive. In this case, the therapist might perform the task with the client, providing appropriate physical support if necessary. For example, the therapist and client may walk up the steps together, with the client placing one hand on the therapist's forearm and holding the railing with the other hand. With exposure to an animal, the client may place a hand on the therapist's arm as the therapist touches the animal. After repeating a given step once or twice with therapist assistance, this support is withdrawn so the client may engage in the exposure task with only as much assistance as necessary to promote progress along the hierarchy of exposure. Progressively, the amount of time spent on each step is extended, until the client can perform the step with relative ease.

The therapist should remain alert to safety behaviors that prevent the client from flexibly performing each step. For instance, the client might be physically rigid while standing on the landing of the fire escape or may hang back toward the building rather than stepping near the outside railing. To use the driving phobia example, the client may be willing to drive on the highway but insist on having the therapist present or driving only in the slow lane. Gradually, the therapist should encourage the client to experiment with letting go of these safety behaviors to perform the step in a free and flexible manner. With the driving example, the client can be encouraged to gradually spend longer periods of time in different, more challenging, lanes of the road. To assist in the transition between accompanied and solo driving, mobile phones can be used as a temporary supportive link to the therapist, although some driving phobics may become dependent on the telephone (Flynn, Taylor, & Pollard, 1992).

Homework assignments to repeat in-session steps without the therapist will facilitate building a sense of mastery in the presence of the phobic stimulus. At each step in this process, therapists should explicitly state the rationale for therapeutic interventions, so clients can learn to be their own therapists by applying the same procedures to new variations of the feared situation. We commonly provide clients with a form for conducting their homework exercise, resembling our record keeping for the exposure session itself. On this form, which can be constructed in just a few minutes on a computer or even by hand, there is space for each step of the homework. The client records exactly what the step involved (e.g., standing on the 7th floor balcony without holding on), along with ratings of anxiety every 5 minutes. Thoughts can also be recorded on this form. This form is then used to plan the next step of treatment, depending on the client's degree of success without the therapist present. An example of a homework exercise form for a client with an elevator phobia is included in figure 3-1.

The efficacy of these gradual exposure procedures, called participant modeling in earlier studies and guided mastery more recently, has been evaluated for a variety of specific phobias, most popularly fears of snakes, spiders, and heights (e.g., Etringer, Cash, & Rimm, 1982; Hellstrom & Ost, 1995; Williams et al., 1985). The treatment has also been used successfully in a group format to treat spider phobia; as we might expect, patients tend to do better in smaller groups of 3–4 than in larger therapy groups of 7–8 (Öst, 1996). Finally, this approach has been used with children as young as 3 years old, to treat phobias of water that interfere with recreational swimming activities (Lewis, 1974; Menzies & Clarke, 1993).

The amount of in-session time permitted for each client has varied across different treatment studies, from 40 minutes (Rimm & Mahoney, 1969) to a maximum of 3 hours (Öst, Salkovskis, & Hellstrom, 1991). In an exposure-based treatment study of height phobia that did not place a limit on the number of session-hours, the mean treatment time was 115 minutes, with a range from 35 to 360 minutes (Bourque & Ladouceur, 1980). The entire treatment has been conducted within one session in several studies (Hellstrom & Öst, 1995; Öst, 1996; Öst, Salkovskis et al., 1991). These very brief treatments have been possible where the nature of the phobia permitted therapists to have good control over the stimulus. That is, phobic stimuli such as heights or snakes allow therapists to control the rate at which clients are exposed to the stimulus. Clients can gradually approach the stimulus and experience a sense of mastery over their fear, while experiencing a steady decline in anxiety.

Some stimuli are more challenging from this perspective, such as fear of

Goal:
Ride elevator to the top of Kline Tower and back to the bottom by myself when the building is empty, and repeat 7 times.

Exposure Step	Time	SUDS (0-100 anxiety)
1. Ride up	_____	_____
2. Ride down	_____	_____
3. Ride up	_____	_____
4. Ride down	_____	_____
5. Ride up	_____	_____
6. Ride down	_____	_____
7. Ride up	_____	_____
8. Ride down	_____	_____
9. Ride up	_____	_____
10. Ride down	_____	_____
11. Ride up	_____	_____
12. Ride down	_____	_____
13. Ride up	_____	_____
14. Ride down	_____	_____

Figure 3.1 Self-Directed Exposure Form.

flying. During in vivo exposure for this problem, unpredictable fear-pro-voking cues can arise. These events include turbulence, sudden noises (such as landing gear retraction, deployment of wing flaps, or seat belt warning chime), and unexpected aircraft movement. Because these cues cannot be controlled or even anticipated by the therapist, they make it harder to pres-ent the stimuli in an orderly way. In these cases, clinicians can prepare cli-ents for such events by reminding them that these events are part of normal flying and do not represent signs of danger. Clients can rehearse such coping statements and imagine themselves in an aircraft experiencing these sensations while reconceptualizing them as normal and safe. The intent is simply to help the client better tolerate unexpected stimuli while flying.

Because the basic procedure for exposure is relatively straightforward, and the rationale readily appreciated by clients, there have been several attempts to construct a manual-based treatment that clients apply on their own. This approach has the obvious appeal of being very inexpensive, but it is clearly less effective than therapist-directed exposure. In two separate studies, Swedish researcher Lars-Göran Öst and his colleagues treated spider phobics. They applied conservative criteria for determining whether a patient had improved in a clinically significant way (not just statistical significance). In order to be considered clinically improved, patients had to improve by two standard deviations on self-rated anxiety and clinician-rated severity *and* allow a spider to crawl on their hands for at least 20 seconds at the end of treatment. After a mean of about 2 hours of treatment, 71–80% of patients treated with therapist assistance achieved this degree of improvement, but only 6–36% of self-exposure patients were clinically improved (Hellstrom & Öst, 1995; Öst, Salkovskis et al., 1991).

Of course, there are some instances in which therapist-directed exposure for specific phobia is impractical. In many rural areas mental health professionals are unavailable; even in urban areas, some clients are unable to afford psychological treatment. Conducting the entire treatment in a single session can be surprisingly effective if the nature of the stimulus allows for this. In those cases in which therapist-assisted exposure is simply not possible, Öst's group has concluded that self-directed exposure can be a reasonable alternative. However, it is important to note that in their studies, clients were provided with spiders if it was impossible to get a friend or relative to collect spiders for the exposure. In one study, a room was set up at the clinic in which jars of spiders were on display; clients did their own exposure in this room, following a manual provided by the clinicians (Hellstrom & Öst, 1995). Obviously, this type of resource has limited utility, as most phobias that come to the attention of clinicians are not readily confined to one room (e.g., driving phobia, fear of flying, claustrophobia).

Variants on Exposure

Systematic Desensitization

Treatments that involve some form of exposure to the feared stimulus have several variants that have been proposed and investigated through the years. One of the earliest variations was Wolpe's systematic desensitization, which was based on a counter-conditioning principle. The idea is that the stimulus, such as a bridge, has become associated with the anxiety response through conditioning. Systematic desensitization involves pairing the stimulus with an anxiety-inhibiting response, such as muscle relaxation. This treatment approach differs from flooding in that the aim in systematic desensitization is to maintain very low levels of anxiety, in order to pair the feared stimulus with a nonfeared state. In contrast, flooding involves exposing the patient to the stimulus at relatively high levels of anxiety, staying with the stimulus until the anxiety habituates, or declines. A secondary aim of flooding is to help clients learn to tolerate the uncomfortable feelings of anxiety until the fear declines.

Thus, in systematic desensitization, the client first learns to reach a deep state of relaxation through progressive muscle relaxation. After constructing a detailed hierarchy, the therapist presents the stimuli in a carefully graded manner, only increasing the intensity of the stimulus with a pace that results in low anxiety for the client. The stimulus can be presented in vivo (e.g., real-life exposure to the snake), imaginally (using a script the therapist has prepared ahead of time), or through proximal stimuli such as slides or photographs (Öst, 1978). Some clients may initially have an adverse reaction to relaxation itself, such as anger (Abramowitz & Wieselberg, 1978) or a paradoxical anxiety response (Heide & Borkovec, 1983). These paradoxical effects are sometimes due to the therapist's failure to properly prepare the client for relaxation and exposure. For clients who are tightly controlled or unaccustomed to relaxing, it may be helpful to describe the typical sensations associated with deep relaxation before commencing the exercise. In addition, these interventions usually benefit from a solid therapeutic alliance.

There are very few studies comparing flooding versus systematic desensitization for specific phobia; most of these comparisons have been made with treatment for agoraphobia. Some of the clients participating in an early study by Marks, Boulougouris, and Marset (1971) had specific phobias; for these clients, flooding and systematic desensitization produced equivalent outcomes. On the other hand, Bandura, Blanchard, and Ritter (1969) found that participant modeling was superior to systematic desensitization in a sample of snake phobics. Note that clients in the Marks et al. study did not receive modeling from therapists, which the clients in the Bandura et al. study did receive, so it is possible that this ingredient boosts the effectiveness of treatment of specific phobia. The habituation model used in flooding treatments also appears be more efficient than systematic desensitization, in the sense that fewer sessions are required to achieve the same treatment goals (Barrett, 1969).

Implosive Therapy

Another exposure-based treatment that has received considerable attention is implosive therapy (Stampfl & Levis, 1967), which is a flooding type of approach based on a psychodynamic understanding of the patient's problems. Because aggressive or sexual impulses are seen as important factors in the psychodynamic model of the development of phobias, these themes are represented among the cues used in exposure. There has been little research on what we call the strong model of implosive therapy, which includes the psychodynamic themes such as aggression, abandonment, or helplessness described by Stampfl and Levis. Several studies purporting to examine implosive therapy have used a weaker model of implosive therapy, excluding the psychodynamic material (Barrett, 1969; McCutcheon & Adams, 1975). This effectively removes the distinctive parts of this treatment, rendering it equivalent to imaginal flooding. Indeed, it seems that regardless of the particular method that the therapist chooses to present feared stimuli, exposure to such stimuli is the key to reduction of the fear (Menzies & Clarke, 1993; Sherman, 1972).

Applied Tension

Clients with blood or injury (B/I) phobia deserve special attention because of the unusual pattern of physiologic responding discussed earlier in this chapter. In an early case study, Cohn, Kron, and Brady (1976) reported on the treatment of a 28-year-old premedical student who regularly lost consciousness at the sight of blood or physical injury. In order to conduct exposure treatment without the client fainting, the therapist searched for a way to elevate blood pressure and heart rate to work against the vasovagal response. Anger, another arousing emotion, was chosen as a solution to this problem. Essentially, the therapist helped the client to become angry during exposure sessions. The therapist initially achieved this goal by role-playing the patient's father, criticizing the patient for his lifestyle. Several other situations associated with especially angry feelings for the patient were used in this same role-playing procedure while the patient simultaneously engaged in exposure to slides of phobic material. Gradually, anger was faded out of the exposure process and the patient was able to volunteer in a city hospital emergency room.

Using a similar rationale, Öst and his colleagues have spent several years developing an applied tension treatment for B/I phobia (Öst & Sterner, 1987). Before commencing with flooding, the client learns to tense the major muscles of the arms, torso, and legs. This tension is maintained for 10–15 seconds, until the client feels warmth rising in the face. After releasing the muscles, the client aims for a return to the baseline state, rather than a relaxed state as in progressive muscle relaxation. In the first phase of this treatment, the client practices cycles of muscle tension and baseline several times a day. (Occasionally, a patient will overdo the tension and produce a headache, but reduction in intensity and frequency of practice usually resolves the problem.) With practice, most clients are able to rapidly effect a rise in blood pressure; color quickly rises to the face.

The second step of the treatment involves several sessions devoted to training the client to detect the earliest signs of a drop in blood pressure. To conduct this training, the therapist presents a series of photographs or slides of wounded or mutilated people. The slides are used to practice producing drops in blood pressure and applying the tension to reverse the response. Finally, in stage three of this treatment, the therapist accompanies the client to progressively more challenging situations, such as a blood donor center or the observation deck of a surgery theater, and encourages gradual progress up the hierarchy, all the while applying tension as needed to prevent fainting. A potential difficulty reported by Öst and Sterner (1987) is that tensing the arms can interfere with venipuncture, such as when a patient has his own blood drawn. Obviously, having blood drawn is an important step in the hierarchy for individuals with injection and blood phobias. Öst and Sterner recommend solving this problem by teaching the patient to relax the nondominant arm while simultaneously tensing the dominant arm, torso, and leg muscles. Blood can then be drawn from the nondominant arm.

In a well-done study, Öst, Fellenius, and Sterner (1991) demonstrated that applied tension was strongly superior to the usual in vivo exposure without muscle tension. After just five sessions of treatment, 90% of those receiving applied tension met stringent criteria for clinical improvement, which was boosted to 100% at one-year follow-up. In contrast, only 40% of clients who had received in vivo exposure without muscle tension were clinically improved. Criteria for clinical improvement included being able to watch color videos of thoracic surgery for 30 minutes without even coming close to fainting and with only moderate anxiety (4.4 or less on a 0–10 scale). Although this study involved 5 sessions of treatment, a more recent study indicates that the treatment can be just as effective when applied in a single session (Öst & Hellstrom, 1992).

Treatment Planning

Timing

There are two obvious timing-related considerations in treatment planning for exposure-based therapies for specific phobia. First, what is the optimal frequency of sessions? Second, how long should each session be? The debate about frequency of sessions has been whether to mass all the sessions close together or space the same number of sessions over time. If sessions occur every day, so the theory goes, clients will not have an opportunity to avoid or escape their feared situation between sessions, thereby providing a consistent learning experience (Foa, Jameson, Turner, & Paynes, 1980). On the other hand, spacing sessions out is usually more convenient for clients, and Barlow (1988) has hypothesized that relapse rates might be lower if sessions are conducted weekly rather than daily.

Studies examining this issue have found no discernible differences between conducting treatment more versus less frequently. In a study providing four sessions of treatment to dental phobics, Ning and Liddell (1991) found that twice weekly or once weekly treatment was equivalent. Chambless (1990) provided ten sessions of treatment to specific phobics and agoraphobics, over the course of 2 or 10 weeks. She found no differences in outcome, dropout rate, relapse rate at 6 months, or how stressful clients perceived the treatment to be. Chambless noted that spacing treatment once weekly does provide clients with an opportunity to carry out homework assignments to practice exposure without the therapist's assistance; homework was not assigned in her study. She concluded that for those clients willing to engage in massed treatment, the clear benefit is improved functioning in 2 weeks rather than 10.

Another consideration is how long to continue each exposure-based session. Clear evidence indicates that longer continuous sessions are more effective than brief or interrupted sessions. Very brief flooding (20 minutes) appears to sensitize rather than diminish the fear response, as compared to 60 minute sessions (McCutchen & Adams, 1975). The important factor seems to be continuing the exposure long enough for a substantial decrease in anxiety to occur (Chaplin & Levine, 1981; Marshall, 1985). Given what we discussed earlier in terms of desynchrony in different channels of anxiety responding, the question is which indication of anxiety the clinician should monitor for signs of decrease. At this point, the scientific literature provides little in the way of guidance. It is not clear whether self-report or some physiological measure should be used to determine that anxiety has declined substantially during a session.

Whether self-report or physiological arousal is used as a guide to terminate the session may influence session length. Andrasik, Turner, and Ollendick (1980) reported that sessions were longer when based on physiological indicators of habituation, but Lande (1982) reported the opposite, that self-report was the slowest indicator to decline during flooding. One strategy might be to monitor both physiological and self-report indicators of anxiety, if possible, and to continue the session until both modes of responding indicate a reduction in anxiety. This method may result in relatively long sessions. Andrasik et al. (1980) reported session lengths based on physiological responding that ranged from 55 to 170 minutes. Some reimbursement plans or organizational structures might not allow the luxury of such long sessions. There are at this point no contraindications for basing the decision to terminate an exposure session on whichever response channel declines most quickly; perhaps this is a solution for those limited to shorter sessions.

Physiological Response

Clinically, it is common to observe that some clients respond to their phobic stimulus with a high level of fear, but without a strong avoidance response. Other clients assiduously avoid the phobic object but show little in the way of objective (physiological) signs of fear. Theoretically, it seems plausible that one could match these patients with a treatment targeted toward their primary response. For avoiders, in vivo exposure would seem to be the likely choice, whereas physiological responders may benefit more from the added relaxation component of systematic desensitization. Although this potential for treatment matching is provocative, studies have shown mixed results. Matching clients with a treatment directed toward their response pattern resulted in superior outcomes in one study of claustrophobia (Öst, Johansson & Jerremalm, 1982) and another study of fear of flying (Huag et al., 1987). A third study with dental phobics did not find that matching the patient's response profile with treatment approach boosted outcome (Jerremalm, Jansson, & Öst, 1986a).

Mental health professionals often tout a lack of side effects as one of the benefits of psychological interventions as compared to pharmacological treatments. However, exposure-based treatments (with the exception of those based on a systematic desensitization model) do produce significant anxiety as a part of the therapy. In an effort to reduce the unpleasantness of these treatments, several investigators have examined the role of medications as an adjunct to exposure. The use of continuously administered medications, such as imipramine or benzodiazepines, appears to have no beneficial effect (Whitehead, Robinson, Blackwell, & Stutz, 1978; Zitrin, Klein, Woerner, & Ross, 1983). Selectively administered benzodiazepines taken just before a session may interfere with the process of exposure because of state-dependent learning effects (Sartory, 1983). On the other hand, exposure conducted during the *waning* phase of a single dose of diazepam (administered several hours in advance of a session) was superior to exposure with pill placebo (Marks, Viswanathan, Lipsedge, & Gardner, 1972). The Marks et al. study noted that diazepam during the *peak* of its effect was not noticeably superior to placebo. Surprisingly, clients who took diazepam before exposure sessions did not find the session to be less unpleasant. On the whole, medications have not demonstrated a promising role in the treatment of specific phobia.

Individual Differences

Because most clients with specific phobia point to the perceived consequences of anxiety and panic as among the most feared aspects of contact with the phobic stimulus, it is reasonable to speculate that sensitivity to anxiety may be an important impediment to exposure-based treatment. For example, Rachman and Levitt (1988) reported that the best predictor of nonhabituation during exposure for claustrophobia was panic-related cognitions, including thoughts of passing out or suffocating. Those clients who are relatively unable to tolerate feelings of anxiety may be more resistant to flooding or anxiety-provoking homework assignments. In addition, these clients may not be prepared to cope if they unexpectedly encounter the feared stimulus even after treatment has concluded. Clients who are high in anxiety sensitivity may require a slower approach to the focal phobia, but they may also require some specific intervention directed toward reducing their fear of the sensations of anxiety. Procedures for reducing fear of bodily sensations have become well established and are described in this volume in the chapter on panic disorder and agoraphobia.

Clients may also doubt their ability to deal effectively with the feared stimulus or feared consequences (e.g., a client fears her high anxiety will cause her to wreck the car). Usually, in vivo exposure with a therapist helps the client gradually engage with the feared stimulus independent of assistance from the therapist, and the client learns to have more confidence regarding the feared situation. Constructing confidence-building homework assignments can also help; thus it is important that homework assignments be manageable yet challenging. An often neglected procedure for helping clients to feel they can deal effectively with the feared situation is to provide factual information. Some clients may hold incorrect beliefs about such things as elevators, snakes, or lightning; the therapist can provide factual information and encourage the client to test the old belief against the new information while engaging in exposure. A few examples of helpful new information include: aircraft struck by lightning while in flight are not in danger because they are not grounded; the experience of dyscontrol during a flood of anxious arousal will not "tip" a person into insanity; elevators cannot free fall because they have automatic brakes.

Specific Recommendations

Conditioning explanations for the etiology of specific phobias have been criticized on a number of grounds. Although learning models may not be able to explain the genesis of every client's phobia, theorizing in this area has led to effective treatments. From treatment studies, we know exposure-based treatment works for most clients and that the improvements observed in therapy are maintained after termination most of the time with no relapse and no symptom substitution (see table 3.2 for overview of exposure treatment). Within the broad category of "exposure-based" treatment, flooding approaches appear to be more efficient than systematic desensitization, which probably take longer to obtain the same therapeutic gains. Participant modeling or guided mastery approaches offers the clinician many tools for helping clients engage in the anxiety-provoking task of exposure to the feared stimulus, while also lending clients a sense of self-confidence in their ability to deal effectively with anxiety and the feared object or situation.

On the other hand, clients with a strong aversion to the feelings of anxiety may not be willing to engage in a flooding-type of exposure. Systematic desensitization may be a better approach for these clients, who would otherwise flee from treatment. It may even be possible to begin with systematic desensitization and then switch to a habituation model of exposure once the client has gained more confidence in the therapist. Alternatively, the clinician may wish to use some of the strategies discussed in the panic disorder

Table 3.2 Overview of Exposure for Treatment of Simple Phobia

---

Psychoeducation
    In the case of blood/injury phobia, give information about the physiology of the vaso-
        vagal response and explain treatment rationale.
    In the case of fears about flying or dentistry, give information about how airplanes fly
        or how dentists perform procedures.
    Explain the nature of panic attacks, if appropriate.
Treatment Planning
    Develop a hierarchy for exposure.
    Evaluate the client's degree of tolerance for anxiety.
Implementing Treatment
    For blood/injury phobia, first develop skills in tensing muscles. Apply these skills
        during exposure.
    Model each step of exposure, followed by client exposure.
    Monitor anxiety level to ascertain degree of habituation.
    Assist the client as necessary by setting smaller exposure goals, providing encourage-
        ment, and correcting misinformation.
    Emphasize the importance of self-directed exposure.
    Introduce imaginal exposure as necessary.
Maintenance
    Develop a plan for continued self-directed exposure in the case of residual symptoms or
        setback.

---

chapter of this volume to help the client become less afraid of the sensations of anxiety. Although implosive therapy may provide a conceptual heuristic for psychodynamically trained clinicians, treatment studies suggest that it is not necessary to specifically expose the client to psychodynamic themes in order for treatment to be effective. On the other hand, those clients with outrageous fantasies about the feared stimulus (e.g., the automobile will be pulled underneath a tractor-trailer while driving on the highway) may benefit from "pushing the limits" of imaginal stimuli as is done in some implosive therapy protocols.

As exposure seems to be the critical ingredient for these various treatments for specific phobia, it is imperative to help clients expose themselves to feared stimuli. At times, practical issues may interfere with plans for exposure. For example, clients with B/I phobia risk fainting during exposure. Planning exposure for situations over which the clinician does not have good stimulus control can also present practical challenges. Specifically, fear-provoking cues in fear of flying (e.g., bumpy flight), driving phobia (e.g., wet roads), or weather (e.g., thunderstorms) cannot be produced by the clinician at the moment in therapy when they would be most useful. For these situations, several variations on exposure have demonstrated utility. Applied tension is a useful way of preventing fainting during exposure for B/I phobics. Imaginal exposure can also be used when exposure in vivo is not practical. While some studies have produced excellent outcome after only a single session, this might be an overly optimistic estimate for treating phobias that provide logistic challenges for exposure.

Even when the nature of the phobia makes exposure convenient from a pragmatic point of view, client resistance may provide other challenges for the clinician planning exposure-based treatment. In order to maximize the amount of contact the client experiences with the phobic stimulus, homework exercises are useful during treatment. Even after treatment has concluded, continued practice facing the phobic stimulus is probably helpful. Extremely motivated clients will not require assistance designing their own self-exposure program once they understand the rationale of treatment. However, the clinician may need to assist most clients in developing a structured plan of programmed practice. Clients with longstanding phobias have often altered their lifestyles to exclude the phobic stimulus. Without changes in daily patterns, they may have little opportunity to practice facing feared stimuli. Once this is recognized, the clinician can help the client to formulate plans to ensure that situations that were formerly avoided are now included in the client's lifestyle.

4 *Social Phobia*

The last 15 years have brought many advances in diagnosis and treatment of social phobia. Perhaps because social anxiety, at least in its mildest form, is a nearly universal experience, only recently have researchers and clinicians come to appreciate the full extent of disability and distress associated with social phobia. In this chapter, we will first discuss the continuum of social anxiety, beginning with shyness. Then we will review many of the complex issues associated with the psychopathology of social phobia, including cognitive features and behavioral manifestations of the disorder, as well as biological findings. Many new tools for assessing social phobia have been developed, and these will be discussed as they apply to clinical practice. Interventions from several perspectives will also be thoroughly outlined, including social skills training, exposure-based approaches, and cognitive techniques. Finally, we will make some recommendations for formulating treatment plans for individual clients. We begin with nonpathological social fears—the sort of social anxiety experienced by most people at one time or another.

TYPOLOGY OF SOCIAL ANXIETY

Social fears become apparent early in life, perhaps beginning with the infant's "stranger anxiety." Some of these fears remain relatively stable, while others fluctuate across developmental stages. Reticence and inhibited behavior have been observed in a sizable minority of toddlers who are faced with a new social situation, and this reserve seems to be relatively stable up to at least school age (Rosenbaum, Biederman, Hirshfeld, Bolduc, & Chaloff, 1991). Children as young as 6 years old express concern about negative social outcomes such as being laughed at or teased by other children (Campbell & Rapee, 1994), and these concerns seem to stay relatively stable over time. Shyness also appears to be relatively constant during development into adulthood (Caspi, Elder, & Bem, 1988). Fears of specific social situations, such as giving a presentation, appear to increase as children grow older (King et al., 1989). The teen years represent a special challenge, rife as they are with social embarrassment and concern over the impression one is making on one's peers.

Trying to delineate where normal shyness ends and social phobia begins can be difficult, primarily because "shy" is not a term that has a broadly accepted definition. At least 40% of people label themselves as shy, and twice as many say that they have been shy at some point in their lives (Pilkonis & Zimbardo, 1979). Characterizing oneself as shy can be based on diverse feelings, such as mild social anxiety upon meeting new people, feeling somewhat uncomfortable sharing personal information, or simply knowing oneself to be a better listener than talker. A self-judgment of shyness may even be based on the fallacious assumption that other people never feel *any* social anxiety. Only the rare person can give a speech without at least some anticipatory anxiety. In fact, one in five people in a metropolitan sample said they were *phobic* about public speaking, but only 2% reported being really distressed about their fear (Pollard & Henderson, 1988).

Stopa and Clark (1993) have offered a compelling characterization of the difference between shyness and social phobia. They suggest that both groups of people enter social situations with anticipatory anxiety and evaluation apprehension. Both shy people and social phobics may initially linger on the periphery of a party, for instance. As the shy person makes some initial attempts to interact, she checks how other people are responding to her. Are people responding as though she is boring or stupid? If not, the shy person can begin to relax in the social situation, opening up and feeling more natural. The person with social phobia, however, does not appear to check what impact his behavior seems to be having on other people, thus missing out on the opportunity to get reassurance about his social performance. In addition, he may misinterpret ambiguous feedback from others as negative, which naturally drives anxiety higher.

Social Phobia

The cardinal feature of social phobia is fear of negative evaluation. Persons with social phobia have a strong fear of situations in which they are open to possible scrutiny from others, and the basic fear in these situations is that of being embarrassed or humiliated. In social situations requiring interaction with others, the phobic person often fears that she will be unable to begin a conversation or that the discussion will quickly sputter to a halt, leaving a mortifying silence for which she will feel responsible. Often, the person with social phobia feels unable to make small talk and worries about how to behave: what to do with her hands, how to sit or stand, what sort of facial expression to adopt (Kaplan, 1972).

People with social phobia also frequently fear situations that do not inherently involve interaction but nevertheless include the possibility of scrutiny from others. These performance situations include musical or dramatic performances, eating or drinking in public, writing in public (e.g., signing a check), using public washrooms, or simply being seen in public (e.g., bowling). Public speaking is the most commonly feared situation, although most people with social phobia fear and avoid more than one situation (Turner, Beidel, Dancu, & Keys, 1986). Perhaps owing to their avoidance of social situations, social phobics achieve less education, have lower incomes, and have less access to social support, including a lower frequency of marriage (Magee, Eaton, Wittchen, McGonagle, & Kessler, 1996). Only about one in five seeks professional help for social anxiety, although 33% consider themselves to be impaired. The most recent estimate for the lifetime prevalence of social phobia based on a community sample is 13.3% (Kessler et al., 1994), affecting only slightly more women than men (Magee et al., 1996).

While social phobia may involve fears of several different specific social settings, the features of each situation that serve to cue (or calm) anxiety are often consistent across situations (Beck, Emery, & Greenberg, 1985). When anticipating entering a social situation, the amount of anxiety that a person expects to encounter will probably be influenced by some of these factors. Many of these factors are undoubtedly related to the degree of social anxiety everyone, not just clients with social phobia, experiences in specific social situations. One factor would be the relative status of social partners, in terms of power or social desirability (including wealth, attractiveness, or poise). Another would clearly be the individual's appraisal of the importance of the situation; how important is it to "do well" in this situation? What are the consequences of failing to conform? For example, one is likely to be more anxious when delivering a sales presentation to customers than when practicing the same presentation in front of supportive friends.

A third factor influencing the amount of social anxiety expected in a given situation is the potential for being "trapped" in the situation (Nichols, 1974). Some situations are naturally more difficult to escape. Leaving in the midst of a small dinner party attracts a lot of attention, less so for a large cocktail party, from which one may slip away unnoticed. Another factor that will influence anxiety across situations is the anticipated response of social partners to social errors or incompetence. If an individual is preparing to ask for a raise from an arrogant and demeaning boss, then the anticipated anxiety will surely be higher than if one is facing a fair and supportive superior—even if the probability of receiving the raise is the same.

Subtypes

As mentioned earlier, most clients with social phobia fear and avoid a variety of social situations. However, some clients are afraid of only one situation, such as giving speeches, using public washrooms, or writing in public. These clients are relatively comfortable in other social situations. Because this symptom profile seems so different from the large numbers of clients with *generalized* social phobia who are afraid of *many* social situations, researchers have examined whether there might be meaningful differences (other than feared stimuli) between clients with generalized social phobia and those whose fear is more circumscribed. Further complicating the picture, many clients with generalized social phobia also meet criteria for avoidant personality disorder. What to make of this overlap has been the subject of some controversy because the criteria for these diagnoses in DSM-IV (and earlier versions of DSM) are very similar. Is this a worthwhile distinction, or are these two diagnostic categories describing head and tail of the same coin?

To address this question, researchers have compared characteristics of three groups of clients with social phobia: specific (also called focal or circumscribed) social phobia, generalized social phobia, and generalized social phobia with avoidant personality disorder. In careful studies comparing clients from all three groups, those with generalized social phobia and avoidant personality tend to be more severe on a variety of dimensions than those without avoidant personality, who are in turn less severe than clients with specific social phobia (Stemberger, Turner, Deborah, & Calhoun, 1995; Tran & Chambless, 1995; Turner et al., 1986). Those with the generalized type are more anxious and depressed, more functionally impaired, less educated, more likely to be single, and more likely to have problems with alcohol.

Thus, most of the identified differences between subgroups of social phobia appear to be issues of severity rather than qualitative differences. There has been one area, however, in which a qualitative difference has been consistently found: physiological response. One would expect that generalized social phobics would show the biggest physiological response when engaging in a frightening situation like giving an impromptu speech, because they are more severe on other dimensions of phobia. Surprisingly, when researchers set up such a situation and asked clients to wear physiological monitoring equipment, those with specific speech phobia showed a sharper rise in heart rate than the generalized social phobics (Heimberg, Hope, Dodge, & Becker, 1990; Hofmann, Newman, Ehlers, & Roth, 1995). The baseline heart rate of those with circumscribed social phobia is often lower than that of clients with the generalized type.

Cognitive Features

Social phobia is different from the specific phobias discussed in the previous chapter in a fundamental way. The core fear is that of being negatively evaluated by other people, but usually other people are polite enough that the threat of negative evaluation must be inferred; it cannot typically be observed. Unlike with a specific phobia, in which the client knows that he is boarding an airplane or riding an elevator, the ambiguity of social situations means that the client's *interpretation* determines whether the feared event is perceived to be happening. For instance, in giving a speech, if an audience member yawns, this is an ambiguous event. Does the yawn indicate that the speaker is boring or that the room is too warm? The speaker's interpretation of the yawn is believed to influence the level of anxiety evoked by the yawn. Cognition thus plays a central role in the psychopathology of social phobia and can be characterized by alterations in perception, attention, self-schema, and implicit social scripts.

Perception

The person with social phobia feels a sense of scrutiny from others in social settings. He perceives disapproval and criticism where there may in fact be none, or else he perceives mild criticism as a strong rebuke. Winton, Clark, and Edelmann (1995) documented this clinical observation by very briefly showing slides of negative and neutral facial expressions to research volunteers. Participants who were fearful of negative evaluation were more likely to rate the face as having had a negative expression. In advance of social situations, socially anxious people anticipate evoking more negative reactions. Afterwards, they interpret interpersonal feedback more negatively than less anxious people (Smith & Sarason, 1975).

Self-Focused Attention

During social interactions, social phobics pay a lot of attention to themselves (Hope, Heimberg, & Klein, 1990). They are busy evaluating their performance, usually rendering negative judgments like "I'm boring" (Beidel, Turner, & Dancu, 1985; Stopa & Clark, 1993). Even shy persons, who lack the intense fear and avoidance associated with social phobia, spend more time focusing on themselves during a social interaction than those who are not shy (Melchior & Cheek, 1990). Focusing excessive attention on oneself during a social interaction has several negative effects. First, self-focus increases social anxiety (Woody, 1996), which in turn magnifies self-focus as the person attends to the discomfort of anxiety (Salovey, 1992), creating an upward spiral of anxiety.

In addition, focusing on the self probably gives social phobics an unfair impression of what they "must look like" to other people (Rapee & Hayman, 1996). When the phobic person becomes self-focused, internal signs of anxiety and negative self-judgmental thoughts become very salient, thus creating the impression that these flaws are obvious to everyone. In fact, socially anxious individuals overestimate how observable their anxiety is, compared to what their peers actually notice (McEwan & Devins, 1983). Thus, persistent self-focused attention increases anxiety and forms an undesirable image that the social phobic may assume other people share. Obviously, for a person who is sensitive to being negatively evaluated, this type of image of one's social performance only serves to further increase anxiety.

Beliefs About the Self

Clients with social phobia often hold global negative beliefs about themselves, such as "I'm inadequate." Unlike depressed clients, whose negative self-views are relatively stable, social phobics have a shifting view of themselves. When in social situations, their self-view can be characterized by low self-confidence and concerns about their general acceptability and self-worth. However, when alone or in social situations that are not threatening, they often have a more positive view of themselves (Clark & Wells, 1995). The sense of being less socially capable and powerful than others (Nichols, 1974) influences their predictions about how social situations will go, particularly those situations involving some conflict or need for assertiveness. In addition, social phobics consistently devalue the quality of their social performance compared to the judgments of observers (Alden & Wallace, 1995; Rapee & Lim, 1992). While feeling that one's social performance has been suboptimal might lead most people to feel a little down, for the social phobic this self-judgment spawns a sense of shame over his assumed weakness, ineptitude, immaturity, or other global character flaws.

Social Scripts

Everyone has social scripts, or ideas about the way social situations ought to go. Violations of these expectations about specific social situations are often sources of humor. If two women are going golfing and one whips a pair of high heels out of the trunk of the car, as though she were planning to wear them on the course, both women would laugh at the incongruity. High heels are part of some other social script, but not one for golf. Depending on the circumstances, violations of social scripts can also be seen in a negative light and the violator subjected to social censure. Loud talking during a symphony performance violates the shared script for the situation and will earn the talker a round of hisses from those seated nearby. Thus, there is some basis in reality for the social phobic's concern, insofar as members of society use shame as a means of enforcing conformity. Other social fears also have a basis in reality, as anxiety does sometimes cause one's mind to go blank or speech to be twisted (Beck et al., 1985). In real life, people do forget names, attribute stories to the wrong people, or experience other minor social embarrassment.

Despite the grain of truth in these fears, there are two ways in which social phobics' ideas regarding social scripts are inaccurate and dysfunctional. First, clients with social phobia often hold perfectionistic standards for performance (Clark & Wells, 1995). These standards might include ideas like "I must have something witty and intelligent to say at all times." Excessively high standards are impossible to achieve, and they do not accurately represent the norms of social scripts held by others. These high standards often involve ideas about wanting to obtain everyone's admiration and respect, and they leave no room for shared responsibility for the success of a social situation. In reality, lags in conversation are common, and no single person is blamed or held up for ridicule for not immediately interjecting an entertaining remark. Social partners work together to keep an interaction flowing smoothly.

Not only do social phobics tend to have excessively high standards for social performance, but also their estimations of the consequences of failing those high standards are blown out of proportion (Beck et al., 1985). They assume dire consequences will come of appearing anxious, ill, or anything other than polished. Thus, relatively common negative social events, such as being turned down for a date, are seen as not merely unpleasant but catastrophic (Foa, Franklin, Perry, & Herbert, 1996). The client also engages in horrified fantasy about the potential for failure or rejection well in advance of important social situations (Nichols, 1974), which again increases the probability of intense anxiety and avoidance.

Behavioral Manifestations

While social phobics as a group certainly underestimate their social performance and make dire predictions about the consequences of leaving a less-than-perfect impression, it is also true that anxiety and a narrow range of social experience make a very real impact on social behavior. The most obvious behavioral impact of social phobia is avoidance of social situations. Persons with social phobia often avoid a wide range of social situations (although not everyone avoids—some courageously endure each situation). For many clients, avoidance has become such a habit that they do not even realize all the subtle ways they are avoiding. For example, turning down an invitation to a party is an obvious avoidance, but making it a habit to have lunch at one's desk could be rationalized as preference or commitment to work. Yet, having lunch at one's desk removes the individual from possible social contacts with co-workers just as effectively as declining to go to a party. Other behavioral components of the anxiety response in social phobia can be seen in social performance deficits and safety behaviors, both of which will be discussed below.

Social Skill

Academic psychologists debate and haggle over whether social phobics really lack social skills or whether anxiety interferes with the production of intact latent skills. For the clinician, it may not be so critical to distinguish these fine points. The bottom line is that many (but certainly not all) clients with social phobia behave in slightly odd or overly restrained ways. Although specific social performance deficits vary from study to study, when chronically socially anxious persons engage in a social situation, they often speak less frequently and less fluently, speak with a quivering voice, and pause excessively or inappropriately (Johnson & Glass, 1989; Monti et al., 1984; Pilkonis, 1977). These behaviors can put off some social partners, diminishing the positive rewards that come from social interactions, as well as decreasing the chances for future social invitations from the same partners. A long history of avoidance of social situations may impair the range of social scripts the client can rely on as a guide when unexpected social events arise.

In general, anticipated evaluation or other anxiety-provoking circumstances inhibit the flexibility with which social phobics respond in social situations. Socially anxious people appear to adopt a self-protective presentation style to avoid making negative impressions. This style primarily involves reticence or the adoption of a structured role such as playing the host. In an interesting study, DePaulo, Epstein, and LeMay (1990) found that socially anxious women told shorter and less personally revealing stories when they believed they were interacting with a wary, judgmental person than when they believed they were interacting with a trusting and open person. Close links with others might also be impaired by the tendency of clients to distract or disconnect during unavoidable social situations. This disconnection is likely to have an impact on social partners, who may interpret the behavior as aloofness or disinterest.

Safety Behaviors

Predictions about terrible consequences that might occur if one is not socially perfect create a strong demand for social phobics to avoid "screwing up" or to hide minor social missteps. Safety behaviors are actions designed to diminish the risk of being negatively evaluated. These behaviors can involve coping strategies aimed at reducing anxiety, such as taking deep breaths or trying to relax. Speech patterns can be involved, as the patient may speak very softly or carefully manage her language to avoid incorrect verb tenses or other minor speaking errors. Safety behaviors can also include the use of props, such as a glass of water to prevent dry mouth or long hair to hide blushing. Drinking alcohol can also be a safety behavior, and up to 40% of socially phobic patients abuse alcohol (Norton et al., 1996). Many people, not just social phobics, use alcohol to feel more comfortable in social situations. Ironically, one study found that alcohol did not effectively decrease subjective anxiety during a speech (Naftolowitz, Vaughn, Ranc, & Tancer, 1994).

On the surface, safety behaviors seem like harmless ways to decrease anxiety, and the caring clinician might be tempted to encourage these coping behaviors. Unfortunately, these behaviors are problematic in several ways

(Wells et al., 1995). First, they prevent the patient from discovering the true consequences of appearing anxious in public or of making a minor social error. The patient is unable to discover that the consequences are not as horrible as she fantasized they would be. Another problematic effect of safety behaviors is that they can make some feared events more likely. Wells et al. give a clinical example of a patient who was afraid of trembling in public and tightly gripped glassware in order to prevent trembling; the tight grip actually caused more of the dreaded tremor.

Biological Findings and Theories

Having discussed the cognitive and behavioral manifestations of social phobia, we now turn to the physiological side. In this section, we will discuss unique physiological responsivity associated with social anxiety and briefly review promising drug treatments and evidence of a genetic contribution to social phobia.

When a socially anxious person enters (or contemplates entering) a social situation, subjective anxiety can be as intense as we would observe in any of the anxiety disorders. The physiological response, on the other hand, may not be as pronounced as in some of the other phobias (Lang, Levin, Miller, & Kozak, 1983). To illustrate, Craske and Craig (1984) asked pianists to perform in front of an audience versus performing alone. Pianists who had performance anxiety were more distressed and played with poorer quality when an audience was present, but nonanxious pianists responded the same way whether an audience was present or not. Despite these differences in distress and performance quality, there were no differences between the anxious and nonanxious pianists on physiological measures in terms of how they responded to having an audience present. This finding brings to mind the desynchrony between different response channels in anxiety discussed in chapter 3.

In general, studies examining physiological responding in social situations have found that most people respond with a surge in sympathetic activity during tasks such as giving a speech (Dimsdale & Moss, 1980), so this is not something that is limited to social phobia. What little research has been done in the neurobiology of social phobia and shyness suggests that biological responses of social phobics cannot reliably be distinguished from those of normals in the same challenge conditions (Nickell & Uhde, 1995). As mentioned earlier, subtypes of social phobia show different patterns: those with circumscribed social phobia show a more consistent increase in heart rate during a speech task than those with generalized social phobia (Hofmann et al., 1995).

Medication Treatment

Several classes of medications have been studied in the treatment of social phobia. The most thoroughly evaluated medications have been the monoamine oxidase inhibitors (MAOI), with at least four controlled trials supporting the efficacy of phenelzine (Gelernter et al., 1991; Heimberg et al., 1998; Liebowitz et al., 1992; Versiani et al., 1992). Phenelzine (Nardil; 15–90 mg per day) is more effective than placebo (Heimberg et al., 1988; Versiani et al., 1992) and more effective than the beta-blocker atenelol (Liebowitz et al., 1992). Patients who took phenelzine in combination with instructions to stop avoiding social situations maintained their improvements at 2-month follow-up, in contrast to patients given alprazolam, who relapsed during the follow-up period (Gelernter et al., 1991). The downside to treatment with phenelzine is that dietary and medication restrictions are necessary to ensure the patient's medical safety. There are some promising signs that the reversible MAOI moclobemide, which can be taken with no dietary restrictions, may also be an effective treatment of social phobia (The International Multicenter Clinical Trial Group on Moclobemide in Social Phobia, 1997). Likewise, paroxetine (Paxil; 20–50 mg per day) has been shown to be effective in one controlled trial (Stein et al., 1998).

Beta-blockers are a class of drugs that reduce some of the peripheral signs of anxiety, such as sweating and heart palpitations. These drugs have been used in many studies of performers who have mild performance anxiety (not social phobia), including professional bowlers, public speakers, students with test anxiety, and musicians (Liebowitz, Gorman, Fyer, & Klein, 1985). The beta-blocker is usually administered just before the performance or competition. Most studies have found that the medication helps maintain a steady heart rate and reduce feelings of nervousness. Although these results would seem to imply that beta-blockers could be a useful treatment for full-scale social phobia, placebo-controlled studies do not bear this out. Three separate studies have shown that neither atenolol (Tenormin; 25–100 mg per day) nor propanolol (Inderal; 160–320 mg per day) was significantly better than placebo in the treatment of social phobia (Falloon, Iloyd, & Harpin, 1981; Liebowitz et al., 1992; Turner, Beidel, & Jacob, 1994).

Genetic Contributions

Family studies reveal a much higher incidence of social phobia among family members of clients who have social phobia (16%) than among comparable nonclient families (5%). Yet, family members of social phobia clients do not appear to have increased rates of other anxiety disorders beyond social phobia (Fyer, Mannuzza, Chapman, Liebowitz, & Klein, 1993). Familial transmission of social phobia could be due to modeling or some other environmental factor, so we have to look to twin and adoption studies for more direct evidence of a genetic contribution. As reviewed by Fyer (1993), twin and adoption studies examining childhood shyness (not social phobia) show only a modest genetic contribution. In a study of over 2,000 female-female twin pairs from the Virginia Twin Registry, researchers attributed 31% of the variance to genetic factors and 68% of the variance to environmental factors (Kendler, Neale, Kessler, Heath, & Eaves, 1992).

One interesting line of research with genetic implications involves studying the emergence of introverted temperament in infancy and early childhood. In a series of studies, Kagan's group at Harvard has identified a subgroup of 10–15% of children who begin as irritable infants, show more fearful behavior than their peers in the preschool years, and are more cautious and introverted at school age (Kagan, Reznick, & Snidman, 1987). At rest, these inhibited children show an elevated heart rate, and when exposed to a mild stressor, their heart rate responsivity is magnified. Thinking that this behavioral pattern could represent a risk factor for later development of anxiety disorders, researchers from this group also examined the parents of children identified as behaviorally inhibited. Compared to the parents of uninhibited children, these parents showed a higher incidence of social phobia and other anxiety disorders, and they recalled symptoms of avoidant and overanxious disorders from their own childhood (Rosenbaum, Biederman, Hirshfeld, Bolduc, Faraone et al., 1991). Approaching the problem from the other direction, researchers also found that 85% of children of parents with panic disorder (without depression) were classified as behaviorally inhibited—compared to the 15% rate for healthy parents or 50% for parents with major depression alone (Rosenbaum et al., 1988).

Having discussed the phenomenology of social phobia, including the response systems of cognition, behavior, and physiology, we now turn to assessment. We will provide a thorough review of assessment procedures useful in the clinical evaluation of symptom severity and functional impairment associated with social phobia.

ASSESSMENT

Differential Diagnosis

Before outlining a plan for comprehensive assessment of social phobia, we need to consider whether the client is best conceptualized as having social phobia, or whether some other diagnosis is more appropriate. Panic disorder (with and without agoraphobia) probably represents the most frequent diagnostic dilemma when evaluating social anxiety. Many of the core features of social phobia can also be present in panic disorder. Patients with panic disorder often fear situations in which they will be the center of attention, because having a panic attack in such a setting would be embarrassing. In addition, social situations like giving a speech or being assertive can provoke at least mild anxiety for almost everyone. Given that panic-disordered patients fear anxiety sensations, it is not uncommon for them to avoid situations that are expected to cause some anxiety—including social situations.

To further confuse things, there is always the possibility that a client may have both social phobia and panic disorder.

Several distinctions between the two disorders may help to clarify which diagnosis better characterizes the client's problems. First, the onset of panic disorder is often much more dramatic than the onset of social phobia. Most patients with panic disorder recall their first panic attack quite clearly, and they date the onset of their problems to that time. In contrast, the beginnings of social phobia can be insidious, as clients often describe having been extremely socially anxious all their lives. A second consideration is the pattern of panic attacks. Spontaneous panic attacks in nonsocial situations (and when not anticipating a social situation) are a relatively clear indication of panic disorder.

The types of feared situations also tend to differ between social phobia and agoraphobia (Amies, Gelder, & Shaw, 1983). The main fears in social phobia tend to involve interactions with others, such as being introduced, meeting persons in authority, or using the telephone. On the other hand, clients with agoraphobia more often list *places* as main fears, including unfamiliar places, public transportation, crowds, or crossing streets. Agoraphobic patients may be afraid to be alone, in case they should need help dealing with panic symptoms; being alone is not a problem for those with social phobia.

The physical symptoms associated with anxiety are also a clue for differential diagnosis. First, social phobics are more likely to report blushing, twitching, stammering, and a dry mouth (Amies et al., 1983; Reich, Noyes, & Yates, 1988). Panic disorder patients often complain of sleep disturbances: waking up in the midst of a panic attack (nocturnal panic) or having insomnia due to generalized anxiety. Social phobics typically do not show sleep disturbance except in extreme cases of anticipatory anxiety before a big social event (Brown, Black, & Uhde, 1994). Second, and more importantly, panic disordered clients are afraid of the symptoms of anxiety. In panic, the fear is not simply that others will notice the symptoms and ridicule the client, although this is also commonly feared. In addition to embarrassment regarding the symptoms, the client with panic disorder fears that the symptoms indicate an impending physical catastrophe, such as a heart attack or stroke. A good question to ask is whether the client would be afraid of these symptoms if she experienced them when alone. Social phobia clients most often respond with something like, "Oh, no. If I knew no one would see me trembling and turning beet red, I would be all right." On the other hand, someone with panic disorder is more likely to say, "Being alone would be terrible. What if it kept getting worse and no one was there to help me?"

At times the distinction between depression and social phobia can be difficult to make, as withdrawal and social avoidance are often a part of major depression. Some of the cognitions associated with depression also bear a strong resemblance to social phobia. These include ideas like "other people are disappointed in me" or "no one enjoys my company" and a hypersensitivity to critical sentiments that are suspected to underlie innocuous remarks made by others. While these cognitions blur the distinction between depression and social phobia, the situation can often be clarified by assessing the client's motivation for social withdrawal. Depressed persons often avoid contact with other people because social activities require more energy than the patient can muster. The depressed person often has difficulty enjoying himself, so social outings do not sound tempting. Patients with social phobia, on the other hand, often yearn for social activity and feel confident they could have a good time if only they were not so anxious or if they knew everyone in attendance. History of the problem can also be a clue. Depression is often an episodic problem, flaring repeatedly over the life span with periods of relatively normal mood in between episodes. Social phobia, on the other hand, tends to be chronic and relatively stable. If social phobia appears to be present even during those periods in the client's life when depression has been in remission, then a dual diagnosis should be considered.

Social Performance

People respond better to an individual who is poised and relaxed in a social situation. Some clients are quite smooth in social settings, despite their anxiety, but others have genuine deficits in social skill. Whether poor performance is due to lack of knowledge about appropriate social behavior or to high anxiety, the clinician needs to determine how a client actually appears in social settings. Some clinicians attempt to evaluate the client's relative poise during the usual clinical interview—whether the client's behavior seems unskilled while talking with the clinician. This method can reveal inadequate social behavior on the part of some clients. The clinician, as an authority figure to whom one reveals personal information, often provokes anxiety in clients with social phobia. However, the clinical interview may not be the best place to assess typical social behavior because clients are not expected to assume responsibility for the progress of the conversation. The course of the interview is steered by the clinician, which relieves the client of the burden of having to come up with conversational topics, initiate a conversation, or end the discussion. The client is also relatively safe from negative evaluation, as therapists are enjoined not to ridicule or openly criticize their clients.

A more formal evaluation of social performance can be conducted to gather direct information about the client's actual behavior in challenging social situations. The best method of doing this is direct observation. In the previous chapter, we discussed behavioral avoidance tests for specific phobias. The same basic methodology can be applied to social phobia, although significant modifications to the procedure are required. Several advance decisions must be made. First, which social situations does the therapist want to sample? Ideally, the initial interview(s) will have revealed several problematic situations in which the therapist suspects a client may have trouble. These may include assertiveness, initiating conversations, arranging social plans, or dating situations, to name a few.

After selecting two or three challenging situations, the therapist next needs to decide who will serve as a conversation partner for the client. Especially at the beginning of treatment, the therapist himself may act as the other conversant in a role-play behavior test, because the client does not yet know the therapist very well. However, some circumstances will require the assistance of a colleague. This colleague need not be a trained professional; someone in the clinic who is bound to the same codes of confidentiality and client respect as the therapist will be fine. We have often used administrative support personnel, fellow clinicians, or trainees in this role. In the ideal world, the characteristics of the conversation partner will match the client's fears. For example, if the client has particular difficulty in conversing with attractive women, then a female assistant would be preferred for the role-play. Likewise if the primary difficulty is some type of public speaking, multiple assistants may be required to act as a small audience. While obtaining the assistance of clinic personnel may seem onerous, in fact the amount of time required of one's colleagues is quite small. We typically limit social situations in behavior tests to 10 minutes or less. In many cases, 2–3 minutes of public speaking or conversation will be more than the client can tolerate at the beginning of treatment.

After the situations are selected and the cooperation of assistants is secured, the therapist should develop scenarios to accompany the situations. For example, if assertiveness is chosen as a situation, an appropriate scenario might be "returning a pair of shoes that did not seem to fit once you got them home." Initiating a conversation might involve "waiting at a busy bus stop." The basic idea is to give the client some context within which to begin the role-play. Sidebar 4-1 contains a number of ideas for scenarios. Assistants should be encouraged to be friendly, with smiles and encouraging body language, but not to carry the burden of the conversation. This can be challenging for gregarious assistants! We have found it helpful to ask this type of assistant to pretend she is shy or preoccupied with some other matter, and we ask assistants to count silently to five before breaking a lull in the conversation.

These behavior tests should ideally be videotaped, because they can be useful for the client to review. If this is not possible, the therapist can still observe the interaction and take notes. What should the therapist be looking for? Avoidance is measured by how long the client was able to continue with the activity (e.g., 2 minutes 34 seconds out of a 5-minute test). In addition, the therapist should note the client's *anticipated* anxiety and peak anxiety *during the task*. Refer to the 0-100 SUDS scale for anxiety described in chapter 3. As for performance quality, the therapist can observe the appropriateness of behaviors such as balance between talking and listening, gaze,

SOCIAL SIMULATIONS FOR EXPOSURE OR COGNITIVE THERAPY

- You are alone at a party and have just caught the eye of someone you find attractive.
- Your physician examines you for a persistent cough and prescribes a medication. You ask about your diagnosis and how the medication will help. The physician says, "Don't worry. Just take these pills and you'll feel much better."
- Friends of yours invite you to go on a picnic with other people you have never met. When you arrive, several people have already begun to arrange the food, but your friends are not yet there.
- A person under your supervision has not been doing satisfactory work.
- Someone with a romantic interest in you asks you out, but you do not want to go.
- Someone in your household is not doing his/her share of the work around the house.
- You are at a party, and the host is offering you something to drink. You would like to talk more with the host, but you prefer to avoid alcohol this evening.
- You are in the middle of a job interview. You are really interested in the job, but the salary they are offering is lower than you are prepared to accept.
- You have just spent an evening at dinner with someone you have only recently met. You would like to end the evening now.
- You have heard that a colleague has been bad-mouthing your work.
- Last week you had dinner with some friends, and they brought along someone you had not previously met. You really enjoyed talking with this person, who is in your line of work, and you are thinking of phoning him to establish a professional contact.
- A friend of yours, who is a high school teacher, asks you to speak to her students on Career Day about your occupation.
- You have noticed the same person waiting at the bus stop with you for several mornings in a row. You begin a conversation.
- You have ordered dinner in a restaurant, and you asked for salad instead of potato with your meal. The meal arrives with a potato.
- You are having a conversation with your friend's new daughter-in-law, whom you just met. The conversation is going well, except that there are frequent long silences.
- You have volunteered some time with a community service group, and this is the first meeting you have attended. The group leader asks you to stand and say a few words of introduction about yourself.

(continued)

Sidebar 4-1 (*continued*)

- You have decided to do a simple home repair that you've never attempted before. You go to the hardware store to ask for advice and obtain the right tools.
- At a neighborhood dinner party, you are talking to a new neighbor who is in your line of work, and she asks your advice about a problem. You feel yourself begin to blush, and she says, "Are you feeling all right? Your face is very flushed."

---

self-manipulative behaviors (i.e., stroking one's hair, face, or limbs), hand gestures, facial expressions, voice quality and tone, and sense of timing.

The appropriateness of the content of the conversation should also be noted. We had one recent client who was asked to role-play striking up a conversation with a new neighbor. Although the conversation began appropriately enough, within one minute he asked our female assistant (ostensibly his "new neighbor") if her boyfriend was going to come after him with a gun for talking to her. His conversation was also peppered with verbal asides critiquing his performance, such as "No, that was a dumb thing to say . . . I'm not being very entertaining here, am I?," after which he would return to the flow of conversation. This client felt frustrated with his inability to form romantic attachments, which was one of his major goals. In this case, the behavior test was extremely valuable because we learned about serious performance deficits that he had been unable to report during an assessment interview. Using similar role-plays during treatment, we were able to give him direct feedback about the appropriateness of these behaviors and give him positive instruction in conversation skills.

Clients often express some resistance to the idea of the behavior test procedure. Sometimes, clients express a belief that the behavior test will be a waste of time because it is not the "real" situation, and they predict they will feel no anxiety in performing the task. Most of the time, these clients change their minds once they engage in the behavior test, as the possibility of any scrutiny provokes anxiety for them. For other clients, resistance to the behavior test simply reflects avoidance of anticipated anxiety. When we do these types of tests, we remind clients that they can stop the test at any time, but that we prefer that they push themselves to complete it if possible. Even at the beginning of treatment, if the length of the test is reasonable (5 minutes or so), most clients will be able to complete it, although they will often be very anxious.

In some settings, it is not feasible to conduct a behavioral assessment of social skill such as the one we have just described. In this case, a questionnaire can be used, such as the Social Performance Survey Schedule (see Appendix A). The SPSS is an inventory of positive and negative social behavior.

The client can complete the scale in reference to himself, or someone who knows the client well can complete the scale. Not only is the scale useful for clients, but also clinicians who are developing social skills training plans for a particular client may find good ideas on the scale. This measure and directions for scoring are included in Appendix A and may be reproduced for use by clinicians.

Fear and Avoidance

While the behavior test can be a good measure of avoidance and anxiety in social situations, it has limitations. Clients with generalized social phobia are afraid of a wide variety of social situations, and the degree of their fear and avoidance may vary across these situations. The behavior test cannot possibly cover all these situations. In addition, the behavior test is costly to administer in terms of therapist time. While the information gained is often worth the cost, it is not a test that one would administer on an ongoing basis. Finally, some clients are less avoidant during the test than they are in real-life situations, because they know the time for the test is restricted. Because of these limitations, the behavior test does not give a complete picture of the client's fear and avoidance patterns. Fortunately, several symptom rating scales that can be administered easily and repeatedly have been constructed for this purpose. A very brief measure was described in chapter 3—the Fear Questionnaire. This measure, reprinted in Appendix A, has a social phobia subscale.

One of the best self-report measures for social phobia is the Social Phobia and Anxiety Inventory (Turner, Beidel, Dancu, & Stanley, 1989; Turner, Stanley, Beidel, & Bond, 1989). It has been extensively tested and discriminates social phobia patients from those with other anxiety disorders. The unique feature of this inventory is that the client makes separate ratings for different social configurations (i.e., with strangers, authority figures, opposite sex, and people in general). For each listed social situation, the client rates how she would feel in that situation with strangers, then rates the situation if authority figures are present, and so on. Although the scale is longer than other measures of social anxiety (and its scoring can be slightly complicated), it represents a more complete sampling of social situations than other instruments. In addition, there is an agoraphobia subscale, which may be subtracted from the total score to control for social anxiety that is more related to agoraphobia-associated concerns. There is also a children's version of the scale that is appropriate for children as young as 8 years of age (Beidel, Turner, & Morris, 1995). The Social Phobia and Anxiety Inventory can be obtained from Multi-Health Systems in Toronto.

The Liebowitz Social Anxiety Scale (Liebowitz, 1987) is a clinician-administered list of 13 performance situations (e.g., eating in public places, urinating in a public bathroom) and 11 interaction situations (e.g., giving a party, calling someone you don't know very well). Each item is rated for degree of fear and for percentage of time the situation is avoided. Although it is designed as an interview, it has been used in a self-report format (Greist, Kobak, Jefferson, Katzelnick, & Chene, 1995). Another measure that is usually completed as an interview is the Brief Social Phobia Scale (Davidson et al., 1991), which follows the same format of rating social situations on fear and avoidance. This scale has fewer situations, and they tend to be more general (e.g., social gatherings, being criticized). The measure also has a subscale assessing the degree to which the client experiences blushing, palpitations, trembling, and sweating in social situations. Both of these measures have also been adapted for computer administration. They can be obtained from Healthcare Technology Systems in Madison, Wisconsin. Information is available on the web at http://www.healthtechsys.com/prodgridnew.html.

Behaving assertively can be challenging for many clients, but social phobics find assertiveness to be a particular problem. Gambrill and Richey (1975) have developed a very useful self-report scale on which clients rate their degree of discomfort with 40 specific assertion behaviors. Clients also rate the likelihood that they would respond in the described way if they were actually presented with the situation. Using both of these indicators allows for characterization of the client as unassertive (high anxiety, low response probability), anxious-performer (high anxiety, high response probability), assertive (low anxiety and high response probability), or unconcerned (low anxiety and low response probability). Even if the measure is not used in a formal way to assess clients, therapists can obtain ideas about practice situations for assertiveness training by consulting the list. The Gambrill and Richey Assertion Inventory is reprinted in Appendix A.

Hierarchies of feared situations were discussed in chapter 3 as they pertain to specific phobia, but constructing a hierarchy of feared social situations is also an important exercise. During discussion of their fears, clients will spontaneously generate many of the items on the hierarchy, but the therapist should also specifically ask about common social situations, focusing on both degree of fear using the SUDS scale and degree of avoidance. Items that should be assessed include performance activities (eating in public, using public restrooms, giving a talk or asking a question in a group, writing in public), interaction situations (parties, meetings, talking to authority figures, initiating conversations, maintaining conversations), and assertiveness (refusing unreasonable requests, asking others to change their behavior). It is useful to do a hierarchy at the beginning of treatment for all socially phobic clients; we have seen several clients who maintained that they had "only a fear of public speaking." When they were asked specifically about these other situations, it turned out that their fear was much more generalized.

The hierarchy should include parameters of other people in the social situations, such as their status, sex, age, or degree of attractiveness. For example, a party at a friend's house would probably elicit different concerns than a party at the company president's house. Situations themselves can be associated with different expectations of the client, and these should also be noted on the hierarchy when possible. For instance, a client may be fine in meetings in which he is expected to be a passive listener, but meetings in which he is scheduled to present information may be a problem. Some of these factors will only become clear as the therapist and client work together to understand cues that provoke anxiety; see the discussion below on social diaries.

Social Functioning

Many clients with social phobia, particularly those with the generalized sub-type, have an impoverished social life. By the time clients seek treatment, they have often had the disorder for 15–20 years, and they have developed entrenched habits of avoidance. Such a restricted lifestyle provides few natural opportunities for social interaction. Becoming less anxious and less actively avoidant does not automatically mean that the person will make the effort to develop and maintain a full, rewarding social life. Because of this problem of passive avoidance, the practitioner should make a point of assessing social functioning.

The format that we have found to be most helpful for evaluating social functioning is self-monitoring, or *social diaries*. Having clients complete a diary of social activities every day provides a wealth of information on clients' social contacts, as well as their experiences during such contacts. These diaries should be relatively simple, yet they should provide the sort of information the clinician needs for ongoing treatment planning. An example of one of these diaries is shown in figure 4.1. It is important to remember that the columns in a social diary can reflect whatever variables the clinician wants to monitor with a given patient. The example given here includes who the other people involved in the situation were, what the situation was, and how long it lasted, as well as the client's thoughts and level of anxiety. One could also include columns for how much enjoyment the client experienced, the client's goals in the situation, whether the client avoided any part of the social situation, or whether the client initiated the contact. Using a word processor, the therapist can print out a diary in a matter of minutes.

The diaries will only be of limited utility without interview follow-up during the session. The therapist should examine the diary, noting the frequency and characteristics of the client's social engagements. The diary provides an opportunity to obtain information on subtle avoidance that the client may not notice or spontaneously report. For example, the therapist may notice that there are no opposite-sex interactions on the diary or that all of the client's interactions last less than 10 minutes. Thus, the diary should be examined for frequency, duration, and diversity of social interactions, as well as anxiety and avoidance. Having the client record her thoughts during social situations (or avoidance) also allows the therapist to observe changes in beliefs. Note that specific treatment goals (e.g., have one

Date	Who was there?	What was the situation?	Duration	SUDS (0–100)	Thoughts
4/3/98	Bob and John	waiting for our wives	10 min.	85	I can't keep the conversation going. I'm such an idiot.
4/4/98	Co-workers	birthday party	avoided	100	I wouldn't know how to act. I'll embarrass myself.

Figure 4.1 Sample Social Diary.

casual conversation at work each day) are easy to assess in the context of social functioning in the diary format. Less specific treatment goals, such as "establish friendly relationships with co-workers," make evaluation of treatment progress more ambiguous.

Cognition

Social diaries are useful for monitoring thoughts during social interactions because they give the therapist direct access to the client's predictions about what might go wrong. As we will discuss later, this information is critical for cognitive interventions. However, there are times when a clinician might want to use a questionnaire for evaluating thoughts about social and evaluative situations. For example, if the therapist wants to monitor progress over time, then a measure that yields a numerical score may be desirable. Diaries can be scored in this way, but obtaining reliable and valid scores from diaries is complicated, whereas questionnaires are user-friendly from this perspective. In the beginning stages of treatment, many clients also have difficulty identifying their thoughts in social situations. A questionnaire that lists common thoughts associated with social anxiety can be helpful.

A widely used instrument for assessing cognition in social phobia is the Social Interaction Self-Statement Test (Glass, Merluzzi, Biever, & Larsen, 1982). This questionnaire evaluates a client's thoughts during a specific situation. Immediately following a social interaction, such as a behavior test or a homework assignment, clients complete the questionnaire indicating the frequency with which they had each of 30 thoughts (15 positive and 15 negative) during the interaction. The Negative subscale of the test is a better predictor of social anxiety and avoidant behavior than the Positive subscale (Arnkoff & Glass, 1989), so it is possible that the cost-effectiveness of the scale would be increased if therapists used only the Negative subscale. The original scale was designed for dyadic interactions, but it can easily be modified for public speaking situations by changing "she/he" to "they" throughout the scale. The scale is reprinted in Appendix A. Dodge, Hope, Heimberg, and Becker (1988) reported clients with social phobia obtained means of 54.75 (SD = 12.68) and 36.21 (SD = 11.44) for the negative and positive subscales, respectively.

Context

In addition to determining a diagnosis and understanding the patient's patterns of fear and avoidance and troublesome cognitions, clinicians should gain some appreciation for the context in which the client lives. Taking a few moments to get contextual and historical information on the client's experiences with family, intimate relationships, school, and employment will be important in understanding the client's social functioning. As pointed out by Butler (1989), the patient's strengths should also be assessed, as these are a source for hopefulness and enjoyment, as well as clues for helping the client to build a social support network. Thus, the clinician should note hobbies, important relationships, appealing personal qualities, and workplace opportunities for socializing.

By repeatedly administering some of these measures, clinicians can document the extent to which clients are improving during treatment. At times, the clinician may also want to get an idea of how well the client is functioning compared to people who do not have social phobia—whether the client is in the "normal" range. Ideally, multiple indices of functioning would be used to make this determination. If data from normal populations is available, some researchers have suggested that treated clients who score in the 84th percentile of normal samples should be considered having obtained high end-state functioning status (Turner, Beidel, Long, Turner, & Townsley, 1993). This indicates that the client performed better than 16% of normals on a given measure. Turner et al. suggest cutoff scores for high end-state status for many of the measures we have discussed in this chapter. This cutoff for the Social Phobia Anxiety Inventory difference scores (after subtracting out the agoraphobia subscale) is a score of 59 or lower. For clients who are asked to give a 10-minute speech, speaking for at least 5.7 minutes with anxiety of 63 or less on a 0–100 scale shows high end-state functioning, as well as Fear Questionnaire social phobia subscale scores of 2 or less (see chapter 3 for a description of the Fear Questionnaire). Using these measures, clinicians can make relatively clear statements about the functional status of their clients vis à vis normal functioning.

In sum, a thorough assessment involves establishing a diagnosis of social phobia and gathering information on performance deficits, degree of fear and avoidance across a wide range of situations, cognitions related to social interactions, and social context and level of functioning. In addition to these information-gathering activities, empirically minded clinicians will want to establish a plan for monitoring progress on important dimensions throughout treatment. We certainly recommend using the social diaries, tailored to specific concerns about each individual client, in nearly all cases. The therapist can use the diary to monitor progress by taking a quick tally of important variables at each session. In addition, several of the questionnaires mentioned in this section can be administered repeatedly, so therapists monitoring progress may want to ask clients to complete them on a monthly or so basis. Again, the clinician's judgment is required to select measures that will evaluate areas of importance to each individual client. Finally, the hierarchy, tailored as it is to each client, is a critical indicator of the work remaining in therapy. At the very least, therapists should formally reevaluate the hierarchy, complete with SUDS and avoidance ratings, on a regular basis and monitor weekly social diaries. Both of these approaches are convenient, inexpensive, and useful for evaluating degree of change on problems that are central to social phobia.

INTERVENTIONS

With the evaluation completed and a plan for monitoring progress prepared, the tools are in place to formulate a specific treatment plan. Three distinct areas of psychosocial interventions have been scientifically investigated, based on separate theoretical models of social phobia. These interventions have been aimed at improving social skills, reducing anxiety, and changing self-defeating cognitions. Current treatment most often combines elements of each of these interventions. We will discuss them in turn, briefly discussing the theoretical model, describing the procedures in detail, and relating the evidence that supports the use of each procedure. After each has been discussed, we will consider the advantages of the current trend of integrating these approaches for a multicomponent therapy of social phobia.

Improving Social Skill

The self-presentation theory of social anxiety (Schlenker & Leary, 1982) maintains that social anxiety results when a person is motivated to make certain impressions on others but doubts that she will be successful in making the desired impression. Elements of this equation include overvaluing the importance of making a certain impression and undervaluing one's own performance abilities. These elements will be discussed below in the section on changing cognitions. Another part of this equation may involve a realistic appraisal of one's own poor social skills; some clients with social phobia feel at a loss as to how to manage common social situations such as making future social plans or initiating a conversation with a stranger. Skills-building interventions inherently involve exposure to social situations, so they may be useful regardless of whether the performance deficits are due to lack of knowledge or simply severe anxiety. Clearly, skills building is not necessary for patients who do not show performance deficits.

Specific Procedures

Social skills training involves a specific sequence of practice and feedback of each specific skill the therapist wishes to teach. We will first discuss this training method, and then we will address basic social skills that clinicians may want to promote. For each basic skill, the clinician will first *provide instruction* on what to do. For example, to initiate a conversation, the client needs to know the types of situations in which initiating conversations is appropriate (e.g., talking to cab drivers, waiters, or someone on the ski lift). In this example, the therapist would instruct the client to observe the person he would like to strike up a conversation with, to see if this person seems to be receptive to a conversation (e.g., not engrossed in conversation with someone else). If the person seems receptive, then the client might start with a stock phrase about some common experience, like "Is this weather supposed to hold out through the weekend?" or "Where are you from?"

After giving the client explicit instructions about how people generally operate in a given social situation, the clinician should involve the client in a role-play, where the clinician *models* the behavior she has just discussed with the client. In our "initiating a conversation" example, the therapist would first suggest a scenario (e.g., standing in a long customer service line). Then the therapist and client would role-play, with the therapist assuming the role of beginning a conversation with the client. Then the therapist and client *switch roles*, so that the client begins a conversation with the therapist (with the same or a different scenario).

The therapist then provides any necessary *corrective feedback*. This feedback should focus on positive things the patient *can* do, rather than solely concentrating on negative things the patient should *refrain* from doing. As an example, "If you look directly at someone when you speak, it is more engaging and invites conversation" is more helpful to the client than, "Don't look at your shoes so much." Ideally, the client practices the behavior again in a second role-play, incorporating the therapist's feedback. Lastly, the therapist and client should formulate concrete plans for practicing the skill in real life during the subsequent week. Because these homework assignments can be very challenging for clients, it is best to help the client decide on a very specific plan: with whom he will initiate a conversation, on what day(s), and in what circumstances. Otherwise, clients often return the following week to report that no opportunities arose to practice the skill.

This basic procedure, involving (a) instruction, (b) modeling, (c) role-play practice, (d) corrective feedback, (e) more practice, and (f) in vivo practice (homework), can be applied to a variety of social skills. The client's degree of performance deficits will determine where to start. Some clients are very unskilled and require basic instruction beginning with nonverbal behavior. Others are quite functional in most areas, but require advanced pointers on delivering a public presentation or dating skills. Any level of social skills can be approached with this model. A key is monitoring the therapeutic relationship as a guide to speed of movement through the steps of the model. The therapist must take care to progress slowly enough that the client has sufficient opportunity to practice, but not so slowly that the client feels belittled by instruction on seemingly basic skills.

What skills should the therapist teach? This chapter does not afford enough space to be able to thoroughly discuss all social skills. However, several popular books provide ideas that are useful for therapists. Some that we have used include *Taking Charge of Your Social Life* (Gambrill & Richey, 1988), *How to Win Friends and Influence People* (Carnegie, 1964), and *Talking with Confidence for the Painfully Shy* (Gabor, 1997). It is important to note that these books were not written for treatment of social phobia, but for helping shy or introverted people to improve their social skills. Many of the exercises recommended in them will probably be too challenging for clients with social phobia to do on their own, but they can be useful to reinforce lessons learned in therapy. We will review some of the basic skills often covered in social skills training.

Nonverbal Behavior

Body language can be just as important to social success as verbal language. Clients need to be able to use appropriate nonverbal behavior to meet their social goals, and they also need to be able to appropriately monitor the nonverbal behavior of others, so as to respond accordingly. For example, if a client decides to strike up a conversation about the upcoming holiday weekend with a co-worker, she might begin by approaching the co-worker and greeting him by name. The co-worker's body language will be important in deciding whether the client should continue with the conversation or postpone it until another time. If the co-worker looks up toward the client, raises his eyebrows, smiles, leans forward, and waves the client closer to his desk, these are all positive signs indicating his receptiveness to conversation. If, on the other hand, the co-worker maintains his working posture with only brief glances toward the client, then the client should understand that the co-worker would prefer not to engage in conversation at this moment. Understanding the nonverbal behavior of others will help the client to appropriately attribute some aborted social interactions as being due to factors involving the other person.

The therapist should also ascertain that the client is able to send appropriate nonverbal signals. The behavior of unskilled persons tends to be more inflexible than that of skilled persons, varying less from situation to situation (Trower, 1980). Thus, nonverbal signals should be assessed and taught in a variety of contexts. The therapist should ascertain that the client maintains an appropriate physical distance from social partners, and that the client understands social norms about touching others. Facial expressions should be compatible with the content of speech, and clients can experiment with the conversation-extending power of a smile. Depending on the culture and context, gazing directly at one's social partner can be engaging or aggressive. The therapist should also take responsibility for giving the client appropriate feedback about physical appearance or odors that may inhibit social interactions.

Socially anxious persons often behave in ways that are designed to avoid attracting attention from others. These behaviors, while useful if the goal is avoiding social interaction, are not helpful in efforts to engage in more rewarding and successful interactions with others. For example, many social phobics use closed body language (slouching the shoulders and lowering the head). Others maintain a soft or monotonic voice regardless of the nature of the communication. In addition, socially anxious persons often have difficulty relaxing enough to use appropriate gestures to accent their speech, or they may unknowingly use gestures that discourage communication, such as covering the mouth with a hand.

Initiating and Maintaining Conversations

Initiating a conversation with a stranger can be challenging for many people. Knowing how to begin a conversation is often half the battle. The therapist can teach clients a set of opening remarks and encourage practice with each of them. For example, conversations can begin with a comment or question on some shared activity. Although we have heard many socially phobic clients complain that talking about the weather will be a sure signal that they have nothing more interesting to say, the weather is an event we all share and often remark on. Another way to begin conversations is complimenting others or asking a casual question about what they are doing. Asking for advice, help, or information is an appropriate way to begin a dialogue, and offering an opinion or advice can also facilitate conversation. One can also simply introduce oneself, although this may not be the best opener in every setting. We have occasionally observed clients who try to compensate for feelings of insecurity in dating situations by using clichés that put others off; corrective feedback about these opening "lines" can be particularly useful.

We suspect that one of the biggest impediments to maintaining conversations is focus of attention. Paying insufficient attention to social partners creates a poor impression (Trower, 1980) and yields fewer social rewards (Jones, Hobbs, & Hockenbury, 1982). In addition, paying attention to one's internal responses can lead one to believe that signs of anxiety are more obvious than they actually are, leading to further anxiety. Thus, helping the client to actively attend to conversational partners can be useful. This can be accomplished by encouraging others to share information about themselves (using open-ended questions like "What did you think of the movie?"), offering reflections of others' feelings, and providing encouraging verbal prompts ("uh huh," "that's true," "yep"). During silences, the client should be encouraged to review things that the other person has been saying, reflecting on the other person and asking follow-up questions. Silences can be another danger spot in maintaining a conversation, as clients again feel the urge to flee. Videotaping conversations and reviewing them with the client can be a powerful demonstration that silences are natural and that they are never as long as they seem to be.

Assertive Behavior

Clients with social phobia are not the only ones who can benefit from assertiveness training; those with depression, agoraphobia, and other problems also avoid assertion. Assertion involves a wide range of social skills, from returning defective merchandise to arranging future social plans. Assertive behavior is involved in ending a conversation, refusing unreasonable requests, and asking for favors. Often clients misunderstand assertive behavior, believing that others will regard it as pushy, selfish, and inappropriate. Being able to ask questions that reveal one's ignorance or confusion, disagreeing with someone's opinion, and asking friends or colleagues to change their behavior are all important parts of clear and honest communication. Finally, an important part of assertiveness skills is knowing what to do when the other person does not comply with a request. Being turned down for a date, for example, can create feelings of disappointment, and it is important that the client be prepared for appropriate behavior in this circumstance.

Assertiveness skills frequently come into play when handling difficult situations. We have all run into social situations in which we must skillfully handle another person's inappropriate or unpleasant behavior; our clients need to be able to deal with these situations as well. For example, when conversing in a group, others may try to interrupt the client before he is finished talking, and specific skills are involved in resisting such interruptions (i.e., raising the voice slightly and maintaining eye contact with those who are listening). Judging when another person has crossed the line from constructive criticism to verbal abuse also requires skill, as does responding appropriately to stand up for oneself.

Scientific Support

Several studies have demonstrated that clients who participate in social skills training show reductions in phobic severity, social inadequacy, and general anxiety and depression (Stravynski, Marks, & Yule, 1982; Trower, Yardley, Bryant, & Shaw, 1978; Wlazlo, Schroeder-Hartwig, Hand, Kaiser, & Munchau, 1990). However, these studies did not use a control group, so other factors may have been responsible for the observed improvements. Studies that have compared social skills training to a waiting-list control inspire more confidence. In a study using this more rigorous research design, patients who received social skills training increased their range of social activities and social contacts (Marzillier, Lambert, & Kellet, 1976). However, no improvements were seen on social anxiety or clinician-rated social adjustment, suggesting that social skills training is by itself insufficient for addressing the full range of problems presented by most socially phobic clients.

One would think that social skills training would be especially useful for clients with poor social performance, compared with clients who are anxious but able to perform adequately. Trower et al. (1978) confirmed this idea in a treatment study. On the basis of an initial evaluation, researchers rated social skills of their socially phobic clients, judging them as either deficient or adequately skilled. Clients were randomly assigned to social skills training or systematic desensitization, so that some clients received a treatment matched to their symptom profile, but other clients received a treatment that was mismatched with their problems. Interestingly, the two forms of treatment were equally useful for clients with adequate social skills. However, clients with poor social skills responded better to social skills training rather than to the systematic desensitization. Clients who participated in social skills training experienced less difficulty in social situations and had more frequent social activities than clients who engaged in systematic desensitization.

Extinguishing the Anxiety Response

As we have previously discussed, whether social phobics lack basic social skills is controversial. Some researchers argue that the effective ingredient in social skills training is the *exposure* inherent in practicing different social situations within the therapy setting and in the real world. Interventions specifically designed to provide exposure have a different theoretical premise that guides the design of the treatment. In social skills training, the idea is to boost social effectiveness, but during treatment with exposure, the object is to allow the client to remain in the social situation long enough to experience a habituation of anxiety. In this section, we will discuss the rationale behind a conditioning model of social phobia and specific procedures to implement exposure-based treatment.

Conditioning Model

A conditioning model of social phobia involves the hypothesis that a traumatic social event has created lasting anxiety associated with performance or social interactions. Subsequent intense anxiety reactions in social situations are considered as conditioned anxiety responses. As formulated by Barlow (1988), biological or psychological vulnerabilities can lay the groundwork so that only a relatively minor life event evoking shame or humiliation may be enough to constitute this initial trauma, particularly if the individual suffers a panic attack at the time of the negative social event. Examples of biological vulnerabilities include genetic influences specific to social phobia or more generally related to anxious apprehension. Sensitivity to shame, humiliation, and negative evaluation may be examples of psychological vulnerabilities. Social phobia can be maintained by the avoidance of anxiety-provoking social situations, because avoiding is reinforced by the anxiety reduction that occurs as a result of avoidance, escape, or even simply making the decision to avoid. See chapter 3 for more background on conditioning theory in phobias in general.

Careful and systematic histories of clients with social phobia have revealed 58% of clients recall a traumatic conditioning event that they associate with the etiology of their phobia (Öst & Hugdahl, 1981). In contrast, only 20% of nonclinical control interviewees report similar traumatic social events. Traumatic conditioning events may be more important in the etiology of specific social phobias than generalized social phobia, if clients' memories of such events are indicative. Clients with specific social phobias such as writing, eating, or drinking in front of others very often report recalling some incident that seemed to mark the beginning of their social phobia (Stemberger et al., 1995).

Maria recalled being on a family car trip when she was a teenager and urgently needing to urinate. After she finally convinced her family she could not wait any longer, the family reluctantly agreed to pull over at a rest stop, and Maria entered the bathroom. Several female members of the family stood outside the stall, urging her to hurry up, reminding her that the whole family was waiting for her so they could continue on their vacation. Despite her desire to be compliant, Maria was unable to relax her pelvic muscles enough to urinate for at least 30 minutes. She felt humiliated and had considerable bladder discomfort. She dated this incident as the beginning of her fear of urinating in public. She was concerned that people would wonder what was "wrong" with her if she took too long in the stall, and her anxiety increased her latency to urinate. By the time she sought treatment, she avoided lengthy social situations and strictly limited her liquid intake before going out. Maria had especially great difficulty in socializing with female friends, as they often volunteered to go to the washroom with her when they were out together. Notably, Maria also had a problem with anorgasmia, which was resolved by helping her and her partner to remove implicit time pressures related to becoming fully aroused.

Basic Exposure Procedures

Similar to the exposure-based treatments for simple phobias discussed in the previous chapter, exposure for social phobia involves encouraging clients to remain in the fearful situation until anxiety has declined. The therapist orchestrates the treatment to gradually increase the difficulty of social situations to which clients are exposed. To maximize generalization, the clinician strives to vary these social situations across settings and mix of social partners. Formulating a specific treatment plan for exposure-based approaches depends heavily on a detailed hierarchy of feared situations, discussed above as a part of assessment procedures. This hierarchy needs to be periodically reevaluated, as clients differ in the degree and pattern of generalization of fear reduction. It is also important that the client understand the rationale behind exposure-based interventions, because this type of treatment requires motivation, persistence, and courage. Repeating the rationale for treatment, along with providing a supportive and encouraging relationship, helps boost motivation for treatment.

After the therapist has carefully constructed a hierarchy, established a plan for monitoring treatment progress, and educated the client about the treatment rationale, within-session exposure may begin. For logistical reasons, it is often more convenient to conduct exposure treatment for social phobia within the context of a group, and this will be discussed later in this chapter. However, arranging a group can be impractical in some settings; practitioners in private practice often have difficulty forming a group within a reasonable period of time. In addition, some clients are reluctant to join a group, either because of severity of social phobia or because of the intimate nature of their fears. Thus, our main discussion of these interventions will be focused on individual treatment, but we will address modifications for and advantages of the group therapy format below.

Typically, the therapist plans in advance for the exposure session by deciding on an exposure scenario, obtaining minimal props for improving realism, and even arranging for confederates. See sidebar 4-1 for suggestions and ideas for exposure scenarios to use within sessions. The first exposure session should involve a scenario the therapist anticipates will provoke a moderate level of anxiety (50–60 on the 0–100 SUDS scale). Subsequent sessions may aim for higher levels of anxiety if the therapist observes that the client is able to tolerate higher anxiety levels and readily habituates within the time permitted for the session. In planning a scenario, the therapist should get input from the client about ways to make the scenario more realistic. For example, in a scenario whereby the client confronts his boss, it may be useful for the client to intentionally wear work clothes to the session rather than more casual attire. Exposure to party situations may be facilitated by allowing the client to hold a cup of soda, as one would do at a party.

In planning the exposure sessions, it is important to remember that while the clients often describe their fear in terms of specific social situations, the core fears are of scrutiny, negative evaluation, and humiliation. Thus, the clinician should pay careful attention to features about a situation that may relate to these basic fears. For example, having a conversation with a gregarious, upbeat stranger who carries the burden of the conversation will not be nearly so challenging as a conversation with a stranger who is distracted, quiet, and seems a little bored. While both are conversations with strangers, the former carries less threat of negative scrutiny. If the therapist uses a confederate, this assistant should be coached on relevant behaviors that are desirable, such as skeptical or challenging comments to the client or looks of boredom or disapproval. Obviously these cues should not be introduced until the therapeutic relationship is solid and the client is ready for such challenges.

Manipulating cues within the exposure scenario can also make a challenging situation somewhat more manageable. At the beginning of treatment, some clients have such intense and pervasive social anxiety that they are unable to think of situations that would be in the "moderate anxiety" range. In planning for these early sessions, the therapist can manipulate cues within the exposure to moderate a challenging situation that the client might otherwise not attempt. For example, one client we treated had difficulty talking with attractive young women. Exposure sessions began with him initiating conversations with a member of our administrative staff in which she was friendly and approachable. During these early sessions, the assistant showed interest and approval toward the client. As he progressed, these conversations became more challenging, as she enacted roles of boredom or irritability.

The therapist should take care to preserve the client's dignity, even when the assistant's job is to "diss" the client in a role-play. One way to do this is to be sure that assistants, if used, are trained properly. They should be encouraged to maintain an attitude of respect while still providing cues that were previously established as difficult for a given client (e.g., yawn, sigh, pointedly look at wristwatch). Despite clients' discomfort during the exposure scenarios, we have found that most respond well to a debriefing session with the therapist (and assistant). In these debriefing sessions, the therapist encourages the client to discuss automatic thoughts that occurred in response to specific statements made by the conversation partner (or audience members). This debriefing reinforces the idea that these cues are being provided because they are triggers for anxiety, rather than because the therapist is trying to ridicule the client. Even when clients "know" the rationale behind a therapist's or assistant's role-play behavior, the cues themselves are powerful enough to elicit anxiety.

The client can also help to plan exposures. Because social situations in the client's real life are not within the therapist's control, it is a good idea to take advantage of naturally occurring situations that arise. The most helpful arrangement is if a client can engage in exposure during the session and then follow that exposure with a similar real life scenario later that week. Take the example of a client we saw who had special difficulty talking with his mother-in-law. He felt that he never had anything to say to her and that she would judge him harshly during what he perceived to be a "flat" conversation. As a result, he avoided being in the room with his mother-in-law unless his wife, Sarah, was also present. During the session before an upcoming family event, the exposure involved a conversation with the therapist, who role-played the mother-in-law. The client was encouraged to allow silences to occur and to remain in the situation in spite of the fact that his "mother-in-law" was saying things like, "Geez, I wonder what is taking Sarah so long in the kitchen" and "You are in a quiet mood today." The client then arranged to have some time alone with his mother-in-law during their visit the following week.

As the preceding example illustrates, exposure in social phobia largely involves role-plays with the therapist (or a confederate if one is available) and self-directed exposure as homework between sessions. See sidebar 4-2 for suggestions about homework, or in vivo, exposure scenarios. When anxiety becomes intense, some clients will fall out of role in the session, turning to the therapist and saying, "I really don't know what to say here." In this event, the therapist should strongly encourage the client not to avoid, but to stay in role as long as possible. Obviously, some social situations, particularly those basic ones like introducing oneself or making eye contact with a store clerk, are by nature very brief. Arranging within-session exposure scenarios for brief social interactions can be challenging unless the format is group therapy.

Sidebar 4-2

SUGGESTIONS FOR HOMEWORK ASSIGNMENTS

- Go into a store and ask for change. Do not buy anything.
- Walk in a straight line through a busy street. Do not step aside for anyone, and look passersby straight in the eye.
- Go to a busy cafeteria (or cafeteria-style restaurant). Select your food, and roam through the sitting area, taking a long time to choose a seat.
- During a break at work, tell fellow employees something about a book you have read or a movie you have recently seen. Ask their opinion, and offer yours.
- Ask several strangers where they bought their coat, bag, tie, etc.
- Visit a busy department store with a clock section. Set off at least one of the alarm clocks. Do not buy it.
- Invite one of your neighbors or a work colleague to have tea or coffee in your home.
- Go into a travel agency and gather information about trips to Portugal for a certain period of time previously decided upon. Ask about inexpensive travel options. Discuss the appeal of travel to Portugal. Maintain the conversation for at least 15 minutes.
- Ask your work supervisor how his or her weekend was.
- Gather information about different kinds of clubs (sports, aerobics, astrology, photo, drama, etc.), and find out whether it is possible to go to one for an introductory lesson. Visit a club that seems interesting to you.
- Start a conversation with a stranger at a social event organized by your church.
- Have lunch alone in a crowded cafeteria.
- Order food in a restaurant. When it comes, send it back to be cooked longer.

Frequent repetition of the situation may be a good stand-in for a lengthy scenario. For example, a therapist in one of our clinics wanted to help a client introduce himself to strangers. That particular exposure session was conducted walking through the halls of the building, where the therapist greeted different staff members. The client would then extend a handshake, greet, and introduce himself. In this way, he was able to practice introducing himself over a dozen times within one session. His homework that week was to introduce himself in a similar way to one person each day, and he and his therapist planned times and places where this would be appropriate.

The actual therapy session usually begins with a review of homework from the last session, and the therapist carefully examines social diaries. Before beginning exposure in a given session, the therapist should offer a brief explanation of the plan for that session. Sometimes, the plan may be modified after consultation with the client. Just before beginning the exposure, the therapist should introduce the assistant (if one is used), and set the stage for the role-play by reminding both the client and the assistant about the scenario. Periodically throughout the exposure, the therapist should ask for SUDS ratings of anxiety. These ratings are used to judge when to end the exposure and are helpful in planning future exposure sessions. At the end of each exposure, the debriefing occurs, in which the therapist asks about moments of peak anxiety and about stimuli that were reassuring or anxiety-provoking. Finally, the exposure ends with a concrete plan for the client to practice the same or a similar situation in real life. In forming plans for homework, the therapist often offers encouragement and instruction about typical social behavior, such as how often one may telephone old friends or extend social invitations to work colleagues.

Empirical Support

A number of studies have demonstrated that real-life confrontation of anxiety-provoking social situations (i.e., exposure) results in measurable improvements in social phobia when compared to waiting list control groups (e.g., Butler, Cullington, Munby, Amies, & Gelder, 1984; Newman, Hofmann, Trabert, Roth, & Taylor, 1994). Exposure by itself may leave clients vulnerable to relapse. Some studies have found that as many as 47% of social phobia clients treated only with exposure went on to seek treatment for their problems again in the few months subsequent to ending exposure therapy (Butler et al., 1984; Mattick & Peters, 1988). In contrast, exposure supplemented by cognitive interventions in these studies was associated with lower rates of clients seeking additional treatment (0%–27%).

These two studies (Butler et al., 1984; Mattick & Peters, 1988) offered clients only 6–7 sessions of treatment, which may not be enough for exposure therapy. In another study that provided 14 sessions, clients maintained their improvement in the 18 months after therapy ended—regardless of whether they received exposure alone or a combination treatment. In general, more sessions do not directly translate into more improvement (Feske & Chambless, 1995), but Scholing and Emmelkamp (1966a; 1996b) found that 16 sessions of exposure (with or without added cognitive interventions) produced more improvement than only 8 sessions of the same treatment.

Including exposure in the treatment plan is probably necessary for a good treatment response. As we will see below, many cognitive interventions include exposure-type activities in which the therapist encourages the client to go into real social situations (although the rationale is markedly different). Cognitive therapy in the *absence* of any exposure procedures was observed to have no immediate effect on three clients with the type of social phobia involving fear of writing in public (Biran, Augusto, & Wilson, 1981). Subsequent exposure with these clients proved substantially effective.

Most recent developments in treatment research for social phobia have not used pure exposure models. One reason for this is the strong cognitive component to social phobia. Perceiving the feared stimulus involves making inferences not required in other phobias; social phobics *presume* others are thinking negatively about them. Because of this cognitive element of social phobia, cognitive interventions have been applied to directly challenge maladaptive thoughts.

Changing Cognitions

The most common combined treatment brings together exposure-based treatment and cognitive therapy to target reductions in anxiety and avoidance at the same time as altering maladaptive thinking associated with social phobia. In the next section, we will briefly discuss the cognitive view of social phobia, describe cognitive interventions in detail, and review the relevant scientific literature.

Cognitive Model

Clinicians working with social phobia can readily point to cognitive patterns they observe in socially anxious patients (Beck et al., 1985). In most social interactions, the cues and feedback are subtle and ambiguous. We usually cannot tell what another person thinks about our behavior or performance in a given social situation. For people who are frightened of the possibility of negative evaluation, neutral social cues can be intolerable, as they are interpreted negatively. Positive associations with social situations, such as memories of past successes or confidence in one's coping resources in the event of a social gaffe, are unavailable or discounted. The ambiguity of most social situations, combined with a mortal fear of being negatively evaluated, leads the social phobic to be hypervigilant in detecting possible threat cues.

As described by Clark and Wells (1995), clients with social phobia have developed a set of assumptions about themselves and about social situations in general. Clients' assumptions include the idea that they are likely to be graceless and behave inappropriately. While this idea alone would be upsetting, it is accompanied by the further assumption that inept social behavior will lead to disastrous results: loss of status, rejection, or humiliation. Even one's own anxiety response is interpreted as evidence that these disasters are imminent. Trembling, or other publicly observable signs of anxiety, is taken as evidence that one is making a fool of oneself. The person with social phobia often incorrectly assumes that her anxiety is apparent to observers. Because most people do not look visibly anxious in social settings, socially phobic clients assume that others simply do not feel social anxiety. Feeling anxious in a social situation is taken as a sign of "differentness," of being weird and inferior to others.

Cognitive interventions explicitly aim to challenge these ideas, including expectations of one's own performance as well as beliefs about the consequences of minor social blunders. It is important to remember, however, that these beliefs may also be changed by other experiences not directly aimed at disconfirming them, such as exposure (Mattick & Peters, 1988). Social skills training may also have the power to change cognition through improved self-efficacy. For example, in learning new assertiveness skills, clients often find that other people do not respond in the negative way that was anticipated by the client. Most people respond to appropriate assertiveness with respect and compliance. The trick, of course, is in persuading the client that the risks of social disaster are small enough to *try* new behaviors like assertiveness. Cognitive interventions can be invaluable here.

Specific Procedures

The cognitive model is not difficult to understand, but cognitive therapy takes practice to learn to do it well. Once the basics are mastered, however, it is not difficult to transfer cognitive therapy skills from one arena (say, depression) to another like social phobia. What is necessary is a thorough understanding of the likely cognitive distortions associated with a given problem, along with an appreciation for likely stumbling blocks. Because of space considerations, here we are able to provide only a brief sketch of some of the procedures involved. Supervised training is necessary to gain competence in cognitive therapy (see Appendix B for a listing of cognitive therapy centers that offer training for professionals). In the absence of opportunities for formal training, another resource is to form peer supervision groups composed of professionals. If some members of the group have a solid background in cognitive therapy, peer supervisors can help other members of the group to develop these skills.

Selling the Cognitive Model

The first step in cognitive therapy for social phobia involves providing a rationale for the treatment. It is in this first step that the therapist and client form a collaborative partnership, where together they begin an investigation into the evidentiary basis of various beliefs held by the client. The therapist shares the cognitive model with the client, as it applies to this specific client, and constantly checks in with the client about how well the model seems to apply to her experiences with social anxiety. The goals of the first stage are to educate the patient about cognitive therapy and about the social anxiety response. In addition, this first stage is the time to discuss the goals of treatment. Some clients may enter treatment with unreasonable expectations, such as wanting never to be anxious in public again or hoping therapy will quickly produce a marriageable partner (Butler, 1989). Shifting these wishes into more reasonable goals will help the client have appropriate expectations about treatment.

Explaining the cognitive model can be accomplished by exploring the three systems of anxiety responding discussed in the last chapter: physiological response, thoughts, and behaviors. The discussion often begins when the therapist asks the client to recount a recent incident involving intense social anxiety. If the client is so avoidant that there have been no recent incidents of social contact, then the clinician can inquire about a recent episode of avoidance or provide a hypothetical scenario (see sidebar 4-1). The therapist should record all of the patient's anxiety responses in that situation, clustering the responses into three lists corresponding to the three channels of anxiety responding. If the client seems to be focusing only on one or two of the anxiety response modes, then the clinician can provide prompts for the client to relate other experiences, with questions like "When your heart starts racing like that, what do you feel like *doing*?" or "As you stood there in the party thinking everyone was looking at you, what was going on in your *body*?". Behavioral responses can be prompted by asking the client what he did to manage his anxiety in this situation.

The client's experiences in social situations, thus written down, can serve as a discussion point for normalizing some of the experiences of anxiety. Nearly everyone has had social anxiety in some situation, and it is important for the client to appreciate this. The sensations associated with anxiety, including hot flushes, dry mouth, or trembling, are products of normal physiological processes. Refer to the discussion on the physiology of anxiety in chapter 2. The point here is that educating the patient about normal anxiety responses provides him with physiological facts. The client can later use these facts to question his previous assumptions about the meaning of anxiety sensations. See the discussion in chapter 5 on helping clients to reevaluate the meaning of bodily sensations associated with anxiety.

Having conceptually separated anxiety into separate channels of responding provides an opportunity to help the client to draw connections between these channels. Most clients can readily acknowledge that thoughts such as "I'm making a fool of myself" serve to increase feelings of anxiety. It is also easy for many clients to see that safety behaviors like keeping one's hands in jacket pockets will temporarily decrease self-conscious thoughts (i.e., about trembling) and anxiety sensations. During this stage of preparing the client for cognitive therapy, the clinician should also discuss the effects of avoidance and disengagement during interactions. From a cognitive perspective, these self-protective behaviors prevent the client from evaluating the true extent of danger in social situations. In avoiding a company picnic, for example, the client denies herself the opportunity to test the truth in her ideas that she is socially incompetent and "different" from everyone else at work. Orienting the client to the cognitive model can be done in as little as a single session for very cognitively minded clients, but it may require as many as 3–4 sessions for clients to whom the process of examining thoughts does not come so easily.

Identifying Automatic Thoughts

The process of identifying automatic thoughts is made easier if the client maintains a social diary, listing social situations attended or avoided, along with thoughts and ratings of anxiety. The early process of identifying automatic thoughts can be facilitated by selective self-disclosure on the therapist's part (Hope & Heimberg, 1993). The goal is to demonstrate that negative automatic thoughts exist for everyone and that alternative ways of viewing any situation are possible. The therapist presents a situation from his own social life that generated significant stress or anxiety. The situation is described and the therapist models a list of automatic thoughts that occurred to him in that situation. It is helpful to write these thoughts on a blackboard or easel where both client and therapist can see them. Table 4.1 lists an example we have used in treatment.

After the thoughts are listed, the therapist and client can together evaluate the validity of the thoughts by asking questions like "How would an objective observer view my situation?" "Is there an alternative explanation?" "What are some other possible outcomes?". The therapist and client can also discuss the client's responses upon hearing that the therapist had these automatic thoughts. In this exercise, the therapist prompts the idea that other people are often supportive rather than rejecting even if they know someone is anxious or worried about social presentation. After exploring the therapist's example, the client will engage in the same activity, describing a recent social activity (from therapy homework or diaries, for instance) and recalling specific thoughts and predictions before and during the activity. Table 4.2 lists several examples of situations and thoughts we have encountered among our socially phobic clients.

Notice in the list of automatic thoughts provided in table 4.2 that some thoughts are better specified than others. For example, "My voice will crack" is not inherently threatening; the client probably associates some threatening idea with that prediction if it is associated with anxiety. The therapist should probe for this meaning—what this event would mean about

Table 4.1 Example of Therapist's Anxious Social Situation and Automatic Thoughts

Situation	Anxiety	Automatic Thoughts
Giving a workshop to 25 colleagues	70 peak; 55 average	I'll be so nervous I won't be able to talk. I will make a bad impression. I will look stupid. I won't be able to get my point across. They will decide I am unprofessional. I will lose career opportunities by looking bad.

Table 4.2 Examples of Clients' Anxious Social Situations and Automatic Thoughts

Situation	Anxiety	Automatic Thoughts
Making small talk with an appealing stranger	90 peak; 75 average	S/he will think I am pushy. S/he will know I am anxious. I will sweat uncontrollably. I will embarrass myself. I will lose control and cry, faint, etc.
Asking a question in class	85 peak; 75 average	The instructor will think I am stupid. The other students will think I am stupid. My voice will crack. I will tremble. Everyone will think I am trying to sound smart.
Stopping someone from cutting in front of me in a long line-up	100 peak; 95 average	S/he will think I am weak. S/he will tell me off in public. Everyone will see me being a doormat. People will push me or swear at me. I will blush, and everyone will know how I feel.

the client or what the consequences would be if the predicted event does occur. Another feature of table 4.2 is that the list contains only statements, not questions such as "What will everybody think of me?". When clients reveal thoughts in the form of questions, it is helpful to ask what predictions or fears underlie the question. How does the client answer the question? Statements are more readily tested than vague questions, and many clients need some assistance in posing their thoughts in a testable way.

Investigating the Validity of Automatic Thoughts

Some anxious thoughts will appear to the client as patently false once they are put to paper in a calm mood. We have often heard clients exclaim, "It does seem silly now, but when I was actually standing there I believed that thought." Others have said that it never occurred to them to question the truthfulness of the thought; they have always treated thoughts as facts. Once prompted to question them, the thoughts often have less power to frighten the client. Needless to say, not every troublesome thought can be dispensed with so easily! Most distorted thoughts will require collaborative investigation from therapist and client. The clinician can rely on a number of specific strategies during this investigation. We will discuss several of these approaches. The basic idea is to prompt the client to question the evidence in support of his predictions about the way social situations will go or about the consequences of suboptimal performance.

One commonly used procedure is to help the client *label thinking errors*. Examples of common cognitive distortions can be found in books on cognitive therapy such as Burns' *Feeling Good: The New Mood Therapy* (1981) or *Cognitive Therapy in Practice: A Case Formulation Approach* by Persons (Persons, 1989). Some versions of these lists of distortions can be long and confusing. Butler and Wells (1995) have narrowed these distortions to four basic errors: *mind-reading* (assuming one knows what another is thinking), *personalization* (inaccurately attaching personal meaning to events or the behavior of others), *catastrophizing* (predicting and focusing on terrible outcomes of a social situation), and *mental filtering* (selectively processing negative information). Some clients readily latch onto these labels for cognitive distortions and are able to use them to gain perspective on automatic thoughts.

Another verbal technique is to *question the evidence* in support of an automatic thought. Depending on the nature of the thought, any of a number of different questions can reveal logical flaws in anxiety-based thinking. For example, the client may believe that others will think she is insincere or shallow if she makes "small talk." The therapist can help the client to question the inevitability and the awfulness of the predicted event, challenge assumptions about the importance of others' opinions, and question the idea that others are being judgmental at all. One of the main ideas is to help clients to stop relying on internally generated information (i.e., sensations of anxiety or mental images of their performance) to judge how they are doing in a social situation. See sidebar 4-3 for questions that may be useful in helping clients to investigate the evidence supporting an automatic thought.

In addition to these verbal techniques, *behavioral experiments* are powerful ways to challenge automatic thoughts. These approaches are similar to exposure in that they involve having the client engage in feared social situations. Where they differ from exposure is in the rationale that guides the therapist's specific interventions. In the cognitive perspective, behavioral exercises are approached as experiments that provide a firm test of the validity of automatic thoughts. These experiments often stem naturally from "if . . . then" statements like "If I eat lunch alone in the cafeteria, then everyone will think I am a weird guy who has no friends." Careful questioning often reveals that feelings of anxiety and self-consciousness are the only evidence supporting these predictions.

After first examining the evidence for this thought, the client can then be encouraged to enter the situation to gather "hard" evidence, including *contrary evidence*. He may find that sitting alone in the cafeteria draws no attention from others, that acquaintances join him at the table, or that several other seemingly normal people are also lunching alone. The process involved in shifting attention from his internal experiences of anxiety and images of social failure to how other people interact and respond to him is also helpful. Simply observing the interactions of others can be educative for the client. We recall a client who had extreme difficulty in approaching

QUESTIONING THE VALIDITY OF AUTOMATIC THOUGHTS

Therapists can engage in a collaborative investigation of the validity of automatic thoughts by helping clients to ask themselves the following questions about the predicted consequence.

1. Do I know for certain that this will happen?
2. What is the probability (out of 100%) that this will occur?
3. What would be the likelihood of its occurrence if someone else were in this situation instead of me?
4. What evidence is there to support my thought?
5. How would an objective observer view my situation?
6. Does this consequence inevitably result from my situation?
7. What other possible outcomes are there?
8. So what if someone does think that about me?
9. Does one person's opinion about me reflect that of everyone else?
10. What would I think of someone else in my same situation?
11. Is this situation really so important that my entire future rests on its outcome?
12. What other reasons could there be for her unfriendliness besides my own inadequacy?
13. Does she seem to be treating other people this way as well?
14. Will people really form a global opinion of me from such a small mistake?
15. How else could I have interpreted their behavior?
16. What other (positive) things might people have noticed about me besides my anxiety and tension?

---

women, frustrating his strong desire to find a girlfriend. He literally felt like a failure each time he said hello to a woman and she failed to respond instantly with enthusiasm! He used the opportunity of being in a crowded cafeteria every day to observe how women respond to other men who greet them—and he quickly learned that typical women do not respond to anyone as he had fantasized they ought to respond to him! Thus, he was able to pursue longer conversations with women without feeling devastated by the thought that he was a failure.

After clients are comfortable with behavioral experiments, *paradoxical strategies* may be a good next step. These strategies involve engaging in feared behavior and observing its effects on others. For example, one of our clients was afraid of riding public transportation because she felt like the center of attention when she boarded a bus. Because she was not familiar with the bus system, she needed to ask directions, and she was afraid she would make an error in counting her fare or drop her money, causing people on the bus to think she was a klutz. She was finally able to purposely pay too much money or too little money and even to drop a coin or two on the floor as she boarded the bus. Rather than giving her disgusted looks, as she had feared, the passengers and driver either paid no attention or actually helped her gather her change. These paradoxical strategies should be used with discretion, as some social behaviors do naturally draw strong negative reactions from others. However, these strategies are appropriate for challenging cognitions about the consequences of minor social errors.

Replace the Automatic Thought With a Coping Response

During the course of examining the validity of automatic thoughts, the client will develop plausible alternative interpretations of events with assistance from the therapist. Continuing with the attitude of inquiry, therapist and patient can also examine evidence for the validity of these alternative interpretations. Typically, these more benign (or even positive) thoughts serve to make clients feel better about social situations and also usually have more evidence to support them. It is important that the clinician refrain from simply asking patients to replace one kind of thought with another or providing alternative suggestions instead of encouraging clients to come up with their own, as these procedures run counter to the collaborative and Socratic nature of cognitive therapy. The idea is to teach the client skills for questioning the validity of thoughts.

Empirical Support

As is evident from some of the procedures used in cognitive therapy for social phobia, separating this treatment approach from exposure can at times be a matter of semantics. Certainly the therapist provides a different rationale for each, but clients usually find both to be compelling rationales. At times, the cognitive approach has some practical advantages over exposure, because arranging exposure scenarios for social phobia can be challenging. For example, some in vivo social situations are naturally very brief, so maintaining them long enough for anxiety to decline (as the habituation model dictates) is impossible. Because cognitive procedures do not place as many theoretical constraints on the presentation of the stimulus (i.e., intensity, duration), they have been a welcome addition to the clinician's repertoire in treating social phobia.

Most of the research investigating the efficacy of cognitive interventions has combined them with exposure-based approaches. Even with purely exposure-based treatment, we look for change in dysfunctional cognitions in order to consider the treatment a success (Beidel et al., 1985; Bruch, Heimberg, & Hope, 1991; Heimberg, Dodge et al., 1990). A number of different cognitive approaches have been developed, such as rational-emotive therapy, self-instructional training, and cognitive therapy closer to the approach outlined by Beck et al. (1985) While individual therapists will undoubtedly prefer one or another of these various cognitively based treatments on the basis of personal style and comfort with the approach, none is clearly superior to another in terms of patient outcomes (DiGiuseppe, McGowan, Sutton-Simon, & Gardner, 1990; Emmelkamp, Mersch, Vissia, & van der Helm, 1985).

Because cognitive change is an important component of recovery from social phobia, and cognitive therapy aims to directly influence this change, some writers have suggested that the combination of cognitive and exposure approaches will be most successful (Butler et al., 1984). Bolstering this opinion, several studies have shown that a combined approach of exposure plus cognitive restructuring achieves better results than exposure alone (Mattick & Peters, 1988; Mattick, Peters, & Clarke, 1989). However, this viewpoint is controversial. In a meta-analysis, Feske and Chambless (1995) concluded that adding cognitive interventions did not improve outcome above and beyond the benefits observed in exposure-based treatment. Notably, some of the studies that have found the most impressive benefits for cognitive therapy were not included in the Feske and Chambless analysis for technical reasons.

Controversy over the relative merits of social skills training, exposure, and cognitive interventions will likely continue for some time. Fortunately, the bottom line from the scientific literature has several specific recommendations for care providers. First, a thorough social skills assessment is necessary to determine the appropriateness of social skills training. If there are true performance deficits, then this approach should be included in the treatment plan. Second, researchers are unanimous in supporting the use of exposure. This powerful intervention should definitely be included either alone or as a component of another approach, such as social skills training or cognitive therapy. Finally, researchers also agree that cognitive change is an essential part of successful social phobia treatment. Such change may be observed as a part of behaviorally oriented approaches, but some clients may require specific cognitive interventions.

Specific Recommendations

We have reviewed the three major scientifically supported approaches to treating social phobia, describing their implementation and relating the evidence regarding efficacy. Before we conclude this chapter, we have a few parting words about actual delivery of the treatment. There have been several attempts to match patients to appropriate treatments, and we will report on the successes and failures from that arena. First, however, we will speak to the advantages of conducting treatment for social phobia in a group format.

Group Treatment for Social Phobia

Group treatment can be challenging to arrange, but the many advantages of this format make the effort worthwhile. Research results also support the effectiveness of a group approach (Heimberg, Dodge et al., 1990). Many clients with generalized social phobia are initially resistant to the idea of group treatment. The reason for this is easy to understand; they have spent many years avoiding groups of people! Despite their initial reluctance, most agree to join the group and readily adjust to the demands of group treatment. With some clients who are very severely anxious and avoidant, we provide individual therapy first, often with an emphasis on social skills training, before encouraging them to begin group treatment.

We do not automatically recommend group treatment for everyone, because some clients have personality styles (i.e., hostile, demanding) that would be destructive in a group setting, particularly with socially anxious group members. In addition, it is important that clients referred for group treatment of social phobia are experiencing social phobia as a primary problem, not secondary (or equal in disturbance) to panic disorder, depression, or alcoholism. A time-limited group format does not provide the specialized attention these clients need for their additional problems.

Group treatment provides many advantages over individual therapy (Hope & Heimberg, 1993). Clients can observe how others cope with similar anxiety, thus learning vicariously through exposure exercises and role-plays involving other clients. In addition, many clients tell us they are relieved to discover that other people have the same problems they do—other people who seem "normal" on the surface. The group also provides a forum for the client to make a public commitment to change, and perhaps adds greater social pressure to comply with homework instructions.

Finally, many clients find the feedback from other group members to be more credible than input from the clinician. The therapist may be suspected of giving positive feedback just to make the client feel better, rather than because the client truly performed well. Observing other anxious persons engage in role-plays allows the client a more objective perspective. As an observer, clients notice that they themselves do not negatively judge someone whose hands are trembling while giving a speech. They may even feel warmer and more sympathetic toward that person. These lessons are valuable later, when the client worries about how others will respond to his visible signs of anxiety.

From the therapist's perspective, there are several logistical advantages of group treatment. The group members provide a wider range of role-play partners without having to involve an assistant (although we do bring role-play assistants into our groups because group members become accustomed to each other). This wider range of potential partners increases the therapist's control over the degree of challenge aimed for in each role-play. For example, the client who is afraid of initiating conversations can first begin with a role-play with a therapist, proceed to a conversation with a same-aged peer, and then begin a conversation with someone in the group who is seen as accomplished or respected. Another obvious advantage of the group approach for clinicians is the greater cost-effectiveness. Hope and Heimberg (1993) recommend six clients and two therapists per group. For information on how to obtain their well-tested treatment protocol using CBT in a group format, please see Appendix B.

Patient-Treatment Matching

As discussed in chapter 3, clients with anxiety disorders do not all respond in the same way when confronted with their feared stimulus. Some clients with social phobia show a marked increase in heart rate in a behavioral test situation; others do not. Some clients experience a barrage of negative cognitions, while others are less troubled by specific thoughts during a social interaction. We have all seen some clients who tenaciously refuse to avoid social situations despite intense anxiety, whereas others avoid social contact as much as possible. Because different treatments for social anxiety aim specifically to change different aspects of the anxiety response, some researchers have speculated that matching a client's response pattern with the treatment approach might result in better outcomes.

Results from this matching approach have thus far met with limited success. In one of the first studies of its kind, Öst and his colleagues investigated the idea that clients with poor social performance might best be treated with social skills training. In contrast, clients showing an intense arousal response were expected to respond better to applied relaxation, in which clients learn to apply relaxation during exposure exercises (Öst, Jerremalm, & Johansson, 1981). (See chapter 5 for a more complete description.) Although there was some support for the utility of this matching strategy, the treatment groups responded with more similarities than differences. In a subsequent study by the same group, clients were classified as cognitive reactors (i.e., many negative thoughts during a social situation) or as physiological reactors (i.e., sharp increase in heart rate during behavior test). The physiological reactors received applied relaxation just like in the 1981 study, but the cognitive reactors received self-instructional training, a form of cognitive therapy. Contrary to their expectations, self-instructional training was superior to applied relaxation regardless of the client's original response pattern (Jerremalm, Jansson, & Öst, 1986b).

Clients' personality styles also seem likely to influence their response to different treatment approaches. Because of the diagnostic overlap between generalized social phobia and avoidant personality disorder, a number of investigators have examined whether clients who meet criteria for the latter

Table 4.3 Overview of Empirically Supported Treatment Options for Social Phobia

Psychoeducation
>   If appropriate, provide information about the physiology of anxiety (see chapter 2) and the
>   nature of panic attacks (see chapter 5) to make bodily symptoms more understandable.

Treatment Planning
>   Develop a hierarchy of anxiety provoking social situations.
>   Establish understanding of client's core fears in social settings through use of question-
>   ing, diaries, and cognition questionnaires.
>   Evaluate the client's social skills related to nonverbal behavior, initiating and maintain-
>   ing conversations, assertiveness, and if appropriate, giving public presentations.

Social Skills Training
>   Provide instruction in a specific social skill.
>   Model the appropriate skill in a role-play, and then switch roles so that the client prac-
>   tices the new skill.
>   Provide corrective feedback in a constructive and positive manner.
>   Plan between-session homework in which the client practices the new skill in a natural
>   setting.

Simulated Exposure
>   Fully discuss rationale for exposure, and consider whether a group setting would be
>   feasible and helpful.
>   Engage in within-session role-play of a feared situation, being sure to include feared
>   elements such as cues that potentially indicate boredom.
>   Enlist the help of colleagues, students, or administrative staff as confederates.
>   Consider using imaginal exposure (see chapter 6) for feared situations that are not feasi-
>   ble for role-play or in vivo exposure.
>   Where possible, use situations for which the client has a naturally occurring opportunity
>   to practice in the coming week.

Cognitive Therapy
>   Help the client develop an understanding of how expectations and interpretations influ-
>   ence anxiety and behavior in social situations.
>   Identify specific automatic thoughts and thinking errors related to social situations.
>   Challenge the validity of automatic thoughts by seeking contrary evidence and consider-
>   ing alternative perspectives.
>   Conduct behavioral experiments to test the validity of the client's predictions about spe-
>   cific social situations.

Maintenance
>   Develop a plan for continued self-directed exposure in the case of residual symptoms or
>   setback.
>   Establish ongoing social activities (such as joining a club or church) that will provide
>   enjoyment as well as opportunities to practice new skills.

might respond differently to cognitive behavioral treatment. In general, avoidant personality disorder is not a significant predictor of treatment response, outside of differences in severity; the same appears to be true of social phobia subtype. Stated more clearly, clients with avoidant personality disorder improve similarly during treatment to those who do not meet criteria for the personality disorder. However, clients meeting criteria for avoidant personality begin treatment more severely impaired, and they continue to be relatively impaired at the conclusion of a standard length of treatment

(Brown, Heimberg, & Juster, 1995; Feske, Perry, Chambless, Renneberg, & Goldstein, 1996).

Beyond the gross categorization of avoidant personality disorder, Alden and Capreol (1993) examined two different types of avoidant personality: cold-avoidant and exploitable-avoidant. These distinctions were based on the circumplex model of interpersonal problems (Horowitz, Rosenberg, Baer, Ureno, & Villasenor, 1988). The cold-avoidant style was characterized by an inability to experience and express positive emotions toward others. In contrast, the exploitable-avoidant style featured an inability to express anger towards others or to resist coercion from others. Clients in this study had received either exposure or social skills training. For the exploitable-avoidant clients, both types of treatment were helpful, although the authors noted that bolstering social skills that are involved in developing and maintaining intimate relationships was particularly useful. On the other hand, the cold-avoidant clients responded only to exposure; social skills training was not useful for these clients.

In summary, the clinician working with social phobia has several therapeutic tools with empirical support. Social skills training, exposure-based treatment, and cognitive therapy have all been demonstrated to be useful approaches. The bottom line here is that social phobia is a complex problem, and assessment must be multimodal in order to evaluate the rate of progress. The client's capacity for skilled social behavior must be formally assessed so that valuable therapy time is not wasted with unnecessary social skills training. On the other hand, if a client lacks basic social skills, the therapist should consider providing skills-based instruction in order to maximize social rewards when the client does interact with others. Diaries are an essential assessment tool for evaluating whether clients are in fact engaging in a more active social life, and cognitive assessment is important even in a behaviorally focused treatment. If all of these modes of anxiety response are evaluated regularly, then the clinician will be able to make informed decisions about whether and when to change the treatment approach or terminate therapy. Table 4.3 provides an overview of treatment strategies for social phobia.

In the next chapter, we will review panic disorder and agoraphobia. Some of the same treatments have been investigated for panic as we saw for social phobia, but there are interesting differences in the actual delivery of the treatment because of the special concerns of clients with panic.

5 *Panic Disorder and Agoraphobia*

Panic disorder (PD) has been intensively studied over the past 15 years. As a result, we now have a better understanding of the features of panic and agoraphobia, their prevalence and patterns in the population, and some of the mechanisms involved in maintaining panic. In addition, several treatment approaches have demonstrated great power in eliminating panic attacks and reducing the extent of agoraphobic avoidance. These treatments have proven to be among the most effective psychological treatments for any mental disorder, and they are equivalent to pharmaceutical treatments during acute treatment of panic disorder (Antony & Swinson, 1996). Furthermore, panic disorder is relatively common, and sufferers frequently seek expensive emergency and specialty services. For these reasons, effective treatment of panic disorder results in more cost savings, in terms of financial burden of illness, than any other psychiatric disorder. Psychiatric care for panic disorder reduces the associated use of nonpsychiatric services by 94% (Salvador-Carulla, Segui, Fernández-Cano, & Canet, 1995).

In this chapter we will address current understanding of panic disorder, with particular emphasis on assessment and treatment procedures. We will first review the features of panic attacks and panic disorder, followed by a discussion of various theoretical perspectives on the problem. Our discussion of assessment and treatment procedures will focus on pragmatics of working with clients with panic and agoraphobia.

DESCRIPTION AND CONCEPTUALIZATION

Phenomenology

As most people are aware, panic disorder usually begins with panic attacks. These attacks are characterized primarily by a sudden wave of fear, alarm, or discomfort. This wave typically begins suddenly and escalates within minutes or seconds to a peak of anxiety, including numerous physical and cognitive symptoms. While the actual attack usually lasts only a few minutes, the after-effects may last for hours. Physical symptoms that occur during panic attacks can include heart palpitations, chest tightness, sweating, choking sensations, trembling, shortness of breath, nausea, dizziness, numbness or tingling in the extremities, chills or hot flushes, and feelings of unreality. Cognitive symptoms usually reflect fears of imminent death, losing control, or going crazy. Feelings of helplessness and thoughts of escape are often the most prominent (Cox, Swinson, Endler, & Norton, 1994).

Panic attacks are not unique to panic disorder, occurring regularly across the anxiety disorders, but there is a difference in the case of panic disorder. In other anxiety disorders, panic attacks are always triggered by a stimulus related to the specific disorder, such as walking into the airport for fear of flying, or suddenly confronting a contaminant for a client with obsessive-compulsive disorder. In contrast, panic attacks that occur as a part of panic disorder are not cued by a frightening stimulus, at least in the beginning. Compared to those with other anxiety disorders, individuals with panic disorder more often experience prominent cognitive symptoms of fear of dying, going crazy, or losing control, as well as somatic symptoms of paresthesias (numbness or tingling), dizziness, dyspnea (difficulty breathing), and feelings of unreality (Rapee, Sanderson, McCauley, & DiNardo, 1992).

Mark described his first panic attack as occurring suddenly, for no apparent reason, on an ordinary day. He was having a coffee in a cafe by himself. "I was minding my own business, feeling O.K., thinking about nothing special when it hit me. Suddenly my heart began to race. I had trouble breathing, and my head began to swim. I couldn't stop it and realized I could die. I was terrified. It passed in about 10 minutes, but I felt shaken up for hours. It is hard to forget those feelings. I watch out for them."

In later stages of the disorder, panic attacks may continue to be unexpected, or they may come to be either completely or intermittently triggered by specific situations. Often these specific situations are places where the client has had a panic attack in the past, or where she or he feels afraid of the consequences of having an attack in that situation. Presumably the terrifying initial panic attacks that appear "out of the blue" sensitize clients and transform previously neutral stimuli into threat cues. Often, sufferers of panic disorder begin to feel predisposed to having panic attacks in certain situations (e.g., the barber's chair, warm crowded rooms).

The degree to which a person begins to avoid these situations (agoraphobia) varies widely, with some people avoiding very little (but taking safety precautions) and others avoiding many places and situations. Some clients with agoraphobia will venture into frightening situations only when accompanied by a trusted companion. Such companions have been identified as "safety signals" due to the reassurance they provide for agoraphobics. Clients who have a "safe person" are more mobile and venturesome in feared situations when accompanied by these individuals. This protective effect of a trusted companion objectively reduces distress, catastrophic cognitions, and physiological arousal during biological challenge experiments (Carter, Hollon, Carson, & Shelton, 1995).

Panic attacks themselves occur relatively frequently in the general population. For example, a cross-validated Canadian study found one-third of young adults had experienced a panic attack in the past year, almost all of which were cued (Norton, Dorward, & Cox, 1986; Norton, Harrison, & Hauch, 1986). Katerndahl and Realini (1993) found lifetime prevalence of panic attacks to be 5.6% in a large community study, using a structured clinical interview to code DSM-III-R diagnoses of panic disorder. Barlow's (1990) review of international rates of panic attacks in the general population suggests that 9–15% of the world population have experienced at least one uncued panic attack. Despite how common the experience of panic is, the attacks themselves seem to have different consequences for those who go on to develop panic disorder. Nonclinical panickers appear to absorb the experience without undo concern. Although immediately upsetting, the casual panicker often attributes a panic attack to life stress or a transient virus. In contrast, clinical panickers are prone to interpret their symptoms in more catastrophic terms, such as a life-threatening cardiac problem. They also become apprehensive about the possibility of future panic attacks and their consequences, thereby generating anticipatory anxiety (Barlow, 1990).

Anticipatory anxiety is a major determinant of agoraphobic avoidance, and strength of agoraphobia is a primary consideration in judging the severity of panic disorder with agoraphobia. Most clients with panic disorder experience anxiety about the consequences of future attacks, and they tend to imagine scenarios of embarrassment, danger, or entrapment. However, severe avoidance of situations like tunnels, large stores, traffic jams, or standing in line can be disabling. Extent of agoraphobia also appears to affect course and outcome of treatment. Goisman and his colleagues (1994) described treatment outcome and course data from a multicenter study involving three groups: panic disorder, panic disorder with agoraphobia (the most common diagnosis), and agoraphobia without a history of panic disorder. Clients with panic disorder had the most favorable outcome and course, while clients with agoraphobia in the context of panic achieved an intermediate outcome, and clients with agoraphobia but no history of panic had the most pessimistic outcome and course. Sidebar 5-1 illustrates the functional limitations imposed by agoraphobia.

Why do some clients develop agoraphobic avoidance in response to panic attacks, while others do not? Growing evidence indicates cognitive variables may be linked to the development of agoraphobia. Agoraphobics tend to expect more panic attacks, focus on the potential negative consequences of an attack (e.g., social humiliation, physical danger), and subsequently feel unable to cope with these events (Clum & Knowles, 1991). Social factors have also been found to play a significant role in agoraphobic avoidance. If

CASE DESCRIPTION

Penny is a 55-year-old single woman who first experienced panic attacks in high school when she had to make a presentation standing in front of the class. She fled the room in distress, unable to complete her talk. Over the next 15 years, Penny experienced limited symptom panic attacks several times a month and full-blown attacks every few years. These full panic attacks tended to occur in groups of two to four attacks over the course of a week. The panic attacks always occurred outside of her home, usually on the street, on the bus, at work, or in social situations. Around age 30, she began to gradually develop agoraphobia. Over the next 3 years she increasingly restricted her travel, and at age 35 she down-graded her employment to a position geographically close to home. By her early 40s, Penny had restricted her travel exclusively to her work, several neighborhood stores, her physician, and her dentist. This pattern continued for almost 10 years whereupon she became unable to work due to her anxiety symptoms and agoraphobia. Several years later she met a new and understanding neighbor who became her close companion. With her new friend, she could resume normal travel within the city; however, she always took the arm of her friend and was unable to leave her house on her own.

the first attack was in public or caused a lot of embarrassment for the client, then avoidance is more likely to result (Amering et al., 1997). The level of perceived social scrutiny in social interactions also seems to be a determinant of avoidance. In a creative study, Whittal and Goetsch (1997) asked clients with panic disorder to locate specified grocery items and then line up in the longest check-out line. If clients were also asked to speak to a store clerk or another customer during their shopping experience, they reliably avoided more tasks than did clients who were not asked to talk with anyone while shopping.

Diagnostic Classification

The first comprehensive account of anxiety disorders was provided by Freud (1895/1962) a century ago. His concept of anxiety neurosis was central to the first editions of the Diagnostic and Statistical Manual (DSM; American Psychiatric Association, 1952; American Psychiatric Association, 1968). Panic disorder was first described in the third edition of the DSM, which replaced the term "neurosis" with specific descriptions of separate anxiety disorders (American Psychiatric Association, 1980). Agoraphobia was classified as distinct from panic disorder in DSM-III as agoraphobia with panic attacks. However, eight years later the DSM-III-R (American Psychiatric Association, 1987) linked panic disorder and agoraphobia into three categories: panic disorder (uncomplicated), panic disorder with agoraphobia, and agoraphobia without a history of panic disorder.

Agoraphobia without a history of panic disorder was a controversial category (Frances, Miele, Widiger, Pincus, & Davis, 1993), but it was clear that primary emphasis in the DSM-III-R had shifted to the experience of panic, with agoraphobia viewed as occurring secondarily. Meanwhile the European perspective, as reflected in the ICD-10 (World Health Organization, 1992), viewed agoraphobia and panic disorder as separate but equally important. Although agoraphobia without a history of panic disorder occurs relatively rarely, new evidence suggests that this disorder should be placed on a continuum with uncomplicated panic disorder and panic disorder with agoraphobia (Goisman et al., 1995). Goisman et al. found evidence of a history of panic-related phenomena in the majority of their patients who had been diagnosed with agoraphobia without a history of panic disorder. These patients had been diagnosed with rigorous procedures, but upon closer inspection, Goisman et al. found that the patients reported experiences consistent with situational panic attacks, limited symptom attacks in conjunction with agoraphobic avoidance, and catastrophic cognitions associated with agoraphobia.

Prevalence and Course

International studies have been fairly consistent in identifying lifetime prevalence rates for panic disorder, with and without agoraphobia, in the range of 1.5% to 3.5% of the general population. A third or more of all individuals with panic disorder also have agoraphobia, but avoidance probably drives more people to seek treatment because of its effects on functioning. Panic disorder is being identified more frequently, and more clients are being referred for treatment, as the disorder becomes better recognized by health professionals (Gerdes, Yates, & Clancy, 1995). Age of onset for panic disorder typically ranges from mid adolescence to the mid-30s, although a recent study indicates that the majority of adult clients with panic disorder report a history of childhood anxiety disorder (Pollack et al., 1996). In this study, childhood anxiety disorders also were linked to comorbid anxiety and depressive disorders, although interestingly, treatment response over time was similar.

Sadly, typical treatments offered to clients with panic disorder and agoraphobia are suboptimal, and prospective follow-up studies in community settings show that these clients usually experience a chronic course of the disorder. Treatment in community settings has usually taken the form of pharmacotherapy, with benzodiazepines being one of the most frequent types of medication prescribed. Ehlers (1995) followed clients with panic disorder in a community setting. By the end of one year, 92% of panic patients still experienced some panic attacks and 41% of patients who had initially remitted had subsequently deteriorated to a point where they again met criteria for a panic disorder diagnosis. A naturalistic follow-up of Danish patients found 75% still had panic disorder and were receiving additional treatment (usually benzodiazepines and supportive psychotherapy) at the point of 3-year follow-up. The remaining 25% no longer met diagnostic criteria for panic disorder, but continued to experience "substantial disability" due to panic symptoms (Rosenberg & Rosenberg, 1994).

A similar picture was observed in a 5-year prospective naturalistic follow-up of Italian panic clients after they had been treated at least once in a manner determined by their attending psychiatrist. During this period, only 12% of clients gained a complete and stable remission of panic symptoms, while 47% experienced a generally positive but partial recovery. The remaining 40% experienced a chronic course of the disorder (Faravelli, Paterniti, & Scarpato, 1995). The presence and extent of agoraphobia, comorbid anxiety disorders, depression, personality disorders, and anxiety sensitivity all contribute to the severity and persistence of panic disorder (Pollack et al., 1990). As we will see later in this chapter, treatment outcome research indicates the prognosis for clients with panic disorder would be considerably better if they had the benefits of cognitive behavior therapy or appropriate antidepressant medication.

Social and developmental factors have also been implicated in the course of panic disorder. For example, in studying clients with panic disorder, parental separation due to death or divorce strongly predicted poor outcome over the course of 7 years (Noyes et al., 1993). In the Noyes et al. study, history of childhood separation from parents was also related to other social variables, including high interpersonal sensitivity, low socioeconomic status, and being unmarried. These factors were in turn associated with a more severe and chronic course among clients with panic disorder.

THEORETICAL PERSPECTIVES

In brief consideration of etiological theories of panic disorder we will note the observations of psychoanalytical theorists before discussing neurobiological and cognitive behavioral formulations.

Psychodynamic Formulations

Historians will likely regard Freud's primary contributions to our understanding of anxiety disorders as the separation of "anxiety-neurosis" from neurasthenia, which gave direction to contemporary classification systems, and his recognition of the temporal relationship between panic and agoraphobia (Freud, 1895/1962). Contemporary psychodynamic theorists have noted, on the basis of case reviews, that adult panic patients often described themselves as having been fearful or nervous as children, and most report stressful interpersonal problems as a precipitant to the onset of panic (Shear, Cooper, Klerman, Busch, & Shapiro, 1993).

The psychodynamic model of panic disorder proposed by Shear and her colleagues (1993) recognizes the role of a neurophysiologically based fear of unfamiliar situations. In common with a number of behavioral and cognitive theorists, Shear et al. argue that unexpected panic attacks are not truly spontaneous but are cued by frightening thoughts, images, or sensations. These psychodynamic theorists further postulate that frightening fantasies, which may be unconscious, spark a fear response when they interact with the temperamental fear of unfamiliar situations. These fantasies are believed to stem from frightening and overcontrolling parental behaviors that have left the client vulnerable to conflicts between dependence and independence as an adult. Fantasies reflecting anxious early life experiences, such as angry separation, critical or unsupportive parents, and relationship entrapment, are hypothesized to subsequently lead to feelings of resentment and discomfort with aggression, which have been found to be common among those who suffer from panic disorder (Shear et al., 1993). Clients with immature defenses, who tend to maintain a problem focus, are believed to be unable to adequately suppress the fear and anxiety associated with the resentment conflict, leaving them feeling unsafe.

Neurobiological Perspectives

Originally, panic disorder was viewed as a neurobiological phenomenon and this theory continues to wield considerable influence (see McNally, 1994, for a review). Klein's early experience in using imipramine with anxious schizophrenic inpatients led to the recognition of panic as a distinct form of anxiety (Klein, 1964). Klein's work further prompted the important differentiation between spontaneous panic, agoraphobic panic, and panic reliably provoked by either exposure or anticipated exposure to phobic stimuli, as in the case of specific phobias (Klein & Klein, 1989). With this new conceptual clarity regarding spontaneous panic attacks, numerous biological theories have been offered to account for the mechanisms responsible for panic attacks.

Some investigators (Charney et al., 1990) have implicated the locus ceruleus in the genesis of panic, through dysregulation in the noradrenergic system. The locus ceruleus is the main source of norepinephrine in the brain, and its noradrenergic neurons project to the cerebral cortex, the limbic system, the thalamus, and the hypothalamus. When Redmond (1977) stimulated the locus ceruleus in monkeys, he noted responses similar to fear and anxiety, which in turn, could be blocked by pharmacologically moderating locus ceruleus activity. In humans, yohimbine has been used to activate the locus ceruleus, and to experimentally increase the frequency of panic in panic patients, but yohimbine produces this effect much less often in (non-panic) psychiatric and normal control groups (Charney et al., 1990).

Another theory proposes that panic disorder results from an inherited pathologically low threshold for provoking a survival-related suffocation alarm (Klein, 1993). This theory proposes that individuals who are hypersensitive to carbon dioxide will experience spontaneous panic when partial carbon dioxide levels fluctuate, triggering the suffocation alarm. Carbon dioxide challenge trials, in which subjects hold a full breath of a mixture of 35% CO_2 and 65% oxygen gas, discriminate well between panic patients and normal controls; self-reported anxiety during a carbon dioxide challenge allows for 86% correct classification of panic patient versus normal control (Battaglia & Perna, 1995).

Biological challenge tests usually induce panic attacks in those with panic disorder but seldom do so in control subjects. These tests use a variety of procedures, including infusions of either sodium lactate or cholecystokinin-tetrapeptide, oral administration of yohimbine, inhalation of CO_2-enriched air, or self-induced hyperventilation. Such studies have been viewed as supportive of biological causation theories of panic. However, several psychological variables appear to moderate the probability of panic in these tests, throwing doubt on purely biological explanations (McNally, 1994). Cognitive factors such as expectation, interpretation, and sense of self-control over the outcome influence whether an individual will have a panic attack in a biological challenge test. Diverse biological theories propose multiple neurobiological pathways by which the surges of autonomic arousal underlying panic attacks can arise. These multiple pathways may be the basis of individual differences in the expression of anxiety and anxiety sensitivity with for example, one individual being sensitive to high cerebral cortex concentrations of the neuropeptide cholecystokinin, while another is subject to noradrenergic dysregulation.

Cognitive Behavioral Formulations

Behavior therapy approaches to panic disorder have traditionally focused on agoraphobic avoidance rather than panic attacks as the focus of therapy. In this view, agoraphobic avoidance is negatively reinforced by the reduction in anxiety that occurs when the person escapes or decides to avoid a feared situation. The relief in anxiety that occurs as a result of repeated avoidance strengthens the agoraphobia over time, according to Mowrer's (1939) two-factor theory of fear and avoidance. Moreover, panic attacks are themselves inherently frightening and represent a powerful unconditioned stimulus. For this reason, the location in which the panic occurred often becomes a conditioned stimulus for provoking future anxiety and hence avoidance.

Some relevant learning experiences may occur in childhood and adolescence, shaping an individual to have an avoidant style of coping and potentially to be afraid of unexplained bodily sensations. Ehlers (1993) explored panic patients' early learning experiences about somatic symptoms, when compared to those with infrequent panic, patients with other anxiety disorders, and normal controls. All patient groups reported more frequent experiences with anxiety symptoms before age 18 and more frequent instructions from their parents to avoid strenuous or social activities, compared to controls. Panickers reported observing more anxiety-related parental sick-role behavior at home, possibly leading to a belief that physical symptoms of anxiety are dangerous. It is not entirely clear whether the communication of parental and subcultural beliefs about bodily sensations immediately sensitize children to certain fears, or whether such communication predisposes them to developing similar beliefs in later years.

More recent investigators began to shift their attention away from agoraphobic avoidance to the nature of panic itself. Likewise, the focus of research moved from a behavioral or conditioning explanation of panic and agoraphobia to the study of cognitive factors related to the occurrence of panic attacks. Clark (1986) proposed a cognitive theory of panic in which he suggested that the basis for panic attacks is a catastrophic misinterpretation of bodily sensations, specifically those sensations typically associated with anxiety (see figure 5.1). As an example, transient lightheadedness (i.e.,

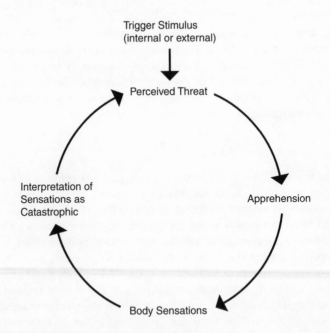

Figure 5.1 A Cognitive Model of Panic Attacks. From Clark, D. M. (1986). A cognitive approach to panic. *Behaviour Research and Therapy, 24,* 461–470. Copyright 1986 by Pergamon Journals, Ltd. Reprinted with permission.

trigger) may be perceived as threatening by individuals who are frightened of unexplained bodily sensations. Perceived threats are naturally followed by anxious apprehension, which exacerbates physical sensations of anxiety. Misinterpreting the lightheadedness to be evidence of a brain aneurism or stroke provides further perception of threat, completing the cycle. The catastrophic outcomes typically imagined by panickers during a panic attack can be loosely grouped into beliefs that they are going to die from an imminent health emergency, go insane, or humiliate themselves socially by losing control. Such convictions, in the presence of physical symptoms of anxiety, escalate fear to acute levels, which in turn exacerbates the experience of somatic symptoms, resulting in a vicious cycle.

Clark (1993) has challenged the neurobiological interpretation of panic provocation experiments, suggesting that panic attacks induced by biological challenge tests are cognitively mediated. He pointed out that clients with panic disorder tend to misinterpret specific bodily sensations compared to controls, and all of these procedures induce physical sensations of some kind. Secondly, Clark noted that cognitions involving the misinterpretation of bodily sensations occur at the time of challenge-induced panic attacks. Finally, Clark pointed to experiments demonstrating that cognitive variables determine whether patients will experience a panic attack during a biological challenge. For example, Sanderson, Rapee, and Barlow (1989) manipulated panic clients' perception of control during a 20 minute test period. Clients were told that they would be able to regulate the gas mixture they were inhaling when a signal light was turned on. When the light was off, clients understood they would not be able to regulate the gas mixture. However, the dial was bogus and did not effect the gas mixture. Although the light was turned on for some of the clients, in reality, all clients inhaled the same 5% CO_2-enriched air. Those clients who had an *illusion* of control over the gas reported fewer catastrophic thoughts compared to those who knew they had no control. Similarly, those clients with a perception of no control were much more likely to experience a panic attack (80%) than those with an illusion of control (20%), despite receiving the same amount of CO_2.

Research by Holt and Andrews (1989) supports Clark's idea of a cognitive process that is particular to panic disorder. Holt and Andrews compared four groups of clients with anxiety disorders (panic with agoraphobia, panic disorder alone, social phobia, and generalized anxiety disorder) with normal control participants who had no psychiatric history. All participants engaged in voluntary hyperventilation and inhaled 5% CO_2 in air, in order to provoke panic attacks. Clients in all four anxiety disorder groups experienced similar increases in somatic symptoms and psychic anxiety relative to control subjects. The factor that distinguished the agoraphobia and panic disorder groups from clients with other anxiety disorders was their strong feeling of impending doom when provoked by these biological provocation procedures.

In addition to catastrophic interpretations and perceptions of uncontrollability during panic attacks, evidence of other psychological features of "cognitive disturbance" has emerged. Agoraphobic patients have been shown to be overly attentive to, or more conscious of, bodily sensations in general. This practice of consciously attending to internal cues or "body vigilance" may be a normal adaptive process, as researchers have found wide variability in how much attention people pay to their bodily sensations even in the general population (Schmidt, Lerew, & Trakowski, 1997). The normal process of attending to internal sensations appears to be exaggerated in those with panic disorder, although the extent to which this vigilance causes or is due to the experience of panic attacks is debatable. During anxious moments, clients with agoraphobia are more aware of autonomic signs of arousal, and they are more afraid of both losing control and being embarrassed, than persons with simple phobia or no anxiety disorder (Belfer & Glass, 1992). Research has demonstrated that clients with panic disorder tend to interpret ambiguous bodily sensations as signs of immediate personal danger. Even more telling, these clients express stronger belief in their interpretations of the bodily sensations than is expressed by normal control subjects, and even other anxiety patients (Clark et al., 1997). Taken together, these findings suggest systematic biases in the way in which clients with panic disorder or agoraphobia process information about physical sensations. For a thorough review, see Eysenck (1997).

Anxiety sensitivity can also be considered as a risk factor in the psychopathology of panic disorder. Anxiety sensitivity is conceptualized as fear of sensations associated with anxiety (Peterson & Reiss, 1987). Schmidt and colleagues (1997) have illustrated the role played by anxiety sensitivity in the development of panic under periods of acute stress. They followed a group of first-year undergraduate cadets through a stressful 5-week period of basic military training. Anxiety sensitivity predicted the development of spontaneous panic attacks, when history of panic attacks and trait anxiety were controlled, and predicted functional impairment and disability due to anxiety.

Of course, panic disorder is a complex phenomenon, with no easy answers about its causes. Researchers generally agree that biological factors represent one causal pathway. A *biological vulnerability* appears to manifest as somatic anxiety largely unrelated to environmental context or as exaggerated biological reactions to stress. The interaction of stressful life events with such a biological vulnerability results in surges of unprovoked and unexplained bodily sensations and fear. Researchers are also in general agreement about a *psychological vulnerability* to panic attacks, which involves a tendency to process emotional information in ways that lead to anxious apprehension. At this point there is some disagreement among theorists as to whether misinterpretation of somatic events is an essential element in the generation of panic, or whether it simply is another source of fear which then becomes learned (e.g., "learned alarm"). A psychobiological model of panic disorder includes information about both biological and psychological factors involved in the development of panic disorder (Barlow, 1990). The occurrence and expression of agoraphobic avoidance is also shaped by social, cultural, and environmental factors (Barlow, 1988).

Although there are overlapping and distinct features between different theoretical models of panic, the psychobiological model provides an explicit integration of diverse research findings. Many questions and issues remain outstanding, such as the role played by the perception of personal control in panic. On the positive side, the intense research interest in panic disorder and agoraphobia in recent decades has spawned a number of effective treatments. Before we discuss those treatments with scientific support, we will first review methods of assessment for panic and agoraphobia.

ASSESSMENT

Diagnostic Assessment

Because panic attacks are common in most of the anxiety disorders, the clinician must pay special attention to the relationship between panic attacks and their situational or ideational triggers, particularly in the onset of the disorder. The DSM-IV identifies three characteristic types of panic attacks. *Unexpected (uncued)* panic attacks are those that are not associated with any situational trigger (i.e., spontaneous, or "out of the blue"). In *situationally bound (cued)* panic attacks, exposure to the situational cue or trigger (or anticipation of exposure to the situation) virtually always induces a panic attack. For example, seeing a snake or dog always triggers an attack. Finally, *situationally predisposed* panic attacks are more likely to occur on exposure to the situational cue or trigger, but they are not invariably associated with the cue. In this case, attacks do not necessarily occur in conjunction with the exposure. For example, a client's attacks are more likely to occur while driving, but there are times when he is able to drive without having an attack or times when the attack occurs after the client has been driving for awhile.

Unexpected panic attacks (at least at the beginning of the disorder) are the hallmark of panic disorder. If the client does not present with a history of uncued attacks, then the case is probably better conceptualized as another anxiety disorder. On the other hand, clients with panic disorder commonly report cued attacks in addition to spontaneous attacks. Within each client, the cued and uncued attacks appear not to differ, in terms of such characteristics as number per week, severity, duration, or number of symptoms (Krystal, Woods, Hill, & Charney, 1991). For clients who do not report spontaneous panic attacks, the diagnosis is related to the nature of the stimulus that provokes cued attacks. In simple phobia, panic attacks, if they occur, are always cued by the feared object or situation. Similarly, panic attacks in the context of social phobia are cued by situations in which the individual feels scrutinized by others. Because clients may feel self-conscious about having even an uncued attack in a public place, the differential diagnosis of social phobia and panic disorder can be difficult. See chapter 4 for a more complete discussion. Finally, panic attacks in posttraumatic stress disorder and obsessive compulsive disorder are cued by stimuli related to the trauma or obsession, respectively.

A number of physical disorders such as hypoglycemia, hyperthyroidism, and seizure disorders can mimic anxiety symptoms. While these disorders are infrequent, clinicians should consider the possibility of an organic disorder in the case of uncued panic attacks. In most cases, clients who seek psychological treatment for panic attacks have already been examined by a primary care physician (and usually several specialists as well). In the rare case where a client has not consulted a physician about anxiety attacks, we recommend that the client be referred to rule out physical disorders causing anxiety symptoms. Even so, organic conditions may coexist and interact with panic disorder, in which case the panic disorder probably warrants independent treatment (Barlow, 1988).

Contextual Factors in Assessment

Diagnostic categories facilitate communication between professionals and provide a shortcut to treatment planning. They are stereotypes, providing a necessary but insufficient amount of information for case formulation and treatment planning. Additional contextual, or background, information is essential to understand the circumstances in which panic and agoraphobia are expressed. Contextual factors relevant to treatment are discussed below.

Index Episode

The first full panic attack should be described in considerable detail, as it often is the most severe and best-remembered of all the panic attacks. Fears and perceptions about that initial attack (or the worst one, if not the initial) may form the basis for anticipatory anxiety and avoidance. If the initial panic attack is many years removed, full investigation of the initial attack is frequently omitted in the interest of time, but at the cost of potentially useful information. We have seen many clients who are less concerned about ostensible heart attacks or brain tumors than they are about reexperiencing that first terrifying attack.

Panic Triggers

Most clients with panic disorder have multiple cues that can trigger a panic attack (e.g., seeing violence on TV, being in crowded public places, drinking alcohol). These cues can be used to build a hierarchy, along the same lines as that discussed in chapter 3. In addition to places and situations, it may be useful to include physical sensations that trigger panic attacks when the individual notices them.

Avoidance and Coping

Almost all clients seeking treatment for panic disorder engage in some type of avoidance or safety-oriented protective behavior. An example of the latter might be a client who continues to go to grocery stores but always uses a rolling shopping cart (even when buying only a few items) because holding the cart handles helps her to feel more steady and less likely to faint. In cataloguing avoidance, it is again useful to build a hierarchy of feared situations in preparation for graded exposure treatment. Each avoided situation should be listed, along with the clients' estimated level of distress in the situation on the SUDS scale of 0 (no anxiety at all) to 100 (most anxiety ever experienced). When constructing the hierarchy, the clinician should ask whether having a trusted person present makes a difference in the estimated anxiety level. If necessary, situations should be listed twice, indicating estimated anxiety when alone and when accompanied.

Comorbidity

Co-occurrence of panic disorder, with or without agoraphobia, and other anxiety disorders is to be expected in general clinical practice. Further, multiple studies show co-occurrence with major depression and Axis II disorders is very common. These realities present clinical management issues. Normally, comorbidity increases severity and probably necessitates longer treatment. As a result, the pace, order, and expectations of treatment, in cases of multiple diagnoses, need to be established collaboratively with the client. Preliminary to this collaboration, the clinician will need to identify all problem areas and formulate a case conceptualization regarding the way the problems are interrelated.

Medication

Concurrent pharmacological treatment for panic disorder needs to be monitored. There are some medications that clients may have been directed to take on an as-needed basis, usually upon the experience or anticipation of anxiety. Concurrent benzodiazepine use may be inadvisable on the grounds that it can interfere with habituation during exposure to feared stimuli and predict relapse (Sanderson & Wetzler, 1993; Wilhelm & Roth, 1997). For example, Otto, Pollack, and Sabatino (1996) contrasted long-term outcome for patients who had entered remission following either cognitive behavioral therapy (CBT) or CBT plus pharmacotherapy (most commonly benzodiazepines). Those patients who were still taking medications when they stopped being symptomatic relapsed sooner than those who entered remission free of medication. Benzodiazepines have their own well-known risks, including rebound effects of anxiety and depression upon withdrawal from the medication. Regardless of the type of medication, therapists should be aware of the status of this issue. For example, clients who terminate psychological treatment while still on medication may have fears about their ability to cope in the absence of medication. Finally, many clients on medications would like to stop taking them, and the therapist may be helpful in providing support or booster sessions while the client tapers the medications under medical supervision.

Life Span Considerations

Onset of panic disorder usually occurs in early adulthood. Almost 12% of adolescents in grade nine report having experienced a panic attack at some time in their lives (Hayward, Killen, & Taylor, 1989), although the prevalence rate of panic disorder is low among high school students and is a rare diagnosis among prepubertal children (McNally, 1994). More common among this age group is separation anxiety, which bears some resemblance to agoraphobia. At the other end of the age spectrum, the prevalence of panic disorder declines sharply by late adulthood. In the elderly, agoraphobic avoidance due to panic symptoms or anticipatory anxiety should be carefully distinguished from avoidance caused by fears of falling, hearing and visual impairments, or other age-related concerns.

MONITORING PROGRESS

There are a number of areas related to functioning that the therapist should assess to gauge the impact of treatment on panic and agoraphobia. Naturally, clients are interested in eliminating panic attacks and decreasing avoidance. In addition, the therapist may want to evaluate anxiety sensitivity and cognitions related to panic attacks. Below we will discuss measures commonly used to guide treatment planning.

Panic Attacks

In our research programs, we often measure frequency of panic attacks in several different ways. Comparing the results of these different methods of assessment for an individual client, we have been amazed at the different estimates clients give, depending on the method of asking. For example, one client estimated she had suffered through 50 panic attacks in the previous week when asked directly by the clinician for an estimate, and she said this was a typical week. When she responded to a questionnaire for the same period of time, she estimated 30 attacks. During the next week before beginning treatment, the client also monitored her attacks in a diary, and she recorded 10 attacks. We could debate the reasons for these different estimates, which might range from the use of different definitions of a panic attack to the effect of memory bias.

Through considering all the issues, we have come to rely on continuous self-assessment of attacks, in a diary format. Assuming the client is willing and able to be reasonably diligent about recording, the diary allows the therapist a consistent means of tallying number and severity of attacks as therapy progresses. In addition, many clients are able to note information about panic triggers by jotting down the situation in which they had the attack as well as the thoughts or sensations they experienced during each attack. Clinicians can develop their own self-monitoring forms that are tailored for each client, depending on the type of information judged to be most useful for shaping the intervention and evaluating the success of treatment.

We have primarily used two types of forms. On the first type (Panic Diary, shown in figure 5.2), clients make an entry each day, indicating the number of panic attacks and whatever other information the therapist has requested. We usually recommend that clients keep this form where they will see it every evening. The bedside stand is a good place. As they retire

Date	Overall anxiety (0–100)	Overall mood (0–100)	Number of panic attacks	Situations in which attacks occurred

Figure 5.2 Panic Diary.

for the night, they review the day and make a record. In figure 5.2, we have included the date, number of panic attacks, severity of the attacks, overall anxiety and depression, and situations in which the attacks occurred. However, it is important to remember that these headings are only suggestions; therapists should adapt the form to target important information for each client. The only real constraint is in not overburdening the client with paperwork.

The second type of form is used only when a client experiences a panic attack. Figure 5.3 (Panic Attack Record) shows a good example of this type of form. For this form, we have adapted the *Panic Attack Record* (Barlow,

---

Panic Attack Record

Date: _____   Time: _____   Duration of attack (in minutes): _____

Whom were you with? (check)

      Alone: ____   Spouse: ____   Friend: ____   Stranger: ____

Was this a stressful situation?   Yes/No   Was the attack expected?   Yes/No

MAXIMUM ANXIETY (circle):

0---------1---------2---------3---------4---------5---------6---------7---------8

   None   Moderate   Extreme

SENSATIONS (check):

Pounding heart ____	Sweating ____	Hot / Cold flash ____
Tight/painful chest ____	Choking ____	Fear of dying ____
Breathless ____	Nausea ____	Fear of going crazy ____
Dizzy ____	Unreality ____	Fear of losing control ____
Trembling ____	Numb / tingle ____	

THOUGHTS AT THE TIME (briefly describe):

_____

_____

Figure 5.3 Panic Attack Record. From D. Barlow, (1988). *Anxiety and its disorders: The nature and treatment of anxiety and panic* (New York: Guilford Press). Copyright 1988 The Guilford Press. Reprinted with permission. Modified to include "Thoughts at the Time (briefly describe)."

1988) developed at the Phobia and Anxiety Disorders Clinic at the State University of New York at Albany. We have added a question about thoughts at the time of the attack. In our clinic, we have had a printing shop create booklets with these forms. Clients carry the booklet with them and tear off a page to record each attack. There is no need to use both of the forms from figures 5.2 and 5.3, as they contain redundant information. The choice between the two formats depends on whichever suits the therapist and client better. For some clients, we have found that getting in the habit of making a notation every day helps them to be consistent with the self-monitoring, so we use the Panic Diary. In addition, the Panic Diary offers the ability to obtain daily ratings of important experiences such as mood or generalized anxiety. For other clients, we may feel the need to better understand their precise experiences during an attack, so the Panic Attack Record is a better choice given its greater detail and focus on each attack.

Agoraphobic Avoidance

One relatively easy way to evaluate degree of agoraphobic avoidance is to ask clients to complete the *Mobility Inventory* (Chambless, Caputo, Jasin, Gracely, & Williams, 1985). This questionnaire evaluates the degree to which respondents avoid a host of typical agoraphobic situations, both when they are alone and when they are accompanied. This measure has been widely used in research and clinical settings and has good reliability and validity. The Mobility Inventory gives a comprehensive view of a client's agoraphobic avoidance. The clinician can also compare the "alone" and "accompanied" subscales for indications of the strength of the effect of being accompanied. The scale is readily understood by clients and can be administered repeatedly over time. Using the questionnaire results in a thorough query about avoidance with very little therapist time involved. Finally, the scale is in the public domain and can be used by clinicians free of charge.

See Appendix A for a copy of this measure. The Mobility Inventory produces two subscale scores. The Agoraphobia Alone subscale is scored by taking the mean of all responses in the "When Alone" column. The Agoraphobia Accompanied subscale is the mean of all responses in the "When Accompanied" column. If a client has not answered an item because the item is not relevant (e.g., "subway" for clients in a rural area), then this item should not be included in the tabulation of the mean. Table 5.1 shows the means and standard deviations of each subscale on the Mobility Inventory before and after treatment from the Chambless et al. (1985) study. The table is included to give clinicians a guide for evaluating severity of agoraphobia based on individual client scores.

Cognition and Anxiety Sensitivity

As we have discussed, cognitions related to panic attacks are readily assessed using the Panic Attack Record. In order to record thoughts in this way,

Table 5.1 Mobility Inventory Scores for 39 Agoraphobic Clients

Subscale	Before Treatment		After Treatment		6-Month Follow-Up	
	Mean	SD	Mean	SD	Mean	SD
Avoidance Alone	3.41	1.02	2.59	0.90	2.12	0.92
Avoidance Accompanied	2.37	0.89	1.81	0.73	1.53	0.60

clients need to be able to identify automatic thoughts. Some clients are able to do this readily, but many others will need instruction and coaching from the therapist. An alternative method is to use a questionnaire that evaluates important panic-related cognitions by directly asking about typical thoughts (rather than having the client generate the thoughts). One well-used questionnaire is the *Anxiety Sensitivity Index* (Peterson & Reiss, 1987), a 16-item questionnaire that measures sensitivity to and fear of symptoms of anxious arousal. Questionnaire items evaluate concern about the potential consequences of anxiety symptoms. Examples include "It scares me when I feel faint," or "Other people will notice when I feel shaky." The Anxiety Sensitivity Index has good psychometric properties and scores on this measure have been shown to decline with successful treatment.

A similar measure of "fear of fear" is the *Agoraphobic Cognitions Questionnaire* (Chambless, Caputo, Bright, & Gallagher, 1984). This 14-item questionnaire is a reliable and valid measure of fearful cognitions in agoraphobics and is both easily administered and quickly scored. This scale is also in the public domain and can be used by clinicians free of charge. See Appendix A for a copy of the ACQ. The ACQ is scored by simply calculating the mean of all rated items. For interpretation of scores, Chambless et al. (1984) report that their sample of 78 agoraphobic clients obtained a mean score of 2.32 (SD = 1.31), and a nonanxious sample of 23 people had a mean score of 0.90 (SD = 0.65).

TREATMENT MODELS AND GUIDELINES

Many therapeutic approaches provide a framework from which to approach treatment of agoraphobia and panic disorder, but few have been subjected to rigorous scientific study. The primary approaches with documented empirical support involve antidepressant medication, behavior therapy, cognitive behavioral therapy (CBT), or a combination of medication and CBT. Each of these three approaches has evolved considerably in the past 15 years. An extensive discussion of recent advances in pharmacotherapy is beyond the scope of this book, as our focus is on psychological interventions. However, we will discuss medication treatment briefly before moving on to consider psychotherapeutic approaches.

Pharmacological Treatments

The objective of pharmacotherapy for panic disorder with agoraphobia has been to suppress both panic attacks and anticipatory anxiety, with the hope that reduction in anxiety will lead to improvements in agoraphobic avoidance. Medications are often used in combination with exposure-based treatments. The idea is that once panic attacks and anticipatory anxiety are controlled thorough medication, the client may be more able to engage in graded exposure for agoraphobia. A number of medications have been evaluated for anxiety reduction in panic disorder with agoraphobia, including tricyclic antidepressants, monoamine oxidase inhibitors, beta-adrenergic blockers, benzodiazepines, and more recently, selective serotonin reuptake inhibitors (SSRIs). Among primary care physicians, SSRIs are usually the first treatment choice for treating panic disorder, in large part because they have fewer cardiac side-effects than the earlier tricyclics. Clients with panic disorder have particular difficulty tolerating heart palpitations and other bodily sensations. As a result, when tricyclics are used, the build-up to therapeutic dose should be very gradual.

In vivo Exposure for Agoraphobia

By the 1970s it became apparent that in vivo exposure, the practice of exposing clients to actual situations or places they have become too frightened to approach, was effective in treating agoraphobia, which otherwise was a chronic condition. International reports of improvement in approximately 70% of agoraphobic clients who completed this behavioral treatment were common. Nevertheless, for those who refused to undertake this treatment, those who dropped out, and those who completed but did not substantially benefit, the limitations of this treatment were evident. Results of exposure treatments for agoraphobia tended to be well maintained at follow-up, and this procedure has become accepted as the treatment of choice for agoraphobia.

Many attempts to improve exposure-based treatments have been undertaken, including self-paced exposure and involving a spouse or significant other in treatment, often with good results. For example, McCarthy and Shean (1966) found that agoraphobics experience more marital conflict, higher interpersonal dependency, and lower self-confidence than controls. Helping the couple to improve their communication skills has been observed to boost the effectiveness of partner-assisted exposure therapy for agoraphobia (Arnow, Taylor, Agras, & Telch, 1985). See sidebar 5-2 for details on this adjunctive therapy approach.

COUPLES COMMUNICATION TRAINING

Communication training can help boost the effectiveness of exposure therapy for agoraphobia. In a study using partner-assisted exposure, Arnow et al. (1985) helped couples learn to communicate better using several specific interventions, adopted from Stuart (1980).

Listening skills. Couples learn to make a commitment to listening to their partner and to wait for the other to complete their message before expressing themselves.

Formulating self-statements. All self-statements begin with the personal pronoun "I". These statements are clear expressions of self-responsibility in which the speaker accepts ownership for what is being said. Self-statements are formatted in the present tense and are made directly, openly, and honestly.

Constructive request-making. Couples learn to make requests from one another in a direct, specific, and positive manner (e.g., "Would you be good enough to walk to the grocery store with me after dinner?"). Making requests often requires that complaints be reformatted into positive and specific requests. For example, rather than requesting that one's partner become "less self-absorbed," one might ask, "Can you please pick up the children on the way home from work this afternoon?", assuming this is one of the issues that has led to the "self-absorbed" stereotype in the past.

Delivering feedback. Couples are encouraged to give feedback communication that is selective (i.e., positive) to the other's behavior, frequent, and timely.

Seeking clarification. This skill involves clarifying messages that have been received. Partners check out or confirm the message to reduce reliance on interpretations of nonverbal communication, an important factor in misunderstandings.

Problem-solving skills. Couples learn to focus on generating alternative solutions to specific problems in a cooperative manner, arriving at a hierarchy of solutions in joint consideration of the pros and cons of each alternative.

Theoretical investigations have also highlighted the importance of cognitions in panic, so research attention subsequently shifted to the nature of the panic attack itself.

Cognitive Behavioral Treatment for Panic

Several research centers have developed treatment protocols based upon theoretical formulations of panic that directly target panic attacks. Barlow and

Craske (1989) developed a cognitive behavioral treatment protocol referred to as panic control treatment (PCT). PCT includes educational and coping (e.g., controlled breathing, relaxation, cognitive reattribution) components designed to help clients reinterpret and control feared bodily sensations which are deliberately provoked (interoceptive exposure) in the therapy setting. In a controlled clinical trial, the 15-week PCT protocol yielded a panic-free rate of 79% by the end of treatment, compared to a 40% panic-free recovery rate for a progressive muscle relaxation group and a 33% panic-free rate for wait-list controls (Barlow, Craske, Cerny, & Klosko, 1989). In separate clinical trials using the PCT protocol with patients having panic disorder, Klosko, Barlow, Tassinari, and Cerny (1990) and Telch et al. (1993) reported almost identical results with, respectively, 87% and 85% of patients being panic-free by the end of treatment. Telch et al. also reported 83% of these patients remained panic-free upon 6-month follow-up. Others have reported panic-free status in excess of 80% of patients at 2-year follow-up.

Meanwhile, researchers at Oxford University reasoned that in vivo exposure, which focuses on agoraphobia, insufficiently addresses the needs of patients who experience panic attacks with mild levels of agoraphobia. Based on cognitive theory of panic disorder (Beck, Emery, & Greenberg, 1985; Clark, 1986; Ehlers, Margraf, Davies, & Roth, 1988; Salkovskis, 1988), which views panic attacks as the consequence of catastrophic misinterpretations of harmless bodily sensations, this team developed a cognitive therapy for panic disorder (Clark, 1989; Salkovskis & Clark, 1991). Cognitive components of this therapy help clients to identify and challenge the evidence for their misinterpretations and to replace them with more logical interpretations, while behavioral components involve inducing feared sensations and conducting behavioral experiments to contradict feared outcomes. A controlled clinical trial using their version of cognitive therapy resulted in 90% of patients attaining panic-free status with 70% remaining panic-free 1 year later (Clark et al., 1994).

Agoraphobia can also be addressed using a combination of cognitive and behavioral interventions. Michelson, Marchione, Greenwald, Testa, and Marchione (1996) found that a cognitive component added to their graded exposure program improved end-state functioning at 1-year follow-up to 37.5% from 71.4% (graded exposure alone) in agoraphobic patients. Cognitive therapy consisted of cognitive restructuring and identifying and altering dysfunctional schemas, beliefs, and misattributions that maintained agoraphobia. Daily records were used to help identify cognitive errors, and behavioral experiments were developed to test the validity of faulty beliefs and provide corrective evidence.

The following procedures for treatment of panic disorder are derived from several well-tested cognitive behavioral treatment manuals. (See table 5.2 for a point form summary.) Most treatment studies on therapy for panic and/or agoraphobia have combined several of these procedures into a com-

Table 5.2 Overview of Cognitive Behavioral Treatment Components for
Panic Disorder and Agoraphobia

Treatment	Components
Psychoeducation	Education about physiology of defensive arousal and other sources of feared bodily sensations
	Orientation to cognitive-behavioral model of panic disorder and agoraphobia
	Benefits of self-monitoring
Coping Skills	
Cognitive Self-Control	Identification of misinterpretations and feared catastrophic outcomes
	Questioning the evidence for interpretations and predicted outcomes
	Development of logical alternatives
	Reevaluating negative imagery
	Developing tolerance for anxiety-related sensations
Applied Relaxation	Recognizing early signs of anxiety
	Learning basic progressive muscle relaxation
	Rapidly achieving a state of relaxation
	Applying rapid relaxation in stressful situations
Controlled Breathing	Diaphragmatic breathing
	Self-pacing technique
Exposure	
Interoceptive	Eliciting sensations associated with anxiety
	Testing the validity of beliefs about the consequences of anxiety-related sensations
Situational	Hierarchy development
	Therapist-accompanied graded exposure (as necessary for agoraphobia)
	Self-directed graded exposure (between sessions)

prehensive treatment plan. Each has some empirical support, although the optimal combination probably varies by client and by therapist. The only relatively clear guidelines we can offer are that in vivo exposure, whether self-directed or therapist-accompanied, appears to be an essential requirement for successful resolution of agoraphobic avoidance. In reference to table 5.2, it should be noted that the "coping skills" (e.g., cognitive restructuring) are initially taught and supervised by the therapist during the active treatment. They become self-management skills as the client develops proficiency in their use and uses them routinely during the maintenance phase.

Psychoeducation

Corrective information about how panic attacks develop and how they are maintained can first be presented to the client as part of the case formulation upon the conclusion of the initial assessment. Psychoeducation normally consumes at least an entire session, and the therapist repeatedly refers to this information throughout therapy. Perhaps most helpful is an understanding of the physiological, cognitive, and behavioral components of the normal anxiety response. This information was presented in detail in chapter 2. How specifically to present the information will depend on the client's education and interest level, but the basics should be offered to every client. Having a solid foundation of knowledge about the body's activities during anxiety will provide a basis for challenging frightening cognitions later in treatment.

When we ask clients about their beliefs regarding the cause of their panic attacks, some point to a "chemical imbalance," anxious parental role models, or having always been a "nervous person." Other clients cautiously state that they do not know the cause, noting that their views on the cause are different depending on whether they are feeling anxious or calm. Some continue to suspect an undetected physical abnormality (e.g., heart problem) despite negative medical findings. These beliefs should be explicitly addressed by providing corrective factual information and by incorporating the beliefs in the explanation of the rationale for treatment. A common theory about panic held by our clients is the chemical imbalance theory. We explain to clients that genes probably contribute to individual differences in baseline anxiety. We further explain that genetic and other biological factors can lead to a "biological vulnerability," contributing to the development and maintenance of panic disorder. We describe an interaction between biological and psychological processes to help ensure that clients have the most accurate current information about their disorder. This perspective also helps clients to view psychological interventions as relevant despite their belief in the chemical imbalance theory.

The CBT model holds that clients interpret benign but unexpected bodily sensations as threatening and dangerous, which elicits acute anxious arousal about physical safety or the possibility of embarrassment. The triggering bodily sensations can arise for a number of reasons. Initial panic attacks often arise in the context of stressful life events, which provoke a relatively high background level of autonomic reactivity. Somatic disorders, even relatively benign conditions such as mitral valve prolapse, can also produce sensations that are not recognized as stemming from the physical disorder but instead are erroneously interpreted as threatening. Even normal bodily sensations caused by routine events such as physical exertion, sexual activity, being in an overheated room, or using caffeine or marijuana can be perceived as alarming.

Individual differences in biological reactivity render some people prone to experience more symptoms during arousal and to respond more readily with vigilance and anxiety in a variety of stressful situations. Accordingly, for these people (often labeled as neurotic), more bodily sensations are available for both misinterpretation and the conditioning of anticipatory anxiety. Theorists from a more behavioral tradition emphasize the conditioned association between fear and internal physiological stimuli (i.e., interoceptive cues) in the development of false alarms (Barlow, 1988). Those from a cognitive tradition place more emphasis on the role of catastrophic misinterpretation of the sensations (Clark, 1986). Regardless of mechanism, once these bodily sensations become associated with threat, individuals become vigilant for early indications of feared bodily sensations. Agoraphobic avoidance often develops as a coping measure to assure health and safety. When discussing agoraphobia with clients, we describe avoidance as very habit-forming due to the gratifying effect of anxiety reduction.

When they enter treatment, many clients report that they are unaware of thoughts and bodily sensations that trigger their panic attacks. From the outset of therapy, we emphasize the benefits of daily self-monitoring using the Panic Diary or Panic Attack Record discussed earlier. These records can help the client to discover the relationship between panic attacks and ambient stress levels, cognitions, manifestations of physical disorders, engagement in arousing activities, hyper-awareness of bodily sensations, and the use of avoidance as a coping strategy. During this educational phase, we set a clear expectation that the client will maintain daily records by carefully reviewing the records at the outset of each session and using them to guide treatment.

On occasion, we have observed a client who experienced spontaneous recovery (with no further intervention necessary) upon hearing a full explanation of this model of panic attacks. This occurrence is rare, and we recommend follow-up within a few months, as our clinical experience suggests relapse is likely under these conditions. Most clients hear the explanation and feel they have a better understanding of panic, but they remain suspicious that an important and dangerous medical condition may underlie their panic experiences. They require more personal experience with the cognitive behavioral model in order to be fully convinced.

Cognitive Strategies

In large part, the experience of anxiety is regulated by an individual's interpretation of the circumstances encountered in daily life. While there are some common cognitive biases across anxiety disorders (e.g., overprediction of feared outcomes), there are some relatively distinct cognitive biases that characterize them as well. Many of the cognitive treatment strategies, including the routine recording of dysfunctional thoughts, identifying automatic thoughts, labeling distortions, and seeking alternative explanations, depend upon the disorder. In panic disorder the focus is on the expectation of physical catastrophe, cued by the misinterpretation of sudden and unexpected physical symptoms of anxious arousal. As we have all noticed in fear-provoking situations, fear often has the effect of suspending rational evaluation. Panickers confronted with alarming bodily sensations are usually unaware of their interpretive biases or the role those misinterpretations play in amplifying autonomic arousal. Instead, the person is usually focused on feared outcomes, commonly referred to as "worst case scenarios" or catastrophic thinking.

The first step in gaining control over the cognitive component of the cycle of anxiety is to help the client identify and list imagined catastrophic outcomes related to bodily sensations. The client first lists those bodily sensations that provoke the most intense fear and worry. Feared outcomes related to those sensations are elicited by asking, "What are you worried will happen when you experience these sensations?" or "What would have happened if you had stayed in the shopping mall instead of leaving when you experienced those sensations?" Often clients will specify basic outcomes such as, "I'll pass out," or "I'll lose control," without elaborating on the implications of these events. When asked what would happen next if this outcome did come to pass, "worst" fears may be revealed (e.g., "If I passed out while driving, I would kill someone," "I won't be competent to care for my children and they'll be taken away from me.").

After feared sensations and their predicted consequences are identified, the second step involves the generation of alternative explanations for the feared bodily sensations. This exploratory process is based on facts about normal physiological components of fear and anxiety, as elaborated in chapter 2. Thus, proceeding with this step relies on a basic understanding of the normal physiology involved in bodily events like the fight-or-flight response, hyperventilation, or exercise. These alternative explanations (based in normal physiology) for worrisome bodily sensations are listed (e.g., "These sensations are due to anxiety," "I often have palpitations and they go away") and used as a rational response to the catastrophic cognitions. Panic attacks are presented as temporary events that are not dangerous and that are usually not detectable by others. It is important to help the client interpret panic attacks as physiologically harmless, as symptoms of anxious arousal which despite their intense and unexpected onset are really painless, private events that will soon pass (i.e., "an inconvenience," at most).

Clients rehearse the logical explanations of their feared bodily sensations and use these explanations to challenge and replace their automatic, catastrophic interpretations of anxious arousal sensations. We encourage clients to ask themselves, "What else might explain what I am feeling?" and "Is this any different from anxious arousal?" When they gain a more rational perspective and can account for their symptoms in terms of a "false alarm" or anxious arousal, they are asked to term this as a "cognitive turnaround." As time goes by, clients monitor the frequency of these "cognitive turnarounds" when experiencing frightening sensations. Monitoring these thoughts facilitates communication with the therapist and more rapid application of alternative explanations in the presence of early signs of escalating anxious arousal.

In addition to these terrible predictions about the consequences of physical sensations, some panickers have vivid imagery of catastrophic outcomes. For example, one woman recently related that she envisioned lying dead on the sidewalk with people gathering around her. These images are certainly based on assumptions about the sensations leading to the imagined scenario (in this woman's case, feeling faint). However, simply discussing normal physiology may not be sufficient to help the client cope with the vividness and emotional impact of the image. Such images can be replaced by coping images, such as imagining stopping for a moment to regain composure after feeling dizzy while walking down the street. These replacement images are more palatable and more realistic, providing an adaptive alternative to the negative imagery. As in the case of cognitive challenges, the coping images need to be rehearsed so that they can be implemented when the panicker is provoked by feared bodily sensations.

Physiological Approaches

An implicit goal of cognitive strategies is to increase the client's tolerance for sensations of anxiety, which is a natural emotion experienced by everyone at times. Despite this goal of helping the client to be able to tolerate sensations of anxious arousal (without feeling a need to escape), the sensation of anxiety is not pleasant and is not a goal in itself. As many clients with panic and agoraphobia experience chronic as well as acute episodes of anxiety, reducing this generalized anxiety is an important goal. Psychopharmacological approaches can address the biological components of panic, and there are several psychological approaches as well. Medications were discussed briefly earlier in the chapter. Discussed below are applied relaxation and diaphragmatic breathing.

Applied Relaxation

Given the state of high arousal involved in panic as well as the perception of uncontrollability, many clients wish for the ability to assert some control over this arousal. The rationale for applied relaxation is to address physiological reactivity as one of three components in anxiety. Increased physiological activity generates additional catastrophic cognitions, which in turn influences behavior related to panic, such as the urge to escape or avoid. Learning how to control the physiological reactivity helps break this cycle, especially if an anxiety reaction can be controlled early, before it gains momentum and reaches its peak (Clark, Beck, & Brown, 1989).

Classical relaxation training programs teach skills in relaxation, but these skills do not always transfer easily to the situations where relaxation is needed. Öst (1987b) developed a relatively powerful applied relaxation technique which addresses many of the shortcomings of conventional relaxation programs. On its own, applied relaxation is a moderately effective treatment for panic disorder (Michelson & Marchione, 1991). An integrative approach is to combine Öst's approach (in modified form) with the cognitive and behavioral strategies we discuss in this chapter. Öst's unabridged format is a highly structured 10-session relaxation treatment program. A modified version of this program can be incorporated into treatment for panic by condensing each session. We have successfully used this approach by introducing relaxation soon after the psychoeducation phase and devoting time to this topic in each session. As we will see, a major aim of applied relaxation is to learn to achieve a relaxed state in a very brief time period. Once this is accomplished, less session time is required to address the more advanced relaxation skills.

Fundamental to applied relaxation is self-awareness of somatic tension. Clients are taught to routinely evaluate their degree of somatic tension on a "0" (completely relaxed) to "100" (maximum tension) scale. These estimates became the means of evaluating pre/post relaxation induction effects. Clients learn that relative relaxation is healthy and desirable and can best be achieved by daily practice. To be most effective against panic, relaxation must be deployed at the earliest sign of anxious arousal and must be practiced on a daily basis. Despite these logistical demands, applied relaxation remains practical since clients learn to achieve relaxation very rapidly, thus being able to apply the relaxation during anxious moments.

Applied relaxation training consists of the following 8 steps, which are based on a procedure developed by Öst and adapted by Clark et al. (1989; for details see Öst, 1987b).

1. *Recognizing early signs of anxiety.* To sharpen early awareness of anxiety, clients self-monitor their reactions in natural situations and record the sensations (e.g., palpitation, lump in throat, abdominal tension), the situation in which the reaction occurred, the intensity of the responses, and action taken.
2. *Progressive relaxation.* The client learns an abbreviated form of traditional progressive relaxation described by Wolpe and Lazarus (1966). Briefly, the body is divided into two parts consisting of large muscle groups. The first session (15–20 minutes) focuses on the hands, arms, face, neck, and shoulders. The second session (15–20 minutes) focuses on the back, chest, stomach, breathing, hips, legs, and feet. Muscle groups are first tensed and then relaxed, with the therapist modeling the procedure and then encouraging the client to practice during the session. Clients rate their degree of relaxation on the 0–100 scale before and after each relaxation induction. As a homework assignment, clients practice twice a day.
3. *Release-only relaxation.* In this stage of applied relaxation, the tension component of the tension-relaxation cycle is deleted, in order to decrease the time taken to fully relax to about 5–7 minutes. The therapist instructs the client to relax the major muscle groups one at a time starting at the top of the head and working down through the feet to achieve full body relaxation. If tension is experienced anywhere during the release-only relaxation procedure, the client is asked to tense the muscles involved and then to relax them. Release-only exercises are practiced in the office and as homework assignments for 1–2 weeks.

4. *Cue-controlled relaxation.* The intent of this phase of applied relaxation is to condition a relationship between the self-command "relax" and the state of relaxation, so that with practice the self-command can reliably produce the relaxation effect. To facilitate the formation of this relationship, the self-command "relax" is tagged on to the natural effect of release experienced upon exhalation in the breathing cycle. After the client has self-induced a state of deep relaxation using the release-only procedure, the therapist says, "Inhale" just prior to an inhalation and, "Relax" just before the exhalation. This is repeated 4 to 5 times, and then the client continues on his own for several minutes more. Cue-controlled relaxation is practiced at home for 1 or 2 weeks before proceeding to the next phase of training. Cue-controlled relaxation can normally produce relaxation in 2 to 3 minutes.

5. *Differential relaxation.* In this phase of training, the goal is to make relaxation practical, that is, to relax all of the muscles not essential for the performance of whatever task the client is engaged in (e.g., driving, walking, or talking to someone). To start, the client relaxes using cue-controlled relaxation while sitting in an armchair. She then practices specific movements with various parts of the body, such as moving the eyes to look about the room with no head movement, lifting an arm, or lifting a leg, while relaxing the rest of the body as fully as possible. This differential relaxation training continues with the client standing, repeating the same exercises done while sitting, striving to remain fully relaxed. The relaxation is eventually applied during more complicated behaviors, such as pretending to answer the phone or walking around the room. These movements are often initially awkward and slow but become smooth and ordinary with practice. Time taken to relax during the differential relaxation training sessions is further reduced to 60–90 seconds.

6. *Rapid relaxation.* The goal of rapid relaxation is to achieve a state of relaxation within 20–30 seconds in natural nonstressful situations. The client practices relaxation 15–20 times a day in naturalistic situations. The relaxation is cued by routine objects or activities, such as looking at one's watch, picking up a pen or pencil, or touching the telephone. These cues are used to practice relaxation every time the client looks at or engages these objects. Öst (1987b) recommends attaching a small colored sticker or tape to these objects in order to help remind the client to practice relaxation. Once cued, the client (a) takes several breaths and slowly exhales; (b) thinks "relax" just before each exhalation; and (c) scans the body for tension while trying to relax as deeply as possible in the selected situation. Clients practice this procedure for a few weeks and usually find they can achieve a comfortable state of relaxation within 20–30 seconds.

7. *Application training.* So far the client has practiced the skill of being able to relax quickly in a variety of nonstressful situations and is now ready to transfer this skill into anxious situations. Application training involves 2–3 sessions of brief exposure (10–15 minutes) to a large range of anxiety-arousing situations. The intention is that the client will not necessarily extinguish all traces of anxiety, but will be able to

induce significant relaxation effects as a coping technique in stressful situations. With continued practice the client should be able to abort anxiety altogether in many situations by applying rapid relaxation, but the therapist should take the precaution of ensuring that the client's expectations are not too high during this transfer phase to anxiety-provoking situations.

8. *Maintenance program.* Like any other skill, ongoing practice is vital to having this useful skill ready for effective application whenever needed. This skill is similar to learning a new sport, such as golf or tennis. Practice is necessary to maintain gains and improve performance; otherwise the person becomes rusty and forgets the feeling of it. Clients are asked to anticipate anxiety-provoking situations and to practice these skills, especially during times of setback.

Diaphragmatic Breathing

A second self-control technique for use in anticipation of or during anxiety-provoking situations is diaphragmatic breathing. Increased respiration is one of the components of autonomic arousal. When the person is at rest, this increased respiration is essentially hyperventilation, as the individual breathes faster than is metabolically required. Sensations associated with hyperventilation include chest tightness, increased heart rate, jittery feelings, numbness or tingling, and, paradoxically, a feeling of being short of breath. These sensations are capable of provoking panic in those individuals who fear the sensations, although in everyday situations clients do not attribute such symptoms to simple hyperventilation as they are unaware they are overbreathing. Diaphragmatic breathing (also called controlled breathing) is a tangible and easily learned coping skill that provides a sense of personal control in an otherwise uncontrollable situation.

Controlled breathing involves limiting the tidal volume of air (i.e., taking normal inhalations, rather than deep breaths), slowing the rate of breathing, and breathing via the diaphragm instead of the chest. The therapist first models controlled breathing, using slow, even breaths. When the client begins to practice, the therapist can assist by counting out loud to pace the interval through a few successive breathing cycles. The concept of diaphragmatic breathing is easily grasped by placing one hand on the upper chest and the other hand over the diaphragm. In diaphragmatic breathing the chest hand remains stationary while the diaphragm hand moves in and out with the breathing cycle. Clients practice diaphragmatic breathing for at least 5 minutes each day. Controlled breathing can also be combined with cue-controlled relaxation, and both can be applied in anxiety-provoking situations.

Behavioral Interventions

Exposure to feared bodily sensations appears to reduce anxiety by several mechanisms. The extinction model holds that through repeated exposure to feared sensations or situations, the client habituates to the stimulus until the conditioned fear response is extinguished. The cognitive model, on the other hand, holds that repeated exposure to feared sensations or situations changes catastrophic beliefs because the feared consequences (e.g., heart attack) fail to occur. Exposure in the context of panic disorder and agoraphobia consists of two basic approaches. Interoceptive exposure focuses on internal bodily sensations, while in vivo exposure is aimed toward situations commonly avoided by agoraphobics.

Interoceptive Exposure

Several noninvasive challenge methods are capable of producing bodily sensations that resemble those occurring during panic attacks. The purpose is to evoke such bodily sensations in a safe setting so that clients' anxiety about the sensations can habituate. Over time clients begin to see the sensations as simply signs of anxious arousal. Rapid breathing is one exercise that serves this purpose. The client breathes deeply and rapidly for a set period of time (usually 1–4 minutes). The therapist models the procedure for the first 30 seconds and periodically thereafter if the client's breathing slows or becomes more shallow. (Alternatively, some therapists accompany the client during the entire procedure, which builds alliance and helps the client to trust that the activity is not dangerous.) The sensations provoked by hyperventilation include lightheadedness, increased heart rate, numbness or tingling in the face or extremities, tightness in the chest, and mild sweating. Although the sensations typically frighten clients, the feelings subside within several minutes after returning to normal breathing.

The therapist should help clients to examine the thoughts they had during the overbreathing exercise—especially those that occurred as the client felt tempted to terminate the exercise. Each time the exposure is repeated, clients state their predictions about what will happen, and these predictions are systematically tested. For example, one client explained that she thought she would faint. When asked what had prevented her from fainting in the first exposure, she guessed that she had not fainted because she was seated at the time. We engaged in overbreathing again, this time standing up in order to test her hypothesis.

Interoceptive exposure is most efficiently conducted by targeting the exercise toward the client's feared sensations. The idea is to evoke sensations that are similar to those the client most fears during panic attacks. This accomplishes several goals. First, the client's conditioned fear response to the stimulus of a bodily sensation is extinguished through repeated safe experiences with the sensation. Second, the therapist is able to help the client test out her fears related to the sensation. Through this process, the client also gradually discovers what safety behaviors she has been using (e.g., clinging to the shopping cart to avoid fainting). These safety behaviors can be dropped one by one until the client fully tests whether the feared event will indeed occur.

Depending on the client's feared sensations, different exercises can be used. For clients who are afraid of dizziness or unsteady feelings, spinning around in a swivel chair or while standing on one foot can reliably evoke these sensations. Feelings of breathlessness or tightness in the chest can be produced by breathing through a straw, holding one's nose if the temptation to cheat is strong. This exercise is useful for helping clients to understand that we need not work at breathing. The objective is to make breathing more difficult, but still possible. As clients learn to relax while breathing through the straw, they find they can get enough air without working at it. Even when the client is experiencing feelings of tightness in the chest or throat constriction, he is exchanging an adequate amount of air. For those clients who have stopped their regular exercise program or who are afraid of feeling overly warm, exercises can be done in the office. The client can do step-ups on a sturdy step-stool or on stairs; calisthenics are also useful.

Some clients are very anxious about evoking these feared bodily sensations and are reluctant to proceed. If clients become distraught, the therapist may temporarily deintensify the stimulus until the client is able to engage in the interoceptive exposure. The stimulus is then slowly increased until the symptoms are experienced at a tolerable level. For those clients who have comorbid medical problems (such as asthma or heart disease), the therapist should obviously coordinate this treatment plan with the client's physician. In most cases, there is no medical reason not to undertake these exposure exercises, but the physician should always be consulted in advance to be sure. Oftentimes, these exercises also frighten therapists, who are not sure what will happen if a client overbreathes for several minutes or stands up immediately afterward. We encourage therapists with these concerns to test them out by engaging in the exercises themselves, before the client arrives for the session.

Situational Exposure

In vivo, or situational, exposure provides a naturalistic environment for confronting feared bodily sensations and consists of systematic graded exposure and behavioral experiments to change beliefs. Together, the therapist and client develop a hierarchy of feared situations ranked in order of intensity of fear (see chapter 3 for a thorough discussion of hierarchies). For clients with severe agoraphobia, each hierarchy item (e.g., shopping malls) can have its own mini-hierarchy. A shopping mall hierarchy, for example, might consist of 8–12 items, ranging from driving to the mall without getting out of the car to shopping alone for an hour in a crowded store, including going through the check-out line. Items for daily exposure tasks are drawn from these hierarchies as a function of comparable difficulty level and the client's activity plans for each day. Assigned tasks can be listed on a recording form.

Clients learn to rate their 0–100 anxiety level before entering the situation and every 5–10 minutes while in the feared situation. We typically recommend that clients remain in the situation until anxiety has dropped by at least 50%. By doing this exposure, clients' conditioned responses to situations where they might have had panic attacks are extinguished. In addition, clients gain a sense of mastery from successfully engaging in anxiety-provoking activities. Finally, clients who have been avoiding a wide variety of situations can begin to live life more fully. For very frightened agoraphobic clients, exposure hierarchies must be finely detailed so as not to make progress too foreboding from one item to the next in the hierarchy.

Table 5.3 lists a hierarchy developed with a 34-year-old, married mother who would only leave her neighborhood with her husband or mother. The only exception was when she was visiting her mother who lived seven blocks away, in which case the client could drive on her own. Travel outside of the city even with her husband had been suspended several years before. Each of her hierarchy items can be further elaborated into mini hierarchies to provide a more fine grained graduation of exposure stimuli, as illustrated in the right-hand column of table 5.3.

Table 5.3 Exposure Hierarchy and Anxiety Ratings for One Client

SUDS	Hierarchy: Travel from Home	SUDS	Detail of One Hierarchy Item
100	Driving on expressway alone more than 20 km from home	100	Driving on expressway alone more than 20 km from home
90	Standing in crowded supermarket check-out line	95	Driving alone on expressway 15 km from home
80	Driving alone downtown, parking and walking around	90	Driving alone, as above, with cell phone
75	Walking alone in the mall on a Saturday	80	Driving accompanied 15 km from home
70	Taking a bus anywhere alone	75	Driving accompanied up to 10 km from home on an expressway
60	Sitting unaccompanied in a movie theatre	70	Driving alone in town up to 10 km from home
55	Spending the evening at home, alone with son (husband away)	65	Driving alone up to 20 blocks from home
50	Walking alone to nearby shopping center		
40	Walking alone in the mall on a quiet weekday		
30	Home with son waiting for husband's return (away 2 hrs.)		
25	Walking with son 2 blocks away from home		
15	Answering unexpected phone calls when home alone		

Note: Mini hierarchies can be created for each of the main hierarchy items, varying fear dimensions (e.g., weather, crowds, day/night).

Similar to the reasoning used in interoceptive exposure, clients can learn to use situational exposure to test out their ideas about what might happen if they enter situations that are frightening to them. These behavioral experiments involve having the client explicitly state predictions about what might happen in advance of each exposure session. After the exposure session, the therapist and client review these predictions and work together to generate explanations for their nonoccurrence. For example, when entering a subway platform, one client predicted she would be disoriented by the arriving train and would faint. She believed other passengers would step on her in the commuting rush. After a session in which she stood on the subway platform while many trains came and went, she was able to list reasons why she did not faint and was able to generate a more plausible scenario of how others would respond if she did.

Pharmacological Treatment as an Adjunct to CBT

Despite potential problems associated with their use (and the availability of more effective medications), benzodiazepines are commonly prescribed to patients with panic disorder. These medications, while useful in helping a patient feel a sense of control over anxiety, may interfere with the effects of CBT. As described above, experiencing the normal sensations of anxiety is an integral part of learning to become less afraid of the sensations. Nevertheless, some clients may benefit from brief use of benzodiazepines in the early stages of CBT. Other clients may be reluctant to discontinue benzodiazepines until they see some tangible result of the psychological approach. Sidebar 5-3 reviews recommendations offered by Sanderson and Wetzler (1993) for using benzodiazepines adjunctively with CBT.

Many clients are on a SSRI medication at the time they present for psychological treatment, and there are no reported interference effects when receiving psychological treatment for panic disorder. These medications can be very helpful in managing comorbid depression and reducing overall distress for highly distressed individuals, allowing them to engage in CBT.

CONSIDERATIONS FOR TREATMENT PLANNING

Treatment Matching

Although there is currently no empirically supported basis for matching clients to either group or individual treatment for panic, group treatment has obvious cost benefits over individual treatment. Belfer, Munzo, Schachter, and Levendusky (1995) outlined a group treatment program for panic disorder and agoraphobia based on Chambless and Goldstein's fear-of-fear principle (Chambless, 1985; Chambless & Goldstein, 1982). Belfer et al. noted

GUIDELINES FOR BENZODIAZEPINE USE IN THE CONTEXT OF CBT

1. Benzodiazepines should be considered for immediate relief of anxiety symptoms in those moderate to severe cases where it is necessary to engage clients who otherwise would not undertake psychological treatment.
2. The effect of benzodiazepine medication on patients engaging in CBT is perhaps most useful during the early stage of treatment (e.g., education, relaxation training), before beginning those procedures that involve evoking anxiety symptoms.
3. Medication should be slowly tapered (with medical supervision) during the beginning of cognitive restructuring and exposure phases of treatment, in order to allow the client to fully engage in behavioral experiments and interoceptive and in vivo exposure. Therapists should then insist upon complete discontinuation and help patients to use their new coping skills to tolerate and experiment with the sensations of anxiety.
4. If possible, the client should be completely free from benzodiazepines by the end of treatment. Even the carrying of a tablet as a "safety signal" represents continued reliance on medication and indicates that the patient remains at risk of relapse.

From W. C. Sanderson & S. Wetzler (1995), Cognitive behavioral treatment of panic disorder. In G. M. Asnis and H. M. van Praag (Eds.), *Panic disorder: Clinical, biological, and treatment aspects* (pp. 330–331) (New York: John Wiley & Sons). Reprinted with permission.

that the agoraphobic's preoccupation with fear of anxiety occurs in the context of interpersonal features that interact with agoraphobia. Childhood separation anxiety, poor assertiveness, social anxiety, and dependency-based relationships are examples of the contextual issues that can affect the expression and course of panic disorder and agoraphobia. Group therapy provides a supportive framework for addressing such social issues. Belfer et al. addressed these issues in a cognitive behavioral, interpersonal process model of group psychotherapy. Results of group cognitive behavioral treatment for panic disorder with or without agoraphobia have been found to be comparable to individual treatment, with 85% of clients panic free after a 8-week group treatment program and 64% estimated conservatively to have achieved full recovery, considering a variety of clinical dimensions.

Minimal and Optimal Interventions

Optimal treatment for panic disorder would stop all panic attacks, remove fear of panic, and eliminate any agoraphobia. A minimal treatment plan should aim to eliminate full panic attacks, reduce fear of panic and agoraphobia by half of their initial value, and include a self-management program directed toward the residual symptoms. Several studies have shown self-directed treatment plus minimal therapist contact can be effective for panic disorder with or without agoraphobia. Gould and Clum (1995) compared the outcome of a self-help procedure against the outcome of a wait-list control group over a 4-week period. Self-help involved reading the book *Coping With Panic* (Clum, 1990), watching a 15-minute educational video about panic attacks and diaphragmatic breathing, practicing progressive muscle relaxation from an audiotape, and having brief telephone progress checks with a therapist. The self-help group showed significant improvement at the end of treatment and maintained the gains when reassessed 2 months later. Similarly, Hecker, Losee, Fritzler, and Fink (1996) compared participants with panic disorder who were either self-directed or therapist-directed (3 sessions) over 12 weeks in working through Barlow and Craske's (1989) *Mastery of Your Anxiety and Panic*. Both groups improved equally and maintained these improvements through the 6-month follow-up period.

These studies show that once clients are properly assessed, clinically meaningful improvements can be attained by providing them with high-quality workbook materials and the expectation of progress review with a professional. Such workbook materials provide a *minimal* intervention in terms of ongoing professional resources. However, for most clients, we believe more therapist involvement will be necessary. Ideally, therapeutic contact should continue until freedom to move between situations and locations is unrestricted and the client is free of panic attacks. Our view is that self-help is a viable option for those who live in remote areas, those who cannot afford professional assistance, or those who have relatively mild and uncomplicated panic.

Michelson, Marchione, Greenwald, Testa, and Marchione (1996) found that a significant number of clients experienced residual panic attacks during follow-up and that the presence of continuing panic attacks predicted relapse and reemergence of agoraphobia. They advocate specifically targeting and eliminating any panic attacks as part of good treatment for agoraphobia, rather than focusing exclusively on the treatment of agoraphobia once treatment has rendered panic attacks infrequent or mild. Their results also suggest that panic-free may be an important criterion, not only because clients obviously prefer this outcome, but also because maintenance of treatment gains related to agoraphobia may depend on the absence of further panic attacks.

As mentioned earlier, there is growing evidence that optimal exposure treatment involves the client's spouse or partner. The quality and quantity of practice in confronting feared situations between therapist sessions is assumed to be enhanced by a supportive partner, both in planning for and carrying out exposure exercises. Barlow, O'Brien, and Last (1984) found that significantly more patients treated for agoraphobia with their spouses responded to treatment, compared to patients treated alone. Others (e.g., Cerny, Barlow, & Craske, 1987; Munby & Johnston, 1980) have shown that the improvements in treatment response with spouse, or partner, involvement in treatment continue to grow over the course of extended follow-up. Because of the restraints that agoraphobia can impose on a relationship, Arnow et al. (1985) theorized that marital strain might compromise outcome despite spouse involvement in treatment. Optimal intervention should assess partner support and interpersonal communication patterns, and address these issues as needed. See sidebar 5-2 for discussion of a couples intervention used as an adjunct to CBT.

Common Problems

Many problems can emerge when asking clients to do things they are afraid to do, in spite of their acceptance in principle of the treatment model provided. We address several common problems and offer suggestions to minimize the impact.

Comorbidity

The presence of multiple diagnoses can interfere with the treatment of panic disorder and agoraphobia. Additional emotional problems can distract clients from focusing on treatment for panic. Motivation for treatment can be reduced if clients feel that *all* their concerns are not being addressed with treatment procedures. An important first step in this case is to review with the client the rationale for the sequence of addressing each problem in the treatment plan. This can help establish boundaries for therapeutic attention to symptoms. The entire symptom picture can be reviewed briefly at the onset of each session, to monitor nontargeted symptoms (especially depression) and to promote symptom tolerance while providing general support (e.g., "It is good that you are not letting your low mood interfere with your exposure assignments.").

Noncompliance

Although theory behind in vivo exposure is straightforward, the application of the procedure can be surprisingly difficult. It is easy for therapists to underestimate the magnitude and consistency of anticipatory fear experienced by clients having agoraphobia, especially as we usually see them in an office setting when they are emotionally composed. The most common challenges involve appropriately grading exposure tasks, providing sufficient structure, and bolstering motivation. Problems in each of these areas can contribute substantially to noncompliance.

Regarding poorly graduated exposure tasks, we find that sometimes the task is simply too difficult and that the client remains avoidant, or seems stuck, seeking exposure tasks of lateral difficulty rather than progressing up the hierarchy. The presence of collaboratively developed program structure (e.g., asking clients what they think they can do in each part of the program over the next week, and to undertake only what they can commit to doing) and active self-monitoring are deterrents against noncompliance. Therapists should watch for common mistakes that clients sometimes make when they are beginning the tough work of exposure. These include infrequent visits to exposure sites, remaining in the exposure location for an insufficient period of time, and avoiding discomfort by being passive or sticking to familiar situations.

Strong program structure (i.e., clear plan and assignments) and the use of self-monitoring provides a ready basis for the client and therapist to review where, how, and why planned assignments failed, and what options are available. Sometimes expectations, or homework requirements, seem too high for clients and it can be helpful to negotiate minimal, desirable, and ideal performance expectations, so the client has some flexibility. If the client commits to doing at least the minimal expectation each week, progress will be slow but steady. Having clients record details of their exposure exercises in a notebook provides a ready record for joint review during treatment sessions, promoting both accountability and opportunities for problem-solving.

Preparing for Termination

Earlier, we drew attention to the widespread observation that improperly treated or untreated panic disorder with and without agoraphobia is a chronic illness with a variable course. Contemporary CBT programs have shown impressive improvements, but clearly not all clients benefit equally. Furthermore, it is well-known that life stress and depression promote relapse. In addition, those clients who are relatively high on the dimensions of neuroticism and trait anxiety are prone to experience the sort of autonomic symptoms that can generate fearful reactions. For these reasons, preparing for periodic relapse can be a useful part of the acute treatment program. The idea is that clients will be careful to notice stress build-up and the prodromal signs of panic and either avert the full attack or minimize its effect. This is easier to do if handling setbacks is discussed in advance.

Although this has not been empirically evaluated, we recommend to clients that they take a very proactive approach to relapse prevention by setting diary dates for monthly review and practice of their program components. In addition to these diary dates, clients can be encouraged to look ahead and anticipate difficult times that may be coming (e.g., child leaving home, change of seasons). These self-directed sessions take about 30 minutes and involve a thorough review and practice of each of the techniques involved in the three main treatment components: exposure, review of the evidence for beliefs about the meaning of bodily sensations, and skills for reducing anxiety. Finally, clients are asked to always consider the unexpected bodily sensations associated with panic as normal and harmless.

In this chapter, we have discussed panic disorder and its frequent companion agoraphobia, noting the abrupt and frightening nature of a panic attack. The client's natural instinct, to take protective action under such frightening circumstances, can lead to avoidance, which only aggravates the situation. Although anxiety has similar processes across clients, including hypervigilance, avoidance, and cognitive bias, each individual nevertheless responds idiosyncratically. In the next chapter, we turn to obsessive-compulsive disorder, where we see clients experiencing loathsome, unavoidable, and distressing thoughts followed by ritualized attempts to prevent or undo the thoughts and their implications.

6   *Obsessive-Compulsive Disorder*

Obsessive-compulsive disorder (OCD) is arguably the most intriguing and challenging of all of the anxiety disorders. Its defining characteristics involve unwanted and abhorrent mental content, such as thoughts or ideas, which are uncontrolled and often followed by either mental or behavioral rituals that function to ease the anxiety provoked by the obsessions. Most OCD sufferers engage in overt rituals or compulsions that logically relate to their worries. Washers clean to rid themselves of contaminants; hoarders save things because one day the items may be critically important to them. Sometimes, however, there is no logical relationship between obsessions and rituals, other than that the rituals function to calm the anxiety induced by obsessions. Those who have obsessions but no behavioral compulsions, for example, frequently engage in mental rituals, often governed by complex rules having no apparent connection with the obsessions that precede them. More so than with other anxiety disorders, OCD sufferers are more often ashamed of their symptoms, which may be less visible and hard for friends and family to understand. Patients with OCD anticipate that other people, even a spouse, would not understand their symptoms, since very often the patients themselves feel embarrassed and mystified by them. OCD can thus be shrouded in secrecy, hidden in people who outwardly seem entirely normal. Severe levels of OCD often result in such functional impairment that sufferers receive disability compensation.

In the past several decades, behavioral treatment for compulsions has demonstrated consistent but limited results against an otherwise bleak therapeutic landscape. In just the last few years, there has been a surge of interest in the cognitive components of OCD. Specifically, researchers have focused on how OCD sufferers interpret the presence of unwanted intrusive thoughts. These interpretations, which we will discuss in more detail later in the chapter, signal strongly held maladaptive beliefs, which may be responsive to cognitive interventions. Research in this area shows exciting promise for the treatment of OCD in general and especially for the treatment of obsessions without overt compulsions, as mental rituals have heretofore been relatively intransigent and less responsive to behavioral treatments.

In addition to the description of OCD itself and prevailing theory of OCD, in this chapter we will review assessment issues related to diagnosis and treatment planning, along with the role of triggers, cognitive appraisals, feared consequences, and avoidance in the occurrence of obsessive thoughts. The heart of the chapter will concentrate on the detailed application of behavioral and cognitive behavioral models of treatment for OCD, since these approaches have been guided by empirical development. Nevertheless, we will also discuss the limitations of current treatment approaches. Finally, as OCD is known to have a chronic course, with many clients still having residual symptoms even after treatment, we will consider factors related to relapse prevention and maintenance of treatment gains.

PHENOMENOLOGY

Typically, OCD sufferers are well aware of the thoughts, images, or impulses that harass them. These cognitions are experienced as intrusive, beyond the individual's control, and distressing. The obsessions are experienced routinely enough to interfere with the ability to carry on with normal day-to-day life. Clients realize that such thoughts are self-generated, but they do not understand why they cannot control the thoughts. More rarely, an individual with OCD is unaware of obsessive thoughts, images, or impulses but is fully aware of overt and usually covert rituals. In such cases, it is possible that over time the relationship between obsessions and rituals has become so automatic that obsessions occur outside of conscious awareness.

The content of obsessional ideation falls into several clusters, with most clients experiencing symptoms from more than one domain (Leckman et al., 1997). Aggressive, religious, and sexual obsessions and their related compulsions represent the first cluster. These obsessions include ideas about harm coming to oneself or other people because of the patient's action or inaction. Thoughts related to blasphemy, piety, or sexual identity also fall into this category. Worry about contamination (and cleaning to purify oneself) represents a second major content area for obsessions. This cluster includes concern with germs, toxic chemicals, and sticky substances. A third domain of obsessional content is ordering, symmetry, and counting, which includes concerns about things not looking or feeling "just right." Collecting and hoarding things represents a final content domain for obsessions. Naturally, there are other obsessions that do not neatly fit these categories, such as those related to special colors or numbers.

Due to the sometimes abhorrent nature of obsessions and the sufferer's inability to control them, obsessions induce anxiety. Rituals are stereotyped, purposeful activities that function to reduce the distress generated by obsessions. Although there are times when rituals are ineffective for calming obsessive fears (such as when the patient is unsure whether the ritual has been performed correctly), the function of the rituals is usually to neutralize potential harm related to the obsession. Neutralization can be defined as "any voluntary, effortful cognitive or behavioral act that is directed at removing, preventing, or attenuating the thought or the associated discomfort" (Freeston & Ladouceur, 1997, p. 344). In some cases, neither overt nor covert compulsions or rituals are apparent. Traditionally referred to as "pure obsessionals," recent studies using more comprehensive assessment procedures have found that virtually all of these individuals do engage in rituals, even though the rituals may be subtle and part of a complex set of mental rules. OCD sufferers are so engrossed in and distracted by their obsessions or compulsions that they often fail to notice contextual information, such as triggers, background beliefs, assumptions about the implications of their obsessions, or the role served by rituals.

Cleaning compulsions are the prototypical ritual and are carried out to rid the individual of imagined contaminants, whether they be germs or industrial toxins or other physical stimuli. Moral "dirt" can carry the same contaminating properties, acquired from activities like touching underwear or reading a magazine containing sexual suggestions. As normal cleaning and grooming habits do vary across persons, washing can be excessive on several dimensions. For example, clients may take a lot of time (such as showering daily for an hour), be unduly frequent (such as washing one's hands 50 times per day), or involve unnecessarily harsh cleaning materials (such as handwashing with bleach). Clients with contamination obsessions may pressure family members into participating in cleaning compulsions or otherwise assisting the patient by facilitating avoidance of places that are somehow associated with a perceived contaminant. On the positive side, such family involvement can diminish secrecy, which ultimately aids identification and assessment. Contamination obsessions are particularly sensitive to threatening cues in news reports, which can even spark a panic attack. For example, one client experienced a crisis when she heard a news report that officials had traced the source of one man's AIDS infection to his dentist. Having recently been to a dentist, the client became terrified that she had become contaminated with HIV during her visit.

Other common OCD rituals involve checking for safety purposes (e.g., doors and windows locked, no pedestrian hit while driving the car, appliances off or unplugged), quality control (e.g., no errors made at work), or the loss of personal items (e.g., identification, money, keys). Other examples include repeating rituals (e.g., until it feels "just right"), ordering rituals (e.g., arranging clothes in the closet by color), or compulsions related to symmetry (e.g., using sentences that end in an even number of words).

Interestingly, both obsessions and routine ways of coping with them are observed in persons without OCD. Rachman and de Silva (1978) found that normal individuals often reported experiencing intrusive thoughts, images, or impulses similar in content to the obsessions of clients with OCD. Unlike with OCD, these thoughts were not associated with distress or concern and were experienced as relatively easy to control, unlike obsessions. Similarly, nonclinical subjects reported using specific strategies to cope with their intrusive thoughts (Freeston, Ladouceur, Thibodeau, & Gagnon, 1991). Nearly everyone (99%) in the Freeston et al. study reported intrusive thoughts, and 92% used strategies to cope with them (e.g., self-reassurance, mentally saying "stop"). Obsessions may best be viewed on a continuum from normal to increasingly abnormal, differing not in the content of thoughts, impulses, or images, but in how they are interpreted, how much distress they cause, and how easy they are to control.

Diagnosis

Criteria for OCD diagnostic classification continue to evolve. The DSM-IV differs from the revised third edition of the DSM in several ways. In DSM-IV, the clinician is reminded to distinguish obsessions from excessive worries about real-life problems, making it easier to rule out generalized anxiety disorder. In addition, DSM-IV criteria for OCD recognize a wider range of insight clients may have about how unreasonable or excessive their symptoms may be, by including a descriptive specification, "with poor insight." This specification recognizes that some clients view their obsessions or compulsions as excessive or irrational during calm moments, but later see them as realistic when confronted with anxiety-provoking stimuli.

The DSM-IV also clarified the nature of compulsions to include mental acts (e.g., counting, thinking "good" thoughts to offset obsessions) as well as overt behaviors. This expansion in the DSM-IV definition of compulsion reflects a new understanding of the manner in which cognitive acts of neutralization occur. Take a recent client of ours, a 23-year-old woman with a 9 year history of intrusive images revolving around themes of violence and aggression perpetrated against her or family members. She felt she would be responsible for provoking such acts if she did not immediately "fix" any intrusive thoughts. These obsessions occurred about 10 times per hour. Rituals involved in "fixing" the thought included thought reversing (dwelling on thoughts that had occurred just prior to the intrusion), counting until she reached a number that felt "right," or imagining the violent image burning up and replacing it with a pleasant image. None of these rituals were outwardly visible, yet they all served to undo her upsetting thought just as an overt compulsion would.

PREVALENCE AND COURSE

Until recently OCD was considered to be a relatively infrequent disorder, since estimates of prevalence were derived from psychiatric clinic populations. The Epidemiologic Catchment Area (ECA) study of five communities in the USA (Karno, Golding, Sorenson, & Burman, 1988) and similar international epidemiological studies (Weissman et al., 1994) have identified lifetime prevalence rates for OCD in the range of 2–3%. These estimates were based on the use of the Diagnostic Interview Schedule (DIS; Robins, Heltzer, Croughan, & Ratcliff, 1981) with lay interviewers. More recent studies with highly experienced clinical interviewers estimated a 1-month prevalence rate of 0.6% (Stein, Forde, Anderson, & Walker, 1997). More definitive estimates await methodological advances in diagnostic determination, although most investigators would likely agree that the true lifetime prevalence rate of OCD is in the 1–1.5% range, rendering it a relatively common psychiatric disorder.

OCD is roughly equally distributed across men and women. The age of onset is typically between 19 and 26 years (Karno et al., 1988), and the course is usually chronic with acute exacerbations occurring at times of stress (Rasmussen & Tsuang, 1984). There also is a considerable range of severity evident in OCD. Overall, those with OCD symptoms tend to marry less often than members of the general population do (Steketee, 1993), and those with moderate to severe levels of OCD often experience considerable impairment in social and occupational functioning. Some 58% of OCD clients experience academic underachievement; 47% report occupational impairment; and 40% are unable to sustain long term employment (Hollander et al., 1996). The economic impact of this disorder in the USA has been estimated to be $2.2 billion for annual direct costs of inappropriate outpatient treatment, $5.0 billion for lifetime hospitalization, and $40.0 billion for lost wages over the life span (Hollander et al.).

THEORETICAL PERSPECTIVES

Cognitive Behavioral Approaches

Behavioral treatments for OCD are founded upon Mowrer's (1960) two-factor theory for the acquisition and maintenance of fear, which was discussed in relation to agoraphobia in chapter 5. In this model, obsessions are thought to be maintained by operant conditioning, wherein fear reduction reinforces compulsions, escape, and avoidance. Experiments by Rachman and Hodgson (1980) demonstrated this mechanism; provoking an obsession resulted in distress that was in turn relieved by engaging in rituals. Consequently, the anxiety associated with obsessions is protected from extinction by the relieving effect of compulsions. This view led early behavior therapists such as Wolpe and Rachman to implement exposure and response prevention. Exposure and response prevention (ERP) involves exposing a client to stimuli related to obsessions (e.g., money or public telephones for a germ-phobic client) and helping to prevent the engagement of compulsions (e.g., washing) by them.

While treatment based on conditioning theory (ERP) has produced dramatic improvements in what had been considered an invariably intractable illness, a number of shortcomings in this theoretical explanation of OCD have become evident. Rachman (1975) drew attention to the inadequacies of the two-factor theory in the face of new evidence (e.g., avoidance behavior can be acquired in the absence of fear reduction) and recommended the expansion and revision of the two-factor theory. Meanwhile, despite the relative success of ERP, it became widely apparent that a minority of OCD clients refused or dropped out of ERP treatment, and that for the majority who were improved, residual obsessions however weak, remained. Furthermore, because a major part of the treatment focuses on preventing the performance of compulsions, clinicians were frustrated in their attempts to treat pure obsessionals for whom no compulsions seem to occur.

The importance of cognitive factors in mediating OCD phenomena has since begun to emerge. Rachman (1976), for example, argued that obsessions not only cause distress but also evoke attempts to "put matters right" via cognitive neutralizing activities, which are functionally equivalent to overt rituals. Salkovskis (1985; 1989) later proposed an influential cognitive behavioral theory to account for the development of OCD. Given that normative intrusive thoughts are similar in content to those seen in OCD, Salkovskis maintains that the difference lies in the interpretation of the meaning of the presence of intrusive thoughts. Specifically, those with OCD appraise intrusive thoughts, which are by definition disturbing, shameful, or abhorrent, in a manner that implies personal relevance. For example, having a thought about a terrible outcome may be perceived as denoting individual responsibility for causing or preventing the potential harm. As an example, we saw a man in the clinic who experienced contamination obsessions of spreading AIDS. Some years ago, he had engaged in unprotected sex. His obsessions about this event convinced him that he would be responsible if a co-worker or family member contracted the virus. As a result, he carefully avoided human contact unless he was wearing gloves, and he engaged in elaborate cleaning rituals to ensure the safety of others.

Salkovskis (1996) feels the pivotal role of responsibility appraisals in OCD is similar to the misinterpretation of bodily sensations in the cognitive account of panic disorder (Clark, 1986), with both appraisals leading to a conclusion that catastrophic events are impending. From the cognitive perspective, compulsions, both covert and overt, are seen as attempts to escape, avoid, or otherwise reduce one's risk of being grossly irresponsible. Compulsions, avoidance, and reassurance seeking all serve to reduce or prevent the anxiety associated with responsibility appraisals (i.e., causing or being able to prevent harm to others) in the short term. However, as discussed above, they also have the effect of preventing the extinction of anxiety and thereby perpetuating the disorder.

Other researchers have demonstrated a link between excessive responsibility and obsessive-compulsive symptoms through experimental manipulations (e.g., Ladouceur, Rhéaume, & Aublet, 1997; Lopatka & Rachman, 1995). Other forms of distorted thinking have also been implicated in OCD by a wide range of investigators from many countries. Freeston, Rhéaume, and Ladouceur (1996) reviewed various types of faulty appraisals that they considered to be operative in clinical obsessions. In addition to the exaggerated responsibility identified by Salkovskis, Freeston et al. identified four additional types of beliefs and faulty appraisals. First, individuals with OCD appear to overestimate the importance of their thoughts. For instance, they may believe that having a thought about a bad outcome will make the event more likely to occur or that random thoughts juxtaposed to a negative event (such as an argument) played a causal role in the event. A second faulty appraisal identified by Freeston et al. is overvaluing the need for perfection and certainty. Feeling pressure to create perfection and feel 100% certain obviously creates anxiety because of the impossibility of this mandate. A third faulty appraisal is overestimating the probability and severity of the consequences of negative events. An example of this is a woman who obsessively checked her refrigerator door out of a fear that if it were left slightly ajar, she and her pets would be poisoned by pathogens in the food. Finally, as Freeston et al. pointed out, some clients with OCD feel that any anxiety associated with unwanted thoughts is unacceptable or even dangerous.

As the importance of beliefs and appraisals in OCD became clear, researchers turned attention to the vexing problem of measuring these cognitive phenomena. An international group of investigators (Obsessive Compulsive Cognitions Working Group, 1997) has been working to develop and evaluate self-report measures about intrusions and beliefs related to obsessions and compulsions. Six belief domains were identified as "likely important to OCD" by this team of researchers. The belief domains include:

Inflated sense of responsibility. The intrusive thought signals potential for future harm. Individuals with OCD interpret the occurrence of the thought as conveying personal responsibility for preventing harm because of the belief that they have influence over the outcome of the negative event. "Not acting to prevent a possible disaster is as bad as causing it."

Overimportance of thoughts. The simple presence of a thought makes it important. "Thinking about something makes it more likely to happen." "Having a thought about something terrible happening means I subconsciously want it to happen."

Control over one's thoughts. Persons with OCD often believe that people generally are able to control all their own thoughts and that intrusive thoughts must be controlled to avoid harm or to be a good person. "If I were a good Christian, I would never have any blasphemous images."

Overestimation of threat. Aversive events are believed to have a high likelihood of occurring and are anticipated to be catastrophic. "There is more danger out there than people realize."

Intolerance of uncertainty. Clients with OCD often have difficulty with decision making, ambiguity, newness, and unpredictable change. "I must be absolutely sure or I'm just asking for mistakes to happen."

Perfectionism. Major and minor mistakes are seen as equally intolerable. "If something is not done right, it is wrong."

The six content areas of dysfunctional assumptions, attitudes, or beliefs identified by the Obsessive Compulsive Cognitions Working Group (1997) parallel the earlier list of five content areas elucidated by Freeston et al., (1996) and span much of the cognitive dysfunction seen by clinicians in OCD. The Obsessive Compulsive Cognitions Working Group has generated preliminary self-report scales that are presently being tested, but many details about the structure, strength, and specificity of OC-related beliefs, as well as their relationship to obsessions and compulsions, remain to be tested. Cognitive research in OCD holds tremendous promise in the identification of dysfunctional cognitions that would be common targets of intervention across content areas of OCD.

BIOLOGICAL APPROACHES

Genetic transmission of OCD is suggested by concordance rates that are higher in monozygotic than dizygotic twins (Billett, Richter, & Kennedy, 1998). However, the relative contribution of environmental and genetic factors cannot be presently determined given the rarity of twin studies where twins are reared apart (Steketee, 1993). Recent brain imaging studies have demonstrated several neurobiological anomalies in those with OCD, but agreement between studies has been patchy. The most consistent findings have suggested frontal or basal ganglia involvement (see Pigott, Myers, & Williams, 1996, for review), and prominent OCD symptoms may occur in many neurological conditions. Structural brain abnormalities have not been observed (Garber, Anuuth, Chiu, Griswold, & Oldendorf, 1989; Hoehn-Saric, 1993). Currently, researchers are unable to positively say whether these observed neurochemical changes are the cause or the effect of OCD.

Most interestingly, both pharmacotherapy and behavior therapy result in measurable brain changes. For example, changes in serotonin activity have been observed after intensive ERP (Neziroglu, Steele, Yaryura-Tobias, Hitri, & Diamond, 1990), and abnormalities in regional brain metabolism rates are normalized effectively by successful treatment with either medication or behavior therapy (Baxter et al., 1992). Clearly, any comprehensive theory of OCD will need to account for both neurochemical evidence and the effectiveness of behavior therapy. Along these lines, Neziroglu and Hsia (1998) have recently proposed a biobehavioral model offering an explanation for how behavior therapy might affect neurochemistry. In their view, behavior therapy may produce neuronal fatigue, so that neurons cannot "reset" after repetitive stimulation. In addition, they propose that as the patient improves, new neural pathways are developed. This may occur because old pathways related to vigilance toward information related to the obsession (e.g., perpetual scanning to be sure the contaminant is not present) are no longer being used.

ASSESSMENT OF OCD

The goals of assessment of OC symptoms are several. First, the clinician obviously wants to make a diagnostic determination regarding OCD and assess for comorbidity. In addition, the strength of obsessive and compulsive symptoms should be evaluated. Finally, the clinician will need to identify idiographic information necessary to establish a case formulation. Such information could include triggers, cognitive appraisals, and the roles that are played by family members.

Differential Diagnosis

Because obsessions and compulsions are unique to OCD and because overt compulsions are relatively easy to recognize, clinicians often agree about the diagnosis of OCD. However, in the absence of overt compulsions, diagnostic disagreements increase (Brown, Moras, Zinbarg, & Barlow, 1993), since the diagnosis is based upon self-reported cognitive activities. In our experience, clients with OCD are sometimes less able to report on their obsessions than their compulsions. Furthermore, they may not recognize cognitive rituals as compulsions. Careful attention is sometimes required to recognize cognitive symptoms of neutralizing (e.g., purposely having "good" thoughts) and avoidance (e.g., not imagining anything associated with breast cancer). Cognitive activities designed to neutralize or avoid obsessions may be even more elusive when they have no logical connection to the obsession (e.g., counting ritual reactive to a sexual image).

Although there are often similarities between OCD and other disorders, differential diagnosis is based on the content of the ideation, cognitive processes, and the presence of distress.

Major Depression

Depression is frequently comorbid with OCD and should routinely be assessed, even during the course of treatment. The relationship between OCD and depression is not well understood, although it appears that depression can follow from the impairment and anxiety associated with OCD. Symptoms of OCD are also clearly exacerbated by episodes of depression. The presence of a moderate or severe major depressive episode can interfere with behavioral treatment for OCD, so pharmacological interventions should be considered in this case. Depression is at times difficult to distinguish from OCD due to the presence of depressive ruminations. In contrast to OCD, the content of depressive ruminations often concerns life problems, and the depressed person typically does not attempt to suppress or ignore ruminations.

Generalized Anxiety Disorder (GAD)

GAD by definition differs from OCD in that the focus of worry in GAD is exclusively on real-life problems (e.g., financial stress, employment problems, social acceptance) and their possible negative outcomes. In contrast, obsessions are seen by the individual to have negative implications about one's personal character (Clark & Claybourn, 1997; Turner, Beidel, & Stanley, 1992). In plain language, clients with GAD worry about terrible things that might happen. People with OCD more frequently worry about being a bad person, based on their unacceptable repetitive thoughts or impulses. When individuals with OCD also worry about real-life problems, these are likely to be realistic difficulties associated with functional impairment due to the OCD (for instance, difficulty holding a job).

Delusional Disorder

A diagnosis of OCD requires that the individual recognize, at some point during the disorder, that the obsessions or compulsions are excessive or unreasonable. If reality testing is absent, and the obsession has reached delusional levels of conviction, then a diagnosis of delusional disorder or psychotic disorder not otherwise specified may be appropriate. For example, we saw a 27-year-old woman in group treatment for OCD. Her OCD symptoms involved cleaning and checking rituals, and she had comorbid major depression. By session five it was apparent that she was becoming more depressed and not relating to the group treatment. Taking her aside after one of the group meetings, we discussed her ideas that she was an evil person when she made a minor mistake or failed to complete her rituals. She reluctantly disclosed a belief in a spiritual entity, "the shadow," that watched her, mocked her inadequacies, and threatened her if she made mistakes. This belief was of delusional proportions, and a revised diagnosis of major depression with mood-congruent psychotic features was considered more appropriate.

Body Dysmorphic Disorder

This disorder is characterized by strong beliefs about a perceived body defect, often resulting in compulsive checking. Recurrent intrusive thoughts are characteristic of body dysmorphic disorder as well as of OCD. At present, the relationship between these two related disorders is not well understood. Many, but not all, clients with body dysmorphic disorder do not experience their beliefs as distressing (i.e., ego-syntonic beliefs). OCD is not diagnosed if the content of the thoughts, impulses, or behaviors is exclusively related to bodily appearance.

Obsessive-Compulsive Personality Disorder (OCPD)

Individuals with OCD and OCPD do have some similarities in terms of perfectionism, inflexibility, preoccupation with rules, and controlling behavior. However, in the case with OCD, these rigid traits are seen only in response to stimuli related to obsessions; in other areas of life, these clients are not usually rule-bound or controlling. A diagnosis of OCPD is warranted when the rigidity and perfectionism is pervasive across domains regardless of the circumstances. Those with OCPD also do not experience obsessions or compulsions. Any repetitive acts are usually ego-syntonic, not provoking distress or efforts to resist them. In contrast, OCD sufferers try to thwart their obsessions and compulsions, at least in the beginning, since they regard them as inappropriate, foreign, and distressing (i.e., ego-dystonic). For these reasons it is usually not difficult to distinguish OCD and OCPD, although the distinction can be more difficult in the case of hoarding rituals.

Mild to moderate hoarders often meet criteria for OCPD and are sometimes dubbed as "pack rats," reflecting their habit of saving things in an austere manner, often for protection against potential hard times ahead. Severe hoarders believe the items collected (e.g., information contained in books, newspapers, taped TV shows) may contain essential important information, and they are substantially preoccupied with the acquisition and storage of such materials. Frost and Hartl (1996) define compulsive hoarding as involving: (1) the acquisition of and failure to discard many possessions that are useless or of limited value; (2) sufficient clutter in living spaces so as to preclude normal use of those spaces; and (3) consequent significant distress or functional impairment.

Symptom Scales

Standardized measures of OCD symptoms permit severity to be quantified and compared across clients with varying types of OCD, and the measures are useful in the measurement of progress during the course of treatment. While there are a number of OCD symptom measures available (For review see Steketee, 1993; Taylor, 1998), two are selected here for discussion due to their widespread use.

The first is the *Maudsley Obsessional-Compulsive Inventory* (MOCI; Hodgson & Rachman, 1977), which is a 30-item true-false questionnaire (see Appendix A). This inventory is scored to produce a total score for obsessions and 5 subscales, reflecting several obsessive-compulsive themes (washing, checking, ruminating, slowness-repetition, and doubting-conscientious). Overall, the MOCI has satisfactory psychometric properties and its subscales allow specific themes, or symptom clusters, to be evaluated. The MOCI is perhaps most useful as a screening instrument or in evaluating highly prototypical symptoms of OCD (i.e., washing and checking).

The *Yale-Brown Obsessive Compulsive Scale* (Y-BOCS; Goodman, Price, Rasmussen, Mazure, Fleischmann et al., 1989) requires a bit more therapist time to administer, but the quality of information is so high that we recommend the Y-BOCS for routine use in evaluating symptoms of OCD. This inventory is completed by a clinical interviewer who first systematically surveys the content of current and past obsessions and compulsions in a checklist format. The advantage here is that a reasonably comprehensive list of obsessions and compulsions are reviewed with the client, reducing the likelihood of missing important symptoms. Using this comprehensive list of current symptoms as a reference, the clinician then asks a series of questions (5 each for obsessions and compulsions) about the severity of the obsessions and compulsions. Each question is graded on a 0–4 scale. The questions evaluate distress associated with the obsessions and compulsions, time occupied by the symptoms, control over the symptoms, degree to which the symptoms are resisted, and degree to which the symptoms cause interference in daily life. A number of other clinically relevant questions are also included, not specific to obsessions or compulsions, such as insight, avoidance, pervasive slowness, and global severity.

The Y-BOCS is contained in Appendix A. Norms for the Y-BOCS have not been published, but to give some idea of what to expect over the course of time-limited treatment, we have listed the means and standard deviations for the obsessions and compulsions subscales as reported by deAraujo et al. (1995). In this study, patients with OCD were assigned to two exposure- and response-prevention treatments which lasted 9 weeks and included follow-up interviews at 20 and 32 weeks. The two subscales are added to yield the Y-BOCS total score at any assessment period.

This instrument has demonstrated reasonably good psychometric qualities (Goodman, Price, Rasmussen, Mazure, Delgado et al., 1989; Goodman, Price, Rasmussen, Mazure, Fleischmann et al., 1989; Woody, Steketee, & Chambless, 1994) and is probably the best means of assessing OC symptoms in practice. First-time administration of the scale takes about 40 minutes, but subsequent administrations require only 15 minutes because the lengthy process of identifying content areas does not need to be repeated. A self-report version of the Y-BOCS (Baer, Brown-Beasley, Sorce, & Henriques, 1993) has been developed, which takes about 10 minutes to complete and discriminates well between clients with and without OCD (Steketee, Frost, & Bogart, 1996). A computerized version of the self-report Y-BOCS can be obtained from Healthcare Technology Systems in Madison, Wisconsin or from www.healthtechsys.com/prodgridnew.html.

Idiographic Assessment

In addition to the ready-made assessments, each client's most specific concerns can be evaluated with self-monitoring to assess the frequency or duration of obsessions and compulsions. Using a diary format that is tailored for each individual client, self-monitoring can be a good indicator of whether symptom frequency or intensity is diminishing over time.

As we have discussed in previous chapters, an essential part of assessment involves developing a *hierarchy* of the stimuli that cause anxiety for the client. (See chapter 2 for an extensive discussion of developing a hierarchy.) Clients with OCD often have several themes, so we usually develop a separate hierarchy for each theme. As with the other anxiety disorders, these hierarchies involve a rank order of items along with 0–100 anxiety ratings for each item. For example, an item low on the hierarchy of a theme of HIV contamination might be watching a movie about someone dying of AIDS. A high item on the same hierarchy might be having blood drawn in a public clinic. Because any particular item may not evoke discomfort if neutralization is permitted, clients rate how much discomfort (0–100) would be experienced if they were to be exposed without opportunity for rituals or escape. In the case of behavior that normally occurs on a regular basis (such as washing one's hands), the clinician may need to specify how long the client must wait before engaging in the behavior (i.e., 4 hours).

We find most clients present with one to three primary themes, although a minority have a few additional themes that are far less intense than the main themes. We suggest that all OC themes be listed, but that only the primary themes be formatted for treatment (e.g., hierarchy developed) during initial assessment because less intense themes are likely to change considerably during treatment directed toward the main themes. At a later point in treatment, more attention can be given to the peripheral symptoms, if they are still found to be problematic. For each primary theme, the therapist inquires about content of and triggers for intrusive thoughts, the client's appraisal of the meaning of the intrusive thought, feared consequences, avoidance pattern, and rituals, as illustrated in the case of Janice in sidebar 6-1.

Eliciting Appraisals

Eliciting appraisals from clients can be difficult since clients seldom think in such terms, as their intrusive thoughts and rituals tend to monopolize their attention. In such cases, the downward arrow technique (Beck, Rush, Shaw, & Emery, 1979) can be useful. To identify the client's unstated beliefs about obsessions, the clinician asks the client to state what she is afraid will happen if she does not engage in a given ritual or if she permits a specific obsessive thought to occur without response from her. After she states her feared consequence, the clinician then asks such questions as, "If that were true, what would it mean to you?" This question is repeated until it comes

CASE EXAMPLE

Janice is a 32-year-old woman who works full-time as a supervisor in the food industry. She presented with two main themes: contamination from germs and general safety. Janice is worried that her normal bodily secretions will contaminate others with germs, so she has difficulty sharing a bathroom and having sex with her partner, with whom she lives. Laundry and showering are protracted and done in a particular order. Related to safety, Janice checks doors and windows repeatedly upon leaving home, and she checks inordinately at work for procedural compliance regarding safety. Janice reports that she has been perfectionistic and concerned about standards of personal hygiene since childhood, but her obsessions and compulsions began 12 years ago, when a toilet malfunctioned in her dormitory, flooding her carpet. She dropped out of university for one year because of the onset of her OCD, and she has been hospitalized once. Symptoms have been more incapacitating in the past 3 years since she began to imagine germs breeding in her pile of dirty clothes at home.

Theme of Contamination from Germs	
Intrusive Thoughts:	I haven't properly washed.
	Germs are on me, under my nails, and I'll spread them to others.
Appraisal:	It will be my fault when others get sick; I'm a carrier.
Feared Consequence:	Someone will die because of being contaminated by my germs.
Avoidance:	• won't allow partner to do her laundry
	• partial avoidance of sex with partner
	• avoids physician visits (if genital examination is anticipated)
	• avoids public swimming
Rituals:	• laundering personal clothes in specific patterns
	• lengthy showering in a particular way or order (30–50 min.)
	• cleaning bathroom in a particular order (1 hour)
	• cleaning and orderliness rituals for household areas (50+ minutes)
	• handwashing prior to departure for work (8–10 separate times)

Anxiety (SUDS)	Hierarchy: Stimulus Situation
100	Touching soles of shoes
90	Sex with partner
80	Cleaning the house
80	Doing own laundry
70	Touching shoelaces
70	Taking out garbage
60	Cleaning bathroom
30	Touching money
25	Sitting on floors at home
20	Dirty dishes on counter overnight
15	Showering
10	Cleaning cat's litter box

to a logical conclusion, which is taken to be the core belief. We continue with our example of Janice, borrowing from an interview conducted by Peter McLean.

Dr. McLean: What are you afraid will happen if you are not careful enough when you wash your hands after using the toilet?

Janice: I'll contaminate someone with my germs, and they'll die.

Dr. McLean: If that were true, what would it mean to you?

Janice: I would be to blame.

Dr. McLean: And what meaning would that have for you, if you were to blame for someone's death?

Janice: I could never live with myself.

Dr. McLean: What does that mean to you?

Janice: I would have to commit suicide.

Note the presence of several appraisals in what Janice has said. First, she indicates a sense of inflated responsibility by taking blame for someone's death from an illness. This same statement also indicates an inflated probability estimate, given the low likelihood of dying from most illnesses spread by contact. In postulating that she would have to commit suicide as a final outcome from failing to wash her hands properly, Janice vividly outlines several dire consequences. She not only sees herself as having an instrumental role in someone else's death, but she also sees herself as unable to cope with the burden of this perceived responsibility; she will have to kill herself. From this brief exchange, we are unable to discern whether Janice will hold herself responsible, or whether she believes others will hold her accountable (or both). This appraisal will be clarified at a later point, using the same basic downward-arrow procedure.

These appraisals provide a basis for challenging underlying assumptions, or beliefs, during treatment. Sometimes there are no obvious appraisals because the only feared consequence is that the client anticipates intense anxiety. This may be true particularly if the client never resists performing rituals. When resisting rituals, however, the client usually experiences an increase in anxiety, whereupon fantasies about feared consequences are easier to access.

Coping with anxiety induced by obsessions can take varied forms, and these behaviors need to be carefully assessed in order to incorporate them into the treatment plan. Three of the most common forms of self-devised anxiety reduction are avoidance of situations, images, or thoughts that trigger obsessions, engaging in neutralizing rituals, and seeking reassurance. The full range of avoidance behavior may not be readily apparent, even to the client. For example, one client believed she had contaminated others with cancer. Over time, she came to believe that she no longer had cancer herself, but she continued to avoid areas of the city where contaminated others might be, as a strategy to avoid being "reinfected" herself. She initially did not report this avoidance in connection with her obsessions about cancer. Her clinician asked her, "Please tell me all the things that you do to feel better about your thoughts or images related to cancer." Asking questions like this often uncovers additional counting, tapping, or other rituals that have the capacity to interfere with treatment. Finally, because clients with OCD often seek reassurance from family members, friends, or experts, the clinician should inquire about who the client talks to when he becomes especially distressed about some event related to OCD worries. One of our clients who was a smoker listened to the news at night in order to ensure that no fatal fires had occurred that day in areas of the city where he had been. Sometimes he would call fire stations directly, seeking the same reassurance.

A minority of OCD sufferers have no overt compulsions (i.e., 'pure obsessions'), and they perform mental rituals in order to neutralize anxiety associated with their obsessions. In this case, both the obsessions and the cognitive neutralizations involved in the maintenance of the obsessional thoughts can be difficult to assess. Treatment for such obsessions is primarily cognitive by necessity, and the assessment of the significance the client attaches to obsessions is key to the discovery of the faulty beliefs that will need to be weakened and replaced. Following Rachman's (1997) suggestion, the following features of the significance of obsessions should be assessed. In what way is the occurrence of obsessive thoughts important to and revealing about the client? In what ways has the client personalized the thought, impulse, or image? How is the obsession alien, or uncharacteristic and disturbing, to the client? What does the client see as potential consequences of having the thought? In what ways are the potential consequences thought to be serious by the client?

Because of the variety of cognitive methods obsessional clients use to cope with their disturbing thoughts, researchers have been at odds to describe cognitive rituals in a way that encompasses all the variations. Rachman (1976) defined neutralizing as acts designed to escape from or avoid an obsession by "putting things right," or undoing the effect of the obsession. Turner and Beidel (1988) added the idea that these mental acts are carried out in a specific manner involving discrete steps. Freeston and Ladouceur (1997) found these definitions to be too narrow. They observed that obsessive clients use a wide range of strategies to reduce the discomfort brought on by obsessional thoughts. These strategies include thought replacement, analyzing the issue, and trying to convince oneself that one is not a bad person. In addition, Freeston and Ladouceur pointed to distractions used as coping strategies, such as talking to others, listening to music, or watching television. Assessment of neutralizing strategies should be widely conceived to include all classes of mental or physical behavior the client uses in an effort to reduce anxiety associated with obsessions or to forestall the occurrence of bad events believed to be related to obsessions.

Family Involvement

Often family members become involved in cooperating with the obsessive fears and rituals. Sometimes family members reluctantly acquiesce to strong pressure from the person with OCD, but we have seen some cases where family members willingly become involved because they are eager to do anything to help relieve the terrible anxiety of OCD. A fairly common example of cooperating with the symptoms involves family members undergoing extensive cleansing procedures upon returning home. A family, or spousal, interview is helpful to assess the nature and extent of such cooperation. This will also allow the clinician to assess family and subcultural attitudes and beliefs on such topics as cleanliness, superstition, and religiosity, which may be relevant to the client's obsessions and appraisals. A further advantage of a family interview is to gain the family's support for changes they may be asked to make in their interactions with the client for purposes of treatment. For example, we needed the cooperation of Janice's partner in changing the household patterns around laundry.

Other Considerations

OCD sufferers wait an average of 10 years before seeking treatment. Even when they do seek help, OCD is often misdiagnosed or unrecognized by caregivers, so on average another 6 years transpires before appropriate treatment is received (Hollander et al., 1996). Clinicians can therefore expect that their clients with OCD have significant experience with treatment failure, and the client's expectations for treatment should be assessed. Also, because clients with OCD often try to hide their fears and rituals and usually have many years of experience in doing so, they may not easily volunteer the full picture of their avoidance, thoughts, coping styles, or social and occupational adjustment. For example, socially isolated clients with OCD usually do not raise social functioning as an issue. The client with OCD is often so absorbed by obsessive fears and the imperative of rituals that other issues seem irrelevant or unimportant.

TREATMENT APPROACHES: EMPIRICAL SUPPORT

Supportive Psychotherapy

There is no empirical evidence that supportive psychotherapy is effective in treating OCD; few anecdotal reports claim effectiveness. Unlike treatment for other disorders such as depression, studies of treatment for OCD have demonstrated little in the way of nonspecific or placebo effects. While supportive psychotherapy alone is clearly insufficient treatment, this approach can have a valuable adjunctive role in the treatment of OCD. Family and partnership strain, occupational interference, and social isolation are all associated problems of OCD that can be disruptive. Such issues can often be addressed in a supportive and problem-solving manner, concurrent with the targeted treatment program, in order to maintain motivation and help the client cope until symptoms improve. We are unaware of any studies employing interpersonal psychotherapy in the treatment of OCD, and psychodynamic psychotherapy has proven disappointing in the treatment of OCD in both adults (Esman, 1989) and children and adolescents (Hollingsworth, Tanguay, & Grossman, 1980).

Pharmacological Treatment

Early studies of antidepressant medication, usually clomipramine (e.g., Marks, Stern, Mawson, Cobb, & McDonald, 1980), showed pharmacological treatment to be effective in improving OCD symptoms only in clients who were initially depressed. Subsequently, more studies using clomipramine have been completed, along with studies examining a number of selective serotonin reuptake inhibitors (SSRIs). Meta-analytic reviews of well-designed studies (Cox, Swinson, Morrison, & Lee, 1993; van Balkom et al., 1994) concluded that behavior therapy, cognitive therapy, and pharmacotherapy were equally effective in reducing OCD symptoms compared to placebo, but were not different from one another. In comparing drug treatments for OCD, Piccinelli, Pini, Bellantuono, and Wilkinson (1995) found clomipramine to be the most effective (61.3% improvement over placebo) compared to fluoxetine, fluvoxamine, and sertraline (28.5%, 28.2%, and 21.6% improvement over placebo, respectively). Pigott and Seay (1998) warn that the apparent superiority of clomipramine may be due to patient selection factors that cannot be ruled out on the basis of available studies.

Combined pharmacotherapy and behavior therapy or CBT is effective in the acute phase of OCD treatment, but the combined treatment is not significantly superior to either treatment modality alone. However, when the client has major depression in addition to OCD, pharmacotherapy is strongly indicated. The tendency for treatment gains to erode upon discontinuation of pharmacotherapy has made exposure and response prevention the treatment of choice for OCD (Antony & Swinson, 1996).

Behavior Therapy

Psychological treatments were considered ineffective for OCD until Meyer (1966) and others demonstrated the efficacy of exposure and response prevention (ERP). Recent reviews using meta-analysis to statistically incorporate data from diverse studies show that most clients treated with ERP for OCD benefit significantly (e.g., Cox et al., 1993; van Balkom et al., 1994). Although most research on ERP has used an individual format, van Noppen, Steketee, McCorkle, and Pato (1996) have preliminary evidence that group and multifamily member behavioral treatment produces comparable results.

Recall from our earlier discussion that ERP consists of two basic inter-ventions, exposure and response prevention. Exposure to feared stimuli pro-duces high anxiety, but over time this anxiety attenuates through the process of habituation discussed in earlier chapters. Exposure by itself is not enough, however, because rituals short-circuit the habituation process by reducing anxiety quickly. Thus, the therapist prevents the client from responding to anxiety with rituals (response prevention). Researchers have investigated many variations of ERP, and several conclusions are warranted (Abramo-witz, 1996).

1. Therapist-assisted exposure is more effective than self-controlled expo-sure. This finding underscores the importance of first modeling the ex-posure and then persuading the client to engage with the feared stimuli in session. Treatment that merely helps the client to plan exposure she will conduct between sessions is usually inadequate. See the discussion of guided mastery in chapter 3 for more on this type of exposure.
2. Complete response prevention is superior to partial response preven-tion. Walking away without checking whether the door is locked, for example, is associated with a better outcome than checking only once or twice. Similarly, no washing eliminates contamination fears faster than time-limited washing. A quick wash, while perhaps normal, some-what defeats the purpose.
3. Combined in vivo and imaginal exposure is more effective than in vivo exposure alone. However, imaginal exposure to the consequences of failing to perform rituals has not been demonstrated to be an effective technique when used alone.

Cognitive Therapy

Emmelkamp and Beens (1991) found rational emotive therapy to be as good as ERP in improving OCD symptoms. The rational emotive therapy in this study primarily involved identifying and challenging irrational cognitions associated with OCD, although home-based exposure occurred in the later stages of cognitive therapy, which makes this study difficult to interpret. van Oppen and her colleagues (1995) tested a form of cognitive therapy with no exposure. In their study, cognitive therapy was equal to ERP in reduction of OCD symptoms and superior to ERP in terms of proportion of clients achieving recovery.

CONDUCTING BEHAVIOR THERAPY

The following guidelines for ERP treatment of OCD stem from typical treat-ment protocols for which efficacy has been established. These guidelines are based upon individual 1–1.5-hour or 2-hour group treatment sessions, spaced weekly.

Psychoeducation

Most clients with OCD have little understanding of the disorder, and they often view themselves as "weird" and not in control of their own mind. Some have the impression that they are the only ones in the world who have a problem with obsessions and compulsions. In particular they cannot understand why they experience unwanted persistent thoughts. Talking about OCD as a problem, and reviewing the expected course of treatment, provides an explanation for symptoms and offers hope to many clients. If not already done as a part of assessment, we review the definition of obsessions and compulsions and explain what is currently known about the phenomenology and course of OCD. This information is usually well received by clients who have felt unique, misunderstood, and ashamed. For the interested client (or family members), we can recommend several excellent paperback books that are widely available: *When Once is not Enough* (Steketee & White, 1990), *Stop Obsessing!* (Foa & Wilson, 1991), *OCD: The Facts* (DeSilva & Rachman, 1992), *The Boy Who Couldn't Stop Washing* (Rapoport, 1989), and *Getting Control* (Baer, 1991).

Building a Collaborative Alliance

Exposure and response prevention are both anxiety-provoking. At the beginning of the treatment, the client still holds beliefs about the harmfulness of having certain thoughts or failing to engage in rituals. Under these conditions, asking clients to engage in exposure or response prevention is equivalent to inviting them to tempt fate or worse. Clients rely on their trust in the therapist to participate in the first few sessions, gradually building faith that session activities are not truly dangerous. Thus, in the first few sessions, the therapist must pay special attention to building a strong collaborative alliance in order to maximize the likelihood that the client will not flee therapy. Usually, the first session or two is devoted to psychoeducation about OCD, developing comprehensive hierarchies for each theme, and preparing the client for what to expect from behavior therapy.

We have learned that some clients perceive ERP treatment as pressure to do what they fear most, and they strongly consider dropping out of therapy once they learn the details of the treatment plan. Clients who are able to trust their therapists and who receive education and modeling are better prepared to endure the anxiety associated with ERP. Even when the actual exposure begins, the therapist should be prepared to offer support, be sensitive to pace and timing, and model each exposure activity before asking the client to do it. Also, the judicious use of humor can be useful in helping clients feel supported and in maintaining a task orientation in the face of fear.

We explain the behavioral model of OCD and illustrate the relationship between triggers and subsequent intrusive thoughts, images, or impulses by way of examples from the client's own story. Clients readily perceive that obsessions cause anxiety, and they easily understand the idea that rituals are maintained by the relief that they experience after a compulsion is performed correctly. We also set the expectation that clients will probably feel anxious during exposure, and we discuss the real consequences of that anxiety. Finally, we reassure clients that there will be no surprises; exposure exercises are discussed in advance and paced appropriately.

Generating a Treatment Plan

Many patients have several OCD themes, for which hierarchies are generated during the initial assessment phase. These hierarchies may need elaboration or revision during treatment, as the therapist learns about stimuli that were inadvertently omitted or as treatment progress in one area generalizes to other themes. We generally select the primary theme to begin exposure, but there are times when we begin with a less central theme if improvement in that area would greatly improve the quality of the patient's life. Within each theme, we start with hierarchy items that are anticipated to provoke anxiety around 60–70 on a 0–100 scale. When there are multiple items at the same level, we try to start with an item that will facilitate work with other stimuli.

For example, one of our clients was a young woman with extreme personal hygiene rituals in addition to a theme of symmetry and exactness. Because she had a lengthy bedtime ritual related to placement of various items in her bedroom, we started exposure with the symmetry theme even though her showering routine was more severe. The rationale for this was that the bedtime rituals prevented her from getting enough sleep, which increased her general stress level. Once she was able to get more rest, she felt better able to cope with anxiety associated with response prevention regarding her showering. Before turning to the personal hygiene theme, we worked on stimuli from her symmetry and exactness theme until all hierarchy items provoked only low to moderate levels of anxiety.

For clients with very severe and longstanding OCD, time may need to be reserved in the treatment plan for helping them to rebuild their lives after many years of disability. We have seen several clients who had spent years performing rituals for as long as 10 hours a day. After the rituals decline significantly, these clients sometimes feel a sense of loss. The clinician may want to consider using some of the methods discussed in the social phobia chapter to help the client to build a social support network, gradually return to work, and gain a sense of identity apart from that of being a person preoccupied with obsessions and compulsions. Without addressing these issues, we are concerned that the client may be at risk for depression and relapse.

Implementing Exposure

The process and rationale for implementing exposure is basically the same for OCD as for the other anxiety disorders we have discussed in earlier chapters (see table 6.1). Starting with the low to moderate items on the client's anxiety hierarchy, the practitioner first models engagement with the feared stimulus or situation and then asks the client to do the same, resisting the urge to perform rituals following the exposure. Using contamination fears as an example, the therapist may touch the floor, garbage can, or sole of her shoe. Usually, the therapist will want to become as engaged with the stimulus as possible, which might involve "contaminating" herself after touching the feared stimulus by rubbing her hands together and subsequently touching her face, hair, neck, arms, and legs. The client then engages in the same activity, giving an anxiety rating before beginning and at 5–10-minute intervals during the exposure.

Exposure with OCD usually involves a little creativity to discover convenient stimuli that provoke fear. For example, a client who is preoccupied with ordering can be asked to remove the elastic band around his carefully ordered identification, money, and credit cards in his billfold and to mix them up randomly, place them in different billfold compartments with some

Table 6.1 Overview of Exposure and Response Prevention Components for Treatment of OCD

Psychoeducation
> Give information about OCD, its definition, phenomenology, course comorbidity.
>> Recommend informative readings.
> Provide examples of normal obsessions.
> Review behavioral model of how obsessions and compulsions relate to each other.

Treatment Planning
> Develop hierarchies for exposure.
> Introduce "Exposure Forms" to help structure between-session exposure.
> Outline expectations and develop a commitment to the treatment plan.

Implementing Treatment
> Model in vivo exposure, followed by client exposure.
> Review and adjust hierarchies as exposure progresses.
> Emphasize self-directed exposure.
> Introduce applied relaxation and other strategies as necessary.

Maintenance
> Develop a schedule for continued exposure.
> Discuss anticipation of setbacks.
> Provide general tips on prevention and reduction of stress.

---

upside down or backwards. At times, creativity is required to generate hierarchy items that are less than maximally fear-producing. For one client who was obsessed with the concept of brain tumor, we began by speaking aloud "brain tumor" 10 times, starting with a whisper and increasing the volume to very loud. Creativity can also be used to sustain the exposure effect. For instance, the client can write "brain tumor" repeatedly on a sheet of paper. Alternatively, the therapist may move on to another topic, but prompt the client every several minutes to repeat "brain tumor" a few times aloud.

The most frequent challenge to ERP treatment for the practitioner is to push the limits to overcome the client's avoidance of progressing to the next level of feared exposure on the hierarchy. Therapists who are new to ERP, reflecting back on their first few cases, often remark, "I should have been more assertive with exposure. I was too accepting of my client's apprehension." Providing clients with methods of anxiety management, such as applied relaxation as outlined in chapter 5, can increase tolerance for both exposure and response prevention. Once clients are engaged in exposure, we have found that their contribution to developing new exposure ideas, as well as thinking of times, places, and new methods for self-exposure outside of the therapy session helps promote the development of anxiety management. Throughout ERP for OCD, however, the primary responsibility of the practitioner is to make sure clients proceed through the hierarchy at a reasonable pace of exposure, thus ensuring adequate levels and duration of anxiety exposure for habituation to occur. Despite their initial understanding and agreement with the model of ERP, virtually all clients balk at moving up to higher levels of exposure and may try to persuade the therapist to continue lateral exposure on related themes in order to avoid exposure to a more feared situation.

For example, a 27-year-old bank employee with obsessions about death avoided portions of his work involving the processing of wills and death certificates. He handled exposure to the obituary column in the daily newspaper and many other moderate level tasks, but he avoided driving by a graveyard or going to a funeral home until the therapist arranged to meet him at the local hospital morgue for a 30-minute exposure session. Thereafter, he was able to visit a graveyard and touch tombstones on his own until his SUDS ratings declined to the 30% range (about 1 hour).

Exposure in imagination is recommended to accommodate a client's particular obsessions where in vivo exposure would not suffice (e.g., catastrophic fears, sexual themes). Some clients admit that they have particularly vivid and horrific mental imagery about the consequences of their perceived potential irresponsibility. One client vividly imagined an apartment fire that resulted in multiple deaths because she neglected to check that all her appliances were unplugged. A male client who normally took extreme precautions to avoid looking at women's bodies (his wife excepted) suspected that he may have glanced at a woman's chest while on the elevator. He visualized this woman informing the entire community that he is "a leering lecher, a pervert;" in his imagery, he was shamed into leaving his family.

Painful images like these are usually fleeting, and clients often exert immediate effort to stop (i.e., avoid) further contemplation of the idea. Imaginal exposure might involve daily tasks in which clients visualize their perceived irresponsible action and all of the possible consequences for 30 minutes. This process can sometimes be gainfully broken down into themes or components of a theme. For example, "On Tuesday you are planning to imagine the court scene and public ridicule in the press directed against you, and on Thursday you are going to imagine the funerals and crying families with the mournful children staring at you. Is that right?" Of course it is essential that clients understand the need for this exposure so that they do not view it as ghoulish, a confirmation of their "sickness," or as flirting with disaster.

Therapists can also encourage clients to change the outcome of their feared consequences by introducing an outcome opposite to those anticipated. This has the effect of making the intrusive thought or image less frightening. For example, Mark, a police officer on highway duty, had obsessive images of pointing his revolver at the faces of people he pulled over for speeding, particularly if they were elderly, cooperative, and had the appearance of innocence. Mark never thought about actually shooting them. Instead he focused on how horrible it would be to thus violate the police code of professional conduct and experience the consequences, such as being dismissed for unprofessional conduct. In imaginal exposure exercises, he imagined being charged and relieved of duty by an internal court, being ridiculed by his colleagues and the media, having his wife divorce him, and living a hermit's life in shame. Later in treatment, the therapist encouraged Mark to change the outcome of his fears by imagining pointing his revolver at the driver, whereupon everyone in the car laughed and congratulated him for being so humorous.

Implementing Response Prevention

It is prudent to make a strong procedural distinction between exposure and response prevention. Clients tend to confuse them, often cutting exposure short to impose response prevention. Exposure is concerned with anxiety elicitation and tolerance until SUDS ratings have dropped significantly, and rituals of neutralization, avoidance, or seeking reassurance is not permitted during this time. However, response prevention continues long after the exposure exercise ends. Some clients can endure exposure with relatively little anxiety, knowing that they will neutralize (e.g., wash) at the first opportunity upon leaving the therapist's office. This plan reflects a poor understanding of the treatment strategy. The therapist needs to be explicit about the duration of both exposure and planned response prevention after exposure, and it is extremely helpful if the client fully understands the rationale for the approach. If response prevention is violated, reexposure to feared cues should be practiced right away.

For example, occasionally an event occurs that requires handwashing for safety reasons during the time that a client is engaging in response prevention. One client was in the habit of leaving the therapy session and going home to walk her dog, which involved scooping poop into a plastic bag— something that normally is followed by a handwash. We first attempted to gain the cooperation of other family members to perform this task so that the client would be able to maintain response prevention, but this was not possible due to scheduling considerations. Thus, we made sure to give the client a "contaminated" article after each exposure session. After walking her dog and washing for 10 seconds, she reexposed herself to the stimulus that had been used in that day's therapy session. Furthermore, she was able to use the "contaminated" article to expose her entire apartment to the feared stimulus, which furthered the goals of exposure.

Clients with OCD commonly lack normative information on issues of threat or moral behavior. It is useful to define acceptable handwashing as lasting no more than 10 seconds and occurring 5 times or less per day (i.e., after using the toilet and before food preparation/eating). The negotiation of exposure exercises is probably the most important issue in keeping clients in treatment. It is not helpful for such negotiations to degenerate into a war of wills, or a perception of widely different personal standards or values, where the clinician is perceived as cavalier, excessively liberal, and ultimately as contaminated or irresponsible. Full effort is required to educate the client and to maintain an open, empathic, and respectful relationship while explaining to the client how and why exposure works and what benefits can be expected. The provocation of anxiety is portrayed as an essential part of the beneficial treatment.

Many clients with OCD have family backgrounds in which excessive standards of cleanliness, security, responsibility, and perfectionism have been consistently modeled and supported. The clinician must first help the client understand the variation in normal practices and then get them to first approximate such community standards and then go beyond them for the full benefit of exposure. For example, one woman believed that her family would die if she did not take extreme food preparation precautions. We began by having her handle her husband's food without first washing her hands. She then moved to purposely touching some food on the floor before he ate it. In this way, she was able to see what happened before doing the same exercises with her children's food.

Between-Session Exposure Exercises

Homework assignments for self-directed exposure are structured with an Exposure Homework Form (figure 6.1). We give clients a pad of these forms, and they complete at least one daily. Each week, exposure homework

Session #: _____   Date: _____

Situation to practice:

_____

_____

Monitor your anxiety:

	SUDS (0 – 100)		SUDS (0 – 100)
Beginning	_____	25 minutes	_____
5 minutes	_____	30 minutes	_____
10 minutes	_____	40 minutes	_____
15 minutes	_____	50 minutes	_____
20 minutes	_____	60 minutes	_____

Response prevention plan:

_____

_____

Figure 6.1 Exposure Homework Form.

is reviewed and adjusted to ensure the adequacy of magnitude and duration of exposure (in terms of SUDS ratings) and response prevention. Generally speaking, minimal exposure is in the range of half an hour per day, and desirable exposure is about 1 hour per day between sessions. If the client is living with a partner or family members, it is usually advantageous to have the partner or a good family representative attend periodic treatment sessions. It is worth keeping in mind how effectively many clients with OCD manage to convince family members to accommodate their fears.

With prior agreement with the client about disclosures, a significant other can be very helpful at home in both exposure and response prevention as well as in motivating and supporting the client emotionally. In the case of children with OCD, parents effectively become the home therapists in a team approach. Supportive partners or family members can be key in encouraging the client, helping to monitor exposure homework, and supporting response prevention (e.g., no longer washing the client's laundry).

Many clients report difficulty in suppressing the urge to engage in compulsions after exposure and report various means of fighting or "staring down" the urge. One interim step in weakening rituals involves completing the ritual in opposite form. One client who had a compulsion to go through doors with his left side turned forward would now go through with the right side of his body first. Another client who engaged in counting rituals involving lucky numbers 4 and 13 agreed to count bad luck numbers 2 and 9 instead. After clients master performing opposite or random rituals following obsessive thoughts, it is often easier for them to suppress rituals altogether as a final step.

COGNITIVE INTERVENTIONS

Cognitive therapy consists of procedures designed to provide clients with alternative and more adaptive appraisals of their obsessions, in order to weaken the perceived importance of the thoughts. In cognitive interventions for OCD, emphasis is placed on faulty appraisals made by the client when interpreting the significance of obsessive thoughts. As discussed earlier, during assessment the clinician identifies faulty appraisals (e.g., inflated responsibility) made by the client. The task involved in cognitive intervention is to weaken the beliefs represented by the appraisals. Usually, these interventions are undertaken while the client and therapist simultaneously work on systematic exposure and response prevention. While waiting for the client's anxiety to decline, the therapist can discuss beliefs and appraisals, encouraging the client to question these ideas and to adopt normative standards. Cognitive interventions are also fruitfully used when a client is afraid to engage in the next step of exposure. By examining beliefs about the exposure, the therapist can often move treatment forward in the face of fearful resistance. In the next few pages, we will discuss basic cognitive therapy as it is applied to OCD. We also refer the reader to previous chapters in which we discussed cognitive interventions, especially chapters 4 and 5.

We wish to emphasize that exposure and cognitive-based therapies are integral. They are complimentary and should be delivered concurrently. We have separated them in this chapter because they have had distinct evolutions, but we recommend a simultaneous approach in conducting treatment. Cognitive techniques of normalization (e.g., "What do you think most other people do about this?" or "How does your immune system deal with germs?") can help to motivate clients, and behavioral exposure can reveal cognitive appraisals that require systematic reevaluation.

Challenging Cognitions (Cognitive Restructuring)

In a collaborative fashion, the therapist and client make a list of intrusive thoughts and the client's associated appraisals, or what the client believes the thought means about her or the future. Often these faulty appraisals or beliefs about thoughts will be consistent across different types of intrusive thoughts. Examples of such beliefs include, "I should be able to control my thoughts," "Bad thoughts reveal that I am bad or evil," and "Not neutralizing means that I want to harm." From this list of appraisals, the therapist then moves to helping clients learn to challenge several aspects of those appraisals:

The importance given to the occurrence of thoughts. For example, one client thought, "If I think about my children's genitals, I must be a pedophile." Over time, she was able to respond to this thought with another, "My thoughts are not erotic, and I'm a good parent, so it doesn't matter."

Estimation of danger. A client focused on the idea that "Germs are disgusting and dangerous. You can get them from anything." Later he noted, "Most day-to-day germs are harmless to the body."

Estimation of consequences. One client expressed her obsession as, "If I don't arrange the house 'just so,' my children might die." Later she was able to gain perspective on the consequences with, "Any dangers my children face have nothing to do with whether the pictures are straight on the walls."

Degree of personal responsibility. Clients often believe that having an awful thought conveys responsibility for preventing the feared outcome. For example, one client said, "If I imagine my mother dead, it must mean that I wish she were dead." Later, the thought changed to, "If mom dies, it will be because she is ill, not because of my thoughts."

Need for certainty. A student who was unable to read textbooks without obsessively checking for complete understanding, felt "If I don't really understand something how can I react?" Over the course of treatment, she was able to reevaluate the depth with which she needed to remember and understand material in her books. "No one can be expert in everything. Most things don't have to be fully understood. It makes no difference to my life if I remember it all."

Need for perfect control over thoughts. Clients sometimes believe that other people have full control over their thoughts—that random bizarre thoughts simply do not occur to normal healthy people. For example, one client believed, "If I can't control my thoughts, I don't know who or what I am." Later, he understood, "There are only occasional situations where full concentration is necessary. The rest of the time stream of consciousness is good, and often creative."

Practitioners trained in cognitive therapy will be aware of many procedures for challenging thoughts, beliefs, and assumptions. Identification of the frightening meanings attached to intrusive thoughts is a continuous exercise during CBT for OCD. As we discussed earlier, the downward arrow technique is helpful in identifying the hidden fear or meaning behind intrusive thoughts and their appraisals. Although the basic techniques are the same as when using cognitive therapy to treat other disorders, the particular types of distortions we see among those with OCD will be different.

Some particularly useful strategies with OCD include identifying double standards, distinguishing subjective versus logical probability, and using cumulative risk as a means of estimating probability of a dangerous outcome. For example, the probability of dropping a lit cigarette on the couch is multiplied by the probability that the client would fail to see the smoke or flames, which is multiplied by the probability the smoke alarm would not sound, resulting in a very small probability.

Another means of normalizing intrusive thoughts is to list advantages and disadvantages of compulsive behavior from the perspective of other people. For example, we saw one client who feared that if he did not perfectly understand things, he would end up knowing nothing. Speculating on how other people might see the situation, he listed the advantages (e.g., knowing what I do know, having certainty about a few things) and disadvantages (self-doubt when I don't succeed, reading less because of distraction) of trying to understand everything. He then challenged the validity of the putative advantages (e.g., "How many times have I been certain about what I've read?"). This helped the client realize he was engaging in a fruitless pursuit of so-called advantages that almost never happened, while suffering the disadvantages of seeking perfect understanding.

Normalizing Intrusive Thoughts

Clients with OCD consistently regard their intrusive thoughts as pathological. The presence of a thought itself is considered meaningful, regardless of what one makes of the thought. From the client's perspective, simply having certain thoughts makes him deranged. In the CBT model, it is the interpretation, not the intrusive thought itself, that is pathological. Clients are often relieved to learn that others experience the same unsavory thoughts. To illustrate this point, the client can be asked to survey 10 other people as to how often they have unwanted thoughts. Prior to conducting the survey, clients are asked to make predictions about how they think the survey will turn out and compare these predictions with actual results.

Behavioral Experiments

Perhaps the most commonly used and most concrete means of weakening obsessive fears is by directly testing behavioral predictions provoked by exposure. This permits an evaluation of evidence for and against alternative appraisals by testing whether feared predictions come true. We discussed the basic principles of this approach in the previous chapter on panic disorder and agoraphobia. Briefly, the idea is to set up behavioral tests of the client's beliefs to see if the predicted events come to pass. If not, then other explanations are explicitly encouraged. This is done within a hierarchy format. For example, if a client believes that thoughts can kill, she is first asked to kill a house plant with her thoughts, then the goldfish, the neighbor's noisy dog, and finally someone she knows—all by thinking. Again, partner or family involvement can be very helpful here. A brother can request that he be killed that night with his sibling's thoughts, as a test of their potency.

To give a case example, we saw one client who feared that if she thought of a crow, God, and a loved one, in close proximity, she would cause the immediate death of the loved one. These disturbing thoughts occurred only at night while she was attempting to sleep. She often used rituals of adjusting the sheets and positioning herself "just right" to compensate. Alternatively, she would get out of bed and think thoughts to undo her bad thoughts until she felt right. When she was 10 years old, this woman had had an encounter with a crow just before her father suddenly died. A few years later, her mother became ill and slowly died. During the mother's illness, the client prayed and promised God that she would be good if her mother were spared. After her mother's death, the client came to believe that God found her inadequate, and she became frightened of God. The behavioral experiment was to taunt the crow and God (e.g., in a blasphemous manner) and then immediately think of either her fiancé or favorite nephew. When she saw that nothing happened to her loved ones, she became accepting of alternative explanations for her fears. Specifically, she came to think, "I had a child's view of magic in that the black crow can kill someone I love and that God is punishing me," and "Black crows are really nothing special and God is forgiving of what I say and knows I'm a good person."

If the obsession involves acting in a physically aggressive or sexual manner, mental visualizations or written scripts can be used to replace physical exposure. Regardless of whether behavioral experiments are conducted physically or by mental visualization, the client and therapist collaborate in specifying the behavioral experiment to be completed. Together, they note the feared consequences, strength of belief that the feared consequence will occur, anxiety levels, actual consequences, and whether thought challenges were utilized. Behavioral experiments are agreed upon in advance, structured in terms of homework assignments (e.g., 3–5 behavioral experiments/week), recorded in terms of probability estimates of specified feared outcomes, and reviewed jointly during the next therapy session.

The objective of cognitive interventions is to help clients generate and evaluate alternative and more adaptive appraisals (i.e., interpretations) of their obsessive thoughts. While they are very aware of their intrusive thoughts, clients are often unaware of the faulty appraisals that follow and therefore are not in a position to be critical of these dysfunctional beliefs and assumptions. The therapeutic task is to employ a variety of procedures to produce and consider alternative interpretations. Behavioral experiments allow predictions based upon faulty appraisals to be defeated in the presence of contradictory information based upon the outcome of the experiment. It is important to fully exploit the contrary information and not let the teachable moment slip away (e.g., "What does this mean in terms of your prediction?").

OBSESSIONS WITHOUT OVERT RITUALS

Until recently there has been no established psychological treatment for those with OCD who do not have overt rituals (Riggs & Foa, 1993). Salkovskis (1985) began encouraging clinicians to conduct a detailed analysis of obsessional thoughts, their meaning to the client, and predicted consequences of having the thought. Freeston, Ladouceur, Gagnon, and Thibodeau (1993) subsequently reported three case studies illustrating the range of subtle neutralization responses that functionally reduce or terminate exposure to obsessive thoughts, thus maintaining the OCD cycle. Examples of subtle neutralization included self-statements minimizing the possibility of the feared outcome or distraction by forcing attention onto something else. In treatment these neutralization responses were targeted for response prevention. Exposure was facilitated by having the client record obsessive thoughts and feared outcomes on an audio tape loop and then listen to it several times a day using a portable audio cassette machine.

Freeston et al. (1997) hypothesized that obsessions are maintained because unrecognized neutralizing responses block access to cognitive structures related to fear, preventing emotional activation. (See the discussion in chapter 7 on emotional activation as it relates to treatment of PTSD.) Applying their ideas to treatment, they obtained good outcome with OCD clients who did not have overt compulsive rituals (Freeston et al.). Their five treatment components are useful guidelines for clients without overt compulsions, although they should be considered as preliminary.

The first component involves providing a *cognitive explanation of obsessions* including distinguishing triggered and spontaneous obsessive thoughts, identifying faulty appraisals, appreciating the anxiety generated by these appraisals, and understanding how cognitive rituals decrease anxiety but leave the appraisal intact. The *rationale for ERP* is presented as a second component. During this phase, the client prepares a loop tape of obsessions for exposure, practices exposure with therapist supervision until successful, and begins daily exposure with loop tape recording as homework. The third component involves *exposure to additional threatening thoughts* higher on the hierarchy. Following the loop tape exposure, exposure hierarchies of additional threatening thought themes are developed. Target thoughts are triggered through in vivo exposure to specific situations associated with the threatening thought.

The fourth component of this approach is *cognitive restructuring* of typical types of dysfunctional appraisals, as outlined earlier in this chapter, such as overvaluing the importance of thoughts, exaggerated responsibility, and perfectionism. Cognitive restructuring can be used before or during exposure and especially in the later part of treatment. Standard methods of cognitive restructuring include techniques like Socratic questioning and behavioral experiments (Beck, Emery, & Greenberg, 1985; Freeston et al., 1996).

The fifth component of the Freeston et al. (1997) approach for treating ob-sessions without overt rituals involves relapse-prevention strategies. These include setting reasonable expectations about residual symptoms and their fluctuations, identifying individual vulnerability factors, and planning cop-ing strategies for setbacks due to stress.

FAMILY INVOLVEMENT

The cooperation of family members in psychological treatment of OCD can be desirable for several reasons. As discussed earlier, family members, de-spite their reluctance, are often pressed into helping OCD sufferers with avoidance and neutralization rituals as well as providing reassurance. Fam-ily members comply with such requests because they want to be helpful or because the client's anxiety and irritation can be difficult to live with. A (carefully selected) trusted family member can act as a coach in both ERP and cognitive challenge exercises at home. Parents can readily learn, for example, to systematically ignore compulsive reassurance seeking on the part of children.

The success of this approach will depend largely on the attitude, patience, and resolve of the partner or family member. In selecting a family member, the client can first nominate someone who is empathic, understanding, and potentially willing to help. If the client identifies someone who may be use-ful in this role, the family member can attend the next session, during which the therapist should evaluate whether the family member is sufficiently sup-portive and prepared to help with both exposure and response prevention. If the family member seems suitable, the therapist can begin by advising that that person not provide reassurance (a form of neutralizing) and by giving recommendations on how to respond instead (e.g., "Yes, there probably are germs on that."). Similarly, guidance to family members about not accom-modating feared exposure or rituals on behalf of the client is most helpful. The family member further serves as an independent observer, which assists in ongoing assessment.

COMMONLY ENCOUNTERED PROBLEMS

Noncompliance with ERP is frequent and predictive of poor outcome. There is some evidence that older men who have never previously been treated for OCD are particularly vulnerable to noncompliance and dropout. This sug-gests that careful management and preparation for therapy during the initial treatment stage is important in building commitment to treatment.

Reassurance-seeking, a form of neutralization, should be distinguished from education. Reassurance-seeking occurs in response to specific anxiety-provoking situations and usually takes the form of asking for reassurance that a feared event did not occur or cannot occur. Education about perceived threats is also a useful component of treatment, but this information is presented apart from its relevance to a specific feared event. For example, clients who are afraid of HIV may benefit from accurate information about how AIDS can be transmitted. Such information is presented on a selective basis, and clients are encouraged to test their feared predictions against what is known about the situation (e.g., communicability of cancer). Education can readily turn to persuasion if the therapist is not careful. Such persuasion can begin to function as reassurance and should be carefully monitored by the therapist. It is better to guide clients in a reassessment of their faulty appraisals, encouraging alternative, normative interpretations.

The therapist should be alert to other forms of safety their presence may provide in the client's eyes. For example, the client may feel secure engaging in behavior perceived to be irresponsible (such as resisting the urge to check whether the car hit a pedestrian) when the therapist is present, out of a belief that if something terrible did happen, then the therapist would say something. One client we saw took this sense of "protection" to such an extreme that exposure in the office came to have little value. The therapist's presence was enough to calm his fears about getting cancer from objects perceived to be contaminated. In this case, telephone sessions proved to be useful, as the therapist guided the client through home-based exposure on the telephone.

Therapists experiencing unexpectedly slow improvement with OCD clients may have not identified all relevant stressors or triggers for neutralization behavior. These often occur only in specific situations (e.g., quick forms of neutralization that are not obvious, such as squeezing fingers together). Sidebar 6-2 provides an illustration of how subtle neutralization can be. Ongoing collaborative assessment is helpful in overcoming this problem. Given the threatening nature of exposure and the embarrassing nature of some OCD themes, clients often don't volunteer information that can be important to treatment planning and success. A strong trusting relationship with clients, in which the therapist recognizes the courage required for compliance with treatment, may foster openness and frank discussion of obsessions and neutralization rituals.

PLANNING FOR THE END OF TREATMENT

Maintenance and Relapse Prevention

Hiss, Foa, and Kozak (1994) demonstrated the utility of adding a relapse prevention module at the conclusion of acute treatment for OCD. In an effort to consolidate treatment gains, Hiss et al. saw clients for four 90-

CASE EXAMPLE

Terry is a 26-year-old part-time student who became unable to carry a full course load due to his obsessions about certainty. He worried in a perfectionistic way that partial knowledge was equivalent to confusion or being ignorant. His concerns about imperfect knowledge grew to involve nonacademic themes, including the need to know why certain musicians wrote their lyrics the way they did, or else he could never understand and hence appreciate their music. Terry had intrusive thoughts about his incomplete knowledge. The obsessions were triggered by reading, listening to music, or interacting with others in a social setting. His appraisal was that if he didn't fully and thoroughly understand things (including others' motivations), he would never know anything worthwhile. The ultimate consequence would be that he would be ignored in life. His rituals involved the application of complex rules governing sentence structure.

Treatment involved exposure to reading, listening to music, and speculating on the motives of people illustrated in magazines who were involved in social conversations. Response prevention involved resisting the urge to engage in covert verbalizations involving sentence structure. Progress was slow until it was accidentally revealed that Terry also practiced covert rituals that involved imagining water stream sounds and head positions that felt "just right." When these rituals were identified and resisted, treatment gains followed.

minute sessions, all within a week, immediately following the completion of 3 weeks of intensive ERP. During these sessions, clients received additional training in self-exposure and cognitive restructuring and planned for changes in lifestyle. A comparison group received relaxation for a comparable amount of time. Six months later, the relaxation group showed deterioration of the gains they had made during the acute treatment phase, while the relapse-prevention group maintained their original treatment benefits.

For many clients with OCD, we conceptualize treatment as helping the client to manage the problem, rather than cure it. Many clients with OCD will continue to struggle with obsessive thoughts throughout their lives, but with regular practice of skills for managing the symptoms, they can keep the OCD from taking over their lives again. Accordingly, clients learn to practice ERP on a reduced basis as long as any discomfort is associated with exposure. Likewise, they learn to be vigilant for signs of subtle avoidance, and implement exposure when they are tempted to avoid.

For example, a 44-year-old electrician worried that he might have hit a child while driving through residential areas. He often parked the car and walked back through the streets to check. He would ask any adult he encountered if there had been an accident, and he would phone the police seeking reassurance there had been no hit-and-run accidents reported in that vicinity. After the acute treatment phase, his anxiety level while driving was less than 20. His maintenance plan to preserve these gains was to deliberately drive through residential alleys (which had previously been particularly challenging) without checking once a month. If he experienced anxiety or obsessions, he was prepared to engage in self-directed ERP.

A second front in an OCD maintenance program involves being alert to the development of new obsessive compulsive content areas. Media coverage of viral outbreaks or environmental pollutants may stimulate new obsessions for those with safety concerns, for example. Practitioners should consider simulating such developments during the later stage of acute treatment and during maintenance or follow-up visits as part of preparation for setbacks (e.g., "If this happened, what would you do to manage the obsessions?"). If clients understand their vulnerabilities related to OCD, such as cognitive biases, the contribution of life stressors, and the tendency to focus on the fear itself rather than seeing it as an "OCD problem," then they can predict and prepare for such events. Otherwise, each new fear introduced by the media, friends, or spontaneous realizations can potentially spark a new episode.

A third area of vulnerability affecting relapses in OCD involves the management of life stressors. Clients with OCD are more prone to relapse under conditions of elevated life stress. Further, depression and social isolation appear to be recurrent difficulties with OCD sufferers. These issues should be routinely addressed in treatment as part of preparation for setbacks prior to discharge from the acute phase of treatment (McKay, 1997). To the extent that life stressors can be predicted and coping strategies rehearsed, clients will be better prepared to absorb and recover from such events. Similarly, brief mood management techniques involving problem solving, social activation, and cognitive restructuring will help prepare the client to tolerate and recover from negative mood swings.

Finally, many clients with OCD live in chronic social isolation due to the degree to which OCD has taken over their lives. Building constructive social involvement brings the attendant advantages of positive feedback to enhance self-esteem. In addition, becoming close with others can help give the client some normative understanding of issues related to OCD. For example, becoming a friend's confidant exposes the client to information about what people worry about, how often they worry, and their motivations for certain behaviors. We suggest therapists refer to strategies outlined in chapter 4 on social phobia for help in building a social network.

When to Conclude Treatment

Many treatment programs are necessarily time-limited, which may impact on treatment goals. Thinking in advance about the number of sessions anticipated will allow the therapist to specify goals and strategies. For short treatments, a main focus may be helping the client to prepare for the self-directed maintenance phase of therapy. For example, a client and therapist may decide that the acute phase of treatment involving weekly office visits will target the following treatment goals: (1) a Y-BOCS score of 13 or less; (2) ability to use public toilets at work, have friends or family over for dinner without decontaminating the apartment afterwards, and shower in less than 10 minutes; and (3) return to work without avoiding touching files and office supplies used by co-workers. Thereafter, treatment would shift entirely to self-directed exposure and appraisal challenge, with monthly review sessions with the therapist, which pending satisfactory progress over several months would phase into a maintenance program of six-month visits for ongoing evaluation and treatment strategy adjustment.

Treatment decisions are often influenced by economic realities, client time availability, and client motivation. If these issues are not limiting, degree of functional improvement is the best guide to the allocation of treatment resources in the acute and maintenance phases of treatment. Symptomatic improvement can be assessed by the Y-BOCS. A score of 10 or less generally indicates further treatment is unnecessary. We recommend reassessment using the Y-BOCS every 4 to 6 weeks during the acute treatment stage and again toward the end of the maintenance stage of treatment. A pattern of repeated administrations of the Y-BOCS can provide a useful context when clients reenter therapy after a setback.

Our next chapter involves a dramatic and often tragic anxiety disorder, posttraumatic stress disorder. While it bears perhaps most resemblance to panic disorder, it also has features similar to OCD, such as intrusive reexperiencing images. While past trauma may seem welded in memory, recent work has shown encouraging results in prevention through early intervention.

7 Posttraumatic Stress Disorder

Throughout history, trauma has been a characteristic of life experience, shaping survival and triggering grief and prolonged stress reactions in many individuals. Exposure to adverse and heart-wrenching life experiences is surprisingly common. Such experience with "toxic" events has been characterized as "violent encounters with nature, technology, or humankind" (Norris, 1992, p. 409). Scientists are rapidly gaining a better understanding of the range, shape, and duration of response to trauma, including mediators of individual differences in response to such events. Posttraumatic stress disorder (PTSD) shares many symptoms with other anxiety disorders, such as avoidance and intrusive thoughts, although some typical PTSD symptoms are unique among anxiety disorders, including flashbacks and nightmares. Basic research into the nature of this disorder, as well as an accumulating body of treatment evaluation studies, provides encouraging direction to practitioners coping with the inevitable volume of PTSD cases.

DESCRIPTION AND CONCEPTUALIZATION

Phenomenology

The hallmark of traumatic experiences is their ability to engender such reactions as shock, horror, disbelief, helplessness, and anxiety. Simply being exposed to horrific events does not automatically trigger PTSD. The focus is necessarily on the *reactions* to traumatic events rather than on the events themselves. Immediately following a traumatic event, survivors commonly experience an acute stress response. The intensity of this reaction will depend on several factors, including the severity and persistence of the traumatic event, the extent of exposure (or proximity to "ground zero"), and the meaning and personal significance the event holds for the individual. The natural course of reaction to trauma is for the individual to adapt and for the stress response to resolve with time. For some victims, however, symptoms are chronic.

Because the degree to which an event is considered to be traumatic is somewhat subject to individual interpretation, a comprehensive and objective list of traumatic events cannot be constructed (Michelson, June, Vives, Testa, & Marchione, 1998). Potent events capable of such effects include war horrors, natural disasters like destructive floods, hurricanes, or earthquakes, major motor vehicle accidents, violent physical assault, torture, hostage takings, explosions, large fires, prisoner of war experiences, terrorist attacks, and sudden confrontation with death, mutilation, or dismemberment. Any grossly shocking and frightening unexpected event, even if it is only observed or threatened, is capable of producing an acute stress reaction which may proceed to PTSD, although not necessarily immediately following the acute stress reaction.

The unfolding of PTSD involves the following temporal sequence: (1) direct exposure to an event that either caused, or had the potential to cause, death or serious injury; (2) a reaction involving intense fear, helplessness, or horror; and (3) the development of three characteristic clusters of symptoms.

The first cluster involves *reexperiencing*, mainly in the form of persistent nightmares and flashbacks reflecting vivid parts or "highlights" of the traumatic event. These intrusive memories are accompanied by distressing emotional responses consistent with those of the original reaction, such as fear, shock, helplessness, and anxiety. Furthermore, the details and personal significance of the event, as well as these emotional reactions, usually foster additional secondary emotional responses, such as guilt, hopelessness, depression, anger, irritability, and feelings of vulnerability.

The second cluster of characteristic symptoms involves *avoidance* of reminders of the event and *numbing* (e.g., psychogenic amnesia, dissociation). The third cluster of PTSD symptoms concerns *hyperarousal*, including hypervigilance, impaired concentration, exaggerated startle response, and insomnia.

Sidebar 7-1

CASE EXAMPLE

Ruth is a 44-year-old nurse who was working the night shift in a community hospital emergency room. At 6:45 a.m. she looked through the window of the locked quiet room and noted the large, young schizophrenic man who was brought in the night before in a disruptive state, now apparently sleeping. The shift was thinly staffed, and rather than wait for a co-worker to return from a ward and accompany her, as protocol required, she decided to take in his oral medications, wake him, and leave. Upon her entry, the patient jumped up and ran out the door and down the hall. Ruth pursued him, calling his name calmly and asking him to come back. Several hospital employees arrived for the 7:00 A.M. shift, oblivious as to what was going on, and went on their way. Alone again, the patient turned on Ruth and started to deliver karate kicks to her midbody. She ran back to the emergency room with him in pursuit. He caught her, threw her down behind the counter and began to punch and then choke her. The only other person on shift ran to get one of the doctors. Ruth was saved by a police officer in a wheelchair awaiting treatment for a broken ankle, who had heard the commotion from the waiting room and pulled the patient off her as the patient was yelling, "You're dead, bitch" to Ruth.

Four months later, upon presentation for treatment, Ruth had not returned to work. She complained of frequent, involuntary, and disturbing "mental replays" of segments of the traumatic event, and she could not drive within the neighborhood of the hospital or watch hospital shows on TV. In addition, she found that her ability to concentrate was gone, that she was hypervigilant, and she felt oddly aloof from others. She also led a sheltered life, avoiding public places and men, unless she was accompanied by her husband.

Like motor vehicle accidents and rape, the above example of assault represents a relatively frequent elicitor of PTSD in western societies, while war and natural disasters are perhaps relatively more common provocateurs in third world societies. Common to the experience of traumatic events that lead to PTSD is intense fear deriving from one's helplessness to prevent real or threatened physical injury or death, along with a shattering of one's expectations about how life should be. Powerful events that are relatively unpredictable and uncontrollable, characteristics typical of natural and technological disasters, are capable of evoking a posttraumatic response (Meichenbaum, 1994).

There are surprisingly large individual differences in response to adversity, making it clear that the severity of the trauma is not the only determinant of the distress that follows. Why do some individuals demonstrate unusual resilience and ability to cope in the face of objectively terrible and terrifying events, while others become defeated, disorganized, and distressed when exposed to milder adversity? Bowman (1997) suggests attending to preexisting factors, rather than basing practice on "the exaggerated idea of the power of life events" (p. vii). Such preexisting factors as personality style and beliefs may mediate the response to objective adversity. For example, the annals of war contain copious accounts of soldiers who feel relieved by having received serious, but not life-threatening injuries, since this ensures removal to a hospital and perceived safety from death. As Malt (1994) points out, "the majority of traumatized persons respond in a controlled and unremarkable way" (p. 108).

Diagnostic Trends

Despite only recently being included as a category in diagnostic classification systems, PTSD is an old phenomenon that has been described by many terms and labels, particularly those relating to battle conditions, such as "shell shock" and "hysteria." PTSD was officially introduced into the psychiatric nomenclature in the third edition of the DSM. In this edition, the diagnosis required a recognizable but extraordinary stressor that would evoke significant and persistent symptoms of distress in almost anyone. In DSM-III-R, PTSD was described in terms of the three clusters of symptoms described earlier, persisting for more than a month, in reaction to an "event that is outside the range of usual human experience and that would be markedly distressing to almost anyone" (American Psychiatric Association, 1987). In DSM-IV (American Psychiatric Association, 1994), the description of the features of trauma have become more specific, pointing to features of the traumatic event itself, such as events involving "actual or threatened death or serious injury, or a threat to the physical integrity of self or others" (p. 427). The criteria have also been expanded to include the *perception* of threat.

Another change in the DSM-IV account of reaction to trauma involves the new diagnostic category, Acute Stress Disorder. The introduction of this diagnostic category underscores the variability in reaction to trauma as a function of the persistence of a stress reaction following the event. The temporal criterion for Acute Stress Disorder requires that "the disturbance lasts for a minimum of 2 days and a maximum of 4 weeks and occurs within 4 weeks of the traumatic event" (p. 432). That is, Acute Stress Disorder begins and resolves within a month. In contrast, PTSD cannot be diagnosed within the first month after the traumatic event. If the symptoms persist beyond one month after the traumatic event and meet the other criteria for PTSD (very similar to those of Acute Stress Disorder), then the diagnosis converts to PTSD. Even within a diagnosis of PTSD, the DSM-IV (American Psychiatric Association, 1994) provides for specification of the timing of the response, as follows: *acute* (symptom duration of 1 to 3 months), *chronic* (symptom duration longer than 3 months), and *delayed onset* (symptoms emerge at least 6 months after exposure to the event).

As clinical attention and experimental investigation focus on PTSD, diagnostic descriptions are evolving rapidly. Perhaps the most obvious issue having both practical and conceptual implications involves the change in the sort of traumatic experiences considered to be likely to provoke a posttraumatic response. In DSM-III-R the trauma had to be outside the realm of usual human experience, yet so many of the traumas likely to cause PTSD are themselves relatively common (e.g., Resnick, Kilpatrick, & Lipovsky, 1991). However, if this criterion were expanded to accommodate more common traumas, some suggest the concept of trauma as a stress-response syndrome would be weakened (March, 1992). Although the nature of the trauma evoking PTSD in DSM-IV has become more specific, the problem is not resolved, especially now that the perception of threat is included to satisfy the requirements for a trauma leading to a diagnosis of PTSD. The question is what degree of focus should be placed on the type of traumatic event required to evoke a response that is labeled as PTSD. DSM-IV has signaled a move away from a focus on the objective characteristics of the traumatic event.

Two lines of inquiry are helpful in addressing the important issue of whether it is the power of the event or the sufferer's interpretation of the event that is most salient in causing PTSD. The first approach involves a review of exposure rates to various traumas experienced within the general population and the distribution of probabilities of PTSD forming as a function of such exposure across trauma types. The second approach is to investigate the role of individual differences in accounting for the development of PTSD, with the intensity of the event considered to be secondary (the "eye of the beholder" hypothesis). Both of these propositions are further addressed later in this chapter.

Prevalence and Course

The most comprehensive source of information currently available on population rates of PTSD comes from the National Comorbidity Survey undertaken in the United States (Kessler, Sonnega, Bromet, Hughes, & Nelson, 1995). The lifetime prevalence rate for PTSD was found to be 7.8%. Women were more than twice as likely (10.4%) as men (5%) to have a lifetime history of PTSD. The National Comorbidity Survey assessed the prevalence of exposure to trauma, regardless of the presence or absence of subsequent PTSD states, and found that 60.7% of men and 51.2% of women reported lifetime exposure to at least one traumatic event. Most of these traumas involved witnessing others being badly injured or killed, exposure to fire or a natural disaster, or being involved in a life-threatening accident. More men than women experienced these three types of trauma, as well as physical attacks, military combat, and threatened assault with a weapon, whereas more women experienced rape and sexual molestation.

The National Comorbidity Survey showed that some traumatic events are more strongly associated with PTSD than others. For example, 65% of men and 46% of women who reported rape as their most upsetting trauma developed PTSD in response to the rape. Similar to other studies, the National Comorbidity Survey found that almost all of the events evoking PTSD were fairly common. However, among the traumatic events reported as "the most distressing" in the National Comorbidity Survey, there were large variations in the probability of subsequently developing PTSD. As a result, it is difficult to categorize stressful events as objectively traumatic or nontraumatic based on these data (Kessler et al., 1995).

As indicated earlier, the National Comorbidity Survey showed that most people experienced posttraumatic symptoms immediately following the most distressing life events. Over time, survivors tended to gradually experience fewer and fewer stress symptoms, with the greatest rate of improvement occurring within the first 12 months. Although improvement was more gradual thereafter, the impact of the trauma continued to diminish for some 6 years after the onset of symptoms. The average length of PTSD symptoms was 64 months for those who did not receive treatment and 36 months for those who did. Fully one-third of those with PTSD in this survey never fully recovered, and 88% of men and 79% of women with a lifetime history of PTSD also experienced at least one other mental disorder during their lifetimes.

The prevalence rates of PTSD reported in the National Comorbidity Survey are similar to those of several other studies also using DSM-III-R criteria (Breslau, Davis, Andreski, & Peterson, 1991; Resnick, Kilpatrick, Dansky, Saunders, & Best, 1993), but they are higher than surveys using DSM-III criteria (Davidson, Hughes, Blazer, & George, 1991; Helzer, Robins, & McEvoy, 1987) or DSM-IV criteria (Stein, Walker, Hazen, & Forde, 1997). Nonetheless, the following conclusions are warranted.

1. Traumatic events are common.
2. Only a minority of individuals who experience a traumatic event go on to develop PTSD.
3. One-third of those with PTSD experience a chronic course of the disorder, regardless of treatment.
4. Treatment is associated with a markedly shorter course of the disorder.
5. Individuals with PTSD often have other comorbid psychiatric diagnoses.

THEORETICAL PERSPECTIVES

A defining feature of PTSD is intrusive imagery involving reexperiencing of the traumatic event. Research in information processing has helped to explain the role of cognitive and emotional factors in memory for understanding both normal and pathological responses to trauma. Intrusive imagery is thought to activate and promote memories of the trauma (van der Kolk, 1996), which incite physiological arousal (locus ceruleus and peripheral sympathetic nervous system activation) and behavioral responding. Traumatic intrusive memories can be expressed during both conscious awareness and sleep, can involve a variety of sensory modalities, and are characterized as intense, vivid, frightening, and uncontrollable. A number of theories have been developed to account for such pervasive effects, and we will briefly describe several of the most comprehensive ones.

Lang's (1979; 1994) bio-informational theory of emotional imagery proposes that emotional memory is arranged in memory networks consisting of perceptual, reactive, and interpretive units, any one of which can activate the network when inputs resemble stored representations in the network (Lang, 1994). In plain language, emotional memory consists of interconnected information about the characteristics of the emotional situation, the individual's reaction to the situation, and the meaning of the situation to the person. When the person later notices something reminiscent of any of these cues, the emotional memory is recalled. When the memory network is activated in this way, by stimuli that match the individual's cognitive, behavioral, or neurophysiological representations of trauma, the network is believed to be strengthened. In this way, the threshold for future network activation is lowered, making it easier for the individual to access memories of the trauma.

Such emotional memory networks are believed to interface with subcortical motivational circuits in the brain. "These are the same subcortical motivational circuits activated by unconditioned appetite and aversive stimuli" (Lang, 1994), and they provide preferential access to neural structures responsible for sympathetic nervous system responding. Furthermore, because emotional memories are believed to activate the sympathetic nervous system through subcortical motivation structures, they are resistant to extinction. van der Kolk (1996) observes that this may account for why memories can be inactive for long periods of time and then be reactivated by stress. Stress may activate emotional memory networks, which in turn provoke intrusive memories.

Applying Lang's (1979) framework to pathological anxiety, Foa, Steketee, and Rothbaum (1989) conceptualized traumatic memory as a fear structure characterized by a large number of response elements relevant to danger and safety. Foa et al. explain the persistence of intrusive memories within this theoretical framework. First, the avoidance that often accompanies intense anxiety makes habituation to trauma cues unlikely. Second, the trauma-related memory structure is believed to increase in size as the victim's preoccupation with safety leads to an ever-expanding assimilation of safety and danger information. In such a scenario, a wider variety of cues can activate the fear network. Finally, the size of the network and relatively low threshold for activation render the trauma-related memories highly accessible (Foa et al., 1989).

In a similar but more comprehensive model, Chemtob, Roitblat, Hamada, Carslon, and Twentyman (1988) propose that information relevant to emotion, cognition, and behavior is processed simultaneously at various sites within a hierarchical structure of neuronal networks, ranging from those that represent muscle movements to those representing more abstract functions, including expectations and goals. As in Lang's theory (1979; 1994), networks are thought to be activated by information that matches elements within the memory structure. In the Chemtob et al. model, threat-related information and arousal receives priority processing and can effect pervasive and chronic influence throughout associated neurophysiological systems, as the "threat-arousal node" works at the highest level in the system. Consequently, trauma survivors are prone to interpret even ambiguous situations as threatening, thereby activating threat-arousal, and hence intrusive, trauma-related imagery. In other words, another consequence of such a significant threat bias in trauma survivors is that many false positive threat interpretations are available to evoke intrusions from memory. In this regard, PTSD sufferers differ from normal individuals looking at the same scene, in that they scan with great care for signs of danger and if they find anything close to danger (i.e., a "match" in their memory network), they are more likely to interpret the situation as dangerous.

These information-processing theories (see Witvliet, 1997 for detailed review) integrate both biological and psychological research findings to account for the cognitive phenomena observed in PTSD. Indeed, the endurance of trauma-related memories in PTSD is striking. In one study, women seeking help for lingering problems related to childhood sexual abuse reported that the trauma occurred 20–30 years previously. At the time of the study, 87% of the women met criteria for PTSD related to their experiences (Rodrieguez, Ryan, Vande Kemp, & Foy, 1997). Similarly, some war veterans have endured PTSD symptoms for many decades. There is not a satisfactory answer as to why some war veterans develop PTSD while others adjust to traumatic war experiences, although indirect evidence suggests that critical developmental conditions, notably family instability and earlier trauma exposure, predisposed both male and female Vietnam veterans to PTSD (King, King, Foy, & Gudanowski, 1996).

Once sensitized by such early experiences, early trauma victims presumably develop the cognitive biases that predispose them to attend to new threatening events and interpret them as dangerous. This tendency may contribute to the individual differences observed in reaction to trauma exposure, in that the same "dose" of traumatic exposure may be processed differently. It may also account for the frequently observed cumulative effect phenomenon in the development of PTSD, wherein serial exposure to disturbing stressors are unremarkable, one at a time, but subsequently an often relatively mild stressor can trigger full PTSD. For example, police or firemen often attend fatal shootings, motor vehicle accidents, industrial accidents, personal threats to safety, and fires. They become accustomed to death, dismembered body parts, and the anguish of family members. While adjustment to each of these events individually is satisfactory and while exposure to such events over the course of one to three decades seldom causes significant adjustment problems, PTSD can be triggered by a relatively mild stressor. In this case, stressors from years ago seem to combine and acquire traumatic significance.

Typically we may think of clients with PTSD as having disturbed memory function related to the horrific aspects of their traumatic experiences, but research on autobiographical memory disturbance in combat-related PTSD has disclosed that clients' memory deficits extend to positive information about themselves in general. McNally, Litz, Prassas, Shin, and Weathers (1994) found that Vietnam combat veterans with PTSD, relative to combat veterans without PTSD, had more difficulty retrieving specific personal memories in response to positive and neutral cue words. These effects were especially pronounced after the veterans had been exposed to reminders of traumatic events by means of a combat video clip. McNally et al. speculated that the veterans may have had trouble recalling personal memories because their preoccupation with intrusive recollections of trauma may consume a disproportionate share of cognitive resources, disrupting other types of thinking. McNally et al. further conjectured that negative attributes dominate the self-representations of people with PTSD, thereby impeding access to positive self-representations.

To evaluate these ideas about self-representation in PTSD, McNally, Lasko, Macklin, and Pitman (1995) asked Vietnam combat veterans to recall a specific personal memory in response to both positive and negative adjectives used as cues. Veterans with PTSD had more difficulty retrieving positive autobiographical memories than did veterans without PTSD. The veterans with PTSD recalled a lower proportion of positive memories about themselves and took longer to produce their first memory. This deficiency in memory recall may facilitate the maintenance of a focus on PTSD symptoms by restricting the availability of positive, counterbalancing memories and by impeding one's ability to envision the future in a positive, adaptive way (McNally et al., 1995).

The three informational theories described above all hypothesize a fear structure, or its equivalent, of neuronal networks involved in emotional processing of fearful information. These theories suggest that modification of fear structure reactivity can occur through two channels: habituation and alteration of meaning (Foa & Kozak, 1986). As discussed in previous chapters, habituation is a physiological process dependent upon exposure, wherein repeated stimulus exposure (e.g., recalling traumatic memories or viewing pictures depicting the traumatic event) leads to diminished emotional reaction to the stimulus. Virtually all theorists agree that fear structures are developed and maintained, in large part, by the implications traumatic experiences hold for the distributed meaning systems of the mind (Horowitz & Reidbord, 1992). As a result, treatments that address the meaning of traumatic experiences and their effect on self-representations are believed to be strategically positioned to modify fear-induced distortions and help restore perspective and a sense of control.

So far the basis for individual differences in the development of PTSD has not been convincingly explained. Ford, Fisher, and Larson (1997) have found that war veterans with PTSD responded differentially to treatment components for PTSD depending upon their object relations test scores. This study is described later in this chapter and represents an initial finding that indicates client characteristics and treatment components may be matched on an empirical basis.

ASSESSMENT

There are a variety of purposes for clinical assessment of trauma victims. The clinician needs to formulate a diagnosis, evaluate specific symptoms, evaluate contextual factors, and plan treatment and the ongoing evaluation of progress.

Diagnosis

Diagnosis of PTSD requires careful attention due to the possibility of multiple trauma experiences, current comorbidity, shared characteristics with other Axis I disorders, and the potential for litigation. There are a number of structured clinical interviews available to the clinician to help in determining diagnostic status. Well-known and frequently used structured clinical interview protocols include the Structured Clinical Interview for DSM-IV (SCID; First, Gibbon, Spitzer, & Williams, 1997), Anxiety Disorders Interview Schedule—Revised (ADIS-IV; Brown, DiNardo, & Barlow, 1994), and the Diagnostic Interview Schedule (DIS-III-R; Robins, Helzer, Cottler, & Goldring, 1988).

We find the ADIS-IV particularly useful in discriminating between the various anxiety disorders and assessing diagnostic status of disorders frequently found to be comorbid with PTSD. Also, the interrater reliability of the ADIS is generally good (Blanchard, Kolb, Gerardi, Ryan, & Pallmayer, 1986), which adds diagnostic confidence. Such structured interview schedules are a requirement in research settings, but they may not be very practical for solo practice clinicians because the time that is required to administer them makes them costly. Nevertheless, we recommend that practicing clinicians become familiar with several of these structured interviews and use them occasionally to sharpen or maintain diagnostic skills.

Differentiating PTSD from other Axis I disorders, particularly generalized anxiety disorder (GAD), panic disorder with agoraphobia, and major depressive disorder (MDD), can be challenging for several reasons. A number of symptoms in these disorders overlap (e.g., avoidance), and symptoms of other disorders may be reactive to earlier PTSD symptoms. For example, PTSD symptoms such as avoidance and withdrawal can provoke an episode of depression. Keane, Taylor, and Penk (1997) asked experienced clinicians to rate the degree to which 90 common symptoms characterized PTSD, GAD, and MDD. They found clinicians accurately distinguished these three diagnostic categories, although clinicians varied significantly in their ratings of symptom intensity in response to vignettes, depending upon the clinician's age and personal experience with trauma. Younger clinicians rated PTSD symptoms more intensely than older clinicians, and combat-experienced clinicians rated PTSD symptoms more mildly than did noncombat experienced clinicians.

Nonetheless, clinicians reliably recognized symptoms *unique* to PTSD, namely reexperiencing traumatic events (awake and in sleep), chronic heightened arousal, avoidance of recollections of traumatic experiences, and anger and frustration over having experienced the life-threatening events in the first place (Keane et al., 1997). Clinicians distinguished PTSD from

MDD by degree of engagement in current activities unrelated to past trauma memories. PTSD was distinguished from GAD primarily on the basis of the scope of stimuli responsible for physiological reactivity. PTSD was viewed as related to specific memories of past traumas, whereas GAD was characterized by anxiety in response to a broad range of stimuli. Individuals with PTSD and those with panic with agoraphobia both experience autonomic reactivity, avoidance, and acute episodes of intense anxiety, which can confuse diagnosis. In our experience, such confusion occurs most often when a client presents with panic complaints and does not volunteer information about past trauma experiences. For this reason, it is prudent to explicitly inquire about traumatic experiences when clients present with this symptom profile.

The clinical interview with PTSD clients requires special sensitivity due to the often tragic details of the trauma and the client's desire to avoid trauma-related memories. Resnick, Kilpatrick, and Lipovsky (1991) recommend a nonjudgmental and supportive approach in taking sexual assault histories. Traumatized clients often use metaphors to describe their reactions to trauma events. These metaphors frequently need to be clarified in order to understand the problem. During treatment, new metaphors can be generated that represent expressions of treatment goals. Meichenbaum (1994) offers an extensive list of metaphors extracted from audiotapes of sessions with PTSD clients, a subset of which appears in table 7.1. Such expressions illustrate the need to clarify the meaning the metaphor holds for the client and to attain a behavioral description of the phenomenon. Clinicians can ask questions like, "When you feel that way, what do you do differently?" and "If that were true, what do you think would happen?" and "When do these thoughts and feelings come and go, how long do they last?"

Estimates of exposure to crime or other traumatic events consistent with PTSD diagnostic criteria are high (U.S. data) and range from 40–70% of the general public (Breslau et al., 1991; Norris, 1992; Resnick, Kilpatrick et al., 1993). A number of self-report screening instruments have been developed that can serve as the first of a two-part assessment procedure. For example, Resnick, Best, Kilpatrick, Freedy, and Falsetti (1993) have developed a brief self-report screening measure specific to crime victimization, including sexual assault. These and similar measures can direct the clinician to a detailed clinical interview to fully elucidate the trauma events and their effects.

Assessment of Symptoms

As discussed earlier, diagnostic criteria for symptoms of PTSD are organized into three groups: (1) intrusions, (2) hyperarousal, and (3) avoidance and numbing. Because symptoms are not always in agreement with one another (Blanchard, Hickling, Taylor, Loos, & Gerardi, 1994), it is possible that they represent different mechanisms. Taylor, Kuch, Koch, Crockett, and

Table 7.1 Client Metaphors Reflecting Dimensions of PTSD Experience
and Healing

Dimension of Experience	Clients' Metaphors
Affective State (emotional sensitivity)	Emotional yo-yo. A pendulum gone mad, swinging wildly. Short fuse. Low boiling point. On hyperdrive. Over the edge, emotional overload, emotional meltdown. Overcome by creepy sensations. Emotional fault-line. Emotionally blind-sided, emotional quagmire.
Feeling Blocked and Trapped (psychic numbing)	Emotional watchfulness. Emotional shut down. Emotional anesthesia. I carry the burden of conscience. My heart and mind have been severed. My mind is dead, fragmented. Emotionally neutered. Zombie-like. My feelings are frozen. Empty vase. End of my rope.
Intrusive Ideation	My thoughts visit me, show up. Cognitive baggage I carry. Like a gusher of ideation. Stop me in my tracks. Indelible images. Crystallized experience. Engraved. An imprint of death. Flashbulb memory. Malignant thoughts. I want to vomit this out. Detoxify my memories.
Sense of Personal Loss	Hole in myself, not complete, a loser. Life is a shambles. A bottomless pit. Live in no man's land between a past and no future. Time slide. Raped my unconscious. Emotional blackmail. Stole my childhood. Cheated me out of my childhood. A meaning vacuum. A void. Sounds of emptiness. Sounds of a soul hurt.
Characteristics of Self (identity) and the Situation	Crippled, phony, dirty, chameleon, Zelig-like character. I carry the stick of Cain. Untouchable, abandoned, skin crawl. Deadened—no guideposts. Just a vulnerable object. Drowning in a sea of chaos. Doormat, garbage pail. An abuser within me.
Past Abusive Events (secrets)	Skeletons in my closet. Memories are not digestible. Malignant (toxic) memories. Unfinished business. Ghosts of old terrors come back to haunt me. My story of abuse was buried, swept under the rug.

(continued)

Table 7.1 Continued

Dimension of Experience	Clients' Metaphors
Expressions of Treatment Goals (hopes for change)	Resolve the hurt. Accept the scars. Move beyond the legacy of my past.
	Doing this for the little girl/boy I used to be.
	I want to be the person I was before all this happened.
	Make peace with the past. Prevent this from happening to others.
	Move from victim to survivor. Move beyond the impasse.
	Join the world, join life. Turn the corner. Find a new path.
	I want to influence the legacies I leave.
	I want to be a gardener, not just the florist. I want to steer a vessel of my own making.
	I want to salvage something positive.
	Trauma can be a catalyst for change.

From D. Meichenbaum (1994), *A clinical handbook/practical therapist manual for assessing and treating adults with post-traumatic stress disorder (PTSD)* (Waterloo, Ontario: Institute Press), pp. 112–116. Reprinted with permission.

Passey (1998) examined the factor structure of PTSD symptoms among a sample of motor vehicle accident victims and a sample of United Nations peacekeepers deployed in Bosnia. In both samples, two correlated factors were identified: (1) intrusions and avoidance, and (2) hyperarousal and numbing. Symptoms from both factors loaded on a single, higher order factor. The authors suggest that intrusive thoughts result in avoidance, and hyperarousal leads to numbing. The authors also speculate that there may be three mechanisms underlying PTSD. First, a general mechanism may account for most PTSD symptoms. Two specific mechanisms may account for the factors of intrusions/avoidance and hyperarousal/numbing. This factor structure provides a conceptual basis by which to view dimensions of PTSD symptoms by prompting a convenient way to think about symptom categories and their hypothesized relationship (intrusions → avoidance, and hyperarousal → numbing).

Several psychometric scales assess PTSD symptoms, some of which are general, while others are specific to the type of trauma. The widely used Clinician Administered PTSD Scale (CAPS; Blake et al., 1990) assesses both symptom frequency and intensity. This instrument provides a thorough assessment following positive diagnosis. Appendix A provides information on how to obtain this scale.

The Impact of Events Scale (IES; Horowitz, Wilner, & Alvarez, 1979) is a short, 15-item, self-report scale (see Appendix A) which contains avoidance and cognitive intrusion subscales. Items on the scale are assigned numerical values depending on how often the client has experienced each item in the preceding week, where "not at all" = 0 points, "rarely" = 1, "sometimes" = 3, and "often" = 5 points. The points are then summed for a total score. Horowitz et al. report total scores for 32 trauma victims; the mean was 43.7 (±17.2) before treatment and 24.3 (±17.8) after treatment. Another popular self-report measure is the PTSD Diagnostic Scale (PSS; Foa, Riggs, Dancu, & Rothbaum, 1993). This is a comprehensive, 49-item scale that provides symptom severity scores and PTSD diagnostic status based on DSM-IV criteria. The PDS is available from National Computer Systems (NCS) in Minnetonka, Minnesota. Both of these scales have good psychometric qualities.

A number of PTSD self-report measures evaluate PTSD symptoms specific to a single type of trauma (e.g., sexual assault). Two excellent scales address PTSD symptoms stemming from combat and rape. The Mississippi Scale for Combat-Related Post-Traumatic Stress Disorder (M-PTSD; Keane, Caddell, & Taylor, 1988) is a 35-item questionnaire that evaluates the full domain of PTSD symptoms required for diagnostic determination. The M-PTSD measures three dimensions: (1) intrusive reexperiencing/numbing-avoidance; (2) anger/lability; and (3) social alienation. This is a psychometrically sophisticated instrument (McFall, Smith, Mackay, & Tarver, 1990) that discriminates well between combat veterans with PTSD and substance-abusing combat veterans without PTSD. The Rape Aftermath Symptom Test (RAST; Kilpatrick, 1988) uses 70 items to evaluate rape related psychological symptoms and potentially fearful stimuli and can be completed in about 15–20 minutes. The RAST is useful in predicting chronic PTSD among rape victims, and has good psychometric qualities (Foa, 1998).

In summary, diagnosis is established based upon a sensitive clinical interview that inquires about all features of the trauma experience, previous experiences with trauma, the meaning such experience has to the individual, and the consequences the trauma has brought about. The presence of PTSD needs to be differentiated from other anxiety disorders and depression, which may develop subsequently to the experience of trauma. PTSD may be prevented when clients are amnesic for an accident or assault in the case of a head injury (Mayou, Bryant, & Duthie, 1993), as they have no recollection of the event. Unfortunately, PTSD frequently follows regardless of amnesia, due to aftermath experiences such as physical disability, pain, and compensation battles (Koch & Taylor, 1995).

Comprehensive exploration of interpretive meaning and related assumptions and beliefs can help identify depression, panic and agoraphobia, and GAD, which can all follow trauma, as well as laying the foundation for treatment planning. The clinical interview allows the clinician to establish the functional relationship among symptoms, which, together with knowledge about their meaning, will help in the selection and sequencing of treatment. This includes the assessment of the impact of related events that follow from the trauma as these sequelae can play a role in the development of PTSD symptoms.

Mr. S. is a 36-year-old cameraman who had been flying in an ultralight aircraft as the sole passenger taking video pictures for his client, a flying school. Structural failure of a wing resulted in an uncontrolled crash into a lake. Mr. S. experienced facial lacerations, lost all his front teeth, and received a back injury. Originally trapped in the sinking aircraft, he was able to escape, although the pilot died. Mr. S. developed an acute stress disorder, which evolved into PTSD, as a result of this accident. His back injury and facial lacerations healed without difficulty. However, the responsible insurance agency contested his demands for quality restorative dental work, which left him feeling humiliated, frustrated, and demoralized. Apparently he had received compliments on the appearance of his teeth over the years and regarded them as a critical feature of his positive social presentation. He was embarrassed by his low quality "false teeth," which he tried to hide, and he felt abandoned by his insurance company with whom he was still in litigation some 2 years after the accident.

This case illustrates the range of conditions that can influence posttraumatic adjustment. These conditions require continuous and rigorous assessment, in their own right as part of comprehensive treatment, but also because they effect a client's ability to engage in PTSD treatment. We have found that trauma victims who develop PTSD and comorbid disorders such as MDD, and who have physical complaints which are subject to ongoing investigations and treatment, along with legal battles, are frequently too exhausted to participate in treatment. Regularly reviewing the treatment plan seems to help clients maintain overall perspective and to see linkages and causal relationships between their symptoms, stressors, coping, and treatment efforts.

Assessing Contextual Factors

Contextual factors can influence the course of treatment. They may become apparent during the initial assessment or later as they interfere with treatment progress. Initial assessment of contextual factors facilitates case formulation. We recommend the following contextual factors be assessed for treatment of PTSD.

Social Support

The range, availability, and quality of social support should be explored, noted, and promoted, as the perception of poor social support, due either to its pretrauma absence or loss following trauma, is normally associated with poorer recovery (Solomon, 1986). Social support can foster a sense of acceptance, approval, self-confidence, and personal effectiveness which are thought to improve one's coping capacity (Sarason, 1994). The relationship between social support and improvement in PTSD may not be linear in the case of women, as there is evidence that too much social support may be experienced as a burden while coping with a traumatic event (see Meichenbaum, 1994, p. 189).

Cognitive Distortions

General measures of cognitive errors and irrational beliefs have failed to distinguish between PTSD and normal subjects (Muran & Motta, 1993). This is no surprise as cognitive distortions related to PTSD are typically quite specific. Foa and Rothbaum (1998) hypothesize that two negative schemata characterize emotional processing underlying the psychopathology of PTSD. First, "The world is completely dangerous." Second, "I am totally inept." Such beliefs require full exploration, elaboration, and documentation in terms of rationale and exemplars, to provide the practitioner with a basis for cognitive challenges and behavioral experiments during treatment.

Another form of cognitive distortion occurs when clients assume traumatic intrusions are historically accurate revisualizations of traumatic events. Merckelbach et al. (1998) found that a substantial proportion of victims or witnesses to a recent trauma showed exaggerated recollection of the traumatic incident, in keeping with a worst case scenario. Further, these exaggerated intrusions were more prone to flashback qualities, including uncontrollability, strong negative affect, bodily sensations, and ease of being triggered by external cues. Accordingly, prudent assessment includes a contrast of traumatic intrusions and a detailed historical account, to detect potential discrepancies in accuracy.

Avoidant Coping

Clinical investigators have found that avoidant coping styles predict posttraumatic distress in victims of bank robbery (Kamphuis & Emmelkamp, 1988) and posttraumatic intrusive thoughts in motor vehicle accident survivors (Bryant & Harvey, 1995). As with several of the anxiety disorders we have discussed thus far in this book, care should be taken to create a detailed hierarchy of stimuli, situations, and places that produce anxiety and avoidance. Many hierarchy themes and items will be obvious, as in the case of circumstances surrounding a traumatic car accident. However, avoidance can be very subtle. Failing to identify and incorporate subtle avoidance into the treatment plan may impair recovery.

Thoughts and images that directly relate to the trauma are one class of avoided stimuli that are often overlooked. The most elusive avoidance takes the form of abandoned interests, restricted activities, and a lack of engagement in many life goals and plans. These avoidance areas may not be routinely identified by the clinician if the client does not consider them to be problematic or related to the PTSD theme. As a result, it is desirable to be proactive by probing for signs of avoidance in these areas. One way to do this is to explain how subtle avoidance can work in PTSD and then enlist the client's assistance in carefully considering pre- and posttrauma functioning in several domains (see figure 7.1). It is often helpful to ask clients to have a knowledgeable family member, or partner, assist in the discovery of avoidance behavior.

Multiple Trauma History

Many clients with PTSD report a history of multiple traumas. Torture, childhood sexual abuse, and combat, for example, are often characterized by a series of discrete traumatic events, any one of which could cause PTSD. Other individuals with PTSD have a history of trauma that is unrelated to their presenting trauma. These trauma themes usually involve childhood sexual or physical abuse, or marital physical abuse. Such prior traumas are often unreported by clients, but nonetheless render them vulnerable and play a significant role in shaping their views of themselves and the world. Mueser et al. (1998) reported that in a population of 275 patients with severe mental illness (e.g., schizophrenia and bipolar disorder), 98% had lifetime exposure to at least one traumatic event. Further, 43% of these patients met DSM-IV criteria for PTSD, although only 2% had this diagnosis in their charts. This study illustrates the concentration of trauma experience in severe mental illness, as well as how remarkably the diagnosis of PTSD can go undetected when it is comorbid with a more obvious mental disorder.

The second notable configuration of multiple trauma exposure involves the presentation of an acute stress reaction that proceeds to PTSD diagnostic status, but which was triggered by a relatively minor traumatic stressor. Although previous stressors within the same theme (e.g., war, rape, motor vehicle accidents) may not have induced a PTSD response, they can have a cumulative effect in some individuals, resulting in PTSD triggered by a relatively minor traumatic stressor. Hence, the careful practitioner will ask about lifetime exposure to traumatic events in general, rather than relying on clients to volunteer such information.

Occupational Adjustment

Depending upon the nature of the trauma theme and severity of the PTSD, clients' occupational adjustment may be affected. When clients are occupationally impaired due to trauma experiences, helping the client return to normal work status may at times involve the practitioner acting as an advocate for the client with the client's employer. For example, in the case of employees missing work due to illness, employers often use a "fit for work" criterion, which means employees are considered able to assume their *full* job responsibilities unless they are considered to be temporarily disabled. This all or nothing approach to employment is often too difficult for those

Please carefully consider and then list examples of things that you used to be able to do easily in each of the following areas <u>before</u> your traumatic experience, followed by how things have <u>now</u> changed.

Thoughts	BEFORE
	NOW
Activities	BEFORE
	NOW
Interests	BEFORE
	NOW
Discussion topics	BEFORE
	NOW
Places	BEFORE
	NOW
Other	BEFORE
	NOW

Figure 7.1 Worksheet for Assessing Avoidance.

suffering from work-related trauma. As an alternative, a negotiated graduated return-to-work program can allow the client to use return to work as an
exposure hierarchy. This request will be foreign to many supervisors and
may require the approval of the human resources representative, who will
want to know a detailed plan for the graduated return-to-work. Union representatives may also need to be consulted. Many return-to-work situations
are regulated by collective agreements that do not address the need for gradual return to work, except in the case of physical disability.

Because of the potential for misunderstanding and bureaucratic inflexibility, the role played by the practitioner in securing a return-to-work schedule
compatible with therapeutic objectives can be pivotal. We have been surprised at how much anxiety and avoidance can be evoked by cues in the
workplace for clients who have been traumatized at work. Clients often feel
prepared to give up the jobs and careers they liked rather than face the
specter of returning to the workplace. In these circumstances, it is sometimes
useful for the victimized employee to initially return to the work environment in a social role, meeting workmates for coffee or lunch, and doing
fairly menial or "make work" tasks, as part of an exposure program. One
can imagine the problems the victim might encounter in trying to explain
the need for this approach, without the assistance of the practitioner.

Physical Injury, Pain, and Litigation

Some clients have experienced physical injuries and prolonged pain. Others
may be involved in litigation as the result of their traumatic experience.
These issues can impact treatment directly by compromising the client's
available time for participation in treatment and indirectly through demoral-
ization. Even without these practical effects on the process of treatment,
injury, pain, and litigation are events that significantly shape the client's
experience of the aftermath of the trauma.

Clients suffering physical injury may not be able to expect a full recovery.
Documentation of client's injuries, planned assessments and treatments, expected outcome, and degree of acceptance of these facts and possibilities
will alert the therapist to a potential competing agenda in terms of client
attention, time, and psychological resources. To illustrate, it is not unusual
to find that a client has 10–20 appointments per week for ongoing investigation and therapy from family physicians, surgeons, physiotherapists, pain
clinics, psychologists or psychiatrists, radiological technicians, and dentists.
If litigation is involved, some or all of the tests will probably be duplicated
by the opposing side.

Chronic pain, when not successfully managed, can result in decreased
compliance with exposure homework. In addition, tolerance of pain may
need to be incorporated into the exposure to trauma-related stimuli. As discussed in chapter 5 related to treatment of panic, anxiolytic medication may
impair habituation to feared stimuli during exposure exercises. Finally, liti-

gation itself can be a disillusioning experience, leading to feelings of anger and betrayal. It may be necessary to help clients with PTSD cope with the added strain of litigation by using stress management techniques (e.g., Meichenbaum & Novaco, 1977). Koch and Taylor (1995, p. 338) for example, used cognitive restructuring to help a motor vehicle survivor cope. "I can't take it personally when their lawyer calls me a malingerer. He's just trying to save the insurance company money and it has nothing to do with me. The judge will make a decision that is fair" (p. 338).

Case Formulation

Once the initial assessment is complete, the clinician is in a position to formulate a coherent explanation that incorporates factors believed to contribute to the development and maintenance of PTSD symptoms. This formulation will serve to direct treatment. In PTSD, case formulations are typically more complex than in other anxiety disorders due to higher probability of sequelae from physical injury, including chronic pain and the potential for litigation. Presenting the case formulation to the client represents an opportunity to motivate the client, build trust, and explain the treatment model. A trusting therapeutic relationship is essential because of the prospect of exposure to trauma-related stimuli. Normally, clients with PTSD find the persistence of their intrusions and emotional disturbance to be puzzling. The case formulation provides an integrated picture for the client, including a model for why symptoms have developed and persisted and how the treatment plan has the potential to result in improvement. It also forms the basis of treatment consent and expectations for treatment in terms of respective roles and tasks.

TREATMENT MODELS AND GUIDELINES

Approaches to intervention will be discussed as they relate to prevention and acute and chronic treatment. Two general approaches have involved treatment with medication and with psychotherapy. In particular, CBT will be featured, as it has been relatively well researched and has posted the most favorable empirical results.

Acute stress disorder (ASD) precedes the development of PTSD, and several studies have shown remarkable success in preventing the development of chronic PTSD through brief CBT. Foa et al. (1995) treated women approximately two weeks after they had been victims of rape or aggravated assault. The women otherwise met DSM-III-R symptom criteria for PTSD. Treatment consisted of 4 weekly 2-hour sessions of individual CBT including: (a) education about common reactions to assault; (b) breathing and relaxation training; (c) imaginally reliving the assault; (d) in vivo exposure; and (e) cognitive restructuring. Compared to an assessment only condition, in which no treatment was received, only 10% of those women who received the CBT intervention still met criteria for PTSD 2 months after the trauma, whereas 70% of the control group continued to meet PTSD criteria. Five months later, while both groups had generally improved, the women who had received CBT showed less depression and fewer reexperiencing symptoms.

A similar study conducted in Australia extended the Foa et al. (1995) study and found even more impressive results (Bryant, Harvey, Basten, Dang, & Sackville, 1998). As a control group, these investigators used a supportive counseling condition designed to account for nonspecific treatment effects. The supportive counseling focused on education about trauma, problem-solving, and unconditional support. The CBT condition consisted of virtually the same treatment components as those used by Foa et al. (1995), and both treatment conditions were delivered on an individual basis over five 1.5-hour weekly sessions. The participants were victims of either motor vehicle or industrial accidents within the previous 2 weeks, and they all met criteria for acute stress disorder. At the end of treatment, 8% of the CBT group met criteria for PTSD compared to 83% of the supportive counseling group. By six months posttrauma, 17% of the CBT group versus 67% of the supportive counseling group were classified as having PTSD. The CBT group also demonstrated statistically and clinically significant improvements in thought intrusions, avoidance, and depression symptoms, compared to the supportive counseling condition. Taken together, these two studies make a strong case for early intervention using CBT techniques to prevent PTSD in the case of acute stress reactions following trauma.

Cognitive Behavioral Therapy for PTSD

For over 100 years, trauma theorists of various persuasions have recognized the need to systematically activate trauma memories in order to bring about recovery (Foa & Kozak, 1986; Horowitz, 1986). Despite the initial discomfort, relief from fear-provoking memories can be obtained as a function of exposure to fear evoking stimuli. How best to introduce victims to frightening reminders has been less clear, as victims tend to avoid such stimuli. In more dramatic forms, traumatic reactions can present as amnesia and dissociative episodes (Christianson & Nilsson, 1984; Spiegel, 1988). Such extreme forms of emotional detachment have usually been viewed as protective, shielding the victim from an unbearable loss of self-identity.

During the past 30 years many forms of exposure to fear-provoking stimuli have been devised in efforts to reduce avoidance and fear, including flooding, systematic desensitization, implosive therapy, eye-movement desensitization and reprocessing (EMDR), self-controlled graduated exposure, and participant modeling (Keane & Kaloupek, 1996). In the past 15–20 years, exposure therapies have been tailored to PTSD, especially as researchers began to test theories about trauma. Particularly influential has been Foa and Kozak's (1985; 1986) emotional processing theory. As stated earlier, this theory proposes that PTSD involves a pathological memory structure that selectively processes trauma-related fear stimuli. This fear structure is thought to be maintained by avoidance and specific beliefs about the dangerousness of the world and the ineffectiveness of the self. PTSD symptoms are seen by victims as dangerous and indicative of personal incompetence. To be successful, exposure treatment must both emotionally engage the client and produce habituation between treatment sessions. Emotional engagement in this context means activating the fear structure by reliving the traumatic memories. Therapists should be suspicious that emotional engagement is being avoided when clients discuss the traumatic event in a detached, matter of fact manner, showing no emotion, while still reporting behavioral or role avoidance and symptoms of hyperarousal and reexperiencing thought intrusions.

When clients are engaged and show good habituation, Jaycox, Foa, and Morral (1998) demonstrated that clients were 8 times more likely to meet rigorous criteria for good endstate functioning, compared to clients who displayed poor habituation despite good initial emotional engagement or those who were moderate or low on both. Foa and Jaycox (In press) have speculated that repeated and systematic exposure to trauma-related stimuli while the client is emotionally engaged reduces anxiety by disconfirming the client's expectation that emotional engagement of trauma memories and PTSD-related arousal is dangerous.

Clients often experience a shift in specific beliefs related to trauma-related stimuli. For example, a sexual assault victim described herself as having previously been known for her friendliness and jocular interpersonal style with men. After she was raped, she saw every man as a potential rapist. Similarly, 6 months after a traumatic car accident, a formerly easygoing man found himself vigilantly scanning oncoming drivers for signs of inattention, impairment, or poor driving skills. After his accident, he believed that he had come to appreciate the true dangerousness of driving, that he had previously been naive to the many risks of driving, and that he would be stupid not to take every precaution. While it is generally acknowledged that behavioral approaches can indirectly ameliorate such anxiety-promoting beliefs, perhaps by disconfirming feared expectations, cognitive interventions directly address dysfunctional beliefs. Doing so can facilitate a shift to more adaptive beliefs and a balanced means of risk assessment. However, it remains unclear whether cognitive interventions aimed at dysfunctional beliefs actually improve therapeutic outcomes in the treatment of PTSD. In more heavily researched disorders, like panic disorder, the value of directly challenging dysfunctional beliefs has become apparent and one might expect the same benefit will be shown to apply to the CBT treatment of PTSD once the appropriate studies are undertaken.

Currently there is no obviously superior treatment of choice for PTSD. Van Etten and Taylor (In press) conducted a meta-analysis on 61 outcome trials for PTSD involving various pharmaceutical and psychological treatments. It should be noted however that the treatments reported in their meta-analysis have not been applied to all trauma types, and there may be differences—especially between combat and civilian PTSD. Selective serotonin reuptake inhibitors (SSRIs), CBT, and eye-movement desensitization and reprocessing (EMDR) proved generally comparable in terms of efficacy and yielded the strongest treatment results. CBT and EMDR showed stronger effects in reducing PTSD symptoms than drug therapies in acute treatment response, although there was a wide range in the efficacy of different medications. Clients tolerated psychological interventions better than drug therapies (14% drop-out for psychological therapies vs. 32% drop-out for pharmacotherapies). Follow-up information has not yet been published for pharmaceutical treatment of PTSD. Follow-up results that are available indicate that behavior therapy and EMDR outcomes are maintained at least 15 weeks posttreatment.

EMDR, although comparable to CBT in the Van Etten and Taylor (In press) review in terms of treatment outcome, has been viewed as controversial. The emergence of EMDR as a treatment for PTSD has had an unusual course in that early studies attesting to its efficacy were of very poor quality. More recent studies have used better designs and have provided evidence that EMDR is better than a waitlist control for civilian PTSD. However, recent well-controlled studies (e.g., Devilly & Spence, 1999) comparing EMDR and CBT show a clear advantage for CBT in terms of treatment effects, including client status at follow-up. Unresolved questions include the mechanism of action and whether EMDR is useful for combat PTSD. Part of the appeal of EMDR has been the lower degree of distress experienced by clients, compared to in vivo or imaginal exposure approaches. Lohr, Lilienfeld, Tolin, and Herbert (1999) point out that EMDR studies have provided minimal controls for nonspecific effects of treatment and offer a number of suggestions for future studies to correct this shortcoming. It remains to be seen whether EMDR contains an active ingredient which is more powerful than nonspecific treatment effects alone.

CBT for PTSD evolved from an exclusive focus on in vivo exposure to include elements of stress inoculation training and cognitive techniques for normalizing dysfunctional beliefs about the safety of the world and one's own competence. Throughout, however, exposure has maintained a role as the essential ingredient of CBT for PTSD. It is worth noting that Van Etten and Taylor (In press) also found moderate treatment effects compared to control conditions, in descending order of strength of treatment effect, for hypnotherapy, relaxation training, and supportive psychotherapy.

Treatment techniques common to virtually all CBT approaches to PTSD, regardless of trauma type, are education, exposure, cognitive control, and relaxation training and are described below. Application issues unique to different classes of trauma will be discussed separately.

Education

Always the first treatment component, education consists of two parts: a detailed interactive discussion about PTSD, followed by the treatment rationale. It is helpful to explain what PTSD is (e.g., symptoms of intrusive imagery and anxious arousal) and what is known about why it develops in some people but not in others. Information about the prevalence and course of PTSD can help prepare the client for treatment requirements. We find it helpful to group and discuss the client's symptoms in terms of the three clusters discussed earlier. *Reexperiencing symptoms* are intrusive and repetitive thoughts, flashbacks, and nightmares involving trauma memories. *Avoidance* includes behavioral avoidance of any reminders of the trauma (e.g., pictures, notes, discussions, or specific locations). Cognitive avoidance involves consciously blocking out thoughts of the trauma itself or blocking the many associated thoughts that could lead to trauma-related thoughts or images (e.g., specific smells and sounds). Avoidance may also include avoidance of feelings associated with the accident (e.g., terror, pain, complete helplessness), replacing such feelings with detachment or numbness. *Arousal symptoms* include startle reactions, muscle tension, poor concentration, insomnia, panic, irritability, and other indications of autonomic arousal.

Clients are prompted to generate examples of their symptoms in each of these categories and explore for signs of subtle avoidance and previously unrecognized cognitive and affective changes. Many clients with PTSD believe that avoidance of trauma-related stimuli should rid them of objective danger and prevent upsetting reminders. During the education phase, avoidance, attentional biases, and dysfunctional beliefs are identified as being responsible for maintaining the disorder. Behavioral and cognitive avoidance are described as preventing recovery by not allowing habituation to feared stimuli or disconfirmation of feared consequences. Further, clients learn that hypervigilance for threat cues and active suppression of trauma-related thoughts can have the ironic effect of increasing both. Finally, cognitive errors, in the form of faulty assumptions and beliefs, as well as overestimation of vulnerability and danger, are presented as factors that work to maintain PTSD symptoms. Such explanations form the basis of the cognitive behavioral model of PTSD.

Because CBT involves asking clients to recall painful memories and engage in frightening tasks, the rationale is extremely important. Clients' full cooperation depends upon trust and understanding of the explanation for their symptoms and the rationale for treatment. This can be a challenge since most clients are unaware of the extent of their avoidance and their cognitive biases. We find both the explanation for symptoms and the treatment rationale represents a continuing educational process.

Exposure

The goal of exposure therapy is to expose the client to trauma-related stimuli with sufficient frequency and intensity to produce habituation and provide opportunities for feared outcomes to be disconfirmed. The procedure necessarily causes marked subjective distress initially, but prolonged and repeated engagement of the feared stimuli weakens the conditioned fear response. Exposure is structured in terms of a fear hierarchy, as discussed in previous chapters (especially chapter 3). Clients engage in exposure exercises during treatment sessions until anxiety significantly declines (within session habituation), and they practice the exposure exercises between sessions, as self-directed homework assignments. The following guidelines describe exposure treatment for PTSD.

The first step is to *select trauma-related stimuli* to use for exposure. The clinician should pay particular attention to stimuli that represent the client's core fear. The core fear is not always readily apparent or volunteered, but it represents the victim's "worst nightmare." It might be straightforward ("I thought I was going to die"), or it may be implied ("Their deaths are my responsibility"). The therapist should be alert to areas of guilt or other personal meaning that can constitute the primary fear for victims, regardless of how irrational the meaning may be.

A behavior analysis of the client's avoidance and escape patterns can help identify useful trauma items or cues. For example, Mary adopted a drab appearance after being raped, foregoing any clothing or grooming practices that might make her stand out or appear fashionable or attractive. She also severely restricted her social life and would abruptly leave work-related functions (e.g., sales meetings or receptions) if she felt scrutinized by a man or if she anticipated crowded circumstances where she might be jostled. In this case a hierarchy of "appearance" involving clothing, hairstyle, and cosmetics was developed that increasingly approximated what the therapist and Mary jointly considered to be conservatively fashionable. Similarly, hierarchies were developed for *places* in which men might be encountered (excluding objectively unsafe places) and *assertive verbal responses* to men who might speak to her in a variety of situations. The practice in assertive responses was designed to provide Mary with a sense of control in interpersonal encounters with men.

After stimuli are identified, the client and therapist collaborate together to construct a hierarchy. As discussed in earlier chapters, the hierarchy represents a graduated arrangement of fear-provoking stimuli that cover a broad range of in vivo and imaginal stimuli related to the trauma. Usually there is one hierarchy per trauma incident, but similar incidents could be combined into the same hierarchy, or discrete parts of the same traumatic incident could be depicted in several hierarchies. The important issues are to ensure that the core fear is represented in the hierarchy and that other significant trauma areas are not omitted. See table 7.2 for an example of a PTSD exposure hierarchy. Some items may not have been part of the original trauma, but are included on the hierarchy because they have subsequently become associated with the trauma and now represent aversive cues. In addition, video material that represents trauma-related associations can be helpful items to include on an exposure hierarchy.

Table 7.2 Example of Exposure Hierarchy for PTSD

Anxiety	Stimulus
100	Empty revolver held to his head and being shouted at, in a car
90	Holding empty revolver to his own head
85	Imagining being shot in the head
80	Imagining details of his own funeral
75	Being handcuffed in the back of a car
70	Bearded men (i.e., convicts), approaching in threatening manner
65	Policeman throwing him against a wall, cuffing him
60	Handling an empty revolver
60	Camping again
60	Being touched by a policeman
45	Imagining salient parts of the 3-day hostage episode
40	Walking through police cell area with prisoners present
30	Talking to a policeman
25	Going into a police station
10	Seeing police cars

Case Description: Bill is a 26-year-old man who was camping with a male friend in a remote area when two recently escaped convicts took them hostage for 3 days. Most of this time was spent in a car with a gun placed periodically to his head. He was repeatedly told he would be killed if the police didn't cooperate with the captors' demands. In apprehending the vehicle, police were unaware of the hostages' status and initially roughed them up. Bill presented for treatment 14 months later due to "stress leave" from work. The local police department assisted with exposure items.

Two rules of thumb apply in *conducting exposure*, which is the next step. As discussed earlier, the client should be fully emotionally engaged with the exposure item, and each session of exposure should continue until the SUDS ratings drop by at least 50%. Exposure sessions require sufficient time for habituation to occur and should last at least 90 minutes. In early sessions, even more time may be required for a 50% decline in SUDS ratings. If a 2-hour session is not possible, then more modest reductions in SUDS may have to be accepted.

Although the procedure is upsetting, the idea is to maximize emotional involvement as the client relives the event. Initially, clients usually avoid detailed description of the trauma event to prevent distress, referring to the event with brief or antiseptic descriptions. Less experienced therapists may feel hesitant to continue exposure on compassionate grounds, when clients are in obvious distress. We find it helpful to encourage distressed clients undergoing exposure to focus on the trauma images and related perceptions, while letting the emotion wash over them without resistance. Reviewing the rationale for treatment and asking the client's permission to continue at the beginning of each session can also make the rigors of exposure easier. Clients who are prone to panic attacks may need some coaching in the means of managing these attacks prior to engaging in exposure exercises. Treatment techniques useful in managing panic attacks are outlined in chapter 5 and can be useful for traumatized clients with panic. Providing a brief course of panic control treatment in advance of and during exposure can help avoid sensitizing clients through the experience of inadvertent panic attacks. These skills should help clients with a history of panic attacks cope with the rigors of exposure.

The starting point for exposure is determined by the SUDS ratings on the hierarchy, aiming for a moderately high level of anxiety. The exposure should be emotionally intense but still manageable. Asking the client to describe the traumatic event typically marks the beginning of exposure. For clarification, the therapist can skip ahead, or backward, ask about background details such as the weather at the time, or scenery, as necessary in order to elaborate the scene and help keep the client engaged with the stimulus or image. Similarly, the therapist can inquire about the client's thoughts and feelings at any point during the self-description of the trauma event. These inquiries serve to ensure that the event, its meaning, associated emotions, and the implications of the event are comprehensively explored. If the descriptions are too short to allow for habituation, the client can repeat them or elaborate more fully so that exposure can continue until anxiety declines sufficiently. During the course of an exposure session, the therapist should regularly inquire about SUDS ratings and use these ratings as a criterion for discontinuing exposure for a hierarchy item.

For stimuli on the hierarchy that can only be experienced imaginally (such as recounting the original trauma), the therapist directs clients to close their eyes and relive the experience starting at an early point in the script. The therapist directs the exposure by periodically inquiring about SUDS ratings and watching for obvious signs of distress. For example, clients may be thinking about the experience in a detached way, which will compromise exposure. The therapist encourages clients to be emotionally engaged by periodically probing with questions such as "What is happening now?," "And then what happened?," and "What were you thinking and feeling?"

Once clients understand how to do imaginal exposure in the office setting, they repeat the exercise for homework. During the homework exposure, clients should keep a record of the times and dates of practice as well as the pre- and postexposure SUDS ratings of each self-directed session. Therapists should ensure that imaginal exposure conducted at home is undertaken for periods of at least 90 minutes or until SUDS ratings have dropped by at least 50%. One difficulty is that sometimes SUDS ratings drop artificially during homework exercises because of distraction or avoidance, so the therapist should be alert to this possibility when reviewing the homework.

Clients can also physically write their story in full detail, including smells, sounds, emotional experiences, and fears, in order to prolong the exposure period. Clients can mix imaginal and written description forms of exposure as long as the two criteria of engagement and duration (i.e., 90 minutes) are met. Sometimes clients become distracted by reactions to their emotions during both imaginal and writing task forms of exposure, by focusing on such reactions as anger, outrage, revenge, or a sense of injustice. While these emotions are understandable, they were most likely not part of the emotional experience at the time of the trauma and therefore should be addressed independently. Instead, clients should be encouraged to think about their fears and feelings (e.g., pain, nausea, terror) that were part of the traumatic experience.

To facilitate cognitive change in maladaptive beliefs, exposure exercises can be usefully formatted as behavioral experiments. Predictions identified by the client before exposure are listed in terms of the worst thing that might happen, followed by an estimate of its probability of occurring, and finally an evaluation of the evidence for and against the likelihood of its occurrence. In addition to the habituation benefits of exposure exercises deriving from behavioral experiments, the therapist is in a position to help clients identify faulty predictions and to develop a habit of balanced risk appraisal. Foa and Rothbaum's (1998) in vivo exposure homework recording form is a useful form for monitoring compliance with homework tasks as well as for identifying predictions and outcomes relating to exposure assignments. Figure 7.2 shows the exposure homework recording form with illustrative client responses. Behavioral experiments can also be used for imaginal exposure since many clients fear loss of control if they "open the lid" on traumatic memories. During in vivo exposure exercises, clients are typically more concerned about danger related outcomes. For example, a client may fear an attack in a relatively benign situation such as shopping at the mall in daylight.

Cognitive Control

As discussed previously, clinical assessment and ongoing treatment will reveal the client's faulty beliefs about the trauma, including the client's potential causal role, other people's reactions, and the future predictions of safety. Furthermore, negative automatic thoughts triggered by trauma memories, emotions, or threat-related environmental cues, along with faulty beliefs, serve to maintain PTSD symptoms. Several approaches serve to help alter these beliefs and cognitions.

Cognitive Restructuring

Involves identifying faulty beliefs relevant to the trauma and then accumulating evidence that challenges these beliefs, leading to a more balanced appraisal. This is not done on a single occasion, but rather is seen as an ongoing exercise. Four general categories of assumptions have been identified, and the therapist may find it useful to cluster the client's faulty beliefs into these categories to more manageably approach them. The first category is the client's causal role in the trauma. Clients often inappropriately blame

---

Date: _May 24, 1998_

Situation practiced: _Walking alone (in the middle of the day) to the area outside of_
the coffee shop where the assault occurred.   .

Instructions: Before performing the <u>in vivo</u> exposure, please answer the following
questions in the spaces provided.

1. What is the worst that could happen in this situation?
    The same two guys could be there, come over and push me around, and then hit
    me in the face again with a baseball bat.   .
2. What is the likelihood that this could happen?
    Not high, maybe 2% or less.
3. Evaluate the evidence for or against the likelihood of this happening.
    When I was attacked it was late at night, the street was deserted, and the
    attackers were loud, like they'd been drinking. This time there will be people
    around.   .
4. Ratings before and after <u>in vivo</u> exposure:

	Time	SUDS
Before	_Noon_	_85_
After	_12:40_	_30_

Comments: _There were lots of people, some who I knew. They talked to me. Those_
I didn't know paid no attention to me. I felt better by the end.

Figure 7.2 Exposure Homework Recording Form. From E. B. Foa & B. O. Rothbaum (1988). *Treating the trauma of rape: Cognitive behavioral therapy for PTSD*
(New York: Guilford Press). Reprinted with permission. (Example added.)

themselves for assaults and accidents, with beliefs such as, "I encouraged
him by not screaming," "It's my fault because I could have driven home
earlier and didn't," or "I kept putting off buying a serious fire extinguisher."
A second category of faulty assumptions involves the reactions of others.
Clients often make negative assumptions about how their friends and family
will see them in relation to the trauma, with thoughts such as, "People see
me as damaged goods," or "Word gets around; people see me as weak.
They feel sorry for me but don't trust my judgment."

The third category of faulty beliefs involves the PTSD symptoms themselves. Clients often have little confidence in their ability to handle the intense emotion evoked by recollections of the trauma, with thoughts such as, "If I go there, I'll cry or run away and embarrass myself," or "These symptoms upset me and flood me with fear; I can't control them." Finally, the fourth general category of faulty beliefs related to the trauma involves future safety concerns. Clients feel generally unsafe, expressing such beliefs as, "Walking alone means I am a walking target," "The inspection process designed to ensure car safety obviously can't be trusted," or "It's foolish to trust anyone."

These and other dysfunctional beliefs can be written in a thought record similar to the one discussed for social phobia in chapter 4. A variation of the thought record for PTSD might include having four columns in the chart: Troublesome Beliefs, Evidence For, Evidence Against, and Balanced View. In this way the client can specifically examine evidence that supports and refutes dysfunctional beliefs. Evidence against maladaptive beliefs can be systematically gathered during behavioral experiments as part of the exposure program. With this approach of explicitly examining the evidence supporting assumptions related to the trauma, the client can come to a more balanced view, such as, "Sometimes I can't control my fears, but it doesn't mean I act irrationally or irresponsibly." Cognitive restructuring should be comprehensive enough to address all faulty beliefs relevant to the trauma. The client should also be encouraged to systematically challenge faulty beliefs both in the office and as they occur outside of the office environment, in order to build the habit of developing a balanced perspective. Clients can benefit from gentle challenges in this regard (e.g., "What did you make of that?" and "What is another way of looking at that?" or "What interpretations might your friends or brother have about this?").

Although many clients naturally try to suppress thoughts related to the trauma, *thought replacement* is a more adaptive strategy. Automatic thoughts associated with the trauma often take the form of unhappy predictions such as, "I will lose control," or "I'll be hit for no reason." Suppressing these trauma-related thoughts actually increases their frequency (Harvey & Bryant, 1998). Clients can learn to challenge these emotional thoughts by identifying at least three logical challenges to each of the negative thoughts. These can be listed on file cards or note paper, so that the client can rehearse the counterarguments as well as add new items that are contrary to the negative thought. The idea here is to help the client develop an active repertoire of counterarguments that are routinely used when negative thoughts intrude. A second technique that clients find helpful in replacing negative thoughts involves guided self-dialogue statements. In this case, coping statements are developed, listed, and rehearsed, so they can be introduced and contemplated by the client in preparation for anxious situations or in reaction to negative feelings. Table 7.3 shows some examples from Foa and Rothbaum (1998).

Table 7.3 Guided Self-Dialogue Examples

Step no.	Step	Questions
1	Preparing for a Stressor	"What is it that I have to do?" "What am I afraid of?" "What is the likelihood that anything bad will happen?" "How bad would it be if it really happened?" "Don't think about how bad I feel; think about what I can do about it." "Don't get caught up in myself. Thinking only about my feelings won't help me cope with the situation." "I have the support and encouragement of people who have experience in dealing with these things." "I have already come a long way toward handling the problem. I can handle the rest."
2	Confronting and Managing the Stressor	"I need to take one step at a time." "Don't think about how afraid or anxious I am; think about what I am doing." "The feeling that I am having now is a signal for me to use my coping exercises." "There is no need to doubt myself. I have the skills I need to get through this." "Focus on my plan. Relax and take a calming breath. I am ready to go."
3	Coping with Feelings of Being Overwhelmed	"When I feel afraid, I will take a breath and exhale slowly, saying to myself, 'calm'." "Focus on what is happening now. What is it that I have to do?" "I can expect my fear to rise, but I can keep it manageable." "This fear may slow me down, but it will not stop me." "This event will pass, and it will be over soon." "I may feel scared and anxious, but I can do it."
4	Self-Reinforcment for Managing a Stressor	"It was much easier than I thought." "I did it — I got through it. And each time will be easier." "When I manage my thoughts in my head, I can manage the feelings in my body." "I am making progress." "I did a good job." "One step at a time."

Adapted with permission from E. B. Foa & B. O. Rothbaum (1998), *Treating the trauma of rape: Cognitive behavioral therapy for PTSD* (New York: Guilford Press).

Relaxation Training

Relaxation training is common to virtually all CBT protocols for PTSD. Relaxation helps clients cope and tolerate exposure without interfering with habituation. We recommend the 8-step applied relaxation training procedure developed by Öst (1987b) and adapted by Clark (1989) as detailed in chapter 5.

Specific Types of Trauma

A number of excellent treatment protocols have been developed for specific traumas in order to address problems particular to those types of trauma. Several of these areas and exemplary treatment programs are identified below.

Sexual Assault

Sexual assault is very prevalent, and victims often respond with social avoidance and relative secrecy about the trauma. Foa and Rothbaum (1998) and Resick and Schnicke (1996) provide comprehensive and scientifically tested treatment recommendations for CBT approaches to PTSD stemming from sexual assault. There has been at least one dismantling study (Echeburua, De Corral, Zubizarreta, & Sarasua, 1997) which has tried to identify the most effective CBT components in the treatment of chronic PTSD in victims of sexual aggression. These investigators found that exposure and cognitive restructuring techniques produced the most immediate and sustained beneficial treatment effects.

Motor Vehicle Accident

Victims of auto accidents usually have special issues involving litigation, injury, and pain that can exacerbate PTSD and interfere with its treatment. Hickling and Blanchard (1997) provide a treatment protocol for PTSD caused by a motor vehicle accident. There has been very little research specifically directed toward treatment of PTSD stemming from road accidents, and this is a welcome start, providing guidelines for brief (9–12 sessions) CBT treatment.

Combat

Combat veterans with PTSD usually represent chronic cases with special problems that relate to dealing with government agencies, substance abuse, and reintegration into the social mainstream. Frueh, Turner, Beidel et al. (1996) have developed a 28-session protocol for chronic combat-related PTSD titled "Trauma Management Therapy." This multicomponent CBT program is very comprehensive in terms of the special problems facing veterans with PTSD and represents a highly structured rehabilitation program. It is based upon treatment components from a number of studies that have established efficacy and to this extent is empirically derived, although to our knowledge, this program has not been tested by itself.

Pharmacological Treatment for PTSD

In a comparative review of pharmacotherapy and psychological therapies for PTSD mentioned earlier, Van Etten and Taylor (In press) concluded that pharmacotherapy in general was more effective than waitlist conditions. However, taken as a whole, medication treatment was found to be less effective in reducing symptoms of PTSD than psychological therapies. While only the most effective drug therapies (i.e., SSRIs and carbamazepine) seemed to work as well as the most effective psychological therapies, the SSRIs provide a further advantage over psychological therapies in reducing depression symptoms. We could find no studies specifically supporting the use of combined CBT and pharmacotherapy in PTSD. However, Gould, Otto, and Pollack (1995) reported that the combination of benzodiazepine medication with behavior therapy was less effective than behavior therapy alone.

In conclusion, the SSRIs appear to yield treatment results comparable to those of psychological therapies during the acute phase of treatment for PTSD. At this time little is known about whether the treatment effects from the acute phase of treatment are maintained during follow-up. Further, the advantage of the SSRIs is that they effectively treat concurrent depression, while their disadvantage is relatively high treatment drop out rates. The relatively high efficacy of SSRIs and carbamazepine in the treatment of PTSD is encouraging despite the attrition rate and lack of follow-up information, and otherwise represents a viable alternative to psychological therapies for PTSD.

Eye-Movement Desensitization and Reprocessing (EMDR)

EMDR was developed specifically for PTSD and has remained controversial primarily because the mechanism of treatment is unknown (e.g., Lilienfeld, 1996) and because efficacy studies have not controlled for nonspecific treatment effects. Several recent reviews have concluded that EMDR is an effective psychological treatment for civilian but not combat-related PTSD (Feske, 1998). Van Etten and Taylor (In press) found EMDR treatment to be as effective as CBT in the treatment of PTSD, although in this study trauma-type was not evaluated separately. There are many calls in the literature for further studies of this intriguing treatment, particularly well-controlled studies that include comparisons to alternative treatments of established efficacy and treatment control conditions. A major stumbling block in more widespread investigation of EMDR is that the training in EMDR treatment is not in the public domain. That is, because EMDR training is copyrighted, therapists must receive training from authorized trainers on a commercial basis. At least initially, this requirement has had the effect of discouraging investigation into EMDR. In conclusion, this is an intriguing treatment with an unknown treatment mechanism that begs further study.

Client-Treatment Matching

Most therapists try to plan treatment to match features of the client's presentation to the specific interventions offered. Even in the case of manual-based treatments, there is usually some provision to allow treatment-component selection or at least to emphasize one treatment component relative to another. Falsetti (1997) has made this process more systematic by outlining a decision-making process of selecting specific treatment components for clients with PTSD related to civilian trauma. The clinical matching here is based on the results of patient requirements as identified through clinical assessment matched conceptually with those components of stress inoculation training, prolonged exposure, cognitive processing therapy, and a combined PTSD and panic control therapy, based on Nezu and Nezu's (1995) problem-solving treatment model. The treatment components available for matching to client characteristics are listed in table 7.4. This clinical-decision-making approach to the treatment of PTSD not only provides flexibility, but also advocates treatment precision based on consideration of trauma history, PTSD symptomatology, behavioral avoidance, comorbid disorders, coping skills, dysfunctional cognitions, and other assessment considerations.

Falsetti's decision-making model represents a "best practices" approach to treatment, where specific treatment components are logically linked to client needs. This represents common practice and is an informal, or best clinical judgment, manner of matching client characteristics with specific treatment components, but the matching process is not empirically derived. On the other hand, Ford, Fisher, and Larson (1997) were able to empirically demonstrate the advantage of matching client characteristics to type of treatment. Specifically, working with a population of inpatient veterans with chronic PTSD, they successfully predicted treatment outcome across a wide range of indicators on the basis of strength of client's object relations. The assessment of object relations was based upon an interview coding system that assessed various components of object relations, broadly reflecting interpersonal judgment and maturity. Moderate as opposed to low scores on the object relation measure consistently and strongly predicted reliable change in outcome measures beyond the influence of other variables such as psychiatric chronicity, demographics, personality disorder, war or childhood trauma exposure, and pretest symptomatic severity.

These findings show that at least a significant subset of combat veterans with chronic PTSD can benefit markedly from treatment. Ford et al. (1997)

Table 7.4 Tips for Treatment Planning

Treatment Phase	Specific Interventions
Education	Education about PTSD.
	If the patient has a comorbid disorder, provide education about that disorder. Otherwise, move on to coping skills phase.
Coping Skills	If the patient has panic attacks, teach diaphragmatic breathing.
	If the patient has poor coping skills or extremely high anxiety, teach coping skills from stress inoculation training.
	If the patient has adequate coping skills, skip the coping skills phase and move on to imaginal exposure phase.
Imaginal Exposure	If the patient has comorbid panic attacks, conduct interoceptive exposure to panic symptoms prior to conducting trauma-related exposure.
	If the patient has good imagery skills, initiate prolonged imaginal exposure to traumatic events.
	If the patient prefers writing and does not have good imagery skills, initiate writing exposure to traumatic events.
Cognitive	Connect events, thoughts, feelings, and behaviors.
	Teach patient to identify and challenge cognitive distortions related to the trauma, panic, or depression.
	Assist patient in implementing cognitive restructuring skills for issues of safety, trust, power, competence, self-esteem, and intimacy.
In vivo Exposure	If the patient has comorbid panic attacks, implement exposure to panic-related cues.
	Develop hierarchies for trauma-related cues, and implement in vivo exposure.
Evaluation	Evaluate panic attacks for patients with comorbid panic attacks.
	Evaluate depressive symptoms for patients with comorbid depression.
	Evaluate substance use for patients with substance abuse.
	Evaluate PTSD symptoms.
	Make decisions about further treatment versus termination.

Adapted with permission from S. A. Falsetti (1997), The decision-making process of choosing a treatment for patients with civilian trauma-related PTSD, *Cognitive and Behavioral Practice, 4,* 99–121.

suggest that clients with better object relations may benefit from the challenge and structure of a combined CBT and existential approach to confronting trauma memories. On the other hand, clients with poorer object relations may better respond to therapy that helps them to contain their overwhelming and diffuse affect, without the potential overstimulation of exposure-based therapies. Further, Ford et al. note that "patients with lower object relations levels tended to recall war-zone trauma experiences through a primitive psychic lens in which terror, guilt, shame, rage and despair seemed not just intense but overwhelming or annihilating" (p. 556). These clients frequently deteriorated over the course of exposure-based treatments. This study makes a strong case for the adaptation of object relations assessment and subsequent treatment matching with this population.

Minimal vs. Optimal Interventions

The overriding consideration for treatment of PTSD is early intervention. Evidence reviewed earlier in this chapter indicates that PTSD can be prevented at the acute stress reaction phase with brief and timely (within 2 weeks of trauma) CBT intervention. Although research is still ongoing, current evidence suggests that the longer treatment is delayed after a trauma, the poorer the prognosis for treatment response. Conversely, early treatment for trauma is likely to involve considerably fewer sessions than delayed treatment. Another issue relevant to treatment planning in PTSD is that trauma experiences frequently result in sustained vulnerability for general psychological distress (Winje, 1996) and development of specific disorders such as panic disorder with agoraphobia (Michelson, June, Vives, Testa, & Marchione, 1998). These studies suggest clients should be monitored every 6 months for several years subsequent to PTSD treatment in order to ensure associated disorders are prevented or managed early.

There is a useful role for family members in the treatment of PTSD both during acute treatment and during follow-up periods. Family members can be key in assisting during in vivo exposure treatments and in challenging dysfunctional beliefs. Further, family members and friends can be pivotal in social reintegration of PTSD clients. We suggest that a partner or family member selected by the client periodically attend treatment sessions, particularly the first and last sessions, in order to be oriented to both the phenomenology of PTSD and the useful role they can play in supporting recovery.

Common Problems

Noncompliance Due to Fear and Avoidance

Fear associated with PTSD might be regarded as particularly intense since the trauma has usually threatened the life of the client. Accordingly, the client and therapist need to work together to carefully prepare for exposure. A solid therapeutic relationship, along with careful gradation of the exposure steps, can provide the client with support needed to engage in exposure exercises. Normalizing the trauma response while reassuring the client of the relative safety of the exposure situation are key. Noncompliance should be addressed early rather than being allowed to become a pattern. Clients often "get stuck" at some point in the trauma sequence and focus on their affective flooding rather than continuing on, perhaps in a less detailed manner, by addressing only key parts of the sequence (e.g., the ambulance ride, parts of the hospital experience). Involvement of the client's partner or a family member can also be helpful in bolstering exposure.

Comorbidity

It is clear from the literature that comorbidity, particularly in the form of depression and substance abuse, is normal in PTSD. This will necessitate clinicians establishing treatment priorities and possibly having to deliver PTSD treatment on a more intermittent basis than is ideal. Clinicians will also face the task of continuously motivating their client and helping to maintain perspective.

Medical and Litigation Complications

These common problems can delay and, occasionally, distort treatment for PTSD. Ongoing physical investigations, clinical levels of pain, "revictimization" by settlement controversies, and the frequent involvement of many specialists, agencies and other "stakeholders" in the client's day-to-day life may easily relegate psychological treatment to a part time and intermittent process. We have found it helpful to review with clients who else is involved in the investigation and treatment of trauma-related symptoms, as well as determining the schedule in progress of any compensation investigation or trauma compensation. In this way, the therapist can be fully informed, act as a client advocate, and more effectively plan treatment.

Treatment Outcome Evaluation and Life Planning

As with OCD, clients with chronic PTSD are best advised to regard their therapeutic objective as one of managing PTSD symptoms rather than as a cure. This position recognizes the fact that chronic PTSD and associated general psychological distress combine to produce a sustained vulnerability, which the client is better able to prepare for if it is understood. Therapists can play a powerful role in relapse prevention, and we recommend that therapists spend at least two full sessions on relapse prevention strategies at the end of acute treatment, updating and rehearsing these strategies as necessary during follow-up visits. As mentioned earlier, it is prudent to conduct 6-month follow-up visits for the first 2 years following treatment and 1 year thereafter for the next several years, depending upon assessed risk. Of particular importance appears to be fostering a strong social network for clients, as the presence of a functional social network appears to promote adjustment.

A final caveat in planning treatment for PTSD clients concerns group treatment, where sensitization can occur. Clients listening to the dramatic stories of other clients in trauma treatment groups may have the unwanted effect of exacerbating distress. Clients with PTSD have often been treated in groups in research, and it is possible that preparing clients before they enter the group may protect them from sensitization effects.

For our last clinical chapter we move on to generalized anxiety disorder. In terms of both focus and intensity of anxiety, this anxiety disorder is the opposite of PTSD. It has a relatively slow onset, and it concerns routine subjects that are pervasive in daily life. Despite the contrasts between these dramatically different disorders, the mechanisms of anxiety provide many similarities, particularly in cognitive symptoms and general arousal level.

8 *Generalized Anxiety Disorder*

Although anxiety has always been a feature of the human condition, we have been slow to understand this disorder of chronic anxiety and worry. Better understanding has come with improved nosology, in which specific anxiety disorders with unique and shared characteristics have been articulated. Once considered the essence of "neurosis," Generalized Anxiety Disorder (GAD) has lagged behind the other anxiety disorders in being reliably diagnosed, conceptualized, and successfully treated. The general or nonspecific nature of this disorder, and attendant problems of classification, help explain why GAD has been relatively neglected despite its prevalence. Fortunately, progress in measurement and theory has identified key cognitive features, which in turn have been targeted by recent treatment trials, early results of which are quite promising and have the potential to parallel the advances made in treating panic disorder. Such developments would be welcome given the personal and social cost of this chronic disorder and its prevalence across the life span.

DESCRIPTION AND CONCEPTUALIZATION

Phenomenology

The defining feature of GAD is worry—chronic, nonspecific, excessive worry that is difficult to control or stop, resulting in distress or (usually mild) impairment of normal functioning. The worry covers multiple themes and is present in an ongoing way, at least half of the time. The chronicity of the worry distinguishes it from specific or social phobias and panic disorder, where worry tends to be experienced more episodically. Worry in GAD is accompanied by somatic symptoms of motor tension, such as feeling shaky, restless, tense, fatigued, jumpy, and cranky, as well as cognitive symptoms of vigilance and scanning, including difficulty concentrating and sleeping.

Interestingly, the content of worry themes among clients with GAD is not remarkably different from that of normal controls. GAD worriers tend to worry about routine things like family, work, and illnesses (Sanderson & Barlow, 1990). These themes are similar to the worries of normal controls, although persons with GAD find their worries to be less realistic and less controllable (Craske, Rapee, Jackel, & Barlow, 1989). Compared to most other anxiety disorders, GAD spans a larger component of the life span, with a relatively early onset and a marked prevalence among the elderly. Furthermore, the themes of worry over the life span tend to shadow developmental stages. Children with GAD identify worry themes related to family or catastrophic events they learn about in school or on TV, such as nuclear war, whereas the elderly tend to worry more about physical illness.

Researchers at Pennsylvania State University examined 162 content areas of worry among clients with GAD (Borkovec, Shadick, & Hopkins, 1991). The main things that clients with GAD seem to worry about are diverse and quite ordinary, such as family and interpersonal relationships. The worry lacks the dramatic intensity of the fear that is characteristic of other anxiety disorders, such as panic disorder or PTSD. Instead, GAD seems to provoke relatively mild to moderate levels of anxiety, which are activated by a broad range of routine circumstances and are experienced most of the time.

Linda is a 29-year-old mother of two who lives with her husband and works full-time as an elementary school teacher. She is widely recognized by friends and family as a competent "worry wart." Her life has a constant foreboding quality to it, whereby she strives to be alert to anything that could go wrong and seeks strategies to prevent or minimize the impact. Her operative mode focuses on "what if . . . ," and she worries about any number of things that might go wrong with her children, husband, students, pets, home, or parents. Her worries are particularly intense if there is any doubt that things are not going exactly as they should, such as if her children are 10 minutes late coming home or if she learns about some misfortune from the news media or colleagues. Her vigilance and attempts to anticipate and prepare for potential stressors have resulted in insomnia, and she feels inefficient in various roles because of poor concentration, fatigue, and bodily tension. Linda's husband has assumed most of the domestic responsibilities in order to reduce her self-imposed pressure, but this has not helped. She says she feels "at the end of my rope" much of the time, for no objective reason.

Worry involved in GAD (pathological worry) can be differentiated from normal worry on a number of grounds, which we will elaborate upon later in the chapter. While the content of immediate, day-to-day concerns are much the same (although GAD clients have a higher frequency of thinking about these concerns), worry about remote future circumstances seems to be particular to clients with GAD (Dugas, Freeston et al., 1998). Furthermore, individuals with GAD seem to have a characteristic cognitive style in which they overestimate the likelihood of future negative events and experience discomfort with both uncertainty about and lack of control over worrisome circumstances. No behavioral disturbances have been characteristically noted among GAD sufferers. However, compared to nonclinical control subjects, clients with GAD make decisions more slowly and require relatively more information in order to make a decision (Lachance, Dugas, Ladouceur, & Freeston, October 1995). Presumably this is a reflection of their relative difficulty tolerating uncertainty.

Among most clients (68%) identified as having GAD, their difficulties are complicated by the presence of an additional mental disorder, and 22% of clients with depressive disorders also meet diagnostic criteria for GAD (Sanderson & Wetzler, 1991). In summary, GAD is qualitatively different from normal worry, general stress, and other anxiety disorders, in the range and number of worries which are processed, the excessive or unrealistic nature of the worry, the cognitive style employed by GAD sufferers, and the degree of comorbidity experienced. The expression of the two primary features of this chronic disorder, worry and somatic tension, are further shaped by cultural influences that may complicate diagnosis. In the relative absence of behavioral markers for GAD, and since many GAD sufferers view their worry as adaptive rather than pathological, the recognition of this disorder rests heavily on the interpretation of symptoms of somatic tension and the experience of uncontrollable worry.

Diagnostic Trends

Although diffuse or "free-floating" anxiety has been recognized for some time (Wolpe, 1958), it was only identified as a separate disorder in DSM-III (American Psychiatric Association, 1980). This definition turned out to be very confusing, mainly because a diagnosis of GAD could not be made unless the client met criteria for no other anxiety or affective disorder (Barlow & DiNardo, 1991). Barlow (1987) found that the agreement in diagnosis for GAD between two independent interviewers was relatively low ($\kappa = .57$) using DSM-III criteria.

The DSM-III-R made a number of changes to the description of GAD that improved diagnostic reliability. For example, excessive or unrealistic worry was identified as the key feature of GAD. The duration criterion was extended to 6 months, and other Axis I diagnoses were permitted as long as the content of the GAD worry themes (two or more life circumstances) were distinct from those of any additional Axis I disorders (e.g., worry about panic attacks). The DSM-III-R criteria were used in several research centers, and after a few years researchers had amassed several large databases from which reliability studies could be conducted (for review see Barlow & DiNardo, 1991). These studies helped pave the way for a more empirically based description of GAD in DSM-IV. It became evident, for example, that different interviewers showed better agreement on worry than on physical symptoms of anxiety (Barlow & DiNardo, 1991).

DSM-IV describes GAD as involving "excessive anxiety and worry (apprehensive expectation), occurring more days than not for at least 6 months, about a number of events or activities" (pp. 435–436, American Psychiatric Association, 1994). The worry is difficult to control and is accompanied by three or more of the following somatic symptoms: restlessness (feeling keyed up or on edge), being easily fatigued, difficulty concentrating (mind going blank), irritability, muscle tension, and sleep disturbance. Further, the diagnosis requires that these symptoms cause clinically significant distress or functional impairment, although the impairment in GAD is often mild in comparison to other anxiety disorders. Finally, the content of the worry cannot be related to the focus of another Axis I disorder. GAD is not diagnosed when the symptoms occur exclusively during a mood disorder. Although the symptoms between generalized anxiety and depression overlap, GAD is chronic rather than episodic (most mood disorders are episodic).

Despite the evolution of GAD diagnostic criteria over successive editions of the DSM, some controversy remains about its validity as a diagnostic entity. Barlow (1991) has suggested anxious apprehension and neurotic depression may have a common cause and lie on the same continuum. Sanderson and Wetzler (1991) speculate that GAD might better be considered a personality disorder. Rapee (1991a) argues that GAD could be considered as a manifestation of high trait anxiety, although he acknowledges that considering a condition to be a disorder requires functional impairment. The improving reliability of diagnostic classification in GAD facilitates the ability of researchers to address validity issues such as these. The identification of the function of worry in GAD should also help to provide conceptual clarification.

Prevalence and Course

The National Comorbidity Survey, discussed in earlier chapters, reported a 12-month prevalence rate of 3.1% and a lifetime prevalence rate of 5.1% for GAD (Kessler et al., 1994). These studies show that GAD is one of the more common anxiety disorders, with prevalence rates comparable to panic disorder. In a study of mental disorder in primary care settings, GAD was found to be the most prevalent (2.9%) of all anxiety disorders (Barrett, Barrett, Oxmann, & Gerber, 1988). Women are almost twice as likely to suffer from GAD as are men.

In terms of onset, most studies show an early onset ranging from mid-teens to the early twenties (Anderson, Noyes, & Crowe, 1984). However, estimating mean age of onset for GAD may not be very accurate as many subjects report experiencing symptoms all their lives, and some studies report onset before age 11 for between 10% and 30% of those with GAD (Rapee, 1989). Of note is Rapee's finding (1985) that over 80% of individuals with GAD could not specifically recall the onset of their disorder. This may reflect the nondramatic and gradual onset of GAD in most cases. The course of GAD is considered to be chronic but fluctuating, with episodes of increased severity occurring at times of stress. For unknown reasons, GAD is particularly prevalent among the elderly with 1-month and 12-month prevalence estimated at 3.7% and 7.1%, respectively (Blazer, George, & Hughes, 1991; Flint, 1994). This is problematic as chronic worry can contribute to other problems in the elderly such as insomnia (Monane, 1992) and depression (Lindesay, Briggs, & Murphy, 1989).

In summary, cross-sectional studies show GAD to have an early, insidious onset with a fluctuating but chronic course over the life span. As a result, this disorder is often viewed as characterological by observers. GAD is not marked by the surges of fear or behavioral avoidance that is characteristic of other anxiety disorders. Instead, GAD sufferers experience a degraded quality of life due to their excessive worry, physical tension, and high rates of comorbidity.

THEORETICAL PERSPECTIVES

Biological Approaches

Compared to panic disorder, the biology of GAD has been relatively neglected (Cowley & Roy-Byrne, 1991). There are a variety of reasons for this disinterest on the part of biological investigators. Perhaps the major difficulties have been the significant changes that have occurred in the definition of GAD since its recognition in DSM-III and the relative difficulty in reliably diagnosing the condition. Furthermore, generalized anxiety is a shared characteristic among the various anxiety disorders. This feature combined with the high rate of comorbidity characteristic of GAD combine to make for boundary problems in defining GAD. GAD is also less tangible and dramatic compared to the other anxiety disorders, perhaps making the biological study of GAD less enticing. Biological studies have identified a state of heightened arousal in GAD, but biological abnormalities per se have not been identified for this disorder. Some investigators have noted that clients with GAD can be differentiated from controls on the basis of weaker skin conductance response (Hoehn-Saric, McLeod, & Zimmerli, 1989). These investigators speculate that clients with GAD have reduced "autonomic flexibility," which may indicate that these individuals take longer to habituate to psychological stressors.

In summary, sleep, psychophysiology, neuroendicrine, and catecholamine studies have been unable to identify a causal mechanism that can account for the expression of GAD. Several problems have hampered these attempts. Identifying challenge stimuli for biological studies of GAD is difficult, as stimuli that evoke worry tend to be less distinctive than fear-producing cues in the other anxiety disorders. Many of the early studies investigating the biology of chronic anxiety were conducted on various populations of people classified as "psychoneurotic," resulting in considerable variation in sample characteristics. The relatively few biological studies on GAD are somewhat inconsistent in their findings, although they do provide reasonable evidence that GAD is distinct from panic disorder, as determined by lactate infusion studies (Cowley & Roy-Byrne, 1991).

Other theorists have conceptualized "nervousness" as heritable. The most influential biological theory of personality has been Eysenck's (1967). In this theory, personality is conceptualized primarily along two independent dimensions. Neuroticism is a normally distributed dimension characterized by extreme emotional reactivity at one end and "stable" individuals at the other end. The biological underpinnings of neuroticism are considered to be differential levels of autonomic nervous system reactivity. Unlike stable individuals, those high on the personality dimension of neuroticism routinely experience more intense autonomic reactions to the same provocations. Eysenck's other personality construct is characterized by introversion at one end of the dimension and extraversion at the other end. Individual differences along this continuum are thought to reflect biologically driven differences in resting levels of cortical arousal.

Eysenck (1967) claimed that individuals seek moderate levels of cortical arousal. Introverts, who have a higher resting level of cortical arousal, therefore avoid additional stimulation from the environment, whereas extraverts seek more stimulation as they have a lower resting level of cortical arousal. Individuals high on both neuroticism and introversion are believed to be particularly vulnerable to the development of emotional disorders and to experiencing relatively high levels of emotional distress, such as anxiety and depression. From this perspective, the trait of neuroticism may be responsible for chronic and pathological worry. There is little in the way of biological studies to support such a model. Various types of studies (e.g., neuroendocrine) have yielded inconclusive or contradictory results. Research has in general been lacking on this topic.

Psychological Approaches

In the past decade, a surge of research into the nature of worry has focused theory and targeted treatment efforts. These developments followed a shift of research attention from autonomic arousal to the cognitive side of GAD. As noted above, research revealed that the content of worry in GAD was not greatly different from that of normal worriers with several exceptions. Individuals with GAD have been found to worry and catastrophize about a wider range of topics than do panickers, for example. "Inability to cope" is the most predominant thought when clients with GAD are anxious, and "loss of self-control" is the most frequent mental image (Breitholtz & Westling, 1998).

Concerns about being able to cope and potential loss of self-control are themes that shadow the general findings of others, who have identified fear of loss of control as a likely maintaining factor in GAD (e.g., Barlow, 1991; Borkovec et al., 1991). Similarly, Davey and Levy (1998) induced worry using a catastrophizing interview technique. They showed that chronic worriers were more prone than nonworriers to catastrophize about new worries and that chronic worriers even catastrophize about positive aspects of their lives. Worriers also felt that information about new (introduced) worries had potential relevance to their existing worries. Further, their thinking style was perseverative, involving repetitive feedback loops. Chronic worriers also tended to account for their worries in terms of their own personal inadequacies, regardless of the worry topic. These findings support the idea that individuals with GAD are particularly concerned about their ability to handle or control hypothetical negative events.

If those with GAD are preoccupied and worried about their ability to cope, is such concern spread across all worries or reserved for only certain types of worry? A group of researchers in Montreal has shed some light on this question. Dugas, Freeston, and their colleagues (1998) assembled three groups of anxiety patients—those with a primary diagnosis of GAD, those with a secondary diagnosis of GAD, and a third group composed of patients with assorted anxiety disorders but not GAD. Both structured and free-recall measures were used to identify worry themes. Their findings revealed differences on high levels of worry about remote future events, which Dugas, Freeston et al. propose may be a distinguishing feature of GAD. Worry about immediate problems did not reliably distinguish the diagnostic groups in this study. Dugas, Freeston et al. speculate that worry about immediate problems may be adaptive, as it can lead to problem-focused coping and information seeking, while worry about remote future events is seldom adaptive.

Other features of worry in GAD have been highlighted. Clark and Claybourn (1997) found that worry in GAD is distinguished by its focus on the possible consequences of negative events, while obsessive intrusive thoughts are more concerned about the personal meaning of the thought. Members of the Montreal team, following clues from clinical experience, empirically investigated the possible role of intolerance of uncertainty in GAD. This cognitive dimension refers to individual differences in perception of information in ambiguous situations (Furnham, 1994) and characteristic ways of responding to this information (Freeston, Rhéaume, Dugas, & Ladouceur, 1994). In a systematic series of studies, this group showed intolerance of uncertainty to be highly related to worry, regardless of anxiety or depression levels (Dugas, Letarte, Rhéaume, Freeston, & Ladouceur, 1995). They also found that intolerance of uncertainty distinguishes worriers who meet diagnostic criteria for GAD from those who do not (Freeston et al., 1994).

Taken together, these intriguing results suggest that individuals with GAD tend to worry about catastrophic consequences of future events as well as their ability to cope with or control such events, and it seems individuals with GAD react strongly and anxiously to uncertainty. The overwhelming question is what function these tendencies serve. In addressing this question it may be instructive to examine the reasons for worrying as stated by clients themselves. Borkovec and Roemer (1995) informally questioned clients participating in a treatment outcome study for GAD. Clients offered six basic reasons for worry: (a) motivation to get tasks done; (b) general problem solving; (c) preparation for the worst; (d) planning ways to avoid negative events; (e) distraction from more emotional thoughts; and (f) superstitious effects on the perceived likelihood of future events.

Borkovec and Roemer (1995) found that "distraction from more emotional topics" particularly discriminated clients with GAD from other comparison groups. They have interpreted this finding as indicating that a main function of worry may be to prevent the experience of negative affect associated with memories of past aversive events. Borkovec et al. (1991) proposed a theoretical model to account for the worry process. They proposed that worry is a form of cognitive avoidance of perceived threat and is largely responsible for the maintenance of anxiety disorders in general. Clients with GAD in particular "have come to depend on conceptual activity as the predominant mode of coping with their world, just as others depend primarily on overt motor avoidance, somatization, or some other protective defensive response" (p. 42). That is, GAD clients are believed to use worry as a tool to cope with past and future catastrophes. In this way, worry provides an illusion of control, or at least some sense of predictability regarding negative events.

According to the Borkovec et al. (1991) theory, clients with GAD fear symptoms of negative physical arousal and affect. In their theory, worry is negatively reinforced because its occurrence interrupts clients' disturbing (arousing) imagery. Avoidance of such imagery helps suppress physiological activation, operating much like agoraphobic avoidance in panic disorder. This latter supposition is supported by the finding that most worry experience is composed of thought (70%), as opposed to images (30%), and that engaging in worrisome thought results in a reduction of somatic activation (Borkovec et al., 1991). Accordingly, worry is believed to diminish somatic sensations through the suppression of upsetting imagery. The "feared stimuli" in GAD are a range of fleeting and emotionally potent mental images of things going terribly wrong. These images are disturbing to contemplate, and worry provides relief by distraction.

Rather than being useful, worry is simply another form of avoidance—a means of escape. Theoretically, worry is pervasive, intense, and uncontrollable because it immediately avoids somatic anxiety without the individual's awareness (Borkovec et al., 1991). Worry may also interfere with the habituating effects of exposure to anxiety-evoking information by inhibiting activation of fear structures (Foa & Kozak, 1986). In this way, adaptive modification of the fear structure in memory is impaired, so the individual is unable to incorporate safety cues into their ideas about potential frightening events. Borkovec et al. argue that repeated exposure to imagery and affect in GAD clients may help reduce the ability of worry to function as a means of avoidance.

A related conceptual model of GAD has been developed by researchers in Montreal (Dugas, Freeston et al., 1998). The model rests on four planks, each believed to represent key cognitive features of GAD: intolerance of uncertainty, belief in the positive value of worry, poor problem orientation, and cognitive avoidance. Intolerance of uncertainty plays a central role in the model (Ladouceur, Talbot, & Dugas, 1997). Intolerance of uncertainty is thought to exacerbate initial "what if . . . " questions or to even invoke these questions in the absence of an immediate stimulus. The second feature of this model involves beliefs about worry. In effect, individuals with GAD justify and advocate worrying on a number of grounds, including "worrying helps avoid disappointment," "worrying protects loved ones," "worrying helps find a better way of doing things" and "worrying can stop bad things from happening" (Freeston et al., 1994).

The third feature of the model is referred to as "poor problem orientation" which is defined as a "set of meta-cognitive processes that reflect awareness and appraisal of everyday problems and one's own problem solving ability" (Dugas, Gagnon, Ladouceur, & Freeston, 1998, p. 217; Maydeu-Olivares & D'Zurilla, 1996). Problem orientation refers to an ability to recognize an existing or developing problem, the evaluation of the problem, and decisions about what, if anything, to do about it. For example, a person who is not a worrier might notice a small discrepancy in her bank statement and conclude that the amount is not worth worrying about, that the problem will resolve itself, or that if the discrepancy becomes important enough, she can always deal with it later.

In contrast, someone prone to pathological worry is likely to engage the issue with alarm and an inadequate approach to resolution, exclaiming, "Oh my God! What are they doing to us now?" Poor problem orientation is associated with a lack of confidence in one's ability to solve problems or to control the problem-solving process. Ladouceur, Blais, Freeston, and Dugas (1998) have shown that clients with GAD have poorer problem orientation than nonclinical moderate worriers, despite being equivalent in their knowledge of problem-solving skills.

The final feature of this model involves cognitive avoidance. Replicating the work of Borkovec and Inz (1990), Freeston, Dugas, and Ladouceur (1996) have demonstrated that worry is composed primarily of thoughts rather than images and that the proportion of thoughts versus images increases with the degree of worry. In agreement with the Penn State group (Borkovec & Lyonfields, 1993), the Montreal group considers the avoidance of threatening mental images to be the key function of GAD-related worry.

This four-component model has successfully discriminated clients with GAD from nonclinical control participants. A discriminant function analysis showed that all four components of the model were highly related to diagnostic group and that intolerance of uncertainty was pivotal in distinguishing GAD patients from controls (Dugas, Gagnon et al., 1998). Taken together, the four features of the model correctly classified 82% of the sample. This is the first study to identify intolerance of uncertainty as the most important component in distinguishing GAD clients from nonclinical control subjects. This model provides clear treatment implications that will be discussed in the treatment section of this chapter.

The relatively high levels of worry related to interpersonal issues that is associated with GAD (Borkovec, Robinson, Pruzinsky, & DePree, 1983) has also encouraged the development of psychodynamic formulations of GAD (Crits-Christoph, Connolly, Azarian, Crits-Christoph, & Shappell, 1996). In this model, earlier frightening or traumatic experiences are believed to foster the development of fears, which in turn threaten the individual's ability to have basic needs met in relationships and in life more generally. Noting the suggestion that clients with GAD avoid thinking of past traumatic events and that the function of worry is really to distract oneself from contemplating painful emotional memories (Borkovec, 1994; Roemer, Borkovec, Posa, & Lyonfields, 1991), psychodynamic theorists propose that the function of worry is defensive (Crits-Christoph et al., 1996). Interpersonally-oriented dynamic therapy bears some similarities to cognitive theories in that both recognize the function of worry as a cognitive avoidance of disturbing emotional themes. Unlike cognitive formulations of GAD, psychodynamic accounts feature interpersonal conflict as the core theme of importance.

ASSESSMENT

The tasks of assessment are to formulate a diagnostic impression, especially as regards differential diagnosis of other anxiety disorders, establish baseline measures of symptoms and cognitions, and evaluate other information relevant to treatment planning.

Diagnosis

The significant changes in diagnostic criteria for GAD between the DSM-III and DSM-IV (e.g., shift to a cognitive focus, 6-month duration requirement) have effectively made the GAD diagnostic criteria more stringent. The diagnosis of GAD relative to other anxiety disorders is difficult because of comorbidity and because general anxiety can be a feature of most other anxiety disorders. For this reason some investigators (e.g., Rapee, 1991b) refer to GAD as the "basic" anxiety. Nonetheless, clinicians will find that an assessment of the focus of anxiety and the nature of anxiety can be helpful in distinguishing between anxiety disorders. Barlow and DiNardo (1991) have differentiated GAD from panic disorder on the basis of the nature of anxiety. In panic disorder anxiety is anticipatory, whereas in GAD it is relatively nonspecific.

The primary way to rule out other anxiety disorders is to identify the focus of anxiety. Put another way, what is the client worrying about? Panic disorder, social phobia, and specific phobia all have both overlapping and distinctive features of cognitive content. The common feature is dread of unwelcome events and physical sensations. Distinctive features of cognitive content for panic disorder include fear of death, fear of medical emergency, or fear of social embarrassment. Worrisome mental content for individuals with social phobia concerns fear of negative evaluations from others, which may not be unlike the interpersonal concerns expressed by persons with GAD. In the case of GAD however, worry content generally goes beyond the concern over being scrutinized. Similarly, GAD can be distinguished quite easily from PTSD and OCD, despite the possibility of overlap in concern about illness and future personal safety. Clients with a primary specific phobia rarely have generalized anxiety and worry. Using discriminant analysis, Riskind et al. (1991) found that cognitive content distinguished clients with pure GAD and dysthymia when the cognitive content involves hopelessness and thoughts of both loss and failure, which are characteristic of dysthymia. However, these investigators could not distinguish between these two groups on the basis of worry and apprehensive expectation.

Comorbidity

One of the most striking features of GAD is its high rate of comorbidity. Simple and social phobias are the disorders most commonly associated with GAD (Sanderson, Di Nardo, Rapee, & Barlow, 1990). The rates of comorbidity between GAD and social phobia (range 23%–29%) and specific phobia (range 21%–32%) reported by Sanderson and Wetzler (1991) were equivalent, although GAD was not often assigned as a secondary diagnosis to other problems. Brown and Barlow (1992) found 18% of GAD patients in their study had an additional diagnosis of dysthymia and another 11% of clients with GAD had a diagnosis of major depression. It is not clear whether the association between these disorders is reflective of depression being reactive to GAD-induced worry, cynical cognitive styles in the case of GAD and dysthymia, or a common affective process, as suggested by Barlow (1991). Certainly, clinicians should be alert to the possibility of social and specific phobias as well as dysthymia and major depression as comorbid disorders in clients with GAD.

Questionnaire Assessment

The Penn State Worry Questionnaire (PSWQ) is a widely used measure of severity of GAD (PSWQ: Meyer, Miller, Metzger, & Borkovec, 1990). This questionnaire consists of 16 items measuring the tendency to worry and the uncontrollability of worry. It has good psychometric qualities and discriminates between GAD patients, those with other anxiety disorders, and normal comparison subjects (Brown & Barlow, 1992; Brown, Moras, Zinbarg, & Barlow, 1993; Meyer et al., 1990). The PSWQ has also been shown to be sensitive to treatment induced changes in levels of worry, when assessed on a weekly basis (Stöber & Bittencourt, 1998). Community norms for the PSWQ have been developed (Gillis, Haaga, & Ford, 1995) and are reprinted in Appendix A along with the questionnaire. In developing these community norms, two nonprobability quota samples (n = 261 and n = 267) were used to match the demographic profile of U.S. adults across variables of gender, race, income, and age for adults between the ages of 18 and 65.

Assessment of Cognitive Content

There are several reasons for a careful cognitive assessment in clients with GAD. The first is to aid the clinician in determining a diagnostic formulation, as discussed earlier. Secondly, a careful exploration of key cognitive variables that have been shown to be distinctive to GAD is essential for the development of treatment targets. In order to identify cognitive content relevant to treatment, we recommend paying particular attention to the four features of the conceptual model identified by the Montreal group (Dugas, Gagnon et al., 1998). Probing these four themes should prove particularly fruitful in developing treatment strategies.

> *Intolerance of Uncertainty.* What kinds of threats are both significant and ambiguous to the client? Threatening situations with ambiguous outcomes involve uncertainty about events that are meaningful and frightening to the client and can be prompted with a series of "what if . . . ," "suppose that . . . ," or other similar probes. The idea here is to document the range of ambiguous situations as well as the client's characteristic ways of perceiving and responding to them in terms of cognitive, emotional, and behavioral reactions.
>
> *Beliefs About Worry.* It will be useful to develop a list of the client's beliefs about worry. Recent studies show that maladaptive beliefs about worry are related to intensity level of the worry (Freeston et al., 1994). Clients can be asked why they think they worry or what ideas they have about the benefits of worrying. Clarification of such beliefs (e.g., "How does this help you?" "What do you think would happen if you didn't . . . ?") is necessary prior to encouraging more balanced appraisals.

Fearful Mental Images. Understanding the client's upsetting images is necessary for exposure during treatment. Fearful mental images may be about death (e.g., "my son in a coffin," "being operated on," "being forced to sell the house," "my husband having an affair with an acquaintance of mine"). The most salient fearful images are likely to be about future threats, and they may be quite vague (e.g., environmental degradation, an economic depression, the absence of an afterlife).

Problem Orientation. Exploring the client's problem orientation involves investigating problem perception, problem attribution, problem appraisal, personal control beliefs, and responses to emotionally threatening content (Maguth, Nezu, D'Zurilla, & Friedman, 1996, November). Since worriers typically have a poorer problem orientation, probing this area will provide the therapist with useful information for treatment purposes. For example, the clinician can trace problem appraisals and problem-solving attempts by asking clients to provide three or four examples of topics they worry too much about. These examples should include details of the event or idea that initiated the worry and what the client has done about the particular problem.

TREATMENT MODELS AND GUIDELINES

Pharmacotherapy of GAD

A range of medications have been shown to be helpful for GAD sufferers (see Antony & Swinson, 1996; Switzer & Rickels, 1991, for reviews). Most of these studies were done before DSM-IV, and we do not know how changes in diagnosis may impact estimates of medication effectiveness. The best efficacy has been established for the benzodiazepines (Switzer & Rickels, 1991). However, one study provided a pharmacological treatment contrast using a fixed dose of 15 mg per day of diazepam (Power, Simpson, Swanson, & Wallace, 1990a; Power, Simpson, Swanson, & Wallace, 1990b), and in this case diazepam treatment was no more effective than the placebo condition. Benzodiazepines tend to work quickly but are associated with cognitive side effects in some patients and a rebound effect of anxiety and depression once the medication is discontinued. Fewer pharmacotherapy studies on the treatment of GAD have been reported than for the other anxiety disorders with the result that clinicians are faced with less empirical knowledge to guide treatment decisions. It is safe to expect that most clients will have had some pharmacotherapy treatment history for GAD as provided by their primary care physician. We are aware of no empirical studies that demonstrate an advantage for combined pharmaceutical and psychological therapies for GAD.

Psychological Treatment Studies

There have been about a dozen empirical studies that have evaluated the efficacy of psychological treatments for GAD. Most of these studies used a cognitive behavioral treatment (CBT) condition contrasted with anxiety management training, analytic psychotherapy, applied relaxation, or nondirective psychotherapy. See Antony and Swinson (1996) for a review. Taken together, the CBT interventions have the best record of treatment efficacy.

The CBT treatments are composite treatments, consisting of a number of highly structured components. For example, the Borkovec and Costello (1993) study involved a combination of self-controlled desensitization and cognitive therapy. Clients were first taught to achieve deep relaxation followed by the engagement of imagined or external anxiety cues. They mentally rehearsed using their relaxation skills in the presence of anxiety-provoking cues (real or imagined), over repeated sessions until the cues no longer generate sustained anxiety. Along with the desensitization procedure, CBT clients also practiced an abbreviated (i.e., 10–15 minutes per session) form of cognitive therapy described by Beck, Emery, and Greenberg (1985), in which clients learned to generate cognitive coping statements and shift their perspectives, as the result of considering new evidence and testing beliefs.

Crits-Christoph and colleagues (1996) have also reported an uncontrolled study of 26 patients who received 16 weekly sessions of supportive-expressive psychodynamic therapy. Therapists followed a treatment manual that focused on the identification of core conflictual relationship themes, as expressed in past and current relationships (including the relationship with the therapist). Following identification of the conflictual relationship themes, they are replaced with healthier ways of understanding and responding in key relationships. The treatment parallels CBT treatment components in terms of exposure to emotionally sensitive themes and an emphasis on adaptive problem-solving. Crits-Christoph et al. found treatment effect sizes in the range typical of CBT outcomes. This represents an encouraging finding and we await randomized controlled trials to more fully document the efficacy of this structured form of psychodynamic treatment for GAD.

New evidence has identified *intolerance of uncertainty* as being highly contributory to OCD (Dugas, Freeston et al., 1998). The Montreal team has recently completed two controlled treatment trials on GAD using both individual and group treatment formats with a CBT approach that specifically targets intolerance of uncertainty and approaches to problem-solving. In a study that has not yet been published, these investigators report strong treatment effects (R. Ladouceur, personal communication, March 22, 1999). Some 78% of clients no longer met DSM-IV criteria for GAD upon the conclusion of treatment, and these results were maintained at 6- and 12-

month follow-up points. The magnitude of change was confirmed on self-report measures including the PSWQ. Group treatment proved to be as effective as treatment offered in the individual format. On the basis of these and several other studies, the following conclusions are warranted.

1. The effects of CBT are seen rather quickly. In one study, Durham et al. (1994) reported that the beneficial effects of CBT were attained within 6–8 treatment sessions. Outcome was not improved by addition of a further 10–12 additional sessions.
2. In all cases where follow-up data were provided, clients treated with CBT maintained their gains or improved during the posttreatment follow-up interval. The typical follow-up period reported in such studies was 6 months (Durham et al., 1994; Power et al., 1990a; Power et al., 1990b), although Borkovec and Costello (1993) report strong treatment effects for CBT continuing through 12 months of follow-up.
3. CBT is as good as (and sometimes superior to) other treatments. In the one study where analytic psychotherapy was compared to cognitive therapy, small to moderate treatment effects were found for analytic psychotherapy (42% improvement) and moderate to strong effects for CBT (76%) (Durham et al., 1994).
4. A number of studies included a nondirective treatment condition as a contrast group. Generally these treatments featured empathic support, exploration of life experiences, self-reflection, and clarification of feelings. The results of nondirective therapy were mixed, and treatment gains typically deteriorated during follow-up.
5. Although CBT produces very robust improvements, applied relaxation generally does as well (e.g., Borkovec & Costello, 1993).
6. The best psychological treatments are imperfect, particularly when end-state functioning is measured, as they leave considerable room for improvement. All of the CBT interventions involved multicomponent treatment packages, so it is unclear what the relative contribution of various treatment components has been.
7. In the two studies that have applied CBT techniques with elderly clients with GAD (Borkovec & Mathews, 1988; Stanley, Beck, & DeWitt Glassco, 1996), CBT performed no better than supportive/nondirective counseling, indicating that specific mediators of GAD in this population are not being successfully targeted.

Cognitive Behavior Therapy

CBT for GAD is based on the theory that this disorder originates in broad-based perceptions of the world as a dangerous place, which results in maladaptive interactions among cognitive, behavioral, and physiological response systems (Newman & Borkovec, 1995). Dysfunctional cognitive responses include intolerance of uncertainty (Dugas, Freeston et al., 1998), attentional bias toward threat cues (Mathews, 1990), and avoidance of negative images through worry (Borkovec & Inz, 1990). As noted in the review of psychological treatment studies for GAD, CBT has consistently produced good, but imperfect, results.

In considering the components of treatment, one might think that imaginal exposure should be used for cognitive avoidance, relaxation for physical tension, and cognitive interventions to reduce worry. Unfortunately, it is difficult to know how the therapeutic effects of treatment targeting one response modality (e.g., relaxation) might affect another. It may well be that improvement is uniform across response modalities no matter which response modality is targeted (e.g., autonomic arousal). By way of comparison, researchers in the area of depression have demonstrated that treatment effects tend to cross over response modalities. For example, an effective medication can improve social functioning, and interventions aimed at improving interpersonal relations tend to have a comparably positive effect on somatic symptoms in depression.

We propose a five-component hybrid treatment protocol for GAD based largely on the work stemming from the research centers at Penn State, Montreal, and Albany, New York. This multicomponent treatment program aims to replace dysfunctional reactions in cognitive, somatic, and behavioral domains with particular emphasis placed on cognition (see table 8.1 for treatment overview).

Table 8.1 Overview of CBT Components for GAD
___

Education About Worry
    Faulty beliefs about the value of worry
    Role of intolerance of uncertainty
    Worry as a means of cognitive avoidance of fearful mental imagery
    Maladaptive problem solving skills
Awareness Training
    Identify immediate and realistic problems
    Identify worries about distant and unlikely events
Worry Interventions
    Problem awareness
        Applying problem solving strategies to current problems
        Making time-limited decisions in the face of uncertainty
    Reevaluate beliefs
        Evaluate beliefs about the advantages of worry
        Clarify the utility versus costs of worry
    Cognitive exposure
        Exposure to anxiety-producing images of unlikely, remote, and unrealistic events
        Practicing covert response prevention
Applied Relaxation
    See chapter 5 for details
Time Management
    Delegation of responsibility
    Assertiveness
    Adhering to agendas
___

Client Education

The goals of client education are to review the model of GAD, preview the treatment plan, and ensure the client's understanding and acceptance of both. Because life is filled with uncertainty, one major goal of the therapy is to change the way the client perceives and responds to emergent issues involving uncertainty. A 2-stage approach involves an acute treatment phase and a maintenance phase involving indefinite self-management and application of skills acquired in treatment. Explaining this approach helps ensure that the client does not view treatment as a brief episode, or cure, after which continuing self-help efforts are unnecessary. At this point the CT model for GAD that emphasizes the role of maintaining factors is reviewed. The contributing role of faulty beliefs about the value of worry is discussed. Similarly, the therapist explains the effect of intolerance for uncertainty in order to provide the client with insight about the powerful role played by this cognitive style.

The adaptive role of worry as cognitive avoidance of feared consequences is also presented. This is a novel concept for most clients, and illustrations of other forms of avoidance in more general areas are helpful before transferring attention to examples of cognitive avoidance. An everyday example of cognitive avoidance can introduce the concept, such as daydreaming when one is facing a deadline. Then the therapist can discuss the use of worry to avoid disturbing mental imagery. Helpful and unhelpful problem-solving skills are contrasted as they apply to anxious problem-solving styles. Finally, the advantages of self-managed relaxation are reviewed. Sidebar 8-1 illustrates the nature of routine worries, feared imagery, beliefs about the advantages of worry, and dysfunctional elements of normal problem-solving, within the context of a case example.

Awareness Training

The object of awareness training is to increase the client's ability to identify situations that lead to worry. In so doing, clients learn to discriminate between two classes of worries: immediate problems with a realistic basis, such as a current financial pinch, versus temporally distant events that are not very realistic, such as the possibility of one's child being killed in a car crash someday. This distinction guides subsequent worry interventions (Ladouceur, Freeston, & Dugas, 1993, November). Clients list 5–10 worries in each of the two classes of worry as a homework assignment. This list provides the therapist and client with worry content for the acute treatment phase. Later, clients are encouraged to upgrade this list as part of their ongoing maintenance program. Immediate and realistic worries are approached with problem-solving, while cognitive exposure is directed toward distant and unlikely worries.

CASE EXAMPLE

Tucker is a 53-year-old married businessman with two adult children in their 20s and a diagnosis of GAD. Viewed by others as astute, pleasant, and successful, Tucker worries excessively about his health, business, marriage, children, parents, and financial security. Assessment revealed the following details, useful to both formulation and treatment planning.

Routine Worries (in order of frequency)	• somatic sensations indicative of impending stroke/ heart attack
	• any significant misadventure/stressor of a family member
	• business problems/risks
Beliefs About Worry	• "Worry got me where I am." (i.e., successful)
	• "If I anticipate problems, then I can solve them."
	• "It pays to be alert and careful."
Problem Orientation	• good problem recognition
	• good causal attributions/appraisals
	• poor personal beliefs about ability to manage situations (characterized by excessive rumination and consultation)
Worst Fears (mental images)	• his own premature death
	• business bankruptcy
	• living alone (wife divorces him)
	• children "write me off"

Worry Interventions

Problem Orientation

Problem orientation, distinct from problem-solving, applies to those worries reflecting immediate problems that are grounded in reality. Problem orientation refers to an individual's general way of reacting to problems, including recognizing the problem, making causal attributions, problem appraisals, and personal beliefs about one's ability to manage the problem, all in the context of one's values, beliefs, and commitments (D'Zurilla, 1986). Deficits in problem orientation interfere with the application of problem-solving skills.

Individuals with GAD are poor in problem orientation, not in problem-solving per se. One significant reason for this is the characteristic intolerance of uncertainty. In this case, clients get bogged down in attempts to gain excessive amounts of information as well as reassurance from others prior to making a decision. They seek this information and reassurance because they cannot be sure how something will turn out, and they feel responsible for contemplating all avenues and potential difficulties. Needless to say, this process can delay or immobilize decision making. This quality is reflected in the unusual lengths that worriers go to collect information for problem-related decisions.

After evaluating the client's problem orientation, the clinician guides the client through normal problem-solving steps, using a problem offered by the client. In this process, the clinician should ascertain that all the key problem-solving steps are applied without unnecessary attention to details and that clients proceed without knowing beforehand how things will turn out (to develop tolerance for uncertainty). Clients should aim for a balanced and flexible point of view in problem-solving, including timely decisions without seeking excessive information to preclude uncertainty (Ladouceur et al., in press). In collaboration, the therapist and client identify 2–3 problem areas per week, ranging in difficulty, for the client to practice problem-solving as homework.

During the session, the therapist reviews the client's written records of each problem, noting the problem-solving steps involved, the time taken, results gained, and the client's satisfaction with these results. For example, Kyle is one of our clients who worries excessively about different ways of conducting home repairs and whether he can do them at all, although he is not a perfectionist. He reads home repair manuals and repeatedly asks advice from hardware store clerks and neighbors. Normally this pattern results in no repairs being done. One of his homework tasks was to make a priority list of the two best ways to repair his towel rack, which has screws that will not stay screwed into the wall. Kyle aimed to make the list of two methods after a brief (10 minutes) review of the options, including a brief consultation with the hardware store clerk. After making the list, he was to apply one of the two solutions. Tasks like these provide the therapist with opportunities to monitor and prompt adaptive problem-solving and cognitive coping (e.g., "It is good enough for now. If it breaks again, then I'll try something else.").

Clients learn to reevaluate their coping approach to problems and to stay focused on the problem situation while identifying all key elements of the problem, but ignoring minor details related to the problem situation. Clients then proceed with the problem-solving process despite its uncertain outcome. Clients with GAD usually need support to remain flexible and balanced while engaging in problem-solving. It is often helpful to ask the client to commit to a deadline for a few problems of differential difficulty. Solutions for one problem can be outlined in the session, prior to tasking the client with the remainder for a homework assignment.

Although most clients with GAD have adequate problem-solving skills, some do not. In this case the clinician should obviously educate the client about how to approach problem-solving, including the steps of problem recognition, generation of alternative solutions, adoption and implementation of a solution, and review of the results. Guidelines for teaching problem-solving are readily available (e.g., D'Zurilla, 1986).

Reevaluation of Beliefs About Worry

Clients with GAD often hold dysfunctional beliefs about the value of worry. Some common beliefs are that worrying can: (1) provide motivation for accomplishing tasks; (2) be useful in general problem-solving; (3) help prepare for "the worst;" (4) help plan ways to avoid negative outcomes; (5) distract from more emotional thoughts; and (6) reduce the probability that something bad will happen (Borkovec & Roemer, 1995). The therapist can challenge the client to systematically examine the advantages and disadvantages of these beliefs. Behavioral experiments may be helpful in testing the value of worrying. For example, the therapist and client may work together to identify two relatively equivalent problems. They can both commit to worrying about one of them while discouraging worry on the other to see if the worry makes any difference to the outcome. The goal of this exercise is to clarify that worry is not a useful approach to problem-solving, and worse, that it promotes GAD and delays or inhibits useful problem-solving.

Cognitive Exposure

Cognitive exposure is used to reduce anxiety associated with the client's images of distant and unlikely awful events. Clients imagine anxiety-provoking images while using covert response prevention, on a daily basis for about half an hour. Disturbing mental images are identified and listed during assessment. (New anxiety-provoking images can be incorporated if they emerge during treatment.) Clients are asked to imagine one particular theme per practice session without distraction, worry, or other forms of cognitive avoidance (i.e., covert response prevention). The intent of this concentrated imaginal exposure is to neutralize the anxiety associated with the images through habituation. It is sometimes useful to structure this exposure by having the client record verbal details of the mental image on a tape recorder using a looped tape for repetitive exposure. As clients become adept at this procedure, they can generalize the exposure to feared outcomes of worries stemming from everyday situations (e.g., broken house window, a bounced check, flat tire).

One of our clients worried that he would be fired from his public relations job for being less competent and productive than his peers despite there being no objective evidence that this was true. He also worried that his children and wife did not respect him and avoided him when they could. His homework exposure tasks involved imagining visual details of both themes without interruption for 30 minutes each. He visualized increasingly confrontational work reviews with his supervisor, being put on probation, and eventually being asked to clean out his office and leave. In his imagery, co-workers became aware of his reputation as "damaged goods" and began to shun him. He imagined himself unsuccessfully trying to get other work, his wife bravely cutting household expenses, and he imagined their neighbors, friends, and extended family feeling sorry for them. In his second theme, this client visualized his children always making excuses to not spend time with him, or not even to communicate with him. He imagined his wife adopting a lifestyle that took her away from him as much as possible, and he imagined eating alone on his birthdays. Interestingly, this client had an active family life and was not depressed. He had heard of cases where these things had happened to others and then selectively recalled negative interpersonal interactions with his family members.

Applied Relaxation

Applied relaxation by itself is established as an effective treatment for GAD. It is well received by clients as being very practical and credible. Clients also tend to feel that applied relaxation is a tangible technique that is in their control, and they seem to appreciate the "hands-on" quality of this self-management technique. Applied relaxation was developed by Öst (1987b). We recommend the 8-step applied relaxation protocol as modified by Clark (1989), which is presented in chapter 5 on the treatment of panic disorder. Applied relaxation has been found to be effective in reducing anxiety across disorders, is widely researched and used, and has several distinct advantages over alternative relaxation protocols. Specifically, it is highly portable and can be quickly deployed. We recommend that the applied relaxation be folded into the GAD treatment program on a session by session basis, such that approximately 20 minutes of each session is devoted to applied relaxation, similar to our recommendations in chapter 5.

Time Management

Many clients with GAD have a sense of time urgency and feel overwhelmed by routine commitments. Consequently, development of time-management strategies can reduce the pressure they feel and contribute to effective problem-solving and a sense of personal control. Brown, O'Leary, and Barlow (1993b) have specified three basic components of a time-management program: delegating responsibility, assertiveness (e.g., saying "no"), and adhering to agendas. Failure to appropriately delegate responsibility may be due to a feeling of being too hurried, perfectionism, or comorbid conditions such as social phobia. It is advisable for therapists to identify a range of situations in which responsibility could be delegated, to role-play these with the client, and then to ask the client to commit to a schedule of implementation, to be reviewed in subsequent sessions.

For example, one client felt overwhelmed at work in her responsibility for providing audio-visual support to several large departments. She had a secretary and a technician, both full-time, who assisted her. Although her two staff members maintained normal working hours, she often skipped her coffee breaks, ate lunch at her desk, stayed late, and took work home with her. Her own performance reviews were positive, but she thought her two staff members were not very efficient. She believed they could not do things as well as she could because they did not have the "big picture." She and her therapist explored obvious problems with her perspective. The therapist then role-played first the client and then each staff member in work delegation scenarios, such as, "John, I've been thinking about the way we handle equipment deliveries and would appreciate it if you'd take that over." "Georgia, I'd like you to learn how to manage and update our inventory records on computer. It really isn't difficult and there is a course coming up in two weeks that would set you up nicely. It would be a good skill for you to have." As would be expected, the client had a variety of reasons why such delegation had not been made before (e.g., "He's careless with record keeping," "It is quicker if I do it"), which were challenged collaboratively.

The second feature of time management, assertiveness, reflects the fact that many individuals with GAD fail to offer sufficient resistance to others making requests of them. As a result, their responsibilities can quickly grow to unmanageable proportions. Again, therapists can help clients identify situations, role-play assertiveness scenarios, and review implementation attempts in subsequent sessions. A client who is unassertive in the face of his boss's unreasonable requests might be prompted to reply, "Well, I could do that, Bill, but I have my hands full. What would you like me to set aside in order to make time to take this on?" Brown, O'Leary et al. (1993) recommend that, where possible, delegation and assertiveness tasks be applied to issues relating to the client's faulty beliefs about the value of worry and personal responsibility. In doing so, delegation and assertiveness assignments can also serve as behavioral experiments (e.g., "Let's see how many complaints you receive from your customers if John handles equipment deliveries").

The third component of the time-management program involves asking clients to commit to daily agendas. Specifically, this involves planning one's day in terms of tasks of different levels of importance, such as things that must be done, desirable tasks, and elective tasks (i.e., if there is time). We ask clients to record their daily plans on an activity sheet (see figure 8.1, for illustration). This schedule involves blocking activities into morning, afternoon, and evening time brackets with the activity listed in advance and prioritized for degree of importance (1, 2, 3) with a column to indicate if the task was completed. A review of 3 or 4 days worth of these agendas will help the therapist to determine what problems the client is having (e.g., planning too many tasks, insufficient planning) and address ways of improving efficiency through adherence to planned agendas.

The two most common problems GAD clients face with planning daily agendas are the failure to (1) identify specific tasks and allocate realistic (i.e., based upon an historical review) time to complete the tasks; and (2) identify task priorities within the day. These problems are likely the result of a stream of consciousness effect, wherein clients with GAD maintain

---

Daily Agenda Planning Record

Instructions:

1. Plan the day in advance, not as you go.

2. Indicate the priority of each activity with 1, 2, or 3.

3. Cross off each agenda item that you complete each day.

MORNING

Take kids to swimming (1)

Shopping (2)

Arrange receipts for taxes (1)

Arrange baby sitter for next week (1)

Ironing (3)

Call Sarah (3)

Lunch (1)

AFTERNOON

Kids to Mom's (1)

Clean downstairs (2)

Car servicing (1)

Schedule dental appointment (2)

Gardening in back (2)

Clean garage (3)

Cook dinner (1)

EVENING

Stories with kids (2)

Call Henry and Jane (3)

Talk to Hans about our budget (2)

Movie with Hans (2)

Figure 8.1 Daily Agenda Planning Record.

heightened awareness for problems—ranging from actual to potential—while not adequately thinking through the relative merits of completing, postponing, or rejecting tasks.

All three of these time-management skills are important in reducing feelings of urgency and being out of control. Because these skills may seem fairly self-evident, many clients will claim awareness of the importance of the issue, but they do not have the requisite skills to implement effective behavior in these areas. Conscientious review of homework tasks and the development of ways of maintaining these skills over time are important tasks.

Common Problems

Demoralization

GAD patients often feel overwhelmed, ineffective, and demoralized. In addition to providing support and encouragement, clinicians should be cautious not to underestimate the difficulty of homework assignments, particularly in the early stages of treatment, which may otherwise lead to failure. To help clients keep their skills development in perspective, we sometimes use sports examples as analogies since most clients can relate easily to them. In learning a new sport, as with learning new ways of thinking, one has to constantly work at skill improvement. Practice and performance review are both important in mastering a new skill, as are anticipating and recovering from setbacks.

Both the content of worry and physiological symptoms will likely vary with clients over time. This can be problematic since clients can feel confident about having subdued their anxiety and worry, only to find new problems and physiological symptoms emerging some time later which can occasion a relapse. These can be approached as problems of treatment generalization and can be addressed toward the end of treatment during discussions of relapse prevention.

Inconsistent Compliance

This problem is by no means unique to GAD. However, it is exacerbated by feelings of being overwhelmed and inefficient time management, characteristic of GAD sufferers. We recommend that clients be encouraged to view the feeling of being overwhelmed as a symptom of their disorder and to use treatment attendance and homework assignments as an opportunity to practice both problem-solving and time-utilization skills. As a precautionary note, we find it important to be very redundant in underscoring the central role of worry in the maintenance of GAD. Clients often underappreciate the subtleties of cognitive strategies they have developed over the years to avoid feared or painful mental images. A routine review of the role of worry in avoiding upsetting mental images should help clients understand the downside of this coping strategy.

Treatment Outcome Evaluation and Life Course Planning

Since life stressors are inevitable and one's coping ability can be variable, periods of vulnerability to relapse can be anticipated. In the final stages of therapy, clients can create a written template of their treatment plan to guide them as they continue to practice the skills that they learned in treatment. When undergoing a stressful period, the template helps them to engage coping strategies before things get out of hand. After treatment has concluded, a routine self-evaluation can also be helpful in noticing when stress is building. During these self-evaluations, clients examine their worry proneness, practice time-management skills, and engage applied relaxation. With such routine self-evaluation and practice, clients can be ready to use self-management skills during periods of predicted stress (e.g., daughter's wedding) or unpredicted stress (e.g., severe illness of a family member).

Having reviewed treatment recommendations for the most common anxiety disorders, the final chapter will return to the general topics discussed at the beginning of the book. In chapter 9, we will discuss means of establishing and maintaining standards for quality care. Measuring quality of care optimizes service to clients, provides professional stimulation to practitioners, and can boost practitioners' economic well-being in the increasingly competitive economic arena of mental health services.

9 *Standards for Quality Care*

In the first chapter of this book, we reviewed recent events that have created enormous changes in the practice of mental health care. We argued for a model of an educated eclectic empiricist as an archetype for the modern practitioner. In this model, clinical work stands on three basic elements: scientific literature (educated), flexible use of tested interventions (eclectic), and sound measurement of client progress (empirical). Sole reliance on any of these three elements would be shortsighted, as each has its own limitations, as we discussed in chapter 1. In the present chapter, we return to the issue of standards of care, having outlined empirically supported treatments for the most prevalent anxiety disorders in the intervening pages. In this chapter, we will discuss concrete steps for evaluating and improving quality of care. Although the examples we use will continue to be centered around clients with anxiety disorders, we have aimed to provide guidance for establishing and maintaining standards of care that are independent of the type of population served. As a first step, we will discuss "quality" as a concept, reviewing indicators of good care at various levels of analysis. The bulk of the chapter will then be devoted to recommendations for how to improve client outcomes at a local level, for instance, within a group practice. Finally, because suggestions for making improvements in patient care necessarily bring up the topic of changing practice patterns, we discuss some ways to learn new interventions and to influence one's colleagues to make positive changes as well.

INGREDIENTS OF QUALITY CARE

Early classic work by Donabedian (1966) outlined basic indicators of quality care from three perspectives, and these indicators are still relevant today.

These three levels are structure, process, and outcome, moving from the more abstract to the more specific.

Structure

Structural indicators of quality include steps undertaken at the professional, legislative, and societal levels to insure that patients receive quality care. These indicators include credentialing procedures, such as licensing and certification, and practice privileges or restrictions regarding which categories of professionals are permitted to practice specific procedures. Professional licenses and certification procedures were designed to protect the public by ensuring standards of education and experience. However, these credentials only protect the public to the extent that the procedures for obtaining and maintaining the credentials are related to quality care.

The particular credentialing rules and procedures vary from one jurisdiction to the next, being under the control of states or provinces rather than the federal government. For example, potential licensees in psychology are examined on material related to *practice* (in contrast to material related to more general knowledge about psychology) in some states, but not in others. Many, but not all, jurisdictions require that licensed psychologists document their participation in continuing education (CE), but few of these jurisdictions provide guidelines for the format or quality of the CE experience. Thus, in Connecticut, there is no requirement for CE; in North Carolina, reading a book and taking a test on the content qualifies as CE. California not only requires workshop attendance for qualifying CE, but not just any workshop will do. The state must certify each workshop presenter in order for attendees to receive credit acceptable to the licensing board.

Most practitioners who have CE requirements as a condition of continued licensing will agree that the requirements can be bothersome. Keeping track of how many credits are needed and making sure that all the proper documentation has been organized—these are not the most exciting parts of a clinician's job. However, without the requirement of CE, a license loses any public-protection value in just a few years. Having loose standards of what qualifies as CE is nearly as bad. Currently, in most jurisdictions there is little assurance that the acceptable forms of CE effectively prepare therapists to competently implement new procedures.

How can clinicians influence these structural aspects of quality mental health care? By becoming involved in state or provincial professional associations and lobbying legislators, clinicians can work to ensure that high standards are maintained. Clinicians who are interested in maintaining high standards of care for mental health consumers can fight for high-quality continuing education by becoming involved in the regulatory process and by demanding that standards be adopted by professional organizations that organize, promote, and endorse CE opportunities. Holding ourselves to high standards promotes professional pride and inspires more confidence from those who seek (or reimburse) our services.

Process

The second indicator of quality outlined by Donabedian (1966) involves process, which encompasses issues of access to services and the efficiency of procedures within an organization. Where impediments prevent patients from being able to access services, this constitutes poor quality care. If a gruff and cranky receptionist scares off anxious clients, then these clients are not being well served. If the clinic building does not allow wheelchair access, then some patients will not be served. Efficiency of procedures is certainly a cost-related issue, but efficiency is also related to quality of care. If clients must wait for many weeks before being able to see a clinician, or if separate trips are required for psychotherapy and medication monitoring, then efficiency is impacting on quality of care. As an example, one of the clinics we work with is extremely cramped for space. Treatment rooms are in use from early in the morning until late at night. Custodial staff find it difficult to coordinate with clinicians to clean the rooms and have at times walked into treatment rooms without knocking while therapy was ongoing. This sort of intrusion, generated by process issues, certainly impacts on the client's experience of care.

Clinicians can work to improve the process of delivering quality mental health care at two levels. Locally, by which we mean in the clinic setting, clinicians should aim for maximum accessibility for their clients. By striving for efficient service, aiming for a diverse staff, and eliminating barriers to access to care, mental health care providers establish a reputation for high-quality service. At a broader community level, clinicians can advocate on behalf of their clients to urge managed-care organizations and insurance companies to provide adequate coverage.

Rapoport and Cantor (1997) made some specific recommendations along these lines for maximizing the quality of care in a managed-care environment. They recommended becoming involved with the managed-care organization, making mental health professionals more visible. Although we may not often like to think in this way, a practice is a business, and clinicians may need to adopt some of the customs of professionals in other businesses, such as networking. Getting to know the plan administrators, corporate sponsors, and gatekeepers of a managed-care organization can create opportunities to provide education about the science and practice of behavioral health care, thereby improving the care available to clients.

Outcomes

Structure and process are not what most clinicians have in mind when they contemplate quality of care. Most of us are focused on the outcomes, or the end results of treatment. This level of analysis involves the "bottom line" of service effectiveness, from the perspectives of the client, the practitioner, and other interested parties (e.g., spouse, employer, judicial system). Outcomes are most directly and obviously tied to quality care, so this is the area in which most clinicians will want to exert their efforts toward improving care. Monitoring outcomes, and using this information to improve the quality of care, can be a complicated undertaking, particularly if there are multiple providers (e.g., family therapist, psychiatrist, and child psychologist).

The infrastructure necessary for using outcomes to improve quality of care involves linking ongoing measurement of patient status to decisions about treatment planning. For example, discharge criteria should be established in advance (e.g., when the client reaches "within normal limits" on a specified measure), so that treatment can be as efficient as possible. While the term "cost-effective" has become a sore spot for many practitioners, it remains true that cost-effectiveness is one component of quality care. To appreciate this point, one needs to recognize that providing more services than necessary is tantamount to providing poor quality care. Generally, people prefer to keep restrictive setting (e.g., hospital) care to a minimum. If one visits the family doctor for simple heartburn and is referred for an exhaustive (and expensive) battery of invasive gastrointestinal tests before first trying antacids, one may reasonably feel ill-served by the physician. Because using outcomes-measurement to improve the quality of care is an elaborate yet important endeavor, we will devote the next few pages to discussing the mechanics of this venture.

CONCRETE STEPS TOWARD IMPROVING OUTCOMES

When different clinicians use greatly differing approaches to clients with similar problems, or when there are wide disparities, depending on who the clinician is, in how well these clients respond, these variations are seen as evidence of poor quality. The process of improvement ideally involves identifying the practice habits of the especially effective clinicians and then helping each clinician to improve quality of care by comparing his or her procedures with the "best practices" standard. Obviously, each component of this process is complicated. In this chapter, there is only time for a brief explanation of the basics involved. More technical references for evaluation of outcomes in clinical practice have become widely available (Forquer & Muse, 1996; Lyons, Howard, O'Mahoney, & Lish, 1997; Ogles, Lambert, & Masters, 1996; Sederer & Dickey, 1996; Yates, 1980). See Appendix C for a listing of vendors who provide outcomes-measurement systems, software, and consultation for behavioral health care.

Step 1: Get Help

The steps we will outline below are time-consuming and, thereby, expensive. They are designed to improve the quality of care in any type or size of practice, but we stress that this task cannot be done alone. As in any business, the single-operator entrepreneur usually works like a dog to produce a quality product. Sharing resources and effort makes the job easier. Some of the larger group practices have been able to secure small grants from managed-care organizations for setting up outcomes-management systems, so this avenue bears exploration. Although the road to establishing such a system may seem long, the potential for improved patient care and better competitiveness are worthwhile goals. In a cost-containment climate, practitioners who demonstrate the flexibility to change practice patterns to strive for better client outcomes will be better able to attract the endorsement of managed care. In this way, effort extended to establish an outcomes-management system is an investment, in both quality care and the business of practice.

Step 2: Establish a Basic Measurement System

There are three major considerations in beginning a regular practice of measurement. *What* should be measured, *how* should it be measured, and *when* should the measurements be done? As with the adoption of any new technology, careful planning is critical. It may be useful to obtain consultation from someone experienced in clinical measurement, if there are no psychologists or similarly trained persons on the professional staff.

What to Measure?

The types of information that should be measured for each client will depend on the setting. In order to begin to establish a measurement system, practitioners need to consider what sort of information is needed by clinicians to facilitate decisions about treatment planning. In addition, the clients' perspective is important; what information is relevant for them? Finally, in some settings, there is an interested other party, such as a judge or an employer, whose interests need thoughtful consideration. In deciding what should be measured, there will inevitably be a trade-off between levels of analysis. Very specific information, such as the degree to which a client avoids driving over bridges, is critical for treatment planning with individual clients. This idiographic type of information is unfortunately more difficult to use when comparing across clients or across therapists. More general information, such as global endorsement of symptoms or indicators of role functioning, are applicable to a wider range of client problems, but they are not very helpful for planning treatment with a particular client. These types of measures can often be insensitive to changes related to specific client goals, such as having fewer arguments within the family.

In approaching this conflict, we recommend including both levels of analysis in the measurement plan. We'll begin by discussing global assessments. *Global measures* of patient status can include wide-ranging symptom measures and indicators of how well a client is functioning in various domains. Symptom measures are widely available, such as the Brief Symptom Inventory, which can be obtained from National Computer Systems in Minneapolis. Such measures typically involve a review of commonly encountered complaints (e.g., nervousness, headaches, insomnia, and worry), often arranged into useful subscales such as Depression or Psychotic.

Indicators of role functioning are also readily available. For example, researchers developed a brief questionnaire for the Medical Outcomes Survey that evaluates functioning as indicated by number of workdays missed, frequency of visits to the family physician, or ability to fully engage in family and home responsibilities. An easily used measure of global functioning is the Global Assessment of Functioning from the DSM-IV (Axis V). Measures of both global symptoms and functioning may not be necessary in all settings. Each measure being considered should be evaluated for how the obtained information will be relevant to the goals of the organization, clinic, or practice. However, we do recommend the use of at least one global measure that applies to every client.

Client satisfaction has recently come into favor as a type of global measure that applies to each client (Hiatt & Hargrave, 1995). Although this measure has been taken as a proxy for good outcomes, there are many dimensions of client satisfaction, going beyond whether the services met the client's needs (Lyons et al., 1997). For example, the client may report being very satisfied with the treatment if she feels that the therapist made a good faith effort. Clients may feel reluctant to make negative comments indicating poor satisfaction with the service due to their positive regard for therapists or staff. While many settings choose to construct their own client satisfaction rating, due to idiosyncrasies in their service environment, there are also several measures available.

Another simple measure of client satisfaction is to survey clients' reasons for leaving treatment. Figure 9.1 shows the results from a survey of 483 mental health consumers. This figure was adapted from data reported by Lyons et al. (1997). The figure gives a quick appreciation for the utility of information gained from even a simple measure asking clients why they ended therapy. When large proportions of clients leave therapy because their problems were resolved, this can be taken as one indication of good quality of care. Data from this type of client survey can be compared across different treatment teams or across time. If one treatment team has comparatively low rates of dissatisfaction, then this team may be using some practices that could be implemented by other teams to improve service quality. Likewise, let us say that clients covered by a given payment plan are much more likely to leave treatment because their benefits are exhausted than because they have reached their treatment goals. Using data such as these, practitioners may be in a position to convince the plan administrators to increase coverage so that their enrollees better match similar clients covered by competitor plans.

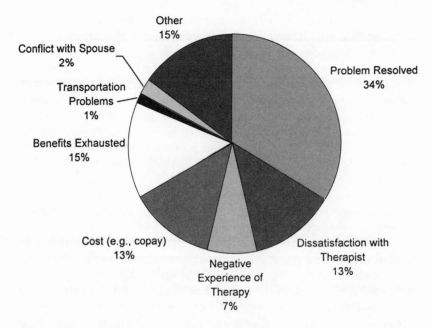

Figure 9.1 Reasons for Ending Therapy. Adapted from data in J. S. Lyons et al. (1997), *The measurement and management of clinical outcomes in mental health* (New York: John Wiley).

Although global information like overall symptoms, functional status, or client satisfaction are important and can be applied to nearly every client being seen, *problem-specific indicators* are often needed to guide treatment planning. In addition, if there are specialty teams (e.g., adolescent treatment team) within a service—even if they are relatively informal—then measures of client outcomes will need to be more specialized if they are to guide outcomes-improvement strategies. We assume that readers of this book have some specialized interest in anxiety disorders, and throughout the book we have provided information on obtaining and using measures that are particularly helpful in assessing problems associated with anxiety disorders. Some of these measures are applicable across several anxiety disorders, such as the Fear Questionnaire. Others are specific to particular anxiety problems, such as the Yale-Brown Obsessive Compulsive Scale. Researchers who constructed these specific scales were generally interested in comparing outcomes within very specific samples, a different situation than faced by most practitioners. The utility of these measures for guiding treatment planning is relatively clear and has been outlined in the preceding chapters. How can clinicians in community settings use these measures to improve outcomes?

There are two strategies for using problem-specific measures to provide feedback on outcomes across clients in a clinical setting. For comparing across clients or therapists, the easiest way is to convert clients' (pre- and posttreatment) scores on these measures to norms, such as percentiles, Z-scores, or *T*-scores. (If several measures are used, they probably will not be on the same scale. Some may use a 0–100 scale, where others are on a 0–4 scale. Standardizing scores with percentiles, Z-scores, or *T*-scores puts all measures in the same metric, so that they can be easily compared.) The basic rudiments of normative data are available for a wide variety of measures, usually published in scoring manuals or journal articles where the measure was initially introduced. Clients' scores can be compared to the published results from other clients with the same problem or those without anxiety problems, with the aim being to help clients reach a numerical goal on the problem-specific measure.

A second way to use these measures to improve outcomes is to identify a subset of clients with a relatively common presenting problem, and follow this subset intensively in lieu of measuring all clients. In a joint project between Yale University and Grove Hill Medical Center in New Britain, Connecticut, we recently began using this method to gather data with the aim of improving outcomes. The Grove Hill Medical Center is a group practice with a behavioral health care section that provides services to clients from diverse backgrounds with a wide array of presenting problems. We decided to study outcomes of panic disorder after a review of records indicated that staff clinicians annually treat over 150 patients with a primary problem of panic. Clients are identified as potential study participants during intake, which triggers a system of ongoing measurement. Therapists collect Panic Records from clients, who also routinely complete the Mobility Inventory and the Beck Depression Inventory. By focusing on a readily identifiable subset of clients, we are able to use targeted measures to document the quality of patient outcomes representing a substantial portion of the patient flow at Grove Hill.

In sum, the type of services offered by the organization will be a primary determinant of *what* needs to be measured. In preparing to implement an outcomes-management system, planners should consider the type of information that will be required, as well as the level of specificity that will be needed. A combination of global and problem-specific measures may provide the benefits of each type of measurement. Once planners have decided what to measure, the questions turn to logistics.

How to Measure?

In considering how information should be gathered, many choice points arise. We certainly want to assess clients' viewpoints about the degree to which their goals are being reached, but for some populations, clinicians' perspectives will be considered to be more important. Furthermore, given the current focus on cost containment, all assessment procedures should be as cost-efficient as possible. How is this best accomplished? Finally, to what degree should outcomes-assessment designers plan to construct their own measures versus using measures previously developed by others? We will discuss each of these topics as a basic outline of some of the measurement issues involved.

There are some types of clinical problems that are notorious for self-deception on the part of the client, including eating disorders, substance abuse, and spousal abuse. In these cases, practitioners obviously need some form of assessment other than self-report. However, even in problems without such obvious need for external indicators, the perspective of a clinician can be important. If a clinician's evaluation is necessary, how should this be obtained? The best method (and the most expensive) is to use an independent evaluator, because therapists' judgments can understandably be clouded by expectations of improvement and by the salience of specific areas of improvement. These biases may prevent the treating therapist from making an objective judgment of the functional status of the client. Independent evaluation is often too expensive to be practical in a community setting, but there are several options to consider. First, if the practice or organization is large enough to support a case manager, then regular brief independent evaluations could be a part of this role (Lyons et al., 1997). Another option to consider for smaller practices is sharing the workload, so that each clinician performs brief evaluations for clients from another clinician. If an established brief measure is used, costs can be held down.

The costs of assessment are a formidable barrier to implementing a basic measurement system. Planners may want to consider computer-assisted evaluation, although most clinicians (including the two of us) initially balk at the idea. In fact, Newman, Consoli, and Taylor (1997) have reviewed numerous studies of computer-based assessments, including popular measures like the Hamilton Scales for Anxiety and Depression, the Diagnostic Interview Schedule, and evaluations of target complaints, suicide risk, and mental status. Computerized versions of these evaluations have shown good reliability and validity when compared with a human interviewer (Newman et al., 1997). There is even some evidence that clients are more revealing of sensitive information when interacting with a computer, and clients (surprisingly) are not put off by the procedure. Computerized assessment has the obvious advantage of cost-efficiency; after the initial start-up costs, the system is relatively inexpensive to operate. Clients can complete computerized questionnaires faster than the paper-and-pencil variety, and the costs of xeroxing and hand-scoring are eliminated.

Throughout this book, we have pointed to a variety of measures that have been thoroughly tested and published. Some of the assessments we recommend are relatively tailored to a client's idiosyncratic concerns, such as the behavioral testing discussed in chapter 3. Others are questionnaires completed by the client or interviews administered by the practitioner. Although there may be times when a measure must be constructed for the particular setting (i.e., client satisfaction evaluations discussed above), generally speaking, existing measures are preferred. In most cases, existing measures have been carefully constructed to be reliable (i.e., repeated adminis-trations of the measure will yield the same result) and valid (i.e., they measure what they say they do). Using an existing instrument permits confi-dence in the psychometric properties of the measure, including norms, with-out doing all the work to establish them.

When to Measure?

The general guideline for when to evaluate clients is *Early* and *Often*. Begin-ning the assessment process early is advisable because a baseline is estab-lished. Setting up a fixed schedule of assessment helps to insure that the evaluations are done frequently. In terms of ease of data collection, baseline data are relatively easy to gather, because clients and therapists are both highly motivated at the outset. From that point on, compliance often goes downhill, if our experiences are any guide. For example, with the Grove Hill project mentioned earlier, therapists are scheduled to collect Panic Re-cords on a weekly basis along with twice monthly measures of agoraphobia and depression. This schedule is somewhat more frequent than is really needed, but this leaves room for the inevitable snags in data collection.

Optimally, data will be collected not only at baseline, but also at the conclusion of treatment, if the data are to be used to guide improvement in quality of care. For example, at the Grove Hill site, there is a larger battery of assessments that is conducted both at baseline and at the conclusion of treatment, including interviews by independent evaluators and both global and problem-specific questionnaires. The expense of this larger evaluation prohibits more frequent data collection, because we are doing this project without the benefit of outside funding.

The biggest measurement challenge has been getting posttreatment data. We have also heard this complaint from others who conduct outcomes as-sessment in practice settings. The problem is that therapists may not know when they are conducting the final session, because clients often simply stop coming to therapy, perhaps after breaking a few appointments. By having a staff person who takes responsibility for telephoning these clients and ex-plaining the rationale behind evaluating their status (in terms of improving quality of services), we are able to dramatically improve our ability to col-lect these endstate assessments. Some clients may feel sheepish about return-ing to the clinic after abruptly ending therapy without saying goodbye, so we have been flexible about conducting evaluations by telephone and mail if necessary. One helpful factor may be that clients are aware when schedul-ing that the evaluator will not be the treating clinician.

We have one last word regarding timing of assessments. In addition to being *Early* and *Often*, they should also be *Brief*. Lyons et al. (1997) advise that evaluators can count on having only about 5 minutes of provider time and 20 minutes of client time. Longer evaluations are possible if good incen-tives are used. For example, in the Grove Hill project, we use about 35–40 minutes of client time for questionnaires at baseline and posttreatment, but we also provide a strong rationale about the purposes of the project. Provider time is at a minimum, limited to about 2 minutes on a weekly basis and 5–10 minutes at the beginning and end of treatment.

In the preceding pages, we have provided suggestions for establishing a basic measurement system within the clinic setting. The planning stage takes quite some time, and actually implementing the measurement system will require working with staff members at all levels of the organization. As we have found in our work in practice settings, there will always be unanticipated problems and glitches. Close communication between staff and those implementing the system will help ensure that problems are identified early. Once the basic measurement system is operational, the information becomes available to move on to the next step involved in improving outcomes.

Step 3: Evaluate Current Practices

In order to be informative, data need to be compared to other data. Simply knowing what percentage of clients feel satisfied with the services they received does not empower the clinician to improve the quality of services. Clearly, a goal of 100% of clients meeting treatment goals or feeling satisfied is not reasonable in behavioral health care. Thus, comparing the current state of client services to some desired state is necessary, but what should that desired state be? A fair comparison would be across clinicians in the same or similar organizations. Comparing client outcomes across clinicians reveals the degree of variation in quality of care within the clinic. Large variations can be seen as evidence of poor quality because some clinicians are able to help clients obtain extremely good outcomes whereas other clinicians are seeing poor outcomes.

Obviously, one must compare apples with apples. Direct comparisons would be inappropriate between the outcomes of Clinician A, whose caseload consists primarily of clients with severe OCD, PTSD, and personality disorders, with those of Clinician B, who sees mostly clients with mild to moderate depression and panic disorder. To *fairly* evaluate whether there are large variations in patient outcomes, the type of caseload must be incorporated into the comparison. Making adjustments for "case mix" includes accounting for caseload factors like the typical severity of the problem, degree to which the problems are acute versus chronic, complexity of the problems, and complexity of the treatment plan (Lyons et al., 1997). These factors can be controlled in the comparison by using statistical tools or by stratifying the comparisons across clinicians (or across treatment teams, etc.) in varying degrees of complexity of the clients.

By measuring and accounting for differences in case mix, practitioners have a context for evaluating the data on patient outcomes. These data can then be used for future planning, such as staff training and development or matching clients to therapists who are likely to be most helpful. Solo practitioners will obviously have some difficulty comparing their outcomes across clinicians. Several of the firms listed in Appendix C, in addition to providing products and services to facilitate outcomes measurement, also provide access to large databases of client outcomes. Those in small group or solo practices may be able to make fair comparisons adjusting for case mix from these resources.

In evaluating patterns of outcome, several comparisons can be made. Outcomes can be compared across clinicians, as we have just discussed, as well as across treatment teams or across sites. In addition, outcomes can also be compared within each clinician, to give feedback on the types of clients with whom each clinician is relatively more and less successful. This type of evaluation has the obvious potential for being threatening to clinicians, so care must be taken to communicate a helpful attitude. By keeping the focus on quality improvement and organizational factors (e.g., membership on treatment teams, targeted case assignment), the process can be less threatening.

This is the Total Quality Management (TQM) approach of making incremental changes to improve the quality of a service or product, and some behavioral health care providers are starting to implement basic strategies from this management philosophy. The TQM approach involves identifying areas where quality can be improved and viewing low quality as a problem to be solved within the system, rather than a problem to be blamed on an individual. To be useful, this approach must be genuinely embraced by the leadership within an organization and must be communicated clearly to everyone involved. Thus, areas in which a clinician's or team's outcomes are relatively strong can serve as practice models for the rest of the organization. Conversely, clinicians or team members can work together to solve problems that are represented by areas of relatively poor outcomes. See sidebar 9-1 for some suggestions for constructive approaches to shoring up weaker areas within an individual clinician, team, or clinic site.

During the process of critically evaluating practice patterns, cost considerations should be kept in mind. Recently, cost-effectiveness has gotten a bad reputation among many clinicians, who perceive that some managed-care organizations appear to cut costs by denying legitimate requests for mental health care. While we do not condone this practice in any way, cost considerations are a reality within every type of payment system. Behavioral health care providers cannot afford to adopt a purist attitude of maintaining that costs are not a relevant topic. Working within the reality that costs need to be balanced by effectiveness does not in any way dehumanize therapy. Olfson, Pincus, and Sabshin (1994) report that only 16% of clients stay in therapy for longer than 20 sessions, but these clients account for 66% of expenditures on mental health services. If these clients are measurably better off *in* therapy than *out of* therapy, then these expenditures are certainly worthwhile, but the question of effectiveness in the face of disproportionate use of resources is appropriate.

A final consideration that should remain on the table when conducting a

IDEAS FOR IMPROVING OUTCOMES

When an examination of the patterns of outcomes across treatment teams, sites, or clinicians reveals that some outcomes are lagging well behind those of other providers, several options can be considered for improving the situation. Some ideas include:

- Reorganize the structure of a group of providers, so that teams or sites include a better mix of clinicians. For example, if the analysis of outcomes in the organization reveals that more experienced clinicians have fewer premature terminations, then teams or sites might be arranged to have seasoned clinicians dispersed relatively evenly throughout them.
- Target providers' special skills in assigning cases. In the above example, try to identify risk factors for premature termination in the client base, and assign higher risk clients to those therapists with especially low drop-out rates. Obviously, every clinician needs a good mix of clients to avoid burnout, but good quality care will involve matching therapists to clients where the data support such a match.
- Arrange for formal supervision between clinicians who have a good track record and those who have been obtaining poor outcomes. Supplemental supervision is likely to work especially well in those cases where patient characteristics of the problem outcomes can be identified. For example, several clinicians who show poor outcomes when treating clients with distressed marriages can be supervised by clinicians who do well with these clients. If supervision is approached from the perspective of enhancing quality of care, rather than as a punitive step, then both supervisors and supervisees are likely to benefit.
- Support training and development within your organization. Make funds (and time off) available for clinicians to enhance their skills in the areas that are identified as needing improvement on the basis of outcomes evaluations.

critical evaluation of one's practice is whether practice patterns are making the best use of scientific findings. Throughout this book, we have tried to make clear that clinical trials do not provide all the answers for clinical decision making. Their current cumbersome structure makes it impossible for them to be flexible enough to address the subtle questions a practitioner faces every day. Like cost considerations, however, empirical research is not made irrelevant by its failure to answer all questions. Clinicians do not typically consult randomized controlled trials when formulating a treatment plan, but we argue that this should be a part of the process. Incorporating research results into practice definitely requires motivation, because research articles are not often written in the most accessible style. The effort to incorporate empirical findings into practice will likely be repaid by better patient outcomes, and later in this chapter we offer some suggestions to facilitate this process.

Step 4: Establish Practice Standards

As reviewed in chapter 1, numerous professional organizations and some managed-care organizations have been writing practice guidelines for specific emotional disorders. The American Psychological Association has also prepared a template for developing practice guidelines. In the main, such guidelines offer general recommendations for types of treatment that should be offered as first-line interventions for specific disorders. However, they do not provide specific instructions in how to conduct the treatments, how to choose from among several alternative treatment approaches, or how to adapt the guidelines for clients who have more complicated problems.

More specific recommendations are probably best developed in local settings, where developers can take into account factors like the types of clients served, the types of clinicians providing services, and resources available. For example, some settings may want to focus on helping clients to maintain gains after a (mostly) single episode, whereas clients in other settings are expected to continue to return for frequent episodes of care, depending on the population served. In the second case, practice standards will reflect recommendations for how to handle a client who has returned for care (e.g., level of assessment required, under what conditions to return to the same clinician).

After a measurement system is in place, and data from the practice have been carefully examined, practice standards can be developed with various degrees of specificity. Practice standards should include recommendations for empirically supported treatments to be offered as an initial step, where these are available. In addition, however, local practice standards should include guidance to clinicians about such things as assessment, treatment and discharge planning, boosting nonspecific treatment effects, and patient-treatment matching. Finally, practice standards, outcomes measurement, and examination of practice patterns are all unlikely to impact on client outcomes unless benchmark mechanisms are developed to provide feedback to clinicians in a timely way.

Assessment

If the basic measurement system as advocated above is already in place within the practice, then much of the guidance for clinicians about what to measure, and how and when, will already be provided by the overall system of outcomes measurement. However, there may be some types of assessment that provide particularly useful information for clients with specific problems that are not covered in a system that is used for all clients. For example, in our clinics, we have found that a behavior test provides extremely useful information for clients with social phobia, but this type of test would not be very practical if applied to all clients across a heterogeneous clinic setting. It is too expensive to implement for each client, and it may not be relevant for clients who do not have significant social anxiety. In addition, there are no available norms for the behavior test, so goals applicable across clients are not readily constructed.

Nevertheless, a behavior test for those clients who do have extreme social anxiety, for example, provides information critical to treatment planning by answering questions the client is not able to address. How does the client come across in a "get to know you" situation? Is social skill a problem, in addition to anxiety? Is the client able to actually give a speech if pressed, or is he so afraid that he routinely avoids, even in a clinic setting? How tolerant is this client of the sensations associated with anxiety, or of the occurrence of normal speech dysfluencies? The behavior test for social phobia is discussed in more detail in chapter 4; these questions are raised as an example. For most client problems, there is likely to be similarly specific information that is important for the clinician to consider in formulating a treatment plan. Throughout the chapters of this book, we have outlined assessment procedures of this type. In addition, clinicians within the organization who have been identified as especially effective in working with particular problems are good resources for specific assessment needs.

Treatment Planning

Most clinicians probably plan treatment strategies in an implicit, rather than explicit, way. Their plans are mentally construed as ideas, rather than being written out on paper. In some settings, treatment planning is mandated, and clinicians are required to specify goals and the methods by which they intend to intervene in the service of those goals. In these settings, there are special forms on which clinicians list goals, methods of measuring progress on those goals, planned interventions, estimated time for reaching the goal, and liaisons with other service providers who are involved in the care of a specific client. While specifying goals can be time-consuming, and few clinicians actually enjoy the task, they are valuable.

For example, in the group therapy program for social phobia at Yale University, clinicians specify 1–4 goals for each client at the outset of the group. Group therapists, while grumbling about constructing the goals, admit that being required to state goals for each client has positively changed the informal aspects of their assessment. They have learned what types of information they need in order to specify client goals, and they have altered their pregroup individual interviews in response. Notably, we recently questioned the utility of committing these goals to paper, given the amount of therapist time required. The primary group therapists, who do most of the work, spoke in favor of continuing to specify these goals, due to the positive effect the procedure has on focusing assessment toward specific client goals rather than more general goals involved in treatment of social phobia.

Being skilled in constructing treatment plans can also facilitate the process of seeking authorization for reimbursement of more sessions from a client's managed-care or insurance company. Staff members who are skilled in constructing these treatment plans can teach other practitioners within the clinic how to efficiently write treatment plans in a way that maximizes the likelihood that the planned treatment will be approved. If treatment plans are required (even for those clients who are paying out-of-pocket), they need to be flexible enough to accommodate new problems that arise. The plans should be written relatively quickly after a client is initially interviewed, in order to help the therapist focus the intervention right away. In addition, the practice standards should specify how often the treatment plan should be reviewed.

Finally, practice standards should give some guidance about planning for discharge. Think about your own cases for a moment. For those clients who are not benefiting from the treatment, do you have an alternative treatment plan? What is your usual approach when you have tried every strategy you can think of? Kendall, Kipnis, and Otto-Salaj (1992) surveyed 315 clinicians and found that 41% planned to continue using the same intervention for clients who were not responding. This sizable minority of practitioners had not developed an alternative treatment plan or made plans to transfer the client to another clinician. Competitive pressures certainly make it difficult for clinicians to refer their clients elsewhere, but what strategy would you want for your own family members if the therapist had tried every treatment approach he knew and the problem was still no better?

Discharge planning for clients who are improving is easier to contemplate but also requires some forethought from clinicians. If the client's benefit plan does not dictate the timing of termination from treatment, when does therapy end? Practice standards can provide guidance to therapists for making these decisions. Even the discussions that go into making the practice standards are likely to benefit clinicians, as they struggle together to define standards of care as they relate to discharge planning.

Nonspecific Treatment Effects

Most of the research that has been done to develop effective psychological treatments for emotional disorders has been designed to compare one intervention to another. These studies often find significant effects for particular treatments, as have been reviewed in earlier chapters. However, the therapeutic relationship often accounts for even more. For example, Najavits and Strupp (1994) tried to differentiate effective and less effective therapists on the basis of their interventions. Relationship ("nonspecific") factors, such as positive attributes of warmth and affirmation and minimizing the negative behaviors of attack and blame, differentiated the more effective therapists. Relationship effects were significantly stronger than technical ("specific") variables, although all therapists in this study were using the same manualized treatment.

Therapist style can have a direct impact on outcomes that are important to clients and their loved ones. Therapist style plays a big role in enhancing motivation for problem drinkers, for example (Miller, Benefield, & Tonigan, 1993). The Miller et al. study found that the more confrontational the therapist was, the more clients drank when evaluated one year later. This finding, certainly contrary to the "tough love" style popular in some recovery programs, points to the need to attend to interpersonal style when implementing psychological treatment. Patterson and Forgatch (1985) found similar results when conducting parent training for parents of children with problem behavior. When therapists used a directive-confrontive style, client resistance during the session increased. Resistance diminished when therapists switched to supportive-reflective styles. Note that these changes in therapist style were intentional and planned in advance, so they were not in *response* to client resistance.

Therapeutic alliance has been shown to be an important facilitator of treatment outcome in many studies across different treatment approaches (Orlinsky, Grawe, & Parks, 1994). Alliance has been conceptualized and measured in a number of ways. Researchers are beginning to understand that alliance is more than simply an emotional bond between therapist and client; recent models of alliance also emphasize technical factors related to the implementation of the treatment (Gaston, Marmar, Gallagher, & Thompson, 1991). Even in very structured or directive treatments, a strong working alliance involves development of a spirit of collaboration between therapist and client, with a sense that there is agreement on the tasks and goals of therapy. This discussion may appear to have run far afield of our point about developing practice standards. Indeed, including nonspecific factors into formalized guidance for therapists may be tricky. There are two ways in which this might be done. First, drawing upon the studies showing the impact of therapist style on outcome, clinical pathways and practice standards can point to the importance of attending to interpersonal style while planning treatment.

The second suggestion for improving nonspecific factors in the pursuit of quality care is more radical. We recommend that groups of practitioners use peer supervision to help boost nonspecific treatment effects. These groups of peer supervisors can help each other point to qualities of a therapist's interpersonal style that the therapist has not previously noticed. In addition, maintaining a good working alliance can be awfully difficult with some types of clients, and these peer supervision groups can be helpful in bolstering clinician morale. Each member of the group can draw on the interpersonal skills of other members to help fashion a thoughtful approach to boosting nonspecific effects. The peer support approach can also be very useful for sharing research results and incorporating them into practice. Practitioners of other professions, such as dentists, accountants, and medical specialists, often organize informal groups to meet regularly to review new research findings and policy changes, or to enhance their technical and professional skills, frequently in the process of reviewing problematic cases. This process can be especially helpful if the group members specify goals for their meetings.

Patient-Treatment Matching

With an organized measurement system in place, focusing on relationship factors leads naturally to considering how the client's characteristics such as interpersonal style or ethnic identity may shape a plan for treatment. This is an issue that practitioners struggle with daily, as they try to figure out what approach would be most useful for a given client. "Should I use an interpersonal approach for working with this client's depression, or would cognitive therapy be more productive?" We often guess at how a client's personality might interact with the therapist's style and planned approach when we assign cases to therapists and plan the treatment. Unfortunately, there has not been much in the way of systematic research on this issue, but some is beginning to appear.

For example, Beutler and his colleagues have demonstrated that directive interventions are better indicated for clients who are relatively less resistant, but these interventions are contraindicated for clients with high state or trait resistance (Beutler, Engle et al., 1991; Beutler, Mohr, Grawe, Engle, & McDonald, 1991). Likewise, behavioral strategies appear to be more effective than nonbehavioral approaches for impulsive clients, whereas the reverse is true for those clients who have good impulse control (Beutler, Engle et al., 1991; Kadden, Cooney, Getter, & Litt, 1989). By comparing a new client's profile on interpersonal factors known to influence treatment with therapists' track records with such clients, it may be possible to maximize quality of outcomes by assigning cases on the basis of such information. At a minimum, practice standards should provide therapists with guidance based on research results or data collected from within the organization to help them adjust treatment strategies where appropriate to accommodate the client's personal style.

The foregoing has not been an exhaustive discussion of practice standards; for that, we would need to write another book! Materials to actually help in the development of practice standards are available elsewhere (Glazer, 1994). Our aim has been to provide some promising possibilities of the type of information that can guide clinicians within an organization toward practices more likely to be associated with good client outcomes. Within that framework, practice standards should include information about empirically supported approaches to treatment as well as indications of appropriate assessment, guidelines for treatment planning, assistance in maximizing nonspecific treatment effects, and recommendations for client-treatment matching. Most of the practices we advocate in this chapter are not yet widely used, although we believe that market forces will encourage their adoption. Nevertheless, after reading this far, you may be thinking, "How would I ever convince my colleagues to adopt such changes to alter their habits of practice?" The next few pages address suggestions to encourage fellow practitioners to adopt new strategies in the pursuit of quality care.

FACILITATING CHANGES

One important implication of doing all the measurement and self-study that we are advocating in this chapter is that clinicians can receive benchmark information. Benchmarking involves having an appropriate comparison for feedback about one's performance. In the traditional model of psychological practice, there is no indication of how well one is doing vis á vis average client outcomes. Consulting with colleagues either promotes telling success stories or discussing very tough cases, but there is no indication of whether one's practice is "up to par," because there is no telling exactly what "par" is. Referring clients to colleagues, or assigning cases within a clinic or group practice, is largely a guessing game. We estimate how a colleague would perform with a particular client based on intuition, using cues from how the colleague discusses other cases, the colleague's general social skills, and how much we personally like the colleague.

Benchmarking

Benchmarking has promise for providing more objective information on which to base decisions. Through benchmarking, clinicians can take an objective measure of their strengths and weaknesses, thereby providing a clear basis for the areas in which one should seek continuing education. This type of procedure can be invaluable for clinicians who are trying to develop new practice skills and who are not sure at what point to stop receiving supervision. On the other hand, benchmarking can initially feel threatening, as it naturally raises fears that one will not measure up. Indeed, if done incorrectly, benchmarking can actually undermine quality of care. For example, if benchmarking and feedback mechanisms are not free of local politics, then there is danger that decisions will be based on considerations of power, authority, and "turf" rather than on client outcomes. To be successful, benchmarking must be implemented out of a genuine desire to help practitioners improve the quality of care delivered to clients. See sidebar 9-2 for suggestions for developing feedback mechanisms.

BENCHMARKING TIPS

Politics within the clinic can get in the way of keeping the focus on improving quality of care. In addition, clinicians who feel threatened by benchmarking may refuse to participate or otherwise undermine the effort to provide practice feedback. Several steps can be taken to reduce the likelihood of these types of problems.

- *Everyone must be involved* in the development of outcomes management and feedback systems. If all clinicians are involved in the development of the system, then there is a greater likelihood that their individual concerns will be included (e.g., a clinician who typically sees very difficult cases will want to make sure that case mix is accounted for in benchmarking).
- *Feedback must be timely.* Unlike in academic studies, where years go by before results are known, in the practice world information quickly gets stale. Prompting a clinician about completing paperwork in a timely way, for example, should be done more or less immediately. This type of administrative procedural feedback cannot be done if there is a lag of several months between collecting data and giving feedback. Even information about clinical outcomes should be less than 6 months old by the time practitioners get the feedback.
- *Feedback must be useful.* Information for clinicians about their performance must be in a format that they can use to shape their actions in providing care to clients. For example, simply telling a therapist that 58.8% of her clients with panic disorder were panic-free within 8 sessions does not tell her where to focus her efforts at improving these results. Information that might be helpful would include knowing how these results compared with those of other clinicians in the practice or with other indicators of her own clients' well-being (e.g., agoraphobic avoidance, marital adjustment, social functioning). Alternatively, she may find it helpful to know that her clients achieved their results in fewer sessions than the clinic average or that she had more premature terminations than her colleagues had.
- *Judgments must be credible.* If clinicians are to be judged on their competence in delivering an intervention, then these judgments should be based on actual in-session behavior. As suggested by Shaw and Dobson (1988), these judgments should also be made by independent judges who are both experienced in the type of therapy being delivered and experienced in the judging of therapists. Another way to increase the credibility of judgments is to ensure that the process of judging is free from local politics. If *all* practitioners, including those in the practice leadership, participate in benchmarking, then the credibility of the process is enhanced.

Obviously, setting up mechanisms to provide feedback and benchmark data to clinicians presupposes that training, supervision, and other skills-building resources will be available and that clinicians will avail themselves of these opportunities. In the traditional practice model, real training is something that stops right after licensure. To be sure, continuing education is required in many jurisdictions, but attending a workshop is a far cry from adequate training for building new skills. There has been an assumption that once one achieves full membership in the guild, no more real training is required. However, as Forquer and Muse (1996) point out, the original purpose of guilds was to ensure quality. With professional knowledge changing all the time, there is need for mechanisms to help practitioners keep up with new innovations in patient care. Benchmarking, as a comparison from one's own practice to the comparable practices of other practitioners, can help achieve these goals.

Using Treatment Manuals

Currently, practitioners gain new knowledge by consulting books on psychotherapy, discussing cases with their colleagues, and attending clinical workshops (Cohen, 1979; Cohen, Sargent, & Sechrest, 1986; Sargent & Cohen, 1983). To these sources, we might fruitfully add treatment manuals. Historically, manuals used to train therapists for clinical trials of a procedure have been difficult to obtain, but this situation is changing. In Appendix B, we have provided information for obtaining detailed treatment manuals as pertinent to the procedures discussed in each chapter. The Psychological Corporation has published several therapist manuals, accompanied in some cases by client workbooks or videotapes of the treatment. In addition, Woody and Sanderson (1998) have published a resource listing of manuals and training opportunities for many well-supported treatments. As of this writing, this resource listing can also be obtained online at www.sscp.nodak.ndsu.edu.

Treatment manuals in themselves are not an adequate means for learning a new therapy, but they have many advantages, as outlined by Addis (1997). Their advantages to researchers are well-known, but treatment manuals have something to offer the practitioner as well. Treatment manuals typically provide a theoretical framework for the approach, along with a discussion of facets of the therapy that distinguish it from others. The biggest value of a treatment manual often lies in its concrete descriptions of technique, along with case examples. Some treatment manuals even provide adherence and competence rating scales to facilitate training.

On the other hand, treatment manuals, having been designed for tightly controlled research, fail to meet many of the needs of practitioners. The biggest shortcoming of most treatment manuals is that they address a single focal problem, rather than the heterogeneous groups of clients from whom the practitioner seeks guidance. Further, some treatment manuals describe the intervention in a specific number of sessions without flexibility for differences in how quickly clients master new skills or make changes in their lives. Finally, there is some concern that implementing manualized procedures in the absence of supervision may lead to rigid step-by-step therapy, destroying the therapeutic alliance that appears to be necessary for any treatment to be effective (Henry, Strupp, Butler, Schacht, & Binder, 1993).

BOOSTING QUALITY OF TREATMENT

As we have discussed above, strict adherence to a manualized treatment does not ensure good therapeutic outcomes. *Reading* the manual to the client might strictly constitute adhering to the therapy, but no one would consider this to be good quality treatment. Several studies have demonstrated that *competence* in delivering the therapy is related to good client outcomes, but not simple *adherence* to the prescribed procedures (Barber, Crits-Cristoph, & Luborsky, 1996; Frank, Kupfer, Wagner, McEachran, & Cornes, 1991). In fact, Barber et al. documented that adherence to the procedures can be *due to* early outcomes in brief dynamic therapy, rather than *influencing* those outcomes. Put another way, therapists were better able to adhere to the treatment manual when the client was doing well. Competence in delivering the therapy (distinct from adherence), on the other hand, was clearly linked to better client outcomes.

Rule-governed behavior, compared to contingency-shaped behavior, tends to be less sensitive to quickly changing environmental contingencies. Experientially, conducting therapy requires adjusting to the contingencies presented by the client. Certainly, maintaining a therapeutic alliance requires these adjustments, and even relatively structured treatments involve tailoring to communicate well with the client. Addis (1997) maintains that rigid adherence to a treatment manual is likely to result in poorer therapy because of the inherent limitations on rule-governed behavior. The question then becomes how to help clinicians learn a new treatment and apply that treatment to the *individuals* in their care, rather than slavishly following the rules enumerated in the manual.

On the face of it, the methods currently in common use to train professionals in a new treatment (i.e., books on psychotherapy, weekend workshops) are inadequate to insure a move from rule-governed to contingency-shaped therapist behavior in the new treatment. Insofar as we are aware, there are no data to even attest to whether these methods provide adequate training for adherence to the new treatment, let alone for developing competence in such a short time. Currently, we have little solid information on the best methods for disseminating new procedures among professionals, as studies have not been conducted in this area. However, ideas and guidelines are beginning to be put forward (Addis, 1997; Calhoun, Moras, Pilkonis, &

Rehm, 1998). Guidelines suggested by Calhoun et al. are summarized in sidebar 9-3.

Throughout this chapter, we have emphasized different facets of quality mental health care, including monitoring outcomes, shaping treatment plans on the basis of ongoing outcomes measurement, using empirically supported treatments where possible, and establishing training and therapist development programs as a regular part of practice. Some of these recommendations will be difficult to implement for the solo practitioner, but forming a consortium of solo practitioners may facilitate the process. Our belief is that in the competitive marketplace, building and maintaining a successful practice will depend on the extent to which practitioners are able to demonstrate cost-efficient high-quality mental health care. Establishing standards of care and shaping practice to strive for improvements in the quality of care has been the focus of this chapter, and the basic premise behind this book.

Sidebar 9-3

GUIDELINES FOR TRAINING IN EMPIRICALLY SUPPORTED TREATMENTS

Guideline 1.   Use videotapes to illustrate the actual procedures involved in administering the treatment. For example, videotapes demonstrating several treatments can now be obtained from The Psychological Corporation. See Appendix B for contact information.

Guideline 2. Use video- or audiotapes of therapy sessions to guide supervision, rather than relying on the therapist's self-report. In a research setting, supervisors have been shown to make reliable ratings of therapist performance based on videotapes ($r = .88$). However, these supervisors' ratings of therapist performance based on videotapes were *unrelated* to their performance ratings of the same therapists when therapist self-report was the basis for the rating (Chevron & Rounsaville, 1983). In a clinic setting, similar results were found; therapist ratings of their own effectiveness were not related to peer ratings of appropriateness of care or to client satisfaction (Hiatt & Hargrave, 1995). Therapists may not be able to objectively report on their own performance, which is necessary for effective supervision. Although clinicians in practice may be reluctant to ask clients' permission to record sessions, we have found that most clients are willing to do this when they understand that the purpose is quality improvement and that the tapes will not identify them and will be erased as soon as possible.

(continued)

Sidebar 9-3 (*continued*)

Guideline 3. Evaluate adherence systematically and frequently. For many treatments, objective adherence ratings scales have been developed. See, for example, the Cognitive Therapy Rating Scale that appears as an appendix to the popular book *Cognitive Therapy of Depression* (Beck, Rush, Shaw, & Emery, 1979). These scales are relatively easy to use if sessions have been recorded, and they provide an objective guide for supervisors (and for trainees). Because adherence may decline in the months following training in a new procedure, these adherence measures should be used repeatedly.

Guideline 4. Use training materials that illustrate common errors in implementing the treatment. In training therapists to do group treatment of social phobia in our own laboratory, we had an experienced therapist videotape mock interviews with a staff member to illustrate common errors along with better approaches. To our knowledge, this sort of resource is not available commercially, but therapists who are experienced in providing and supervising others in a given treatment should have no trouble creating such materials.

Guideline 5. Consider group supervision as a cost-effective way of training several therapists in the same new procedure. In a group setting, each therapist has the opportunity to learn from other therapists' cases. For this approach to work, therapists should be at roughly the same skill level and should be comfortable receiving feedback in front of their peers.

Guideline 6. Allow for a lengthy learning process. Calhoun and colleagues (1998) suggest that therapists need be supervised on three to four prototypical cases (e.g., uncomplicated panic disorder) and four more nonprototypic cases (e.g., comorbid conditions, atypical presentation) in order to develop competence in a new therapy.

Guideline 7. Include instruction in outcomes assessment related to the client's response to the treatment. This instruction should also include explicit discussion of when to change strategies within the treatment and when to change to a different treatment approach based on client nonresponse.

These guidelines were adapted from K. S. Calhoun, K. Moras, P. A. Pilkonis, & L. P. Rehm (1998). Empirically supported treatments: Implications for training. *Journal of Consulting and Clinical Psychology, 66,* 151–162.

Appendix A

Useful Measures for Anxiety Disorders

This questionnaire has two parts. Below are some thoughts or ideas that may pass through your mind when you are nervous or frightened.

1. Indicate how often each thought occurs when you are nervous. Rate from 1–5 using the scale below.

    1 Thought never occurs.
    2 Thought rarely occurs.
    3 Thought occurs during half of the times I am nervous.
    4 Thought usually occurs.
    5 Thought always occurs when I am nervous.

2. Circle the three ideas that occur most often when you are nervous.

    ____ I am going to throw up.
    ____ I am going to pass out.
    ____ I must have a brain tumor.
    ____ I will have a heart attack.
    ____ I will choke to death.
    ____ I am going to act foolish.
    ____ I am going blind.
    ____ I will not be able to control myself.
    ____ I will hurt someone.

    ____ I am going to have a stroke.
    ____ I am going to go crazy.
    ____ I am going to scream.
    ____ I am going to babble or talk funny.
    ____ I will be paralyzed by fear.
    ____ Other ideas not listed (Please describe and rate.)

From D. L. Chambless, G. C. Caputo, P. Bright, & R. Gallagher (1984). Assessment of fear in agoraphobics: The body sensations questionnaire and the agoraphobic cognitions questionnaire. *Journal of Consulting and Clinical Psychology, 52,* 1090–1097. Reprinted with permission.

FEAR QUESTIONNAIRE

Choose a number from the scale below to show how much you would avoid each of the situations listed below because of fear or other unpleasant feelings. Then write the number you chose in the box opposite each situation.

| 0 | 1 | 2 | 3 | 4 | 5 | 6 | 7 | 8 |

| Would not avoid it | Slightly avoid it | Definitely avoid it | Markedly avoid it | Always avoid it |

1. Main phobia you want treated (describe in your own words)

_____ □

2. Injections or minor surgery.............................. □
3. Eating or drinking with other people................. □
4. Hospitals .... □
5. Travelling alone by bus or train .... □
6. Walking alone along busy streets...................... □
7. Being watched or stared at .... □
8. Going into crowded shops................................ □
9. Talking to people in authority.......................... □
10. Sight of blood.. □
11. Being criticized.. □
12. Going alone far from home .... □
13. Thought of injury or illness .... □
14. Speaking or acting to an audience .... □
15. Large open spaces... □
16. Going to the dentist.. □
17. Other situations (describe:)_____ □

Leave blank → □   □   □   □

Ag + BI + Soc = Total

Now choose a number from the scale below to show how much you are troubled by each problem listed, and write the number in the box opposite.

| 0 | 1 | 2 | 3 | 4 | 5 | 6 | 7 | 8 |

| Hardly at all | Slightly troublesome | Definitely troublesome | Markedly troublesome | Very severely troublesome |

18. Feeling miserable or depressed..................................... □
19. Feeling irritable or angry.. □
20. Feeling tense or panicky.. □
21. Upsetting thoughts coming into your mind.................... □
22. Feeling you or your surroundings are strange or unreal □
23. Other feelings (describe:) _____ □

How would you rate the present state of your phobic symptoms on the scale below? Please circle one number between 0 and 8.

0	1	2	3	4	5	6	7	8

No phobias present	Slightly disturbing/ Not really disabling	Definitely disturbing/ disabling	Markedly disturbing/ disabling	Very severely disturbing/ disabling

Mean pre- and post-treatment subscores for each diagnostic subgroup (from sample of 26 phobic patients)

		Phobic patient subgroup					
		Agoraphobia ($n = 9$)		Social ($n = 8$)		Other* ($n = 9$)	
Subscore (each 5-item total, range 0-40)		Mean	SD	Mean	SD	Mean	SD
Agoraphobia	Pre	21.6	(12.1)	7.3	(7.1)	12.0	(11.6)
	Post	10.0	(9.1)	4.8	(6.8)	8.7	(8.5)
Social	Pre	14.5	(10.2)	21.5	(8.2)	10.8	(9.0)
	Post	10.5	(7.4)	15.8	(10.8)	10.9	(11.9)

*Travelling by train, sitting in an audience, waiting in lines, small enclosed places, being alone at home, the thought of dying, talking to a stranger, giddiness, sleeplessness, and breathing difficulties.

From I. M. Marks & A. M. Mathews (1979). Brief standard self-rating for phobic patients, *Behaviour Research and Therapy, 17*, 263–267. Reprinted with permission from Elsevier Science.

GAMBRILL-RICHEY ASSERTION INVENTORY

Many people experience difficulty in handling interpersonal situations requiring them to assert themselves in some way, for example, turning down a request, asking a favor, giving someone a compliment, expressing disapproval or approval, etc. Please indicate your degree of discomfort or anxiety in the space provided before each situation listed below. Utilize the following scale to indicate your degree of discomfort:

	1	2	3	4	5
Discomfort:	None	A little	A fair amount	Much	Very much

Then, go over the list a second time and indicate after each item the probability or likelihood of your displaying the behavior if actually presented with the situation.* For example, if you rarely apologize when you are at fault, you would mark "4" after that item. Utilize the following scale to indicate response probability:

	1	2	3	4	5
Response Probability:	Always do it	Usually do it	Do it about half the time	Rarely do it	Never do it

*NOTE: It is important to cover your discomfort ratings (located in front of the items) while indicating response probability. Otherwise, one rating may contaminate the other and a realistic assessment of your behavior is unlikely. To correct for this, place a piece of paper over your discomfort ratings while responding to the situations a second time for response probability.

Degree of Discomfort	Situation	Response Probability
_____	1. Turn down a request to borrow your car	_____
_____	2. Compliment a friend	_____
_____	3. Ask a favor of someone	_____
_____	4. Resist sales pressure	_____
_____	5. Apologize when you are at fault	_____
_____	6. Turn down a request for a meeting or date	_____
_____	7. Admit fear and request consideration	_____
_____	8. Tell a person with whom you are intimately involved when s/he says or does something that bothers you	_____
_____	9. Ask for a raise	_____
_____	10. Admit ignorance in some area	_____
_____	11. Turn down a request to borrow money	_____

	1	2	3	4	5
Discomfort:	None	A little	A fair amount	Much	Very much

	1	2	3	4	5
Response Probability:	Always do it	Usually do it	Do it about half the time	Rarely do it	Never do it

Degree of Discomfort	Situation	Response Probability
_____	12. Ask personal questions	_____
_____	13. Turn off a talkative friend	_____
_____	14. Ask for constructive criticism	_____
_____	15. Initiate a conversation with a stranger	_____
_____	16. Compliment a person you are romantically involved with or interested in	_____
_____	17. Request a meeting or a date with a person	_____
_____	18. Your initial request for a meeting is turned down and you ask the person again at a later time	_____
_____	19. Admit confusion about a point under discussion and ask for clarification	_____
_____	20. Apply for a job	_____
_____	21. Ask whether you have offended someone	_____
_____	22. Tell someone that you like him or her	_____
_____	23. Request expected service when such is not forthcoming, for example, in a restaurant	_____
_____	24. Discuss openly with a person his or her criticism of your behavior	_____
_____	25. Return a defective item to a store	_____
_____	26. Express an opinion that differs from that of the person with whom you are talking	_____
_____	27. Resist sexual overtures when you are not interested	_____
_____	28. Tell a person when you feel he or she has done something that is unfair to you	_____
_____	29. Accept a date	_____

—continued

	1	2	3	4	5
Discomfort:	None	A little	A fair amount	Much	Very much

	1	2	3	4	5
Response Probability:	Always do it	Usually do it	Do it about half the time	Rarely do it	Never do it

Degree of Discomfort	Situation	Response Probability
_____	30. Tell someone good news about yourself	_____
_____	31. Resist pressure to drink	_____
_____	32. Resist a significant person's unfair demand	_____
_____	33. Quit a job	_____
_____	34. Resist pressure to use drugs	_____
_____	35. Discuss openly with a person his or her criticism of your work	_____
_____	36. Request the return of a borrowed item	_____
_____	37. Receive compliments	_____
_____	38. Continue to converse with someone who disagrees with you	_____
_____	39. Tell a friend or co-worker when he or she says or does something that bothers you	_____
_____	40. Ask a person who is annoying you in a public situation to stop	_____

Lastly, please indicate the situations you would like to handle more assertively by placing a circle around the item number.

Means and Standard Deviations of Discomfort and
Response Probability Subscales for Two Samples

Sample		Discomfort		Response Probability	
		Mean	SD	Mean	SD
College Students (n = 313)	Male (n = 116)	94.4	19.5	104.9	16.5
	Female (n = 197)	96.3	20.2	104.0	15.3
Women in Assertion Training (n = 19)	Before Treatment	107.7	22.4	104.8	22.6
	After Treatment	82.0	19.5	87.9	20.1

Adapted from E. Gambrill & C. A. Richey (1975). An assertion inventory for use in assessment and research. *Behavior Therapy*, 6, 547–549. Reprinted with permission.

IMPACT OF EVENT SCALE

On _____ you experienced _____.
Below is a list of comments made by people after stressful life events. Please check each item, indicating how frequently these comments were true for you DURING THE PAST SEVEN DAYS. If they did not occur during that time, please mark the "not at all" column.

	Not at all	Rarely	Sometimes	Often
1. I thought about it when I didn't mean to.				
2. I avoided letting myself get upset when I thought about it or was reminded of it.				
3. I tried to remove it from memory.				
4. I had trouble falling asleep or staying asleep, because of pictures or thoughts about it that came into my mind.				
5. I had waves of strong feelings about it.				
6. I had dreams about it.				
7. I stayed away from reminders of it.				
8. I felt as if it hadn't happened or it wasn't real.				
9. I tried not to talk about it.				
10. Pictures about it popped into my mind.				
11. Other things kept making me think about it.				
12. I was aware that I still had a lot of feelings about it, but I didn't deal with them.				
13. I tried not to think about it.				
14. Any reminder brought back feelings about it.				
15. My feelings about it were kind of numb.				

See chapter 7 text for scoring instructions. From M. Horowitz, N. Wilner, & W. Alvarez (1979). Impact of Event Scale: A measure of subject stress. *Psychosomatic Medicine, 41*, 209–218. Reprinted with permission.

MAUDSLEY OBSESSIONAL-COMPULSIVE INVENTORY

Instructions: Please answer each question by putting a circle around the "T" for True and "F" for False. There are no right or wrong answers. Work quickly, and do not think too long about the exact meaning of the question.

T F   1. I avoid using public telephones because of possible contamination.

T F   2. I frequently get nasty thoughts and have difficulty in getting rid of them.

T F   3. I am more concerned than most people about honesty.

T F   4. I am often late because I can't seem to get through everything on time.

T F   5. I don't worry unduly about contamination if I touch an animal.

T F   6. I frequently have to check things (e.g., gas or water taps, doors, etc.) several times.

T F   7. I have a very strict conscience.

T F   8. I find that almost every day I am upset by unpleasant thoughts that come into my mind against my will.

T F   9. I do not worry unduly if I accidentally bump into someone.

T F   10. I usually have serious doubts about the simple everyday things I do.

T F   11. Neither of my parents was very strict during my childhood.

T F   12. I tend to get behind in my work because I repeat things over and over again.

T F   13. I use only an average amount of soap.

T F   14. Some numbers are extremely unlucky.

T F   15. I do not check letters over and over again before mailing them.

T F   16. I do not take a long time to dress in the morning.

T F   17. I am not excessively concerned about cleanliness.

T F   18. One of my major problems is that I pay too much attention to detail.

T F   19. I can use well-kept toilets without any hesitation.

T F   20. My major problem is repeated checking.

T F   21. I am not unduly concerned about germs and diseases.

T F   22. I do not tend to check things more than once.

T F   23. I do not stick to a very strict routine when doing ordinary things.

T   F   24. My hands do not feel dirty after touching money.

T   F   25. I do not usually count when doing a routine task.

T   F   26. I take rather a long time to complete my washing in the morning.

T   F   27. I do not use a great deal of antiseptics.

T   F   28. I spend a lot of time every day checking things over and over again.

T   F   29. Hanging and folding my clothes at night does not take up a lot of time.

T   F   30. Even when I do something very carefully I often feel that it is not quite right.

From R. J. Hodgson & S. Rachman (1977). Obsessional compulsive complaints. *Behavioural Research and Therapy, 15*, (389–395). Reprinted with permission.

MAUDSLEY OBSESSIONAL-COMPULSIVE INVENTORY SCORING KEY

Total Score
1. Score 1 point if the following items are marked "True": 1, 2, 3, 4, 6, 7, 8, 10, 12, 14, 18, 20, 26, 28, 30.
2. Score 1 point if the following items are marked "False": 5, 9, 11, 13, 15, 16, 17, 19, 21, 22, 23, 24, 25, 27, 29.
3. Sum the scores from the previous two steps for the Total Score.

Checking Subscale
1. Score 1 point if the following items are marked "True": 2, 6, 8, 14, 20, 26, 28.
2. Score 1 point if the following items are marked "False": 15, 22.
3. Sum the scores from the previous two steps for the Checking Subscale score.

Washing Subscale
1. Score 1 point if the following items are marked "True": 1, 4, 26.
2. Score 1 point if the following items are marked "False": 5, 9, 13, 17, 19, 21, 24, 27.
3. Sum the scores from the previous two steps for the Washing Subscale score.

MOBILITY INVENTORY

Please indicate the degree to which you avoid the following places or situations because of discomfort or anxiety. Rate your amount of avoidance when you are with a trusted companion and when you are alone. Do this by using the following scale:

1 Never avoid
2 Rarely avoid
3 Avoid about half the time
4 Avoid most of the time
5 Always avoid

(You may use numbers half-way between those listed when you think it is appropriate. For example, 3 1/2 or 4 1/2.)

Write your score in the blanks for each situation or place under both conditions: when accompanied and when alone. Leave blank those situations that do not apply to you.

Places	When Accompanied	When Alone
Theatres	_____	_____
Supermarkets	_____	_____
Classrooms	_____	_____
Department stores	_____	_____
Restaurants	_____	_____
Museums	_____	_____
Elevators	_____	_____
Auditoriums or stadiums	_____	_____
Parking garages	_____	_____
High places	_____	_____
Tell how high _____		
Enclosed spaces (e.g., tunnels)	_____	_____
Open spaces: Outside (e.g., fields, wide streets, courtyards)	_____	_____
Inside (e.g., large rooms, lobbies)	_____	_____
Riding in: Buses	_____	_____
Trains	_____	_____
Subways	_____	_____
Airplanes	_____	_____
Boats	_____	_____
Driving or riding in a car: At any time	_____	_____
On expressways	_____	_____

Places	When Accompanied	When Alone
Situations: Standing in lines	_____	_____
Crossing bridges	_____	_____
Parties or social gatherings	_____	_____
Walking on the street	_____	_____
Staying at home alone	_____	_____
Being far from home	_____	_____
Other (specify)	_____	_____

We define a panic attack as:

1. a high level of anxiety accompanied by
2. strong body reactions (heart palpitations, sweating, muscle tremors, dizziness, nausea) with
3. the temporary loss of the ability to plan, think, or reason, and
4. intense desire to escape or flee the situation. (Note this is different from high anxiety or fear alone).

Please indicate the total number of panic attacks you have
had in the last 7 days.   _____
Please rate the severity of these attacks, on a 0–8 scale,
where 8 is the worst.   _____

From D. L. Chambless, G. C. Caputo, S. E. Jasin, E. J. Gracely, & C. Williams (1985). The mobility inventory for agoraphobia. *Behaviour Research and Therapy, 23*, 35–44. Reprinted with permission.

PENN STATE WORRY QUESTIONNAIRE

For each of the following statements, please indicate how often the statement is characteristic of you.

	Not at all Typical of Me				Very Typical of Me
1. If I do not have enough time to do everything, I do not worry about it.	1	2	3	4	5
2. My worries overwhelm me.	1	2	3	4	5
3. I do not tend to worry about things.	1	2	3	4	5
4. Many situations make me worry.	1	2	3	4	5
5. I know I should not worry about things, but I just cannot help it.	1	2	3	4	5
6. When I am under pressure I worry a lot.	1	2	3	4	5
7. I am always worrying about something.	1	2	3	4	5
8. I find it easy to dismiss worrisome thoughts.	1	2	3	4	5
9. As soon as I finish one task, I start to worry about everything else I have to do.	1	2	3	4	5
10. I never worry about anything.	1	2	3	4	5
11. When there is nothing more I can do about a concern, I do not worry about it any more.	1	2	3	4	5
12. I have been a worrier all my life.	1	2	3	4	5
13. I notice that I have been worrying about things.	1	2	3	4	5
14. Once I start worrying, I cannot stop.	1	2	3	4	5
15. I worry all the time.	1	2	3	4	5
16. I worry about projects until they are all done.	1	2	3	4	5

From T. J. Meyer, M. L. Miller, R. L. Metzger, & T. D. Borkovec (1990). Developmental validation of the Penn State Worry Questionnaire. *Behaviour Research and Therapy, 28*, 487–496. Adapted and reprinted with permission.

Percentile Scores for the Penn State Worry Questionnaire

Percentile	Full Community Sample	18–44 Age Group	45–65 Age Group
10th	28	29	28
20th	32	32	31
25th	33	34	32
30th	35	35	33
40th	37	39	35
50th	41	44	37
60th	44	46	38
70th	48	49	41
75th	49	50	43
80th	51	53	44
90th	57	60	50

Note: The Penn State Worry Questionnaire is scored by adding scores from all items. Items 1, 3, 8, 10, and 11 are reverse-scored.

From M. M. Gillis, D. A. F. Haaga, & G. T. Ford (1995). Normative values for the Beck Anxiety Inventory, Fear Questionnaire, Penn State Worry Questionnaire, and Social Phobia and Anxiety Inventory. *Psychological Assessment, 7,* 450–455. Reprinted with permission.

SOCIAL INTERACTION SELF-STATEMENT TEST

It is obvious that people think a variety of things when they are involved in different social situations. Below is a list of things that you may have thought to yourself at some time before, during, or after the interaction in which you were engaged. Read each item and decide how frequently you were thinking a similar thought before, during, and after the interaction.

Circle the number from 1 to 5 for each item. The scale is interpreted as follows:

1 = *hardly ever* had the thought
2 = *rarely* had the thought
3 = *sometimes* had the thought
4 = *often* had the thought
5 = *very often* had the thought

Please answer as honestly as possible.

1. When I can't think of anything to say I can feel myself getting very anxious.

1	2	3	4	5
Hardly ever	Rarely	Sometimes	Often	Very often

2. I can usually talk to women pretty well.

1	2	3	4	5
Hardly ever	Rarely	Sometimes	Often	Very often

3. I hope I don't make a fool of myself.

1	2	3	4	5
Hardly ever	Rarely	Sometimes	Often	Very often

4. I'm beginning to feel more at ease.

1	2	3	4	5
Hardly ever	Rarely	Sometimes	Often	Very often

5. I'm really afraid of what she'll think of me.

1	2	3	4	5
Hardly ever	Rarely	Sometimes	Often	Very often

6. No worries, no fears, no anxieties.

1	2	3	4	5
Hardly ever	Rarely	Sometimes	Often	Very often

7. I'm scared to death.

1	2	3	4	5
Hardly ever	Rarely	Sometimes	Often	Very often

8. She probably won't be interested in me.

1	2	3	4	5
Hardly ever	Rarely	Sometimes	Often	Very often

9. Maybe I can put her at ease by starting things going.

1	2	3	4	5
Hardly ever	Rarely	Sometimes	Often	Very often

10. Instead of worrying I can figure out how best to get to know her.

1	2	3	4	5
Hardly ever	Rarely	Sometimes	Often	Very often

11. I'm not too comfortable meeting women, so things are bound to go wrong.

1	2	3	4	5
Hardly ever	Rarely	Sometimes	Often	Very often

12. What the heck -the worst that can happen is that she won't go for me.

1	2	3	4	5
Hardly ever	Rarely	Sometimes	Often	Very often

13. She may want to talk to me as much as I want to talk to her.

1	2	3	4	5
Hardly ever	Rarely	Sometimes	Often	Very often

14. This will be a good opportunity.

1	2	3	4	5
Hardly ever	Rarely	Sometimes	Often	Very often

15. If I blow this conversation, I'll really lose my confidence.

1	2	3	4	5
Hardly ever	Rarely	Sometimes	Often	Very often

16. What I say will probably sound stupid.

1	2	3	4	5
Hardly ever	Rarely	Sometimes	Often	Very often

—continued

17. What do I have to lose? It's worth a try.

1	2	3	4	5
Hardly ever	Rarely	Sometimes	Often	Very often

18. This is an awkward situation, but I can handle it.

1	2	3	4	5
Hardly ever	Rarely	Sometimes	Often	Very often

19. Wow—I don't want to do this.

1	2	3	4	5
Hardly ever	Rarely	Sometimes	Often	Very often

20. It would crush me if she didn't respond to me.

1	2	3	4	5
Hardly ever	Rarely	Sometimes	Often	Very often

21. I've just got to make a good impression on her or I'll feel terrible.

1	2	3	4	5
Hardly ever	Rarely	Sometimes	Often	Very often

22. You're such an inhibited idiot.

1	2	3	4	5
Hardly ever	Rarely	Sometimes	Often	Very often

23. I'll probably "bomb out" anyway.

1	2	3	4	5
Hardly ever	Rarely	Sometimes	Often	Very often

24. I can handle anything.

1	2	3	4	5
Hardly ever	Rarely	Sometimes	Often	Very often

25. Even if things don't go well it's no catastrophe.

1	2	3	4	5
Hardly ever	Rarely	Sometimes	Often	Very often

26. I feel awkward and dumb; she's bound to notice.

1	2	3	4	5
Hardly ever	Rarely	Sometimes	Often	Very often

27. We probably have a lot in common.

	1	2	3	4	5
	Hardly ever	Rarely	Sometimes	Often	Very often

28. Maybe we'll hit it off real well.

	1	2	3	4	5
	Hardly ever	Rarely	Sometimes	Often	Very often

29. I wish I could leave and avoid the whole situation.

	1	2	3	4	5
	Hardly ever	Rarely	Sometimes	Often	Very often

30. Ah! Throw caution to the wind.

	1	2	3	4	5
	Hardly ever	Rarely	Sometimes	Often	Very often

Scoring Key for the Social Interaction Self-Statement Test

Positive (Facilitative) Thoughts Item #	Negative (Debilitative) Thoughts Item #
2	1
4	3
6	5
9	7
10	8
12	11
13	15
14	16
17	19
18	20
24	21
25	22
27	23
28	26
30	29

Both subscale scores are calculated by simply adding the numerical responses for each of the 15 items.

Note: Although many items are worded for men who have completed an interaction with a woman, pronouns can be reversed to make the scale appropriate for female respondents (e.g., "she" changed to "he").

From C. R. Glass, T. V. Merluzzi, J. L. Biever, & K. H. Larsen (1982). Cognitive assessment of social anxiety: Development and validation of a self-statement questionnaire. *Cognitive Therapy and Research*, 6, 37–55. Reprinted with permission.

SOCIAL PERFORMANCE SURVEY SCHEDULE

This survey is a measure of social behavior. It can be used to assess your own social behaviors or those of someone else. This assessment involves rating how often you (or the person you're rating) engage in the behaviors described in the survey.

Rate how often you (or the person) demonstrate the behaviors in those situations where they might occur. For example, the item "shares what (s)he has with others" refers only to situations where sharing might occur; it does not imply that a person should share everything (s)he has with others.

Items are written in the third person, so if you are rating yourself, read the "he or she" headings as referring to yourself. *Be sure* to rate how often each behavior is *actually* demonstrated, *not* what you think a "good" response would be. Your answers will be kept strictly confidential.

He or she . . .	Not at all 0	A little 1	A fair amount 2	Much 3	Very much 4
1. has eye contact when speaking.					
2. reacts with more anger than a situation calls for.					
3. seeks others out too often.					
4. shows enthusiasm for others' good fortunes.					
5. keeps secrets or confidential information to himself/herself.					
6. is aggressive when (s)he takes issue with someone.					
7. initiates contact and conversation with others.					
8. shares what (s)he has with others.					
9. puts himself/herself down.					

He or she . . .	Not at all 0	A little 1	A fair amount 2	Much 3	Very much 4
10. takes advantage of others.					
11. is pessimistic.					
12. makes other people laugh (with jokes, funny stories, etc.)					
13. interrupts others.					
14. tries to work out problems with others by talking to them.					
15. gives the impression that (s)he's an expert on everything.					
16. seems impatient for others to finish their remarks.					
17. shows appreciation when someone does something for him/her.					
18. says little in conversations (s)he has.					
19. demonstrates concern for others' rights.					
20. talks negatively about others when they are not present.					
21. reveals personal information and feelings to those with whom (s)he is close.					
22. talks readily to people (s)he hasn't met before.					

—continued

He or she . . .	Not at all 0	A little 1	A fair amount 2	Much 3	Very much 4
23. insults others.					
24. is able to accept other people despite their faults.					
25. smiles when (s)he first sees someone (s)he knows.					
26. threatens others verbally or physically.					
27. is able to make people who are anxious or up-set feel better by talking to them.					
28. makes others feel (s)he is competing with them.					
29. rejects or criticizes other people before knowing much about them.					
30. when facing conflict with others, knows what to do or say to avoid offending them.					
31. hurts other people while striving to reach his/her goals.					
32. talks repeatedly about his/her problems and worries.					
33. asks others how they've been, what they've been up to, etc.					
34. laughs at other people's jokes and funny stories.					

He or she . . .	Not at all 0	A little 1	A fair amount 2	Much 3	Very much 4
35. gets into arguments.					
36. listens when spoken to.					
37. is a sore loser.					
38. keeps the significance of his/her accomplishments in perspective.					
39. remembers and discusses topics previously discussed with others.					
40. shows interest in what another is saying (e.g., with appropriate facial movements, comments, and questions).					
41. gives unsolicited advice.					
42. knows when to leave people alone.					
43. directs rather than requests people to do something.					
44. makes embarrassing comments.					
45. directs conversation with other people toward topics the other person is interested in.					
46. stays with others too long (overstays his/her welcome).					
47. makes fun of others.					

—continued

He or she . . .	Not at all 0	A little 1	A fair amount 2	Much 3	Very much 4
48. takes or uses things that aren't his/hers without permission.					
49. shows appreciation when people seek him/her out.					
50. blames others for his/her problems.					
51. asks questions when talking with others.					
52. admits to mistakes or errors (s)he makes.					
53. hurts others when teasing them.					
54. gives positive feedback to others.					
55. considers the opinions given by others.					
56. speaks in a monotone.					
57. does things others like to do.					
58. dominates conversations (s)he has.					
59. is sarcastic.					
60. is able to recognize when people are troubled.					
61. keeps in touch with friends.					
62. tells people what (s)he thinks they want to hear.					

He or she . . .	Not at all 0	A little 1	A fair amount 2	Much 3	Very much 4
63. apologizes when (s)he wrongs someone.					
64. refuses to change his/her opinions or beliefs.					
65. finds something to be optimistic about in hard times.					
66. criticizes people when (s)he talks to them.					
67. shows a willingness to compromise to resolve conflicts.					
68. compliments others on their clothes, hairstyle, etc.					
69. complains.					
70. perceives insults or criticism when none were intended.					
71. tries to help others find solutions to problems they face.					
72. reacts to injustices with a desire for revenge.					
73. makes facial gestures (e.g., shaking his/her head) or sounds (e.g., sighs) which indicates disapproval of others.					
74. easily becomes angry.					
75. stands up for his/her rights.					

—continued

He or she . . .	Not at all 0	A little 1	A fair amount 2	Much 3	Very much 4
76. tries to manipulate others to do what (s)he wants.					
77. allows others to do things for him/her without reciprocating in some way.					
78. has eye contact when listening.					
79. stands up for his/her friends.					
80. acts like (s)he's superior to other people.					
81. expresses concern to others about their misfortunes.					
82. does not reveal his/her feelings.					
83. focuses conversation on his/her accomplishments and abilities.					
84. shares responsibility equally with the members of groups (s)he belongs to.					
85. seems bored when interacting with others.					
86. takes care of others' property as if it were his/her own.					
87. gloats when (s)he wins.					
88. asks if (s)he can be of help.					

He or she . . .	Not at all 0	A little 1	A fair amount 2	Much 3	Very much 4
89. gets to know people in depth.					
90. talks too much about himself/herself.					
91. discusses a variety of topics with others.					
92. explains things in too much detail.					
93. reevaluates his/her position when (s)he receives new information.					
94. makes sounds (e.g., burping, sniffling) that disturb others.					
95. considers the effects of his/her statements and actions on others' feelings.					
96. mentions people's names when talking to them.					
97. criticizes behaviors or practices of other people which (s)he engages in himself/herself.					
98. keeps commitments (s)he makes.					
99. talks about interesting topics.					
100. deceives others for personal gain.					

From M. R. Lowe & J. R. Cautela (1978). A self-report measure of social skill. *Behavior Therapy, 9*, 535–544. Reprinted with permission.

SCORING KEY FOR THE SOCIAL PERFORMANCE
SURVEY SCHEDULE

Positive Behavior Subscale
Scores assigned to the positive behavior subscale are as follows:

Not at all = 0   A little = 1   A fair amount = 2   Much = 3   Very much = 4

The Positive Behavior subscale is the sum of the scores on the following
items:
1, 4, 5, 7, 8, 12, 14, 17, 19, 21, 22, 24, 25, 27, 30, 33, 34, 36, 38, 39, 40,
42, 45, 49, 51, 52, 54, 55, 57, 60, 61, 63, 65, 67, 68, 71, 75, 78, 79, 81,
84, 86, 88, 89, 91, 93, 95, 96, 98, 99

Negative Behavior Subscale
Scores assigned to the negative behavior subscale are as follows:

Not at all = 4   A little = 3   A fair amount = 2   Much = 1   Very much = 0

The Negative Behavior subscale is the sum of the scores on the following
items:
2, 3, 6, 9, 10, 11, 13, 15, 16, 18, 20, 23, 26, 28, 29, 31, 32, 35, 37, 41, 43,
44, 46, 47, 48, 50, 53, 56, 58, 59, 62, 64, 66, 69, 70, 72, 73, 74, 76, 77,
80, 82, 83, 85, 87, 90, 92, 94, 97, 100

Total SPSS Score
The total score for the Social Performance Survey Schedule is the sum of the
Positive and Negative Behavior subscales.

SOURCES FOR PTSD MEASURES

Clinician Administered PTSD Scale (CAPS)
　　Copies and instruction manual available from:
　　　　M. Friedman, MD, Ph.D., Executive Director
　　　　National Center for PTSD
　　　　Psychiatric Services (116A)
　　　　White River Junction VAMC
　　　　White River Junction, VT 05001

Mississippi Scale for Combat-Related PTSD (M-PTSD)
　　Available from:
　　　　Dr. T. Keane
　　　　National Center for PTSD (116B2)
　　　　VA Boston Healthcare System
　　　　150 South Huntington Ave.
　　　　Boston, MA 02130

YALE-BROWN OBSESSIVE COMPULSIVE SCALE
(Y-BOCS)

Symptom Checklist

Check all that apply, but clearly mark the principal symptoms with a "P". (Rater must ascertain whether reported behaviors are bona fide symptoms of OCD, and not symptoms of another disorder such as simple phobia or hypochondriasis. Items marked as "*" may or may not be OCD phenomena.)

Current   Past

Aggressive obsessions

_____   ____   Fear might harm self

_____   ____   Fear might harm others

_____   ____   Violent or horrific images

_____   ____   Fear of blurting out obscenities or insults

_____   ____   Fear of doing something else embarrassing*

_____   ____   Fear will act on unwanted impulses (e.g., to stab friend)

_____   ____   Fear will steal things

_____   ____   Fear will harm others because not careful enough (e.g., hit/run car accident)

_____   ____   Fear will be responsible for something else terrible happening (e.g., fire, burglary)

_____   ____   Other _____

Contamination obsessions

_____   ____   Concerns or disgust with bodily waste or secretions (e.g., urine, feces, saliva)

_____   ____   Concerns with dirt or germs

_____   ____   Excessive concern with environmental contaminants (e.g., asbestos, radiation, toxic waste)

_____   ____   Excessive concern with household items (e.g., cleansers, solvents)

_____   ____   Excessive concern with animals (e.g., insects)

_____   ____   Bothered by sticky substances or residues

_____   ____   Concerned will get ill because of contaminant

_____   ____   Concerned will get others ill by spreading contaminant (aggressive)

—continued

—— —— No concern with consequences of contamination other than how it might feel

—— —— Other _____

Sexual obsessions

—— —— Forbidden or perverse sexual thoughts, images, or impulses

—— —— Content involves children or incest

—— —— Content involves homosexuality*

—— —— Sexual behavior toward others (aggressive)*

—— —— Other _____

Hoarding/saving obsessions
[distinguish from hobbies and concern with objects of monetary or sentimental value]

—— —— _____

Religious obsessions (scrupulosity)

—— —— Concerned with sacrilege and blasphemy

—— —— Excess concern with right/wrong, morality

—— —— Other _____

Obsession with need for symmetry or exactness

—— —— Accompanied by magical thinking (e.g., concerned that mother will have accident unless things are in the right place)

—— —— Not accompanied by magical thinking

Miscellaneous obsessions

—— —— Need to know or remember

—— —— Fear of saying certain things

—— —— Fear of not saying just the right thing*

—— —— Fear of losing things

—— —— Intrusive (nonviolent) images

—— —— Intrusive nonsense sounds, words, or music*

—— —— Bothered by certain sounds/noises*

—— —— Lucky/unlucky numbers

—— —— Colors with special significance

—— —— Superstitious fears

—— —— Other _____

Somatic obsessions

—— —— Concern with illness or disease*

_____ _____ Excessive concern with body part or aspect of appearance (e.g., dysmorphophobia)*

_____ _____ Other _____

Cleaning/washing compulsions

_____ _____ Excessive or ritualized handwashing

_____ _____ Excessive or ritualized showering, bathing, toothbrushing, grooming, or toilet routine

_____ _____ Involves cleaning of household items or other inanimate objects

_____ _____ Other measures to prevent or remove contact with contaminants

_____ _____ Other _____

Checking compulsions

_____ _____ Checking locks, stove, appliances, etc.

_____ _____ Checking that did not/will not harm others

_____ _____ Checking that did not/will not harm self

_____ _____ Checking that nothing terrible did/will happen

_____ _____ Checking that did not make mistake

_____ _____ Checking tied to somatic obsessions

_____ _____ Other _____

Repeating rituals

_____ _____ Rereading or rewriting

_____ _____ Need to repeat routine activities (e.g., in/out door, up/down from chair)

_____ _____ Other _____

Counting compulsions

_____ _____ _____

Ordering/arranging compulsions

_____ _____ _____

Hoarding/collecting compulsions
[distinguish from hobbies and concern with objects of monetary or sentimental value (e.g., carefully reads junk mail, piles up old newspapers, sorts through garbage, collects useless objects)]

_____ _____ _____

Miscellaneous compulsions

_____ _____ Mental rituals (other than checking/counting)

_____ _____ Excessive listmaking

—continued

———— ———— Need to tell, ask, or confess

———— ———— Need to touch, tap, or rub*

———— ———— Rituals involving blinking or staring*

———— ———— Measures (not checking) to prevent harm to self, harm to others, or terrible consequences

———— ———— Ritualized eating behaviors*

———— ———— Superstitious behaviors

———— ———— Trichotillomania*

———— ———— Other self-damaging or self-mutilating behaviors*

———— ———— Other _____

YALE-BROWN OBSESSIVE COMPULSIVE SCALE (Y-BOCS)

Y-BOCS TOTAL SCORE (add items 1–10) _____

	None	Mild	Moderate	Severe	Extreme
1. Time spent on obsessions	0	1	2	3	4

	No Symptoms	Long	Moderately Long	Short	Extremely Short
1b. Obsession-free interval (do not add to subtotal or total score)	0	1	2	3	4

	None	Mild	Moderate	Severe	Extreme
2. Interference from obsessions	0	1	2	3	4
3. Distress from obsessions	0	1	2	3	4

	Always Resists				Completely Yields
4. Resistance	0	1	2	3	4

	Complete Control	Much Control	Moderate Control	Little Control	No Control
5. Control over obsessions	0	1	2	3	4

Obsession subtotal (add items 1–5) _____

	None	Mild	Moderate	Severe	Extreme
6. Time spent on compulsions	0	1	2	3	4

	No Symptoms	Long	Moderately Long	Short	Extremely Short
*6b. Compulsion-free interval (do not add to subtotal or total score)	0	1	2	3	4

	None	Mild	Moderate	Severe	Extreme
7. Interference from compulsions	0	1	2	3	4
8. Distress from compulsions	0	1	2	3	4

	Always Resists				Completely Yields
9. Resistance	0	1	2	3	4

	Complete Control	Much Control	Moderate Control	Little Control	No Control
10. Control over compulsions	0	1	2	3	4

Compulsion subtotal (add items 1–5) _____

	Excellent				Absent
11. Insight into O-C symptoms	0	1	2	3	4

	None	Mild	Moderate	Severe	Extreme
12. Avoidance	0	1	2	3	4
13. Indecisiveness	0	1	2	3	4
14. Pathologic Responsibility	0	1	2	3	4
15. Slowness	0	1	2	3	4
16. Pathologic Doubting	0	1	2	3	4
17. Global Severity	0	1	2	3	4	5	6
18. Global Improvement	0	1	2	3	4	5	6

19. Reliability	Excellent = 0	Good = 1	Fair = 2	Poor = 3

—continued

Means and Standard Deviations for the Y-BOCS Across Brief Treatment

	Pre-treatment	Active Treatment		Follow-up	
		4 weeks	9 weeks	20 weeks	32 weeks
Obsessions					
ERP	14.7 (±3.2)	9.4 (±4.2)	7.6 (±4.9)	9.0 (±6.4)	8.6 (±5.9)
ERP + imaginal	13.6 (±2.7)	8.3 (±2.5)	6.8 (±3.6)	7.6 (±4.4)	7.0 (±3.0)
Compulsions					
ERP	14.1 (±2.7)	10.5 (±2.7)	7.9 (±3.9)	8.8 (±5.4)	8.0 (±5.9)
ERP + imaginal	13.8 (±2.1)	8.8 (±2.3)	7.5 (±3.2)	8.0 (±4.0)	7.0 (±2.9)

Note: Y-BOCS subscale scores (Obsessions and Compulsions) for 46 clients receiving 9 weeks (1.5 hrs/wk.) of either live exposure and response prevention (ERP), or both live and imaginal exposure and response prevention (ERP + imaginal). The range of possible scores on each subscale is 0–20. Total Y-BOCS scores are calculated by summing the subscale scores.

Data were taken from L. A. de Araujo, L. M. Ito, I. M. Marks, & E. Deale (1995). Does imagined exposure to the consequence of not ritualising enhance live exposure for OCD? A controlled study: I. Main outcome. *British Journal of Psychiatry, 167,* 65–70.

Appendix B

Educational Resources for Professionals

Treatment Manuals

Generalized Anxiety and Worry

Brown, T., O'Leary, T., & Barlow, D. H. (1994). Generalized anxiety disorder. In D. H. Barlow (Ed.), *Clinical Handbook of Psychological Disorders*. New York: Guilford.

Anxiety Management for Generalized Anxiety and *Controlling Anxiety*. (Available for £2 each. Contact: Secretary, Department of Psychology, Warneford Hospital, Headington, Oxford, U.K. OX3 7JX.) *These treatment manuals cover anxiety management and CBT approaches for treating GAD.*

Mastery of Your Anxiety and Worry by R. Zinbarg, M. Craske, & D. Barlow. Available from The Psychological Corporation, San Antonio, TX at 1-800-228-0752 or www.PsychCorp.com. *The Psychological Corporation offers a series of tools, including therapist guides, videotapes, and client workbooks.*

Obsessive-Compulsive Disorder

Riggs, D. S., & Foa, E. B. (1994). Obsessive compulsive disorder. In D. H. Barlow (Ed.), *Clinical Handbook of Psychological Disorders*. New York: Guilford.

Steketee, G. (1993). *Treatment of Obsessive Compulsive Disorder*. New York: Guilford. *This very readable treatment guide provides comprehensive instruction in treatment of OCD.*

Steketee, G. S. (1999). *Overcoming obsessive-compulsive disorder*. Oakland, CA: Harbinger Press. *This series involves both a therapist manual and a client workbook.*

Mastery of Your Obsessive-Compulsive Disorder by M. Kozak & E. Foa. Available from The Psychological Corporation, San Antonio, TX at 1-800-228-0752 or www.PsychCorp.com. *The Psychological Corporation offers both a therapist guide to treatment of OCD and a client workbook.*

Panic Disorder and Agoraphobia

Barlow, D. H., & Cerney, J. A. (1988). *Psychological Treatment of Panic*. New York: Guilford.

Clark, D. M. (1989). Anxiety states: Panic and generalized anxiety. In K. Hawton, P. Salkovskis, J. Kirk, & D. M. Clark (Eds.), *Cognitive behavior therapy for psychiatric problems*. Oxford, UK: Oxford University Press.

Hecker, J. E., & Thorpe, G. L. (1992). *Agoraphobia and panic: A guide to psychological treatment*. Boston: Allyn & Bacon.

Mastery of Your Anxiety and Panic by M. Craske, E. Meadows, & D. Barlow. Available from The Psychological Corporation, San Antonio, TX at 1-800-228-0752 or www.PsychCorp.com. *The Psychological Corporation materials include therapist guides and videotapes in addition to client workbooks and videos.*

Post-Traumatic Stress Disorder

Foa, E. B., & Rothbaum, B. O. (1998). *Treating the trauma of rape: Cognitive-behavioral therapy for PTSD*. New York: Guilford.

Resick, P. A., & Schnicke, M. K. (1996). *Cognitive processing therapy for rape victims: A treatment manual*. Newbury Park, CA: Sage Publications.

Social Phobia

A Manual for the Conduct of Exposure Treatment for Social Phobia by D. Hope & R. Heimberg. Contact: Deborah Hope, Ph.D., Department of Psychology, University of Nebraska-Lincoln, Lincoln, NE 68588-0308. Cost = $10.00.

Cognitive Behavioral Group Therapy for Social Phobia by R. Heimberg. Contact: Richard G. Heimberg, PhD, Social Phobia Program, Department of Psychology, Temple University, Weiss Hall, 1701 North 13th Street, Philadelphia, PA 19122-6085. Cost = $20.00.

Social Effectiveness Therapy: A Program for Overcoming Social Anxiety and Phobia (Contact: Multi-Health Systems at 908 Niagara Falls Blvd., North Tonawanda, NY 14120-2060. Phone 416-424-1700 or Fax 416-424-1736.)

Specific Phobia

Marks, I. (1978). *Living with fear*. New York: McGraw-Hill.

Mastery of Your Specific Phobia by M. Craske, M. Antony, & D. Barlow. Available from The Psychological Corporation, San Antonio, TX at 1-800-228-0752 or www.PsychCorp.com.

Supervised Training

American Institute for Cognitive Therapy
30 E. 60th Street
Suite 1007
New York, NY 10022
Phone: 212-308-2440
E-mail: AICT@aol.com

Anxiety and Phobic Disorders Program
   Harlan R. Juster, Ph.D.
   1A Pine West Plaza
   Washington Avenue Extension
   Albany, NY 12205
   Phone: 518-862-1665
   E-mail: hjuster@juno.com

Anxiety Disorders Center
   C. Alec Pollard, Director
   St. Louis Behavioral Medicine Institute
   1129 Macklind Avenue
   St. Louis, MO 63110
   E-mail: pollarda@sluvca.slu.edu

Atlanta Center for Cognitive Therapy
   1772 Century Boulevard
   Atlanta, GA 30345
   Phone: 404-248-1159
   E-mail: acct@cognitiveatlanta.com
   Website: www.cognitiveatlanta.com

Beck Institute for Cognitive Therapy and Research
   Judy S. Beck, Ph.D.
   GSB Building—Suite 700
   City Line & Belmont Avenues
   Bala Cynwyd, PA 19004-1610
   Phone: 610-664-3020

Boston VA Medical Center
   Women's Health Sciences Division
   (I 16 B-3) and Behavioral Science Division (I 16 B-2)
   Boston, MA 02130

Center for Cognitive Therapy
   1101 Dove Street
   Suite 240
   Newport Beach, CA 92660
   Phone: 714-646-2044

Center for Cognitive Therapy
   University of Pennsylvania Medical School
   3600 Market Street, Room 754
   Philadelphia, PA 19104
   Phone: 215-898-4100

Cleveland Center for Cognitive Therapy
   24100 Chagrin Boulevard
   Suite 470
   Beachwood, OH 44122
   Phone: 216-831-2500

Cognitive Therapy Training Program
  Cognitive Therapy Center of New York
  120 E. 56th Street
  Suite 530
  New York, NY 10022
  Phone: 212-588-1998 extension 5

Laboratory for the Study of Anxiety Disorders
  Michael J. Telch, Director
  Department of Psychology
  Mezes 330
  University of Texas at Austin
  Austin, TX 78712

National Center for PTSD
  Educational Division (323EI12)
  Palo Alto VA Medical Center
  Palo Alto, CA 94304

National Crime Victims Research & Treatment Center
  Department of Psychiatry & Behavioral Sciences
  Medical University of South Carolina
  171 Ashley Avenue
  Charleston, SC 29425

Social Phobia Program
  Richard G. Heimberg, PhD
  Department of Psychology
  Temple University, Weiss Hall
  1701 North 13th Street
  Philadelphia, PA 19122-6085
  Email: rheimber@nimbus.ocis.temple.edu

UCLA Anxiety Disorders Behavioral Program
  Michelle Craske, Ph.D.
  Department of Psychology
  405 Hilgard Avenue
  Los Angeles, CA 90095-1563
  Email: Craske@psych.sscnet.ucla.edu

Appendix C

Outcomes Measurement Systems Vendors

The following companies provide outcomes measurement systems to behavioral health care organizations. They all provide measures that target a variety of client problems, and the systems are flexible, allowing for additional instruments to be integrated within the package. Most of these firms also have large databases of clients against which users can compare typical outcomes.

Behavioral Health Outcomes Systems (BHOS, Inc.)
689 Mamaroneck Avenue
Suite 102
Mamaroneck, NY 10543
Phone: (800) 494-2467 or (914) 381-7784
Fax: (914) 381-1725
Contact Person: Bill Berman, President
Website: www.bhos.com

Beaumont Outcome Software System (BOSS)
Parrot Software
P.O. Box 250755
West Bloomfield, MI 48325
Phone: (800) 727-7681
Fax: (248) 788-3224
Contact Person: Fred Meltzer
Website: www.parrotsoftware.com
E-mail: support@parrotsoftware.com

Compass Information Services, Inc.
1060 First Avenue
Suite 410
King of Prussia, PA 19406
Phone: (610) 992-7000
Fax: (610) 992-7046
Contact Person: Rick Jackson
Website: www.integra-ease.com

DeltaMetrics
2005 Market Street
Suite 1120
Philadelphia, PA 19103
Phone: (215) 665-2888
Fax: (215) 665-2892
Contact Person: John Cacciola

UNI/CARE Systems, Inc.
150 Preston Executive Drive
Suite 202
Cary, NC 27513
Phone: (919) 467-9295
Fax: (919) 467-3005
Contact Person: Michelle Means, Vice President of Sales & Marketing
Website: www.unicaresys.com

Velocity Healthcare Informatics
Object Products
8441 Wayzata Blvd.
Suite 105
Minneapolis, MN 55426
Phone: (800) 844-5648 or (612) 797-9997, ext. 12
Fax: (612) 797-9993
Contact Person: Ellen White, President
Website: www.objectproducts.com

References

Abramowitz, J. S. (1996). Variants of exposure and response prevention in the treatment of obsessive-compulsive disorder: A meta-analysis. *Behavior Therapy, 27,* 583–600.

Abramowitz, S. I., & Wieselberg, N. (1978). Reaction to relaxation and desensitization outcome: Five angry treatment failures. *American Journal of Psychiatry, 135,* 1418–1419.

Addis, M. (1997). Evaluating the treatment manual as a means of disseminating empirically validated treatments. *Clinical Psychology: Science and Practice, 4,* 1–11.

Agras, W. S., Sylvester, D., & Oliveau, D. (1969). The epidemiology of common fears and phobias. *Comprehensive Psychiatry, 10,* 151–156.

Alden, L. E., & Capreol, M. J. (1993). Avoidant personality disorder: Interpersonal problems as predictors of treatment response. *Behavior Therapy, 24,* 357–376.

Alden, L. E., & Wallace, S. T. (1995). Social phobia and social appraisal in successful and unsuccessful social interactions. *Behaviour Research and Therapy, 33,* 497–505.

American Psychiatric Association. (1952). *Diagnostic and statistical manual of mental disorders.* Washington, DC: Author.

American Psychiatric Association. (1968). *Diagnostic and statistical manual of mental disorders.* (2nd ed.). Washington, DC: Author.

American Psychiatric Association. (1980). *Diagnostic and statistical manual of mental disorders.* (3rd ed.). Washington, DC: Author.

American Psychiatric Association. (1987). *Diagnostic and statistical manual of mental disorders (DSM-III-R).* (3rd. rev. ed.). Washington, DC: Author.

American Psychiatric Association. (1994). *Diagnostic and statistical manual of mental disorders (DSM-IV).* (4th ed.). Washington, DC: Author.

Amering, M., Katschnig, H., Berger, P., Windhaber, J., Baischer, W., & Dantendorfer, K. (1997). Embarrassment about the first attack predicts agoraphobia in panic disorder patients. *Behaviour Research and Therapy, 35,* 517–521.

Amies, P. L., Gelder, M. G., & Shaw, P. M. (1983). Social phobia: A comparative clinical study. *British Journal of Psychiatry, 142,* 174–179.

Anderson, D. J., Noyes, R. J., & Crowe, R. R. (1984). A comparison of panic disorder and generalized anxiety disorder. *American Journal of Psychiatry, 141,* 572–575.

Andrasik, F., Turner, S. M., & Ollendick, T. H. (1980). Self-report and physiologic responding during in vivo flooding. *Behaviour Research and Therapy, 18,* 593–595.

Andrews, G. (1996a). Comorbidity in neurotic disorders: The similarities are more important than the differences. In R. M. Rapee (Ed.), *Current controversies in the anxiety disorders.* New York: Guilford.

Andrews, G. (1996b). It is the same penny: We see the head and they see the tail. In R. M. Rapee (Ed.), *Current controversies in the anxiety disorders.* New York: Guilford.

Andrews, G., Crino, R., Hunt, C., Lampe, A., & Page, A. (1994). *Treatment of anxiety disorders.* New York: Cambridge University Press.

Antony, M. M., & Swinson, R. P. (1996). *Anxiety disorders and their treatment: A critical review of the evidence based literature.* Ottawa: Health Canada.

Arnkoff, D. B., & Glass, C. R. (1989). Cognitive assessment in social anxiety and social phobia. *Clinical Psychology Review, 9,* 61–74.

Arnow, B. A., Taylor, C. B., Agras, W. S., & Telch, M. J. (1985). Enhancing agoraphobia treatment outcome by changing couple communication patterns. *Behavior Therapy, 16,* 452–467.

Arntz, A., Lavy, E., van den Berg, G., & van Rijsoort, S. (1993). Negative beliefs of spider phobics: A psychometric evaluation of the Spider Phobia Beliefs Questionnaire. *Advances in Behaviour Research and Therapy, 15,* 257–277.

Ax, A. F. (1953). The physiological differentiation between fear and anger in humans. *Psychosomatic Medicine, 15,* 433–442.

Baer, L. (1991). *Getting control: Overcoming your obsessions and compulsions.* Boston, MA: Little, Brown.

Baer, L., Brown-Beasley, M. W., Sorce, J., & Henriques, A. (1993). Computer-assisted telephone administration of a structured interview for obsessive-compulsive disorder. *American Journal of Psychiatry, 150,* 1737–1738.

Ball, S. G., & Otto, M. W. (1994). Cognitive-behavioral treatment of choking phobia: 3 case studies. *Psychotherapy and Psychosomatics, 62,* 207–211.

Bandura, A. (1977). Self-efficacy: Toward a unifying theory. *Psychological Review, 84,* 191–215.

Bandura, A., Blanchard, E. B., & Ritter, B. (1969). Relative efficacy of desensitization and modeling approaches for inducing behavioral, affective, and attitudinal changes. *Journal of Personality and Social Psychology, 13,* 173–199.

Barbee, J. G. (1993). Memory, benzodiazepines, and anxiety: Integration of theoretical and clinical perspectives. *Journal of Clinical Psychiatry, 54* (10 suppl.), 86–101.

Barber, J. P., Crits-Cristoph, P., & Luborsky, L. (1996). Effects of therapist adherence and competence on patient outcome in brief dynamic therapy. *Journal of Consulting and Clinical Psychology, 64,* 619–622.

Barlow, D. H. (1985). The dimensions of anxiety disorders. In A. H. Tuma & J. Maser (Eds.), *Anxiety and the anxiety disorders* (pp. 479–500). Hillsdale, NJ: Lawrence Erlbaum.

Barlow, D. H. (1987). The classification of anxiety disorders. In G. L. Tischler (Ed.), *Diagnosis and classification in psychiatry: A critical appraisal of DSM-III.* Cambridge, England: Cambridge University Press.

Barlow, D. H. (1988). *Anxiety and its disorders: The nature and treatment of anxiety and panic.* New York: Guilford.

Barlow, D. H. (1990). Long-term outcome for patients with panic disorder treated with cognitive-behavioral therapy. *Journal of Clinical Psychiatry, 51*, 17–23.

Barlow, D. H. (1991). The nature of anxiety: Anxiety, depression, and emotional disorders. In R. M. Rapee & D. H. Barlow (Eds.), *Chronic anxiety: Generalized anxiety disorder and mixed anxiety-depression*. New York: Guilford.

Barlow, D. H., & Barlow, D. G. (1995, May/June). Practice guidelines and empirically validated psychosocial treatments: Ships passing in the night? *Behavioral Healthcare Tomorrow*.

Barlow, D. H., & Craske, M. G. (1989). *Mastery of your anxiety and panic*. Albany, NY: Graywind Publications.

Barlow, D. H., Craske, M. G., Cerny, J. A., & Klosko, J. S. (1989). Behavioral treatment of panic disorder. *Behavior Therapy, 20*, 261–282.

Barlow, D. H., & DiNardo, P. A. (1991). The diagnosis of generalized anxiety disorder: Development, current status, and future directions. In R. M. Rapee & D. H. Barlow (Eds.), *Chronic anxiety: Generalized anxiety disorder and mixed anxiety-depression*. New York: Guilford.

Barlow, D. H., DiNardo, P. A., Vermilyea, B. B., Vermilyea, J. A., & Blanchard, E. B. (1986). Co-morbidity and depression among the anxiety disorders: Issues in diagnoses and classification. *Journal of Nervous and Mental Disease, 174*, 63–72.

Barlow, D. H., Hayes, S. C., & Nelson, R. O. (1984). *The scientist practitioner: Research and accountability in clinical and educational settings*. Boston: Allyn & Bacon.

Barlow, D. H., O'Brien, G. T., & Last, C. G. (1984). Couples treatment in agoraphobia. *Behavior Therapy, 15*, 261–282.

Barrett, C. L. (1969). Systematic desensitization versus implosive therapy. *Journal of Abnormal Psychology, 74*, 587–592.

Barrett, J. E., Barrett, J. A., Oxmann, T. E., & Gerber, P. D. (1988). The prevalence of psychiatric disorders in a primary care practice. *Archives of General Psychiatry, 45*, 1100–1106.

Battaglia, M., & Perna, G. (1995). The 35% CO_2 challenge in panic disorder: Optimization by receiver operating characteristics (ROC) analysis. *Journal of Psychiatric Research, 24*, 111–119.

Bauer, D. H. (1976). An exploratory study of developmental changes in children's fears. *Journal of Child Psychology and Psychiatry, 17*, 69–74.

Baxter, L. R., Schwartz, J. M., Bergman, K. S., Szuba, M. P., Guze, B. H., Mazziotta, J. C., Alazraki, A., Selin, C. E., Ferng, H. K., Munford, P., & Phelps, M. E. (1992). Caudate glucose metabolic rate changes with both drug and behavior therapy for obsessive-compulsive disorder. *Archives of General Psychiatry, 49*, 681–689.

Beck, A. (1974). *Cognitive therapy and the emotional disorders*. New York: International Universities Press.

Beck, A. T. (1996). Beyond belief: A theory of modes, personality, and psychopathology. In P. M. Salkovskis (Ed.), *Frontiers of cognitive therapy* (pp. 1–25). New York: Guilford.

Beck, A. T., Emery, G., & Greenberg, R. I. (1985). *Anxiety disorders and phobias: A cognitive perspective*. New York: Basic Books.

Beck, A. T., Rush, A. J., Shaw, B. F., & Emery, G. (1979). *Cognitive therapy of depression*. New York: Guilford.

Beidel, D. C., Turner, S. M., & Dancu, C. V. (1985). Physiological, cognitive, and behavioral aspects of social anxiety. *Behaviour Research and Therapy, 23*, 109–117.

Beidel, D. C., Turner, S. M., & Morris, T. L. (1995). A new inventory to assess childhood social anxiety and phobia: The Social Phobia and Anxiety Inventory for Children. *Psychological Assessment, 7,* 73–79.

Belfer, P. L., & Glass, C. R. (1992). Agoraphobic anxiety and fear of fear: Test of a cognitive-attentional model. *Journal of Anxiety Disorders, 6,* 133–146.

Belfer, P. L., Munzo, L. S., Schachter, J., & Levendusky, P. G. (1995). Cognitive-behavioral group psychotherapy for agoraphobia and panic disorder. *International Journal of Group Psychotherapy, 45,* 185–205.

Bernadt, M. W., Silverstone, T., & Singleton, W. (1980). Behavioural and subjective effects of beta-adrenergic blockade in phobic subjects. *British Journal of Psychiatry, 137,* 452–457.

Beutler, L. E., & Davison, E. H. (1995). What standards should we use? In S. C. Hayes, V. M. Follette, R. M. Dawes, & K. E. Grady (Eds.), *Scientific standards of psychological practice: Issues and recommendations* (pp. 11–24). Reno, NV: Context Press.

Beutler, L. E., Engle, D., Mohr, D., Daldrup, R. J., Bergan, J., Meredith, K., & Merry, W. (1991). Predictors of differential response to cognitive, experiential, and self-directed psychotherapeutic procedures. *Journal of Consulting and Clinical Psychology, 59,* 333–340.

Beutler, L. E., Mohr, D. C., Grawe, K., Engle, D., & McDonald, R. (1991). Looking for differential effects: Cross-cultural predictors of differential psychotherapy efficacy. *Journal of Psychotherapy Integration, 1,* 121–141.

Billett, E. A., Richter, M. A., & Kennedy, J. L. (1998). Genetics of obsessive-compulsive disorder. In R. P. Swinson, M. M. Antony, S. Rachman, & M. A. Richter (Eds.), *Obsessive-compulsive disorder.* New York: Guilford.

Biran, M., Augusto, F., & Wilson, G. T. (1981). In vivo exposure vs. cognitive restructuring in the treatment of scriptophobia. *Behaviour Research and Therapy, 19,* 525–532.

Blake, D., Weathers, F., Nagy, L., Kaloupek, D., Klauminzer, G., Charney, D., & Keane, T. (1990). *Clinician administered PTSD scale (CAPS).* Boston: National Center for Post-Traumatic Stress Disorder, Behavioral Science Division—Boston VA.

Blanchard, E. B., & Hersen, M. (1976). Behavioral treatment of hysterical neurosis: Symptom substitution and symptom return reconsidered. *Psychiatry, 39,* 118–129.

Blanchard, E. B., Hickling, E. J., Taylor, A. E., Loos, W. R., & Gerardi, R. J. (1994). Psychological morbidity associated with motor vehicle accidents. *Behaviour Research and Therapy, 32,* 283–290.

Blanchard, E. B., Kolb, L. C., Gerardi, R., Ryan, P., & Pallmayer, T. P. (1986). Cardiac response to relevant stimuli as an adjunctive tool for diagnosing post-traumatic stress disorder in combat veterans. *Behavior Therapy, 17,* 592–606.

Bland, R. C., Orn, H., & Newman, S. C. (1988). Lifetime prevalence of psychiatric disorders in Edmonton. *Acta Psychiatrica Scandinavica, 77*(Suppl. 338), 24–32.

Blaney, P. H. (1986). Affect and memory: A review. *Psychological Bulletin, 99,* 229–246.

Blatt, S. J., Sanislow, C. A., Zuroff, D. C., & Pilkonis, P. A. (1996). Characteristics of effective therapists: Further analyses of data from the National Institute of Mental Health Treatment of Depression Collaborative Research Project. *Journal of Consulting and Clinical Psychology, 64,* 1276–1284.

Blazer, D., George, L. K., & Hughes, D. (1991). The epidemiology of anxiety disorders: An age comparison. In C. Salzman & B. D. Lebowitz (Eds.), *Anxiety in the elderly.* New York: Springer.

Bodden, J. L. (1991). Accessing state-bound memories in the treatment of phobias: Two case studies. *American Journal of Clinical Hypnosis, 34*, 24–28.

Borkovec, T. D. (1994). The nature, functions, and origins of worry. In G. C. L. Davey & F. Tallis (Eds.), *Worrying: Perspective on theory, assessment, and treatment*. New York: John Wiley.

Borkovec, T. D., & Costello, E. (1993). Efficacy of applied relaxation and cognitive-behavioral therapy in the treatment of generalized anxiety disorder. *Journal of Consulting and Clinical Psychology, 61*(4), 611–619.

Borkovec, T. D., & Inz, J. (1990). The nature of worry in generalized anxiety disorder: A predominance of thought activity. *Behaviour Research and Therapy, 28*, 153–158.

Borkovec, T. D., & Lyonfields, J. D. (1993). Worry: Thought suppression of emotional processing. In H. W. Krohne (Ed.), *Attention and avoidance* (pp. 101–108). Seattle, WA: Hogrefe & Huber Publishers.

Borkovec, T. D., & Mathews, A. M. (1988). Treatment of nonphobic anxiety disorders: A comparison of nondirective, cognitive, and coping desensitization therapy. *Journal of Consulting and Clinical Psychology, 56*, 877–884.

Borkovec, T. D., Robinson, E., Pruzinsky, T., & DePree, J. A. (1983). Preliminary exploration of worry: Some 39 characteristics and processes. *Behaviour Research and Therapy, 21*, 9–16.

Borkovec, T. D., & Roemer, E. (1995). Perceived functions of worry among generalized anxiety disorder subjects: Distraction from more emotionally distressing topics? *Journal of Behaviour Therapy and Experimental Psychiatry, 26*, 25–30.

Borkovec, T. D., Shadick, R. N., & Hopkins, M. (1991). The nature of normal and pathological worry. In R. M. Rapee & D. H. Barlow (Eds.), *Chronic anxiety: Generalized anxiety disorder and mixed anxiety-depression*. New York: Guilford.

Bourdon, K. H., Boyd, J. H., Rae, D. S., Burns, B. J., Thompson, J. W., & Locke, B. Z. (1988). Gender differences in phobias: Results of the ECA community study. *Journal of Anxiety Disorders, 2*, 227–241.

Bourque, P., & Ladouceur, R. (1980). An investigation of various performance-based treatments with acrophobics. *Behaviour Research and Therapy, 18*, 161–170.

Bower, G. H. (1981). Mood and memory. *American Psychologist, 36*, 129–148.

Bowman, M. (1997). *Individual differences in post-traumatic response: Problems with the adversity-distress connection*. Mahwah, NJ: Lawrence Erlbaum.

Breitholtz, E., & Westling, B. E. (1998). Cognitions in generalized anxiety disorder and panic disorder patients. *Journal of Anxiety Disorders, 6*, 567–577.

Breslau, N., Davis, G. C., Andreski, P., & Peterson, E. (1991). Traumatic events and posttraumatic stress disorder in an urban population of young adults. *Archives of General Psychiatry, 48*, 216–222.

Brook, R. H., & Lohr, K. N. (1985). Efficacy, effectiveness, variations, and quality: Boundary-crossing research. *Medical Care, 23*, 710–722.

Brown, E. J., Heimberg, R. G., & Juster, H. R. (1995). Social phobia subtype and avoidant personality disorder: Effect on severity of social phobia, impairment, and outcome of cognitive behavioral treatment. *Behavior Therapy, 26*, 467–486.

Brown, T. A., & Barlow, D. H. (1992). Comorbidity among anxiety disorders: Implications for treatment and DSM-IV. *Journal of Consulting and Clinical Psychology, 60*, 835–844.

Brown, T. A., DiNardo, P., & Barlow, D. (1994). Anxiety Disorders Interview Schedule-IV (ADIS-IV). San Antonio, TX: The Psychological Corporation.

Brown, T. A., Moras, K., Zinbarg, R. E., & Barlow, D. (1993). Diagnostic and symptom distinguishability of generalized anxiety disorder and obsessive-compulsive disorder. *Behavior Therapist, 24,* 227–240.

Brown, T. A., O'Leary, T. A., & Barlow, D. H. (1993). Generalized anxiety disorder. In D. H. Barlow (Ed.), *Clinical handbook of psychological disorders: A step by step treatment manual* (2nd ed.). New York: Guilford.

Brown, T. M., Black, B., & Uhde, T. W. (1994). Sleep architecture in social phobia. *Biological Psychiatry, 35,* 420–421.

Bruch, M. A., Heimberg, R. G., & Hope, D. A. (1991). States of mind model and cognitive change in treated social phobics. *Cognitive Therapy and Research, 15,* 429–441.

Bryant, R. A., & Harvey, A. G. (1995). Avoidant coping style and post-traumatic stress following motor vehicle accidents. *Behaviour Research and Therapy, 33,* 631–635.

Bryant, R. A., Harvey, A. G., Basten, C., Dang, S. T., & Sackville, T. (1998). Treatment of acute stress disorder: A comparison of cognitive-behavioral therapy and supportive counseling. *Journal of Consulting and Clinical Psychology, 66,* 862–866.

Burke, M., & Mathews, A. (1992). Autobiographical memory and clinical anxiety. *Cognition and Emotion, 6,* 23–35.

Burns, D. D. (1981). *Feeling good: The new mood therapy.* New York: Signet.

Butler, G. (1989). Issues in the application of cognitive and behavioral strategies to the treatment of social phobia. *Clinical Psychology Review, 9,* 91–106.

Butler, G., Cullington, A., Munby, M., Amies, P., & Gelder, M. (1984). Exposure and anxiety management in the treatment of social phobia. *Journal of Consulting and Clinical Psychology, 52,* 642–650.

Butler, G., & Wells, A. (1995). Cognitive-behavioral treatments: Clinical applications. In R. G. Heimberg, M. R. Liebowitz, D. A. Hope, & F. R. Schneier (Eds.), *Social phobia: Diagnosis, assessment, and treatment* (pp. 310–333). New York: Guilford.

Calhoun, K. S., Moras, K., Pilkonis, P. A., & Rehm, L. P. (1998). Empirically supported treatments: Implications for training. *Journal of Consulting and Clinical Psychology, 66,* 151–162.

Campbell, M. A., & Rapee, R. M. (1994). The nature of feared outcome representations in children. *Journal of Abnormal Child Psychology, 22,* 99–111.

Campos, P. E., Solyom, L., & Koelink, A. (1984). The effects of timolol maleate on subjective and physiological components of air travel phobia. *Canadian Journal of Psychiatry, 29,* 570–574.

Carnegie, D. (1964). *How to win friends and influence people.* New York: Pocket Books.

Carter, M. M., Hollon, S. D., Carson, R., & Shelton, R. C. (1995). Effects of a safe person on induced distress following a biological challenge in panic disorder with agoraphobia. *Journal of Abnormal Psychology, 104,* 156–163.

Caspi, A., Elder, G. H., Jr., & Bem, D. J. (1988). Moving away from the world: Life-course patterns of shy children. *Journal of Abnormal Child Psychology, 24,* 824–831.

Cerny, J. A., Barlow, D. H., & Craske, M. (1987). Couples treatment of agoraphobia: A two-year follow-up study with interview, self-report, and behavioral data. *Behavior Therapy, 17,* 580–591.

Chambless, D. (1985). Agoraphobia. In M. Hersen & A. Bellack (Eds.), *Handbook of behavior therapy with adults.* New York: Plenum.

Chambless, D. L. (1987). *Gender and phobia.* Paper presented at the European Association for Behavior Therapy Congress, Amsterdam.

Chambless, D. L. (1990). Spacing of exposure sessions in treatment of agoraphobia and simple phobia. *Behavior Therapy, 21,* 217–229.

Chambless, D. L. (1996). In defense of dissemination of empirically supported psychological interventions. *Clinical Psychology: Science and Practice, 3,* 230–235.

Chambless, D. L., Baker, M. J., Baucom, D. H., Beutler, L. E., Calhoun, K. S., Crits-Christoph, P., Daiuto, A., DeRubeis, R., Detweiler, J., Haaga, D. A. F., Johnson, S. B., McCurry, S., Mueser, K. T., Pope, K. S., Sanderson, W. C., Shoham, V., Stickle, T., Williams, D. A., & Woody, S. R. (1998). Update on empirically validated therapies, II. *The Clinical Psychologist, 51*(1), 3–16.

Chambless, D. L., Caputo, G. C., Bright, P., & Gallagher, R. (1984). Assessment of fear of fear in agoraphobics: The body sensations questionnaire and the agoraphobic cognitions questionnaire. *Journal of Consulting and Clinical Psychology, 52,* 1090–1097.

Chambless, D. L., Caputo, G. C., Jasin, S. E., Gracely, E. J., & Williams, C. (1985). The mobility inventory for agoraphobia. *Behaviour Research and Therapy, 23,* 35–44.

Chambless, D., & Goldstein, A. (Eds.). (1982). *Agoraphobia: Multiple perspectives on theory and treatment.* New York: Wiley.

Chaplin, E. W., & Levine, B. A. (1981). The effects of total exposure duration and interrupted versus continuous exposure in flooding therapy. *Behavior Therapy, 12,* 360–368.

Chapman, L., & Chapman, J. (1967). Genesis of popular but erroneous psychodiagnostic observations. *Journal of Abnormal Psychology, 72,* 193–204.

Chapman, T. F., Fyer, A., Mannuzza, S., & Klein, D. F. (1993). A comparison of treated and untreated simple phobia. *American Journal of Psychiatry, 150,* 816–818.

Charney, D. S., Woods, S. W., Price, L. H., Goodman, W. K., Glazer, W. M., & Heninger, G. R. (1990). Neurobiology dysregulation in panic disorder. In J. C. Ballenger (Ed.), *Neurobiology of panic disorder* (pp. 91–105). New York: Wiley-Liss.

Chemtob, C., Roitblat, H. L., Hamada, R. S., Carslon, J. G., & Twentyman, C. T. (1988). A cognitive action theory of post-traumatic stress disorder. *Journal of Anxiety Disorders, 2,* 253–275.

Chevron, E., & Rounsaville, B. J. (1983). Evaluating the clinical skills of psychotherapists: A comparison of techniques. *Archives of General Psychiatry, 40,* 1129–1132.

Christianson, S.-A., & Nilsson, L.-G. (1984). Functional amnesia as induced by a psychological trauma. *Memory and Cognition, 12,* 142–155.

Clark, D. A., Beck, A. T., & Brown, G. (1989). Cognitive mediation in general psychiatric outpatients: A test of the content-specific hypothesis. *Journal of Personality and Social Psychology, 56,* 958–964.

Clark, D. A., Beck, A. T., & Stewart, B. (1990). Cognitive specificity and positive-negative affectivity: Complementary or contradictory views on anxiety and depression? *Journal of Abnormal Psychology, 99,* 148–155.

Clark, D. A., & Claybourn, M. (1997). Process characteristics of worry and obsessive intrusive thoughts. *Behaviour Research and Therapy, 35,* 1139–1141.

Clark, D. M. (1986). A cognitive approach to panic. *Behaviour Research and Therapy, 24,* 461–470.

Clark, D. M. (1989). Anxiety states: Panic and generalized anxiety. In K. Hawton, P. Salkovskis, J. Kirk, & D. M. Clark (Eds.), *Cognitive behaviour ther-*

apy for psychiatric problems: A practical guide. Oxford, UK: Oxford University Press.

Clark, D. M. (1993). Cognitive mediation of panic attacks induced by biological challenge tests. *Advances in Behaviour Research and Therapy, 15*, 75–84.

Clark, D. M., Salkovskis, P. M., Hackmann, A., Middleton, H., Anastasiades, P., & Gelder, M. (1994). A comparison of cognitive therapy, applied relaxation and imipramine in the treatment of panic disorder. *British Journal of Psychiatry, 164*, 759–769.

Clark, D. M., Salkovskis, P. M., Ost, L.-G., Breitholtz, E., Koehler, K. A., Westling, B. E., Jeavons, A., & Gelder, M. (1997). Misinterpretation of bodily sensations in panic disorder. *Journal of Consulting and Clinical Psychology, 65*, 203–213.

Clark, D. M., & Wells, A. (1995). A cognitive model of social phobia. In R. G. Heimberg, M. R. Liebowitz, D. A. Hope, & F. R. Schneier (Eds.), *Social phobia: Diagnosis, assessment, and treatment* (pp. 69–93). New York: Guilford.

Clement, P. W. (1996). Evaluation in private practice. *Clinical Psychology Science and Practice, 3*, 146–159.

Clum, G. A. (1990). *Coping with panic.* Pacific Grove, CA: Brooks/Cole.

Clum, G. A., & Knowles, S. L. (1991). Why do some people with panic disorders become avoidant? A review. *Clinical Psychology Review, 11*, 295–313.

Cohen, L. H. (1979). The research readership and information source reliance of clinical psychologists. *Professional Psychology, 10*, 780–786.

Cohen, L. H., Sargent, M. M., & Sechrest, L. B. (1986). Use of psychotherapy research by professional psychologists. *American Psychologist, 41*, 198–206.

Cohn, C. K., Kron, R. E., & Brady, J. P. (1976). A case of blood-illness-injury phobia treated behaviorally. *Journal of Nervous and Mental Disease, 162*, 65–68.

Compton, A. (1992). The psychoanalytic view of phobias. Part IV: General theory of phobias and anxiety. *Psychoanalytic Quarterly, 61*, 426–446.

Cowley, D. S., & Roy-Byrne, P. P. (1991). The biology of generalized anxiety disorder and chronic anxiety. In R. M. Rapee & D. H. Barlow (Eds.), *Chronic anxiety: Generalized anxiety disorder and mixed anxiety-depression.* New York: Guilford.

Cox, B. J., & Swinson, R. P. (1994). Overprediction of fear in panic disorder with agoraphobia. *Behaviour Research and Therapy, 32*, 735–739.

Cox, B. J., Swinson, R. P., Endler, N. S., & Norton, R. (1994). The symptom structure of panic attacks. *Comprehensive Psychiatry, 35*, 349–353.

Cox, B. J., Swinson, R. P., Morrison, B., & Lee, P. S. (1993). Clomipramine, fluoxetine, and behavior therapy in the treatment of obsessive-compulsive disorder: A meta-analysis. *Journal of Behaviour Therapy and Experimental Psychiatry, 24*, 149–153.

Craske, M. G., & Craig, K. D. (1984). Musical performance anxiety: The three-systems model and self-efficacy theory. *Behaviour Research and Therapy, 22*, 267–280.

Craske, M. G., Rapee, R. M., Jackel, L., & Barlow, D. H. (1989). Qualitative dimensions of worry in DSM-III-R generalized anxiety disorder subjects and nonanxious controls. *Behaviour Research and Therapy, 27*, 397–402.

Crits-Christoph, P., Connolly, M. B., Azarian, K., Crits-Christoph, K., & Shappell, S. (1996). An open trial of brief supportive-expressive psychotherapy in the treatment of generalized anxiety disorder. *Psychotherapy, 33*, 418–430.

Darwin, C. (1872/1965). *Expression of the emotions in man and animals.* Chicago: University of Chicago Press.

Davey, G. C. L. (1989). Dental phobias and anxieties: Evidence for conditioning processes in the acquisition and modulation of a learned fear. *Behaviour Research and Therapy, 27,* 51–58.

Davey, G. C. L., & Levy, S. (1998). Catastrophic worrying: Personal inadequacy and a perseverative iterative style as features of the catastrophizing process. *Journal of Abnormal Psychology, 107,* 576–586.

Davidson, J. R. T., Hughes, D., Blazer, D., & George, L. K. (1991). Posttraumatic stress disorder in the community: An epidemiological study. *Psychological Medicine, 21,* 1–19.

Davidson, J. R. T., Potts, N. L. S., Richichi, E. A., Krishnan, R., Ford, S. M., Smith, R. D., & Wilson, W. (1991). The Brief Social Phobia Scale. *Journal of Clinical Psychiatry, 52,* 48–51.

Davis, M. (1992). The role of the amygdala in fear and anxiety. *Annual Review of Neuroscience, 15,* 353–375.

Dawes, R. (1994). *House of Cards.* New York: Simon & Schuster.

de Araujo, L. A., Ito, L. M., Marks, I. M., and Deale, E. (1995). Does imagined exposure to the consequence of not ritualising enhance live exposure for OCD? A controlled study: I. Main outcome. *British Journal of Psychiatry, 167,* 65–70.

de Jongh, A., Muris, P., ter Horst, G., van Zuuren, F., Schoenmakers, N., & Makkes, P. (1995). One-session cognitive treatment of dental phobia: Preparing dental phobics for treatment by restructuring negative cognitions. *Behaviour Research and Therapy, 33,* 947–954.

DePaulo, B. M., Epstein, J. A., & LeMay, C. S. (1990). Responses of the socially anxious to the prospect of interpersonal evaluation. *Journal of Personality, 58,* 623–640.

Depression Guideline Panel (1993). *Depression in primary care: Volume 2. Treatment of Major Depression, Clinical Practice Guideline, Number 5* (Washington, DC: US Government Printing Office AHCPR Publication No. 93-0551): Department of Health and Human Services, Public Health Service, Agency for Healthcare Policy and Research.

DeSilva, P., & Rachman, S. (1992). *Obsessive-compulsive disorder: The facts.* Oxford, UK: Oxford University Press.

Devilly, G. J., & Spence, S. H. (1999). The relative efficacy and treatment distress of EMDR and a cognitive-behavior trauma treatment protocol in the amelioration of posttraumatic stress disorder. *Journal of Anxiety Disorders, 13,* 131–157.

Devine, D. A., & Fernald, P. S. (1973). Outcome effects of receiving a preferred, randomly assigned, or non-preferred therapy. *Journal of Consulting and Clinical Psychology, 41,* 104–107.

DiGiuseppe, R., McGowan, L., Sutton-Simon, K., & Gardner, F. (1990). A comparative outcome study of four cognitive therapies in the treatment of social anxiety. *Journal of Rational-Emotive and Cognitive-Behavior Therapy, 8,* 129–146.

Dimsdale, J. E., & Moss, J. (1980). Plasma catecholamines and stress and exercise. *Journal of the American Medical Association, 243,* 340–342.

DiNardo, P. A., O'Brien, G. T., Barlow, D. H., Waddell, M. T., & Blanchard, E. B. (1983). Reliability of DSM-III anxiety disorder categories using a new structured interview. *Archives of General Psychiatry, 40,* 1070–1074.

Dodge, C. S., Hope, D. A., Heimberg, R. G., & Becker, R. E. (1988). Evaluation of the Social Interaction Self-Statement Test with a social phobic population. *Cognitive Therapy and Research, 12,* 211–222.

Donabedian, A. (1966). Evaluating the quality of medical care. *Milbank Memorial Fund Quarterly, 44,* 166–206.

Doogan, S., & Thomas, G. V. (1992). Origins of fear of dogs in adults and children: The role of conditioning processes and prior familiarity with dogs. *Behaviour Research and Therapy, 30,* 387–394.

Dugas, M. J., Freeston, M. H., Ladouceur, R., Rheaume, J., Provencher, M., & Boisvert, J. M. (1998). Worry themes in primary GAD, secondary GAD, and other anxiety disorders. *Journal of Anxiety Disorders, 12,* 253–261.

Dugas, M. J., Gagnon, F., Ladouceur, R., & Freeston, M. (1998). Generalized anxiety disorder: A preliminary test of a conceptual model. *Behaviour Research and Therapy, 36,* 215–226.

Dugas, M. J., Letarte, H., Rhéaume, J., Freeston, M., & Ladouceur, R. (1995). Worry and problem solving: Evidence of a specific relationship. *Cognitive Therapy and Research, 19,* 109–120.

Durham, R. C., Murphy, T., Allan, T., Richard, K., Treliving, L. R., & Fenton, G. W. (1994). Cognitive therapy, analytic psychotherapy and anxiety management training for generalized anxiety disorder. *British Journal of Psychiatry, 165,* 315–323.

D'Zurilla, T. J. (1986). *Problem-solving therapy: A social competence approach to clinical intervention.* New York: Springer.

Echeburua, E., De Corral, P., Zubizarreta, I., & Sarasua, B. (1997). Psychological treatment of chronic posttraumatic stress disorder in victims of sexual aggression. *Behavior Modification, 21*(4), 433–456.

Ehlers, A. (1993). Somatic symptoms and panic attacks: A retrospective study of learning experiences. *Behaviour Research and Therapy, 31,* 269–278.

Ehlers, A. (1995). A 1-year prospective study of panic attacks: Clinical course and factors associated with maintenance. *Journal of Abnormal Psychology, 104,* 164–172.

Ehlers, A., Margraf, J., Davies, S., & Roth, W. T. (1988). Selective processing of threat cues in subjects with panic attacks. *Cognition and Emotion, 2,* 201–219.

Emmelkamp, P. M. G., & Beens, H. (1991). Cognitive therapy with obsessive-compulsive disorder: A comparative evolution. *Behaviour Research and Therapy, 29,* 293–300.

Emmelkamp, P. M. G., Bouman, T. K., & Blaauw, E. (1994). Individualized versus standardized therapy: A comparative evaluation with obsessive-compulsive patients. *Clinical Psychology and Psychotherapy, 1,* 95–100.

Emmelkamp, P. M. G., Mersch, P. P. A., Vissia, E., & van der Helm, M. (1985). Social phobia: A comparative evaluation of cognitive and behavioral interventions. *Behaviour Research and Therapy, 23,* 365–369.

Esman, A. (1989). Psychoanalysis in general psychiatry: Obsessive-compulsive disorder as a paradigm. *Journal of American Psychoanalytical Association, 37,* 319–336.

Etringer, B. D., Cash, T. F., & Rimm, D. C. (1982). Behavioral, affective, and cognitive effects of participant modeling and an equally credible placebo. *Behavior Therapy, 13,* 476–485.

Eysenck, H. J. (Ed.). (1967). *The biological basis of personality.* Springfield, IL: Charles C. Thomas.

Eysenck, H. J. (1968). A theory of the incubation of anxiety/fear responses. *Behaviour Research and Therapy, 6,* 309–321.

Eysenck, H. J. (1982). Neurobehavioristic (S-R) theory. In G. Wilson & Francks (Eds.), *Contemporary Behavior Therapy.* New York: Guilford.

Eysenck, M. (1997). *Anxiety and cognition: A unified theory.* Hove, UK: Psychological Press.

Eysenck, M. W., & Mogg, K. (1992). Clinical anxiety, trait anxiety, and memory bias. In S.-A. Christianson (Ed.), *The handbook of emotional memory: Research and theory* (pp. 429–450). Hillsdale, NJ: Lawrence Erlbaum.

Falloon, I. R., lloyd, G. G., & Harpin, R. (1981). The treatment of social phobia: Real-life rehearsal with non-professional therapists. *Journal of Nervous and Mental Disease, 169,* 180–184.

Falsetti, S. A. (1997). The decision-making process of choosing a treatment for patients with civilian trauma-related PTSD. *Cognitive and Behavioral Practice, 4,* 99–121.

Faravelli, C., Paterniti, S., & Scarpato, A. (1995). 5-year prospective, naturalistic follow-up study of panic disorder. *Comprehensive Psychiatry, 36,* 271–277.

Feske, U. (1998). Eye movement desensitization and reprocessing treatment for posttraumatic stress disorder. *Clinical Psychology: Science and Practice, 5*(2), 171–181.

Feske, U., & Chambless, D. L. (1995). Cognitive behavioral versus exposure only treatment for social phobia: A meta-analysis. *Behavior Therapy, 26,* 695–720.

Feske, U., Perry, K. J., Chambless, D. L., Renneberg, B., & Goldstein, A. J. (1996). Avoidant personality disorder as a predictor for treatment outcome among generalized social phobics. *Journal of Personality Disorders, 10,* 174–184.

First, M. B., Gibbon, M., Spitzer, R. I., & Williams, J. B. W. (1997). Structured Clinical Interview for DSM-IV Axis I Disorders: Clinician Version. New York: American Psychiatric Press.

Flint, A. J. (1994). Epidemiology and comorbidity of anxiety disorders in the elderly. *American Journal of Psychiatry, 151,* 640–649.

Flynn, T. M., Taylor, P., & Pollard, C. A. (1992). Use of mobile phones in the behavioral treatment of driving phobias. *Journal of Behaviour Therapy and Experimental Psychiatry, 23,* 299–302.

Foa, E. B. (1998). *Treating the trauma of rape: Cognitive-behavioral therapy for PTSD.* New York: Guilford.

Foa, E., Franklin, M. E., Perry, K. J., & Herbert, J. D. (1996). Cognitive biases in generalized social phobia. *Journal of Abnormal Psychology, 105,* 433–439.

Foa, E. B., Hearst-Ikeda, D., & Perry, K. (1995). Evoluation of a brief cognitive-behavioral program for the prevention of chronic PTSD in recent assault victims. *Journal of Consulting and Clinical Psychology, 63,* 948–955.

Foa, E. B., Jameson, J. S., Turner, R. M., & Paynes, L. L. (1980). Massed vs. spaced exposure sessions in the treatment of agoraphobia. *Behaviour Research and Therapy, 18,* 333–338.

Foa, E. B., & Jaycox, L. H. (1999). *Cognitive-behavioral theory and treatment of post-traumatic stress disorder.* In D. Spiegel (Ed.), Efficacy and cost-effectiveness of psychotherapy (pp. 23–61). Washington, DC: American Psychiatric Association.

Foa, E. B., & Kozak, M. J. (1985). Treatment of anxiety disorders: Implications for psychopathology. In A. H. Tuma & J. D. Maser (Eds.), *Anxiety and the anxiety disorders* (pp. 421–452). Hillsdale, NJ: Lawrence Erlbaum.

Foa, E. B., & Kozak, M. J. (1986). Emotional processing of fear: Exposure to corrective information. *Psychological Bulletin, 99,* 20–35.

Foa, E. B., Riggs, D. S., Dancu, C. V., & Rothbaum, B. O. (1993). Reliability and validity of a brief instrument for assessing posttraumatic stress disorder. *Journal of Traumatic Stress, 6,* 459–473.

Foa, E. B., & Rothbaum, B. O. (1998). *Treating the trauma of rape: Cognitive-behavioral therapy for PTSD.* New York: Guilford.

Foa, E. B., Steketee, G., & Rothbaum, B. (1989). Behavioral/cognitive conceptualizations of post-traumatic stress disorder. *Behavior Therapy, 20,* 155–176.

Foa, E. B., & Wilson, R. (1991). *Stop obsessing!* New York: Bantam.

Fonagy, P., & Target, M. (1996). Should we allow psychotherapy research to determine clinical practice? *Clinical Psychology Science and Practice, 3,* 245–250.

Ford, J. D., Fisher, P., & Larson, L. (1997). Object relations as a predictor of treatment outcome with chronic posttraumatic stress disorder. *Journal of Consulting and Clinical Psychology, 65*(4), 547–559.

Forquer, S. L., & Muse, L. C. (1996). Continuous quality improvement: Theory and tools for the 1990s. In B. L. Levin & J. Petrila (Eds.), *Mental health services: A public health perspective.* New York: Oxford University Press.

Frances, A., Miele, T. A., Widiger, H. A., Pincus, D. M., & Davis, W. W. (1993). The classification of panic disorders: From Freud to DSM-IV. *Journal of Psychiatric Research, 27*(Suppl. 1), 3–10.

Frank, E., Kupfer, D. J., Wagner, E. F., McEachran, A. B., & Cornes, C. (1991). Efficacy of interpersonal psychotherapy as a maintenance treatment of recurrent depression: Contributing factors. *Archives of General Psychiatry, 48,* 1053–1059.

Fredrikson, M. (1981). Orienting and defensive reactions to phobic and conditioned fear stimuli in phobics and normals. *Psychophysiology, 18,* 456–465.

Fredrikson, M., Annas, P., Fischer, H., & Wik, G. (1996). Gender and age differences in the prevalence of specific fears and phobia. *Behaviour Research and Therapy, 34,* 33–39.

Freeston, M. H., Dugas, M. J., & Ladouceur, R. (1996). Thoughts, images, worry and anxiety. *Cognitive Therapy and Research, 20,* 265–273.

Freeston, M. H., & Ladouceur, R. (1997). What do patients do with their obsessive thoughts? *Behaviour Research and Therapy, 35,* 335–348.

Freeston, M. H., Ladouceur, R., Gagnon, F., & Thibodeau, N. (1993). Beliefs about obsessional thoughts. *Journal of Psychopathology and Behavioral Assessment, 15,* 1–21.

Freeston, M. H., Ladouceur, R., Gagnon, F., Thibodeau, N., Rhéame, J., Letarte, H., & Bujold, A. (1997). Cognitive-behavioral treatment of obsessive thoughts: A controlled study. *Journal of Consulting and Clinical Psychology, 65,* 405–413.

Freeston, M. H., Ladouceur, R., Thibodeau, N., & Gagnon, F. (1991). Cognitive intrusions in a non-clinical population. I. Response style, subjective experience and appraisal. *Behaviour Research and Therapy, 29,* 585–597.

Freeston, M. H., Rhéaume, J. L., Dugas, M. J., & Ladouceur, R. (1994). Why do people worry? *Personality and Individual Differences, 17,* 791–802.

Freeston, M. H., Rhéaume, J., & Ladouceur, R. (1996). Correcting faulty appraisals of obsessional thoughts. *Behaviour Research and Therapy, 34,* 433–446.

Freud, S. (1895/1962). On the grounds for detaching a particular syndrome from neurasthenia under the description "anxiety neurosis." In J. Strachey (Ed.), *The Standard Edition of the Complete Psychological Works of Sigmund Freud* (Original work published 1895 ed., Vol. 3, pp. 90–115). London: Hogarth Press.

Freud, S. (1933). *The problem of anxiety.* New York: Norton.

Friedman, S. (Ed.). (1977). *Cultural issues in the treatment of anxiety.* New York: Guilford.

Frost, R. O., & Hartl, T. L. (1996). A cognitive-behavioral model of compulsive hoarding. *Behaviour Research and Therapy, 34,* 341–350.

Frueh, B. C., Turner, S. M., Beidel, D. C., Mirabella, R. F., & Jones, W. J. (1996). Trauma management therapy: A preliminary evaluation of a multicomponent behavioral treatment for chronic combat-related PTSD. *Behavior Research and Therapy, 34,* 533–543.

Furnham, A. (1994). A content, correlational and factor analytic study of four intolerance of ambiguity questionnaires. *Personality and Individual Differences, 16,* 403–410.

Fyer, A. J. (1993). Heritability of social anxiety: A brief review. *Journal of Clinical Psychiatry, 54*(12, Suppl.), 10–12.

Fyer, A. J., Mannuzza, S., Chapman, T. F., Liebowitz, M. R., & Klein, D. F. (1993). A direct interview family study of social phobia. *Archives of General Psychiatry, 50,* 286–293.

Gabor, D. (1997). *Talking with confidence for the painfully shy.* New York: Crown.

Gaind, R., Suri, A. K., & Thompson, J. (1975). Use of beta blockers as an adjunct in behavioral techniques. *Scottish Medical Journal, 20,* 284–286.

Gambrill, E., & Richey, C. A. (1975). An assertion inventory for use in assessment and research. *Behavior Therapy, 6,* 547–549.

Gambrill, E., & Richey, C. (1988). *Taking charge of your social life.* Berkeley, CA: Behavioral Options.

Garb, H. N. (1994). Cognitive heuristics and biases in personality assessment. In L. Heath, R. S. Tindale, J. Edwards, E. J. Posavac, F. B. Bryant, E. Henderson-King, Y. Suarez-Balcazar, & J. Myers (Eds.), *Applications of heuristics and biases to social issues* (pp. 73–90). New York: Plenum.

Garber, H., Anuuth, J., Chiu, L., Griswold, V., & Oldendorf, W. (1989). Nuclear magnetic resonance of obsessive-compulsive disorder. *American Journal of Psychiatry, 146,* 1001.

Gaston, L., Marmar, C. R., Gallagher, D., & Thompson, L. W. (1991). Alliance prediction of outcome beyond in-treatment symptomatic change as psychotherapy processes. *Psychotherapy Research, 1,* 104–112.

Gauthier, J., & Ladouceur, R. (1981). The influence of self-efficacy reports on performance. *Behavior Therapy, 12,* 436–439.

Gelernter, C. S., Uhde, T. W., Cimbolic, P., Arnkoff, D. B., Vittone, B., Tancer, M. E., & Bartko, J. J. (1991). Cognitive-behavioral and pharmacological treatments of social phobia: A controlled study. *Archives of General Psychiatry, 38,* 938–945.

Gerdes, T. G., Yates, W. R., & Clancy, G. (1995). Increasing identification and referral of panic disorder over the past decade. *Psychosomatics, 36,* 480–486.

Gillis, M. M., Haaga, D. A. F., & Ford, G. T. (1995). Normative values for the Beck Anxiety Inventory, Fear Questionnaire, Penn State Worry Questionnaire, and Social Phobia and Anxiety Inventory. *Psychological Assessment, 7,* 450–455.

Glass, C. R., Merluzzi, T. V., Biever, J. L., & Larsen, K. H. (1982). Cognitive assessment of social anxiety: Development and validation of a self-statement questionnaire. *Cognitive Therapy and Research, 6,* 37–55.

Glazer, W. M. (1994). What are "best practices?": Understanding the concept. *Hospital and Community Psychiatry, 45,* 1067–1068.

Goisman, R. M. (1983). Therapeutic approaches to phobia: A comparison. *American Journal of Psychotherapy, 37,* 227–234.

Goisman, R. M., Warshaw, M. G., Lind, M. A., Peterson, M. D., & Rogers, M. P. (1994). Panic, agoraphobia, and panic disorder with agoraphobia. *Journal of Nervous and Mental Disease, 182,* 72–79.

Goisman, R. M., Warshaw, M. G., Steketee, G. S., Fierman, E. J., Rogers, M. P., & Goldenberg, I. (1995). DSM-IV and the disappearance of agoraphobia without a history of panic disorder: New data on a controversial diagnosis. *American Journal of Psychiatry, 152,* 1438–1443.

Goldfried, M. R., & Wolfe, B. E. (1996). Psychotherapy practice and research: Repairing a strained alliance. *American Psychologist, 51,* 1007–1016.

Good, J. G., & Kleinman, A. M. (1985). Culture and anxiety: Cross-cultural evidence for the patterning of anxiety disorders. In A. H. Tuma & J. Maser (Eds.), *Anxiety and the anxiety disorders* (pp. 297–323). Hillsdale, NJ: Lawrence Erlbaum.

Goodman, W. K., Price, L. H., Rasmussen, S. A., Mazure, C., Delgado, P., Heninger, G. R., & Charney, D. S. (1989). The Yale-Brown obsessive compulsive scale. II: Validity. *Archives of General Psychiatry, 46,* 1012–1016.

Goodman, W. K., Price, L. H., Rasmussen, S. A., Mazure, C., Fleischmann, R. L., Hill, C. L., Heninger, G. R., & Charney, D. S. (1989). The Yale-Brown obsessive-compulsive scale, I: Development, use and reliability. *Archives of General Psychiatry, 40,* 1006–1011.

Gould, R. A., & Clum, G. A. (1995). Self-help plus minimal therapist contact in the treatment of panic disorder: A replication and extension. *Behavior Therapy, 26,* 533–546.

Gould, R. A., Otto, M. W., & Pollack. (1995). A meta-analysis of treatment outcome for panic disorder. *Clinical Psychology Review, 15,* 819–844.

Gray, J. A. (1987). *The psychology of fear and stress.* (2nd ed.). New York: Cambridge University Press.

Greenberg, D. B., Stern, T. A., & Weilburg, J. B. (1988). The fear of choking: Three successfully treated cases. *Psychosomatics, 29,* 126–129.

Greist, J. H., Kobak, K. A., Jefferson, J. W., Katzelnick, D. J., & Chene, R. L. (1995). The clinical interview. In R. G. Heimberg, M. R. Liebowitz, D. A. Hope, & F. R. Schneier (Eds.), *Social phobia: Diagnosis, assessment, and treatment* (pp. 185–201). New York: Guilford.

Hare, R. D., & Bleving, G. (1976). Defensive responses to phobic stimuli. *Biological Psychology, 3,* 1–13.

Harvey, A. G., & Bryant, R. A. (1998). The effect of attempted thought suppression in acute stress disorder. *Behaviour Research and Therapy, 36,* 583–590.

Hayward, C., Killen, J. D., & Taylor, C. B. (1989). Panic attacks in young adolescents. *American Journal of Psychiatry, 146,* 1061–1062.

Hecker, J. E., Losee, M. C., Fritzler, B. K., & Fink, C. M. (1996). Self-directed versus therapist-directed cognitive behavioral treatment for panic disorder. *Journal of Anxiety Disorders, 10,* 253–265.

Heide, F. J., & Borkovec, T. D. (1983). Relaxation-induced anxiety: Paradoxical anxiety enhancement due to relaxation training. *Journal of Consulting and Clinical Psychology, 51,* 171–182.

Heimberg, R. G., Dodge, C. S., Hope, D. A., Kennedy, C. R., Zollo, L. J., & Becker, R. E. (1990). Cognitive behavioral group treatment for social phobia: Comparison with a credible placebo control. *Cognitive Therapy and Research, 14,* 1–23.

Heimberg, R. G., Hope, D. A., Dodge, C. S., & Becker, R. E. (1990). DSM-III-R subtypes of social phobia: Comparison of generalized social phobics and public speaking phobics. *Journal of Nervous and Mental Disease, 178,* 172–179.

Heimberg, R. G., Liebowitz, M. R., Hope, D. A., Schneier, F. R., Holt, C. S., Welkowitz, L. A., Juster, H. R., Campeas, R., Bruch, M. A., Cloitre, M., Fallon, B., & Klein, D. F. (1998). Cognitive behavioral group therapy vs. phenelzine therapy for social phobia. *Archives of General Psychiatry, 55,* 1133–1141.

Hellhammer, D. (1992). Psychoendocrinology: The brain, hormones, and behavior. In A. Ehlers, W. Fiegenbaum, I. Florin, & J. Margraf (Eds.), *Perspectives and promises of clinical psychology.* New York: Plenum.

Hellstrom, K., & Öst, L.-G. (1995). One-session therapist directed exposure vs. two forms of manual directed self-exposure in the treatment of spider phobia. *Behaviour Research and Therapy, 33,* 959–965.

Helzer, J. E., Robins, L. N., & McEvoy, L. (1987). Post-traumatic stress disorder in the general population. *The New England Journal of Medicine, 317,* 1630–1634.

Henry, W. P., Strupp, H. H., Butler, S. F., Schacht, T. E., & Binder, J. L. (1993). Effects of training in time-limited dynamic psychotherapy: Changes in therapist behavior. *Journal of Consulting and Clinical Psychology, 61,* 434–440.

Hiatt, D., & Hargrave, G. E. (1995, July/August). The characteristics of highly effective therapists in managed behavioral provider networks. *Behavioral Healthcare Tomorrow,* 19–22.

Hickling, E. J., & Blanchard, E. B. (1997). The private practice psychologist and manual-based treatments: Post-traumatic stress disorder secondary to motor vehicle accidents. *Behaviour Research and Therapy, 35*(3), 191–203.

Hillman, J., & Ventura, J. (1993). *We've had a hundred years of psychotherapy-and the world's getting worse.* San Francisco, CA: Harper.

Hiss, H., Foa, E. B., & Kozak, M. J. (1994). Relapse prevention program for treatment of obsessive-compulsive disorder. *Journal of Consulting and Clinical Psychology, 62,* 801–808.

Hodgson, R. J., & Rachman, S. (1977). Obsessional compulsive complaints. *Behavioural Research and Therapy, 15,* 389–395.

Hoehn-Saric, R. (1993). *Regional cerebral blood flow in obsessive-compulsive disorder patients before and during treatment with fluoxetine.* Paper presented at the 1st International OCD Conference Abstracts, Isle of Capri, Italy.

Hoehn-Saric, R., McLeod, D. R., & Zimmerli, W. D. (1989). Somatic manifestations in women with generalized anxiety disorder: Psychophysiological responses to psychological stress. *Archives of General Psychiatry, 46,* 1113–1119.

Hofmann, S. G., Newman, M. G., Ehlers, A., & Roth, W. T. (1995). Psychophysiological differences between subgroups of social phobia. *Journal of Abnormal Psychology, 104,* 224–231.

Hollander, E., Kwon, J., Stein, D., Broatch, J., Rowland, C. T., & Himelein, C. A. (1996). Obsessive-compulsive and spectrum disorders: Overview and quality of life issues. *Journal of Clinical Psychiatry, 57*(Suppl. 8), 3–6.

Hollingsworth, C., Tanguay, P., & Grossman, L. (1980). Long-term outcome of obsessive-compulsive disorder in childhood. *Journal of American Academy of Child Psychiatry, 19,* 134–144.

Holt, P. E., & Andrews, G. (1989). Provocation of panic: Three elements of the panic reaction in four anxiety disorders. *Behaviour Research and Therapy, 27,* 253–261.

Hope, D. A., & Heimberg, R. G. (1993). Social phobia and social anxiety. In D. H. Barlow (Ed.), *Clinical handbook of psychological disorders* (2nd ed., pp. 99–136). New York: Guilford.

Hope, D. A., Heimberg, R. G., & Klein, J. F. (1990). Social anxiety and the recall of interpersonal information. *Journal of Cognitive Psychotherapy, 4,* 185–195.

Horowitz, L. M., Rosenberg, S. E., Baer, B. A., Ureno, G., & Villasenor, V. S. (1988). Inventory of Interpersonal Problems: Psychometric properties and clinical applications. *Journal of Consulting and Clinical Psychology, 56,* 885–892.

Horowitz, M., Wilner, N., & Alvarez, W. (1979). Impact of event scale: Measure of subjective distress. *Psychosomatic Medicine, 41,* 209–218.

Horowitz, M. J. (1986). *Stress Response Syndrome.* (2nd ed.). Northvale, NJ: Jason Aronson.

Horowitz, M. J., & Reidbord, S. P. (1992). Memory, emotion and response to trauma. In S. A. Christianson (Ed.), *The handbook of emotion and memory: Research and therapy* (pp. 343–356). Hillsdale, NJ: Lawrence Erlbaum.

Houlihan, D., Schwartz, C., Miltenberger, R., & Heuton, D. (1993). The rapid treatment of a young man's balloon (noise) phobia using in vivo flooding. *Journal of Behaviour Therapy and Experimental Psychiatry, 24,* 233–240.

Huag, T., Brenne, L., Johnsen, B. H., Berntzen, D., Gostestam, K.-G., & Hugdahl, K. (1987). A three-systems analysis of fear of flying: A comparison of a consonant versus a non-consonant treatment method. *Behaviour Research and Therapy, 25,* 187–194.

The International Multicenter Clinical Trial Group on Moclobemide in Social Phobia. (1997). Moclobemide in social phobia: A double-blind placebo-controlled clinical study. *European Archives of Psychiatry and Clinical Neuroscience, 247,* 71–80.

Isaacs, B. (1978). *Recent advances in geriatric medicine.* (Vol. 1). London: Churchill Livingstone.

Jacobson, N. S., Schmaling, K. B., Holtzworth-Munroe, A., Katt, J. L., Wood, L. F., & Follette, V. M. (1989). Research-structured vs clinically flexible versions of social learning-based marital therapy. *Behaviour Research and Therapy, 27,* 173–180.

Jang, K. L., Livesley, W. J., & Vernon, P. A. (1996). Heritability of the Big Five personality dimensions and their facets: A twin study. *Journal of Personality, 64*(3), 577–591.

Jang, K. L., McCrae, R. R., Angleitner, A., Riemann, R., & Livesley, W. J. (1998). Heritability of Facet-level Traits in a Cross-Cultural Twin Sample: Support for a Hierarchical Model of Personality. *Journal of Personality and Social Psychology, 74,* 1556–1566.

Jaycox, L. H., Foa, E. B., & Morral, A. R. (1998). Influence of emotional engagement and habituation exposure therapy for PTSD. *Journal of Consulting and Clinical Psychology, 66,* 185–192.

Jerremalm, A., Jansson, L., & Öst, L.-G. (1986a). Individual response patterns and the effects of different behavioral methods in the treatment of dental phobia. *Behaviour Research and Therapy, 24,* 587–596.

Jerremalm, A., Jansson, L., & Öst, L.-G. (1986b). Cognitive and physiological reactivity and the effects of different behavioral methods in the treatment of social phobia. *Behaviour Research and Therapy, 24,* 171–180.

Johnson, R. L., & Glass, C. R. (1989). Heterosocial anxiety and direction of attention in high school boys. *Cognitive therapy and research, 13,* 509–526.

Johnson, W. R., & Smith, E. W. L. (1997). Gestalt empty-chair dialogue versus systematic desensitization in the treatment of a phobia. *Gestalt Review, 1,* 150–162.

Jones, W., Hobbs, S., & Hockenbury, D. (1982). Loneliness and social skill deficits. *Journal of Personality and Social Psychology, 42*, 682–689.

Kadden, R. M., Cooney, N. L., Getter, H., & Litt, M. D. (1989). Matching alcoholics to coping skills or interactional therapies: Posttreatment results. *Journal of Consulting and Clinical Psychology, 57*, 698–704.

Kagan, J. (1994). *Galen's prophecy.* New York: Basic Books.

Kagan, J., Reznick, J. S., & Snidman, N. (1987). The physiology and psychology of behavioral inhibition in children. *Child Development, 58*, 1459–1473.

Kamphuis, J. H., & Emmelkamp, P. M. G. (1988). Crime-related trauma: Psychological distress in victims of bankrobbery. *Journal of Anxiety Disorders, 12*, 199–208.

Kaplan, D. M. (1972). On shyness. *International Journal of Psychoanalysis, 53*, 439–453.

Karno, M., Golding, J. M., Sorenson, S. B., & Burman, M. A. (1988). The epidemiology of obsessive-compulsive disorder in five US communities. *Archives of General Psychiatry, 45*, 1094–1099.

Katerndahl, D. A., & Realini, J. P. (1993). Lifetime prevalence of panic states. *American Journal of Psychiatry, 150*, 246–249.

Keane, T. M., Caddell, J. M., & Taylor, K. L. (1988). Mississippi Scale for combat-related posttraumatic stress disorder: Three studies in reliability and validity. *Journal of Consulting and Clinical Psychology, 56*, 85–90.

Keane, T. M., & Kaloupek, D. G. (1996). Cognitive behavior therapy in the treatment of posttraumatic stress disorder. *The Clinical Psychologist, 41*, 7–8.

Keane, T. M., Taylor, K. L., & Penk, W. E. (1997). Differentiating post-traumatic stress disorder (PTSD) from major depression (MDD) and generalized anxiety disorder (GAD). *Journal of Anxiety Disorders, 11*, 317–328.

Kendall, P. C., Kipnis, D., & Otto-Salaj, L. (1992). When clients don't progress: Influences on and explanations for lack of therapeutic progress. *Cognitive Therapy and Research, 16*, 269–281.

Kendler, K. S., Neale, M. C., Kessler, R. C., Heath, A. C., & Eaves, L. J. (1992). The genetic epidemiology of phobias in women: The interrelationship of agoraphobia, social phobia, situational phobia, and simple phobia. *Archives of General Psychiatry, 49*, 273–281.

Kessler, R. C., McGonagle, K. A., Zhao, S., Nelson, C. B., Hughes, M., Eshleman, S., Wittchen, H.-U., & Kendler, K. S. (1994). Lifetime and 12-month prevalence of DSM-III-R psychiatric disorders in the United States: Results from the National Comorbidity Survey. *Archives of General Psychiatry, 51*, 8–19.

Kessler, R. C., Sonnega, A., Bromet, E., Hughes, M., & Nelson, C. B. (1995). Posttraumatic stress disorder in the national comorbidity survey. *Archives of General Psychiatry, 52*, 1048–1060.

Kilpatrick, D. G. (1988). Rape Aftermath Symptom Test. In M. Hersen & A. S. Bellack (Eds.), *Directory of behavioral assessment techniques.* Oxford, UK: Pergamon Press.

King, D. W., King, L. A., Foy, D. W., & Gudanowski, D. M. (1996). Prewar factors in combat-related posttraumatic stress disorder: Structural equation modeling with a national sample of female and male Vietnam veterans. *Journal of Consulting and Clinical Psychology, 64*, 520–531.

King, N. J., Ollier, K., Iacuone, R., Schuster, S., Bays, K., Gullone, E., & Ollendick, T. H. (1989). Fears of children and adolescents: A cross-sectional Australian study using the Revised-Fear Survey Schedule for Children. *Journal of Child Psychology and Psychiatry, 30*, 775–784.

Klein, D. F. (1964). Delineation of two drug-responsive anxiety syndromes. *Psychopharmacologia, 5*, 397–408.

Klein, D. F. (1993). False suffocation alarms, spontaneous panic, and related conditions: An integrative hypothesis. *Archives of General Psychiatry, 50*, 306–317.

Klein, D. F., & Klein, H. M. (1989). The definition and psychopharmacology of spontaneous panic and phobia. In P. Tyrer (Ed.), *Psychopharmacology of anxiety* (pp. 135–162). New York: Oxford University Press.

Klorman, R., Weerts, T. C., Hastings, J. E., Melamed, B. G., & Lang, P. J. (1974). Psychometric description of some specific fear questionnaires. *Behavior Therapy, 5*, 401–409.

Klosko, J. S., Barlow, D. H., Tassinari, R., & Cerny, J. A. (1990). A comparison of alprazolam and behavior therapy in the treatment of panic disorder. *Journal of Consulting and Clinical Psychology, 58*, 77–84.

Koch, W. J., & Taylor, S. (1995). Assessment and treatment of motor vehicle accident victims. *Cognitive and Behavioral Practice, 2*, 327–342.

Kokotovic, A. M., & Tracey, T. J. (1987). Premature termination in a university counseling center. *Journal of Counseling Psychology, 34*, 80–82.

Kramer, M., German, P. S., Anthony, J. C., Von Korff, M., & Skinner, E. A. (1985). Patterns of mental disorders among the elderly residents of eastern Baltimore. *Journal of the American Geriatric Society, 33*, 236–245.

Krystal, J., Woods, S. W., Hill, C. L., & Charney, D. S. (1991). Characteristics of panic attack subtypes: Assessment of spontaneous panic, situational panic, sleep panic, and limited symptom attacks. *Comprehensive Psychiatry, 32*, 474–480.

Kuch, K., Cox, B. J., Evans, R. E., & Shulman, I. (1994). Phobias, panic, and pain in 55 survivors of road vehicle accidents. *Journal of Anxiety Disorders, 8*, 181–187.

Lachance, S., Dugas, M. J., Ladouceur, R., & Freeston, M. H. (October, 1995). Mesures conportementales de l'intolérance à l'incertitude (Behavioral measures of intolerance of uncertainty). Poster presented at the annual convention of the Quebec Society for Research in Psychology in Ottawa, Ontario.

Ladouceur, R., Blais, F., Freeston, M. H., & Dugas, M. J. (1998). Problem solving and problem orientation in generalized anxiety disorder. *Journal of Anxiety Disorders, 12*, 139–152.

Ladouceur, R., Freeston, M. H., & Dugas, M. J. (November, 1993). L'intolérance à l'incertitude et les raisons pour s'inquiéter dans le trouble d'anxiété généralisée [Intolerance of uncertainty and worry appraisal in Generalized Anxiety Disorder]. Poster presented at the annual convention of the Quebec Society for Research in Psychology in Québec City, Québec.

Ladouceur, R., Freeston, M. H., Gagnon, F., & Thibodeau, N. (1993). Idiographic consideration in the behavioral treatment of obsessional thoughts. *Behaviour Research and Therapy, 24*, 301–310.

Ladouceur, R., Rhéaume, J., & Aublet, F. (1997). Excessive responsibility in obsessional concerns: A fine-grained experimental analysis. *Behaviour Research and Therapy, 35*, 423–427.

Ladouceur, R., Talbot, F., & Dugas, M. J. (1997). Behavioral expressions of intolerance of uncertainty in worry: Experimental findings. *Behavior Modification, 21*, 355–371.

Lande, S. D. (1982). Physiological and subjective measures of anxiety during flooding. *Behaviour Research and Therapy, 20*, 81–88.

Lang, P. (1968). Fear reduction and fear behavior. In J. Shlein (Ed.), *Research in psychotherapy*. Washington, DC: American Psychiatric Association.

Lang, P. J. (1979). A bio-informational theory of emotional imagery. *Psychophysiology, 16*, 495–512.

Lang, P. J. (1994). The motivational organization of emotion: Affect-reflex connections. In S. Van Goozen, N. E. Van de Poll, & J. A. Sergeant (Eds.), *Emotions: Essays on emotion theory* (pp. 61–93). Hillsdale, NJ: Lawrence Erlbaum.

Lang, P. J., Levin, D. N., Miller, G. A., & Kozak, M. J. (1983). Fear behavior, fear imagery, and the psychophysiology of emotion: The problem of affective response integration. *Journal of Abnormal Psychology, 92*, 276–306.

Lazarus, R. S. (1966). *Psychological stress and the coping process*. New York: McGraw-Hill.

Leckman, J. F., Grice, D. E., Boardman, J., Zhang, H., Vitale, A., Bondi, C., Alsobrook, J., Peterson, B. S., Cohen, D. J., Rasmussen, S. A., Goodman, W. K., McDougle, C. J., & Pauls, D. L. (1997). Symptoms of obsessive-compulsive disorder. *American Journal of Psychiatry, 154*, 911–917.

LeDoux, J. E. (1995). Emotion: Clues from the brain. *Annual Review of Psychology, 46*, 209–235.

Lewis, S. (1974). A comparison of behavior therapy techniques in the reduction of fearful avoidance behavior. *Behavior Therapy, 5*, 648–655.

Liberman, B. L. (1978). The role of mastery in psychotherapy: Maintenance of improvement and prescriptive change. In J. D. Frank, R. Hoehn-Saric, S. D. Imber, B. L. Liberman, & A. R. Stone (Eds.), *Effective ingredients of successful psychotherapy*. New York: Brunner/Mazel.

Liebowitz, M. R. (1987). Social phobia. *Modern Problems of Pharmacopsychiatry, 22*, 141–173.

Liebowitz, M. R., Gorman, J. M., Fyer, A. J., & Klein, D. F. (1985). Social phobia: Review of a neglected anxiety disorder. *Archives of General Psychiatry, 42*, 729–736.

Liebowitz, M. R., Schneier, F. R., Campeas, R., Hollander, E., Hatterer, J., Fyer, A., Gorman, J., Papp, L., Davies, S., Gully, R., & Klein, D. F. (1992). Phenelzine vs atenolol in social phobia: A placebo-controlled comparison. *Archives of General Psychiatry, 49*, 290–300.

Lief, H. I. (1968). Generic and specific aspects of phobic behavior. *International Journal of Psychiatry, 6*, 470–473.

Lilienfeld, S. O. (1996). EMDR treatment: Less than meets the eye? *Skeptical Inquirer, January/February*, 25–31.

Lindesay, J., Briggs, K., & Murphy, E. (1989). The Guy's/Age concern survey: Prevalence rates of cognitive impairment, depression, and anxiety in the urban elderly community. *British Journal of Psychiatry, 155*, 317–329.

Logan, A. C., & Goetsch, V. L. (1993). Attention to external threat cues in anxiety states. *Clinical Psychology Review, 13*, 541–559.

Lohr, J. M., Lilienfeld, S. O., Tolin, D. F., & Herbert, J. D. (1999). Eye movement desensitization and reprocessing: An analysis of specific versus nonspecific treatment factors. *Journal of Anxiety Disorders, 13*, 185–207.

Lonigan, C. J., Carey, M. P., & Finch, A. J. (1994). Anxiety and depression in children and adolescents: Negative affectivity and the utility of self-reports. *Journal of Consulting and Clinical Psychology, 62*, 1000–1008.

Lopatka, C., & Rachman, S. (1995). Perceived responsibility and compulsive checking: An experimental analysis. *Behaviour Research and Therapy, 33*, 673–684.

Luborsky, L., McLellan, A. T., Woody, G. E., O'Brien, C. P., & Auerbach, A. (1985). Therapist success and its determinants. *Archives of General Psychiatry, 42*, 602–611.

Lyons, J. S., Howard, K. I., O'Mahoney, M. T., & Lish, J. D. (1997). *The measurement and management of clinical outcomes in mental health.* New York: John Wiley.

Magee, W. J., Eaton, W. W., Wittchen, H.-U., McGonagle, K. A., & Kessler, R. C. (1996). Agoraphobia, simple phobia, and social phobia in the National Comorbidity Survey. *Archives of General Psychiatry, 53,* 159–168.

Maguth, N. C., Nezu, A. M., D'Zurilla, T. J., & Friedman, S. H. (November, 1996). Problem-solving assessment and therapy: Clinical practice applications. Workshop presented at the Annual Convention of the Association for Advancement of Behavior Therapy, New York.

Maller, R. G., & Reiss, S. (1992). Anxiety sensitivity in 1984 and panic attacks in 1987. *Journal of Anxiety Disorders, 6,* 241–247.

Malt, U. F. (Ed.). (1994). *Traumatic effects of accidents.* New York: Cambridge University Press.

March, J. S. (Ed.). (1992). *What constitutes a stressor?* Washington, DC: American Psychiatric Press.

Marks, I., Boulougouris, J., & Marset, P. (1971). Flooding versus desensitization in the treatment of phobic patients: A crossover study. *British Journal of Psychiatry, 119,* 353–375.

Marks, I. M. (1987). *Fears, phobias, and rituals.* New York: Oxford University Press.

Marks, I. M., & Mathews, A. M. (1979). Brief standard self-rating for phobic patients. *Behaviour Research and Therapy, 17,* 263–267.

Marks, I. M., Stern, R. S., Mawson, D., Cobb, J., & McDonald, R. (1980). Clomipramine and exposure for obsessive-compulsive rituals. *British Journal of Psychiatry, 136,* 1–25.

Marks, I. M., Viswanathan, R., Lipsedge, M. S., & Gardner, R. (1972). Enhanced relief of phobias by flooding during waning diazepam effect. *British Journal of Psychiatry, 121,* 493–505.

Marshall, W. L. (1985). The effects of variable exposure in flooding therapy. *Behavior Therapy, 16,* 117–135.

Marzillier, J. S., Lambert, C., & Kellet, J. (1976). A controlled evaluation of systematic desensitization and social skills training for socially inadequate psychiatric patients. *Behaviour Research and Therapy, 14,* 225–238.

Mathews, A. (1990). Why worry? The cognitive function of anxiety. *Behaviour Research and Therapy, 28,* 455–468.

Mathews, A., & MacLeod, C. (1986). Discrimination of threat cues without awareness in anxiety states. *Journal of Abnormal Psychology, 95,* 131–138.

Mattick, R. P., & Peters, L. (1988). Treatment of severe social phobia: Effects of guided exposure with and without cognitive restructuring. *Journal of Consulting and Clinical Psychology, 56,* 251–260.

Mattick, R. P., Peters, L., & Clarke, J. C. (1989). Exposure and cognitive restructuring for social phobia: A controlled study. *Behavior Therapy, 20,* 3–23.

Mattson, M. E. (1995). Patient-treatment matching. *Alcohol, Health and Research, 18,* 287–295.

Maydeu-Olivares, A., & D'Zurilla, T. J. (1996). A factor analysis of the Social Problem-Solving Inventory using polychoric correlations. *European Journal of Psychological Assessment, 11,* 98–107.

Mayou, B., Bryant, B., & Duthie, R. (1993). Psychiatric consequences of road traffic accidents. *British Medical Journal, 307,* 647–651.

McCarthy, L., & Shean, G. (1966). Agoraphobia and interpersonal relationships. *Journal of Anxiety Disorders, 10,* 477–487.

McCutcheon, B. A., & Adams, H. E. (1975). The physiological basis of implosive therapy. *Behaviour Research and Therapy, 13,* 93–100.

McEwan, K. L., & Devins, G. M. (1983). Is increased arousal in social anxiety noticed by others? *Journal of Abnormal Psychology, 92,* 417–421.

McFall, M. E., Murburg, M. M., Smith, D. E., & Jensen, C. F. (1991). An analysis of criteria used by VA clinicians to diagnose combat-related PTSD. *Journal of Traumatic Stress, 4,* 123–136.

McFall, M. E., Smith, D. E., Mackay, P. W., & Tarver, D. J. (1990). Reliability and validity of Mississippi scale for combat-related posttraumatic stress disorder. *Journal of Consulting and Clinical Psychology, 2,* 114–121.

McKay, D. (1997). A maintenance program for obsessive-compulsive disorder using exposure with response prevention: 2-year follow-up. *Behaviour Research and Therapy, 35,* 367–369.

McNally, R. J. (1995). Automaticity and the anxiety disorders. *Behaviour Research and Therapy, 33,* 747–754.

McNally, R. J. (1994). *Panic disorder: A critical analysis.* New York: Guilford.

McNally, R. J., Lasko, N. B., Macklin, M. J., & Pitman, R. K. (1995). Autobiographical memory disturbance in combat-related posttraumatic stress disorder. *Behaviour Research and Therapy, 33,* 619–630.

McNally, R. J., Litz, B. T., Prassas, A., Shin, L. M., & Weathers, F. W. (1994). Emotional priming of autobiographical memory in post-traumatic stress disorder. *Cognition and Emotion, 8,* 351–367.

McNally, R. J., & Steketee, G. S. (1985). The etiology and maintenance of severe animal phobias. *Behaviour Research and Therapy, 23,* 431–435.

Meichenbaum, D. (1994). *A clinical handbook/practical therapist manual for assessing and treating adults with post-traumatic stress disorder (PTSD).* Waterloo, Ontario: Institute Press.

Meichenbaum, D., & Novaco, R. (1977). Stress inoculation: A preventive approach. In C. Speilberger & I. Sarason (Eds.), *Stress and Anxiety* (Vol. 5). New York: Halstead Press.

Melchior, L. A., & Cheek, J. M. (1990). Shyness and anxious self-preoccupation during a social interaction. *Journal of Social Behavior and Personality, 5,* 117–130.

Menzies, R. G. (1996). Individual response patterns and treatment matching in the phobic disorders: A review. *British Journal of Clinical Psychology, 35,* 1–10.

Menzies, R. G., & Clarke, J. C. (1993). A comparison of in vivo and vicarious exposure in the treatment of childhood water phobia. *Behaviour Research and Therapy, 31,* 9–15.

Merckelbach, H., Muris, P., Horselenberg, R., & Rassin, E. (1998). Traumatic intrusions as 'worst case scenarios'. *Behaviour Research and Therapy, 36,* 1075–1079.

Meyer, T. J., Miller, M. L., Metzger, R. L., & Borkovec, T. D. (1990). Development and validation of the Penn State Worry Questionnaire. *Behaviour Research and Therapy, 28,* 487–495.

Meyer, V. (1966). Modification of expectations in cases with obsessional rituals. *Behaviour Research and Therapy, 4,* 273–280.

Michelson, L., June, K., Vives, A., Testa, S., & Marchione, N. (1998). The role of trauma and dissociation in cognitive-behavioral psychotherapy outcome and maintenance for panic disorder with agoraphobia. *Behaviour Research and Therapy, 36,* 1011–1050.

Michelson, L. K., & Marchione, K. (1991). Behavioral, cognitive, and pharmacological treatments of panic disorder with agoraphobia: Critique and synthesis. *Journal of Consulting and Clinical Psychology, 54,* 100–114.

Michelson, L. K., Marchione, K. E., Greenwald, M., Testa, S., & Marchione, N. J. (1996). A comparative outcome and follow-up investigation of panic disorder with agoraphobia: The relative and combined efficacy of cognitive therapy, relaxation training and therapist-assisted exposure. *Journal of Anxiety Disorders, 10*, 297–330.

Michelson, L., & Mavissakalian, M. (1983). Temporal stability of self-report measures in agoraphobia research. *Behaviour Research and Therapy, 21*, 695–698.

Milgram, S. (1974). *Obedience to authority: An experimental view.* New York: Harper.

Miller, W. R., Benefield, G., & Tonigan, J. S. (1993). Enhancing motivation for change in problem drinking: A controlled comparison of two therapist styles. *Journal of Consulting and Clinical Psychology, 61*, 455–461.

Mineka, S., Davidson, M., Cook, M., & Keir, R. (1984). Observational conditioning of snake fear in rhesus monkeys. *Journal of Abnormal Psychology, 93*, 355–372.

Mohl, P. C., Martinez, D., Ticknor, C., Huang, M., & Cordell, M. D. (1991). Early dropouts from psychotherapy. *Journal of Nervous and Mental Disease, 179*, 478–481.

Monane, M. (1992). Insomnia in the elderly. Roundtable Conference: Low dose benzodiazepine therapy in the treatment of insomnia (1991, Chicago, Illinois). *Journal of Clinical Psychiatry, 53*, 23–28.

Monti, P. M., Boice, R., Fingeret, A. L., Zwick, W. R., Kolko, D., Munroe, S. M., & Grunberger, A. (1984). Midi-level measurement of social anxiety in psychiatric and non-psychiatric samples. *Behaviour Research and Therapy, 22*, 651–660.

Moore, R., Brodsgaard, I., & Birn, H. (1991). Manifestations, acquisition, and diagnostic categories of dental fear in a self-referred population. *Behaviour Research and Therapy, 29*, 51–60.

Moras, K. (1993). The use of treatment manuals to train psychotherapists: Observations and recommendations. *Psychotherapy, 30*, 581–586.

Morey, L. C., & Ochoa, E. S. (1989). An investigation of adherence to diagnostic criteria: Clinical diagnosis of the DSM-III personality disorders. *Journal of Personality Disorders, 3*, 180–192.

Mowrer, O. H. (1939). A stimulus-response analysis of anxiety and its role as a reinforcing agent. *Psychological Review, 46*, 553–565.

Mowrer, O. (1960). *Learning theory and behaviour.* New York: Wiley.

Mueser, K. T., Goodman, L. B., Trumbetta, S. L., Rosenberg, S. D., Osher, F. C., Vidaver, R., Auciello, P., & Foy, D. W. (1998). Trauma and posttraumatic stress disorder in severe mental illness. *Journal of Consulting and Clinical Psychology, 66*, 493–499.

Munby, J., & Johnston, D. W. (1980). Agoraphobia: The long-term follow-up of behavioral treatment. *British Journal of Psychiatry, 137*, 418–427.

Muran, E. M., & Motta, R. W. (1993). Cognitive distortions and irrational beliefs in post-traumatic stress, anxiety, and depressive disorders. *Journal of Clinical Psychology, 49*, 166–176.

Naftolowitz, D. F., Vaughn, B. V., Ranc, J., & Tancer, M. E. (1994). Response to alcohol in social phobia. *Anxiety, 1*, 96–99.

Najavits, L. M., & Strupp, H. H. (1994). Differences in the effectiveness of psychodynamic therapists: A process-outcome study. *Psychotherapy, 31*, 114–123.

Nelson-Gray, R. O. (1996). Treatment outcome measures: Nomothetic or idiographic? *Clinical Psychology Science and Practice, 3*, 164–167.

Newman, M. G., & Borkovec, T. D. (1995). Cognitive-behavioral treatment of generalized anxiety disorder. *The Clinical Psychologist, 48*(4), 5–7.

Newman, M. G., Consoli, A., & Taylor, C. B. (1997). Computers in assessment and cognitive behavior therapy of clinical disorders: Anxiety as a case in point. *Behavior Therapy, 28,* 211–235.

Newman, M. G., Hofmann, S. G., Trabert, W., Roth, W. T., & Taylor, C. B. (1994). Does behavioral treatment of social phobia lead to cognitive changes? *Behavior Therapy, 25,* 503–517.

Neziroglu, F., & Hsia, C. (1998). Reconceptualization of behavior therapy for obsessive-compulsive disorder from a learning and neurochemical perspective. *CNS Spectrums, 3*(7), 47–53.

Neziroglu, F., Steele, J., Yaryura-Tobias, J.A., Hitri, A., & Diamond, B. (1990). Effect of behavior therapy on serotonin level in obsessive-compulsive disorder. In C. N. Stefanis (Ed.), *Psychiatry: A world perspective.* New York: Elsevier Science.

Nezu, C. M., & Nezu, A. M. (1995). Critical decision making in everyday practice: The science in the art. *Cognitive and Behavioral Practice, 2,* 1704–1718.

Nichols, K. A. (1974). Severe social anxiety. *British Journal of Medical Psychology, 47,* 301–306.

Nickell, P. V., & Uhde, T. W. (1995). Neurobiology of social phobia. In R. G. Heimberg, M. R. Liebowitz, D. A. Hope, & F. R. Schneier (Eds.), *Social phobia: Diagnosis, assessment, and treatment* (pp. 113–133). New York: Guilford.

Ning, L., & Liddell, A. (1991). The effect of concordance in the treatment of clients with dental anxiety. *Behaviour Research and Therapy, 29,* 315–322.

Norris, F. H. (1992). Epidemiology of trauma: Frequency and impact of different potentially traumatic events on different demographic groups. *Journal of Consulting and Counselling Psychology, 60,* 409–418.

Norton, G. R., Dorward, J., & Cox, B. J. (1986). Factors associated with panic attacks in non-clinical subjects. *Behaviour Research and Therapy, 17,* 239–252.

Norton, G. R., Harrison, B., & Hauch, J. (1986). Characteristics of people with infrequent panic attacks. *Journal of Abnormal Psychology, 94,* 216–221.

Norton, G. R., McLeod, L., Guertin, J., Hewitt, P. L., Walker, J. R., & Stein, M. B. (1996). Panic disorder or social phobia: Which is worse? *Behaviour Research and Therapy, 34,* 273–276.

Noyes, R., Clancy, J., Woodman, C., Holt, C. S., Suelzer, M., Christianson, J., & Anderson, D. J. (1993). Environmental factors related to the outcome of panic disorder: A seven-year follow-up study. *Journal of Nervous and Mental Disease, 181,* 529–537.

Nunes, J. S., & Marks, I. M. (1975). Feedback of true heart rate during exposure in vivo. *Archives of General Psychiatry, 32,* 933–936.

Nunes, J. S., & Marks, I. M. (1976). Feedback of true heart rate during exposure in vivo: Partial replication with methodological improvement. *Archives of General Psychiatry, 33,* 1346–1350.

Obsessive Compulsive Cognitions Working Group. (1997). Cognitive assessment of obsessive-compulsive disorder. *Behaviour Research and Therapy, 35,* 667–681.

Ogles, B. M., Lambert, M. J., & Masters, K. S. (1996). *Assessing outcome in clinical practice.* Boston: Allyn and Bacon.

Olfson, M., Pincus, H. A., & Sabshin, M. (1994). Pharmacotherapy in outpatient psychiatric practice. *American Journal of Psychiatry, 151,* 580–585.

Orlinsky, D. E., Grawe, K., & Parks, B. K. (1994). Process and outcome in psychotherapy—Noch einmal. In A. E. Bergin & S. L. Garfield (Eds.), *Handbook of psychotherapy and behavior change* (4th ed., pp. 270–376). New York: John Wiley.

Öst, L.-G. (1978). Fading vs. systematic desensitization in the treatment of snake and spider phobia. *Behaviour Research and Therapy, 16,* 379–389.

Öst, L.-G. (1987a). Age of onset in different phobias. *Journal of Abnormal Psychology, 96,* 223–229.

Öst, L.-G. (1987b). Applied relaxation: Description of a coping technique and review of controlled studies. *Behaviour Research and Therapy, 25,* 397–409.

Öst, L.-G. (1996). One-session group treatment of spider phobia. *Behaviour Research and Therapy, 34,* 707–715.

Öst, L.-G., Fellenius, J., & Sterner, U. (1991). Applied tension, exposure in vivo, and tension-only in the treatment of blood phobia. *Behaviour Research and Therapy, 29,* 561–574.

Öst, L.-G., & Hellstrom, K. (1992). One versus five sessions of exposure in the treatment of injection phobia. *Behavior Therapy, 23,* 263–282.

Öst, L.-G., & Hugdahl, K. (1981). Acquisition of phobias and anxiety response patterns in clinical patients. *Behaviour Research and Therapy, 19,* 439–447.

Öst, L.-G., Jerremalm, A., & Johansson, J. (1981). Individual response patterns and the effects of different behavioral methods in the treatment of social phobia. *Behaviour Research and Therapy, 19,* 1–16.

Öst, L.-G., Johansson, J., & Jerremalm, A. (1982). Individual response patterns and the effects of different behavioral methods in the treatment of claustrophobia. *Behaviour Research and Therapy, 20,* 445–460.

Öst, L.-G., Salkovskis, P. M., & Hellstrom, K. (1991). One-session therapist-directed exposure vs. self-exposure in the treatment of spider phobia. *Behavior Therapy, 22,* 407–422.

Öst, L.-G., & Sterner, U. (1987). Applied tension: A specific behavioral method for treatment of blood phobia. *Behaviour Research and Therapy, 25,* 25–29.

Öst, L.-G., Sterner, U., & Lindahl, I.-L. (1984). Physiological responses in blood phobics. *Behaviour Research and Therapy, 22,* 109–117.

Otto, M. W., Pollack, M. H., & Sabatino, S. A. (1996). Maintenance of remission following cognitive therapy for panic disorder: Possible deleterious effects of concurrent medication treatment. *Behavior Therapy, 27,* 473–482.

Pallack, M. S. (1995). Managed care and outcomes-based standards in the health care revolution. In S. C. Hayes, V. M. Follette, R. M. Dawes, & K. E. Grady (Eds.), *Scientific Standards of Psychological Practice: Issues and Recommendations* (pp. 73–77). Reno, NV: Context Press.

Patterson, G. R., & Forgatch, M. S. (1985). Therapist behavior as a determinant for client noncompliance: A paradox for the behavior modifier. *Journal of Consulting and Clinical Psychology, 53,* 846–851.

Persons, J. B. (1989). *Cognitive therapy in practice: A case formulation approach.* New York: Norton.

Peterson, R. A., & Reiss, S. (1987). *Test manual for the Anxiety Sensitivity Index.* Orland Park, IL: International Diagnostic Systems.

Piccinelli, M., Pini, S., Bellantuono, C., & Wilkinson, G. (1995). Efficacy of drug treatment in obsessive-compulsive disorder: A meta-analytic review. *British Journal of Psychiatry, 166,* 424–443.

Pigott, T. A., Myers, K. R., & Williams, D. A. (1996). Obsessive-compulsive disorder: A neuropsychiatric perspective. In R. M. Rapee (Ed.), *Current Controversies in the Anxiety Disorders*. New York: Guilford.

Pigott, T. A., & Seay, S. (1998). Biological treatments for obsessive-compulsive disorder: Literature review. In R. P. Swinson, M. M. Antony, S. Rachman, & M. A. Richter (Eds.), *Obsessive-compulsive disorder: Theory, research, and treatment* (pp. 298–326). New York: Guilford.

Pilkonis, P. (1977). The behavioral consequences of shyness. *Journal of Personality, 45*, 596–611.

Pilkonis, P. A., & Zimbardo, P. G. (1979). The personal and social dynamics of shyness. In C. E. Izard (Ed.), *Emotions in personality and psychopathology*. New York: Plenum.

Pincus, H. A. (1994). Treatment guidelines: Risks are outweighed by the benefits. *Behavioral Healthcare Tomorrow, 4*, 35–39.

Pollack, M. H., Otto, M. W., Rosenbaum, J. F., Sachs, G. S., O'Neil, C., Asher, R., & Meltzer-Brody, S. (1990). Longitudinal course of panic disorder: Findings from the Massachusetts General Hospital naturalistic study. *Journal of Clinical Psychiatry, 51*, 12–16.

Pollack, M. H., Otto, M. W., Sabatino, S., Majcher, D., Worthington, J. J., McArdle, E. T., & Rosenbaum, J. F. (1996). Relationship of childhood anxiety to adult panic disorder: Correlates and influence of course. *American Journal of Psychiatry, 153*, 376–381.

Pollard, C. A., & Henderson, J. G. (1988). Four types of social phobia in a community sample. *Journal of Nervous and Mental Disease, 176*, 440–445.

Power, K. G., Simpson, R. J., Swanson, V., & Wallace, L. A. (1990a). A controlled comparison of cognitive-behaviour therapy, diazepam, and placebo, alone and in combination, for the treatment of generalized anxiety disorder. *Journal of Anxiety Disorders, 4*, 267–292.

Power, K. G., Simpson, R. J., Swanson, V., & Wallace, L. A. (1990b). Controlled comparison of pharmacological and psychological treatment of generalized anxiety disorder in primary care. *British Journal of General Practice, 40*, 289–294.

Quality Assurance Project (1982a). A methodology for preparing 'ideal' treatment outlines in psychiatry. *Australian and New Zealand Journal of Psychiatry, 16*, 153–158.

Quality Assurance Project (1982b). A treatment outline for agoraphobia. *Australian and New Zealand Journal of Psychiatry, 16*, 25–33.

Quality Assurance Project (1985). Treatment outlines for the management of obsessive-compulsive disorders. *Australian and New Zealand Journal of Psychiatry, 19*, 240–253.

Rachman, S. (1975). The passing of the two-stage theory of fear and avoidance: Fresh possibilities. *Behaviour Research and Therapy, 14*, 125–131.

Rachman, S. (1976). The modification of obsessions: A new formulation. *Behaviour Research and Therapy, 14*, 437–443.

Rachman, S. (1977). The conditioning theory of fear acquisition: A critical examination. *Behaviour Research and Therapy, 15*, 375–387.

Rachman, S. (1980). Emotional processing. *Behaviour Research and Therapy, 18*, 51–60.

Rachman, S. (1984). Anxiety disorders: Some emerging theories. *Journal of Behavioral Assessment, 6*, 281–299.

Rachman, S. J. (1990). *Fear and Courage*. (2nd ed.). New York: W. H. Freeman.

Rachman, S. (1994). The overprediction of fear: A review. *Behaviour Research and Therapy, 32*, 683–690.

Rachman, S. (1997). A cognitive theory of obsessions. *Behaviour Research and Therapy, 35*, 793–802.

Rachman, S., & Cuk, M. (1992). Fearful distortions. *Behaviour Research and Therapy, 30*, 583–589.

Rachman, S., & DeSilva, P. (1978). Abnormal and normal obsessions. *Behaviour Research and Therapy, 16*, 233–248.

Rachman, S., & Hodgson, R. (1974). I. Synchrony and desynchrony in fear and avoidance. *Behaviour Research and Therapy, 12*, 311–318.

Rachman, S., & Hodgson, R. (1980). *Obsessions and compulsions*. Englewood Cliffs, NJ: Prentice-Hall.

Rachman, S., & Levitt, K. (1988). Panic, fear reduction, and habituation. *Behaviour Research and Therapy, 26*, 199–206.

Rapee, R. M. (1985). Distinctions between panic disorder and generalized anxiety disorder: Clinical presentations. *Australian and New Zealand Journal of Psychiatry, 19*, 227–232.

Rapee, R. M. (1989). Boundary issues: GAD and psychophysiological disorders. Paper presented for the generalized anxiety disorders subcommittee for DSM-IV.

Rapee, R. M. (1991a). Generalized anxiety disorder: A review of clinical features and theoretical concepts. *Clinical Psychology Review, 11*, 419–440.

Rapee, R. M. (1991b). Psychological factors involved in generalized anxiety. In R. M. Rapee & D. H. Barlow (Eds.), *Chronic anxiety: Generalized anxiety disorder and mixed anxiety-depression*. New York: Guilford.

Rapee, R. M., & Hayman, K. (1996). The effects of video feedback on the self-evaluation of performance in socially anxious subjects. *Behaviour Research and Therapy, 34*, 315–322.

Rapee, R. M., & Lim, L. (1992). Discrepancy between self and observer ratings of performance in social phobics. *Journal of Abnormal Psychology, 101*, 727–731.

Rapee, R. M., Sanderson, W. C., McCauley, P. A., & DiNardo, P. A. (1992). Differences in reported symptom profile between panic disorder and other DSM-III-R anxiety disorders. *Behaviour Research and Therapy, 30*, 45–52.

Rapoport, J. L. (1989). *The boy who couldn't stop washing: The experience and treatment of obsessive-compulsive disorder*. New York: Dutton.

Rapoport, M. H., & Cantor, J. J. (1997). Panic disorder in a managed care environment. *Journal of Clinical Psychiatry, 58*(Suppl. 2), 51–55.

Rasmussen, S. A., & Tsuang, M. T. (1984). Epidemiology of obsessive compulsive disorder: A review. *Journal of Clinical Psychiatry, 45*, 450–457.

Redmond, D. E., Jr. (1977). Alternations in the function of the nucleus locus corruleus: A possible model for studies in anxiety. In I. Hanin & E. Usdin (Eds.), *Animal models in psychiatry and neurology* (pp. 293–304). Oxford, UK: Pergamon Press.

Reich, J., Noyes, R., & Yates, W. (1988). Anxiety symptoms distinguishing social phobia from panic and generalized anxiety disorders. *Journal of Nervous and Mental Disease, 176*, 510–513.

Reiss, S., & McNally, R. J. (1985). The expectancy model of fear. In S. Reiss & R. R. Bootzin (Eds.), *Theoretical issues in behavior therapy* (pp. 107–121). New York: Academic Press.

Reiss, S., Peterson, R. A., Gursky, D. M., & McNally, R. J. (1986). Anxiety sensitivity, anxiety frequency, and the prediction of fearfulness. *Behaviour Research and Therapy, 24*, 1–8.

Rescorla, R. A. (1988). Pavlovian conditioning: It's not what you think it is. *American Psychologist, 43*, 151–160.

Resick, P. A., & Schnicke, M. K. (1996). *Cognitive processing therapy for rape victims: A treatment manual.* Newbury Park, CA: Sage Publications.

Resnick, H. S., Best, C. L., Kilpatrick, D. G., Freedy, J. R., & Falsetti, S. A. (1993). *Trauma assessment for adults-self-report.* Charleston, SC: The National Crime Victims Research and Treatment Centre, Medical University of South Carolina.

Resnick, H. S., Kilpatrick, D. G., Dansky, B. S., Saunders, B. E., & Best, C. L. (1993). Prevalence of civilian trauma and posttraumatic stress disorder in a representative national sample of women. *Journal of Consulting and Clinical Psychology, 61,* 984–991.

Resnick, H. S., Kilpatrick, D. G., & Lipovsky, J. A. (1991). Assessment of rape-related posttraumatic stress disorder: Stressor and symptom dimensions. *Psychological Assessment, 4,* 561–572.

Riggs, D. S., & Foa, E. B. (Eds.). (1993). *Obsessive compulsive disorder.* New York: Guilford.

Rimm, D. C., & Mahoney, M. J. (1969). The application of reinforcement and participant modeling procedures in the treatment of snake-phobic behavior. *Behaviour Research and Therapy, 7,* 369–376.

Riskind, J. H., Moore, R., Harman, B., Hohmann, A. A., Beck, A. T., & Stewart, B. (1991). The relation of generalized anxiety disorder to depression in general and dysthymic disorder in particular. In R. M. Rapee & D. H. Barlow (Eds.), *Chronic anxiety: Generalized anxiety disorder and mixed anxiety-depression* (pp. 153–171). New York: Guilford.

Robins, L., Helzer, J., Cottler, L., & Goldring, E. (1988). NIMH Diagnostic Interview Schedule Version III Revised (DIS-III-R). St. Louis, MO: Washington University Press.

Robins, L. N., Helzer, J. E., Croughan, J., & Ratcliff, K. S. (1981). The National Institute of Mental Health Diagnostic Interview Schedule: Its history, characteristics and validity. *Archives of General Psychiatry, 38,* 381–389.

Robins, L. N., Helzer, J. E., Weissman, M. M., Orvaschel, H., Gruenberge, E., Burke, J. D., & Regier, D. A. (1984). Lifetime prevalence of specific psychiatric disorders in three sites. *Archives of General Psychiatry, 41,* 949–958.

Rodrieguez, N., Ryan, S. W., Vande Kemp, H., & Foy, D. W. (1997). Posttraumatic stress disorder in adult female survivors of childhood sexual abuse: A comparison study. *Journal of Consulting and Clinical Psychology, 65,* 53–54.

Roemer, L., Borkovec, M., Posa, S., & Lyonfields, J. (1991). *Generalized anxiety disorder in an analogue population: The role of past trauma.* Paper presented at the annual convention of the Association for the Advancement of Behavior Therapy, New York.

Rosenbaum, J. F., Biederman, J., Gersten, M., Hirshfeld, D. R., Meminger, S. R., Herman, J. B., Kagan, J., Reznick, J. S., & Snidman, N. (1988). Behavioral inhibition in children of parents with panic disorder and agoraphobia: A controlled study. *Archives of General Psychiatry, 45,* 463–470.

Rosenbaum, J. F., Biederman, J., Hirshfeld, D. R., Bolduc, E. A., & Chaloff, J. (1991). Behavioral inhibition in childhood: A possible precursor to panic disorder or social phobia. *Journal of Clinical Psychiatry, 52*(Suppl.), 5–9.

Rosenbaum, J. F., Biederman, J., Hirshfeld, D. R., Bolduc, E. A., Faraone, S. V., Kagan, J., Snidman, N., & Reznick, J. S. (1991). Further evidence of an association between behavioral inhibition and anxiety disorders: Results from a family study of children from a non-clinical sample. *Journal of Psychiatric Research, 25,* 49–65.

Rosenberg, N. K., & Rosenberg, R. (1994). Three years follow-up of panic disorder patients: A naturalistic study. *Scandinavian Journal of Psychology, 35*, 254–262.

Salkovskis, P. M. (1985). Obsessional-compulsive problems: A cognitive-behavioral analysis. *Behaviour Research and Therapy, 25*, 571–583.

Salkovskis, P. M. (1988). Phenomenology, assessment and the cognitive model of panic. In S. Rachman & J. Maser (Eds.), *Panic: Psychological Perspectives*. Hillsdale, NJ: Lawrence Erlbaum.

Salkovskis, P. M. (1989). Obessions and intrusive thoughts: Clinical and nonclinical aspects. In P. Emmelkamp, F. Everaerd, F. Kraaymatt, & M. van Son (Eds.), *Annual series of European Research in Behaviour Therapy* (Vol. 4). Amsterdam: Swets.

Salkovskis, P. M. (1996). Cognitive-behavioral approaches to the understanding of obsessional problems. In R. M. Rapee (Ed.), *Current Controversies in the Anxiety Disorders*. New York: Guilford.

Salkovskis, P. M., & Clark, D. M. (1991). Cognitive therapy for panic disorder. *Journal of Cognitive Psychotherapy, 5*, 215–226.

Salovey, P. (1992). Mood-induced self-focused attention. *Journal of Personality and Social Psychology, 62*, 699–707.

Salvador-Carulla, L., Segui, J., Fernández-Cano, P., & Canet, J. (1995). Cost and offset effect in panic disorders. *British Journal of Psychiatry, 166*(Suppl. 27), 23–28.

Salzman, L. (1968). Obsessions and phobias. *International Journal of Psychiatry, 6*, 451–476.

Sanderson, W. C. (1997). The importance of empirically supported psychological interventions in the new healthcare environment. In L. Vandecreek, S. Knapp, & T. Jackson (Eds.), *Innovations in Clinical Practice: A Source Book* (Vol. 15, pp. 387–399). Sarasota, FL: Professional Resource Exchange.

Sanderson, W. C., & Barlow, D. H. (1990). A description of patients diagnosed with DSM-III-R generalized anxiety disorder. *The Journal of Nervous and Mental Disease, 178*, 588–591.

Sanderson, W. C., Di Nardo, P. A., Rapee, R. M., & Barlow, D. H. (1990). Syndrome comorbidity in patients diagnosed with DSM-III-R anxiety disorder. *Journal of Abnormal Psychology, 99*, 309–312.

Sanderson, W. C., Rapee, R. M., & Barlow, D. H. (1989). The influence of an illusion of control on panic attacks induced via inhalation of 5.5% carbon dioxide-enriched air. *Archives of General Psychiatry, 46*, 157–162.

Sanderson, W. C., & Wetzler, S. (1991). Chronic anxiety and generalized anxiety disorder: Issues in cormorbidity. In R. M. Rapee & D. H. Barlow (Eds.), *Chronic anxiety: Generalized anxiety disorder and mixed anxiety-depression*. New York: Guilford.

Sanderson, W. C., & Wetzler, S. (1993). Observations on the cognitive-behavioral treatment of panic disorder: Impact of benzodiazepines. *Psychotherapy, 30*, 125–132.

Sanderson, W. C., & Woody, S. R. (1995). Manuals for empirically validated treatments. *The Clinical Psychologist, 48*, 7–11.

Sarason, I. (1994). *Stress and social support*. Paper presented at the NATO Conference on Stress, Coping and Disaster, Bonas, France.

Sargent, M., & Cohen, L. (1983). Influence of psychotherapy research on clinical practice: An experimental survey. *Journal of Consulting and Clinical Psychology, 51*, 718–720.

Sartory, G. (1983). Benzodiazepines and behavioural treatment of phobic anxiety. *Behavioural Psychotherapy, 11*, 204–217.

Schlenker, B., & Leary, M. (1982). Social anxiety and self-presentation: A conceptualization and model. *Psychological Bulletin, 92,* 641–669.

Schmidt, N. B., Lerew, D. R., & Trakowski, J. H. (1997). Bodily vigilance in panic disorder: Evaluating attention to bodily perturbations. *Journal of Consulting and Clinical Psychology, 65,* 214–220.

Scholing, A., & Emmelkamp, P. M. G. (1996a). Treatment of fear of blushing, sweating, or trembling: Results at long-term follow-up. *Behavior Modification, 20,* 338–356.

Scholing, A., & Emmelkamp, P. M. G. (1996b). Treatment of generalized social phobia: Results at long-term follow-up. *Behaviour Research and Therapy, 34,* 447–452.

Schulte, D., Kunzel, R., Pepping, G., & Schulte-Bahrenberg, T. (1992). Tailor-made versus standardized therapy of phobic patients. *Advances in Behaviour Research and Therapy, 14,* 67–92.

Schwartz, J. M., Stoessel, P. W., Baxter, L. R., Martin, K. M., & Phelps, M. E. (1996). Systematic changes in cerebral glucose metabolic rate after successful behavior modification treatment of obsessive-compulsive disorder. *Archives of General Psychiatry, 53,* 109–113.

Sederer, L. I., & Dickey, B. (Eds.). (1996). *Outcomes assessment in clinical practice.* Baltimore, MD: Williams & Wilkins.

Shaw, B. F., & Dobson, K. S. (1988). Competency judgments in the training and evaluation of psychotherapists. *Journal of Consulting and Clinical Psychology, 56,* 666–672.

Shear, M. K., Cooper, A. M., Klerman, G. L., Busch, F. N., & Shapiro, T. (1993). A psychodynamic model of panic disorder. *American Journal of Psychiatry, 150,* 859–866.

Sherman, R. A. (1972). Real life exposure as a primary therapeutic factor in the desensitization treatment of fear. *Journal of Abnormal Psychology, 79,* 19–28.

Smith, G. R., & Hamilton, G. E. (1994). Treatment guidelines: Provider involvement is critical. *Behavioral Healthcare Tomorrow, 4,* 40–45.

Smith, R. E., & Sarason, G. (1975). Social anxiety and the evaluation of negative personal feedback. *Journal of Consulting and Clinical Psychology, 43,* 429.

Snaith, R. P. (1968). A clinical investigation of phobias. *British Journal of Psychiatry, 114,* 673–697.

Solomon, S. D. (Ed.). (1986). *Mobilizing social support networks in times of disaster.* (Vol. 2). New York: Brunner/Mazel.

Speltz, M. L., & Bernstein, D. A. (1976). Sex differences in fearfulness: Verbal report, overt avoidance, and demand characteristics. *Journal of Behaviour Therapy and Experimental Psychiatry, 7,* 117–122.

Spiegel, D. (1988). Dissociation and hypnosis in posttraumatic stress disorder. *Journal of Traumatic Stress, 1,* 17–33.

Spielberger, C. D. (1971). Trait-state anxiety and motor behavior. *Journal of Motor Behavior, 3,* 265–279.

Spielberger, C. D. (1972a). Anxiety as an emotional state. In C. D. Spielberger (Ed.), *Anxiety: Current trends in theory and research* (Vol. 1). New York: Academic Press.

Spielberger, C. D. (1972b). Current trends in theory and research on anxiety. In C. D. Spielberger (Ed.), *Anxiety: Current trends in theory and research* (Vol. 1). New York: Academic Press.

Stampfl, T. G., & Levis, D. J. (1967). Essentials of implosive therapy: A learning-theory-based psychodynamic behavioral therapy. *Journal of Abnormal Psychology, 72,* 496–503.

Stanley, M. A., Beck, J. G., & DeWitt Glassco, J. (1996). Treatment of generalized anxiety in older adults: A preliminary comparison of cognitive-behavioral and supportive approaches. *Behavior Therapy, 27,* 565–581.

Stein, M. B., Forde, D. R., Anderson, G., & Walker, J. R. (1997). Obsessive-compulsive disorder in the community: An epidemiologic survey with clinical reappraisal. *American Journal of Psychiatry, 154,* 1120–1126.

Stein, M. B., Liebowitz, M. R., Lydiard, R. B., Pitts, C. D., Bushnell, W., & Gergel, I. (1998). Paroxetine treatment of generalized social phobia (social anxiety disorder): A randomized, controlled study. *Journal of the American Medical Association, 280,* 708–713.

Stein, M. B., Walker, J. R., Hazen, A. L., & Forde, D. R. (1997). Full and partial posttraumatic stress disorder: Findings from a community survey. *American Journal of Psychiatry, 154,* 1114–1119.

Steketee, G. S. (1993). *Treatment of Obsessive Compulsive Disorder.* New York: Guilford.

Steketee, G., Frost, R., & Bogart, K. (1996). The Yale-Brown obsessive compulsive scale: Interview versus self-report. *Behaviour Research and Therapy, 34,* 675–684.

Steketee, G. S., & White, K. (1990). *When Once is Not Enough.* Oakland, CA: New Harbinger Press.

Stemberger, R. T., Turner, S. M., Deborah, D. C., & Calhoun, K. S. (1995). Social phobia: An analysis of possible developmental factors. *Journal of Abnormal Psychology, 104,* 526–531.

Stöber, J., & Bittencourt, J. (1998). Weekly assessment of worry: An adaptation of the Penn State Worry Questionnaire for monitoring changes during treatment. *Behaviour Research and Therapy, 36,* 645–656.

Stopa, L., & Clark, D. M. (1993). Cognitive processes in social phobia. *Behaviour Research and Therapy, 31,* 255–267.

Strauss, C. C., & Last, C. G. (1993). Social and simple phobias in children. *Journal of Anxiety Disorders, 7,* 141–152.

Stravynski, A., Marks, I., & Yule, W. (1982). Social skills problems in neurotic outpatients: Social skills training with and without cognitive modification. *Archives of General Psychiatry, 39,* 1378–1385.

Stuart, R. B. (1980). *Helping Couples Change.* New York: Guilford.

Switzer, E., & Rickels, K. (1991). Pharmacotherapy of generalized anxiety disorder. In R. M. Rapee & D. H. Barlow (Eds.), *Chronic anxiety: Generalized anxiety disorder and mixed anxiety-depression.* New York: Guilford.

Szymanski, J., & O'Donohue, W. (1995). Fear of Spiders Questionnaire. *Journal of Behaviour Therapy and Experimental Psychiatry, 26,* 31–34.

Task Force on Promotion and Dissemination of Psychological Procedures (1993). Training in and dissemination of empirically-validated psychological treatments. *The Clinical Psychologist, 48,* 3–23.

Task Force on Psychological Intervention Guidelines (1995). *Template for developing guidelines: Interventions for mental disorders and psychosocial aspects of physical disorders*: American Psychological Association, Washington, DC.

Tata, P. R., Leibowitz, J. A., Prunty, M. J., Cameron, M., & Pickering, A. D. (1996). Attentional bias in obsessional compulsive disorder. *Behaviour Research and Therapy, 34,* 53–60.

Taylor, S. (1998). Assessment of obsessive-compulsive disorder. In R. S. Swinson, M. M. Antony, S. Rachman, & M. A. Richter (Eds.), *Obsessive-Compulsive Disorder: Theory, Research and Treatment* (pp. 229–257). New York: Guilford.

Taylor, S., Kuch, K., Koch, W. J., Crockett, D. J., & Passey, G. (1998). The structure of posttraumatic stress symptoms. *Journal of Abnormal Psychology, 107*, 154–160.

Taylor, S., & Rachman, S. J. (1994). Stimulus estimation and the overprediction of fear. *British Journal of Clinical Psychology, 33*, 173–181.

Telch, M. J., Lucas, J. A., Schmidt, N. B., Hanna, H. H., Jaimez, T. L., & Lucas, R. A. (1993). Group cognitive-behavioral treatment of panic disorder. *Behaviour Research and Therapy, 31*, 279–287.

Telch, M. J., Valentiner, D., & Bolte, M. (1994). Proximity to safety and its effects on fear prediction bias. *Behaviour Research and Therapy, 32*, 747–751.

Thorpe, S. J., & Salkovskis, P. M. (1995). Phobic beliefs: Do cognitive factors play a role in specific phobias? *Behaviour Research and Therapy, 33*, 805–816.

Torgersen, S. (1983). Genetic factors in anxiety disorders. *Archives of General Psychiatry, 40*, 1085–1089.

Tran, G. Q., & Chambless, D. L. (1995). Psychopathology of social phobia: Effects of subtype and of avoidant personality disorder. *Journal of Anxiety Disorders, 9*, 489–501.

Trower, P. (1980). Situational analysis of the components and processes of behavior of socially skilled and unskilled patients. *Journal of Consulting and Clinical Psychology, 48*, 327–339.

Trower, P., Yardley, K., Bryant, B., & Shaw, P. (1978). The treatment of social failure: A comparison of anxiety-reduction and skills-acquisition procedures on two social problems. *Behavior Modification, 2*, 41–60.

Turner, S. M., & Beidel, D. C. (1988). *Treating obsessive-compulsive disorder.* New York: Pergamon Press.

Turner, S. M., Beidel, D. C., Dancu, C. V., & Keys, D. J. (1986). Psychopathology of social phobia and comparison to avoidant personality disorder. *Journal of Abnormal Psychology, 95*, 389–394.

Turner, S. M., Beidel, D. C., Dancu, C. V., & Stanley, M. A. (1989). An empirically derived inventory to measure social fears and anxiety: The Social Phobia and Anxiety Inventory. *Psychological Assessment, 1*, 35–40.

Turner, S. M., Beidel, D. C., & Jacob, R. G. (1994). Social phobia: A comparison of behavior therapy and atenolol. *Journal of Consulting and Clinical Psychology, 62*, 350–358.

Turner, S. M., Beidel, D. C., Long, P. J., Turner, M. W., & Townsley, R. M. (1993). A composite measure to determine the functional status of treated social phobics: The Social Phobia Endstate Functioning Index. *Behavior Therapy, 24*, 265–275.

Turner, S. M., Beidel, D. C., & Stanley, M. A. (1992). Are obsessional thoughts and worry different cognitive phenomena? *Clinical Psychology Review, 12*, 257–270.

Turner, S. M., Stanley, M. A., Beidel, D. C., & Bond, L. (1989). The Social Phobia and Anxiety Inventory: Construct validity. *Journal of Psychopathology and Behavioral Assessment, 11*, 221–234.

van Balkom, A., van Oppen, P., Vermeulen, A., van Dyck, R., Nanta, M., & Vost, H. (1994). A meta-analysis on the treatment of obsessive-compulsive disorder: A comparison of antidepressants, behavior and cognitive therapy. *Clinical Psychology Review, 14*, 359–381.

van der Kolk, B. A. (1996). Trauma and memory. In B. A. van der Kolk, A. C. McFarlane, & L. Weisaeth (Eds.), *Traumatic stress: The effects of overwhelming experience on mind, body, and society* (pp. 279–302). New York: Guilford.

Van Etten, M. L., & Taylor, S. (In press). Comparative efficacy of treatments for posttraumatic stress disorder: A meta-analysis. *Clinical Psychology and Psychotherapy.*

Van Noppen, B., Steketee, G., McCorkle, B. H., & Pato, M. (1996). Group and multi-family behavioral treatment for obsessive compulsive disorder: A pilot study. Unpublished study.

van Oppen, P., deHaan, E., van Balkom, A. J. L. M., Spinhoven, P., Hoogduin, K., & van Dyck, R. (1995). Cognitive therapy and exposure in vivo in the treatment of obsessive compulsive disorder. *Behaviour Research and Therapy, 33,* 379–390.

Versiani, M., Nardi, A. E., Mundim, F. D., Alves, A. B., Liebowitz, M. R., & Amrein, R. (1992). Pharmacotherapy of social phobia: A controlled study with moclobemide and phenelzine. *British Journal of Psychiatry, 161,* 353–360.

Watson, D., Clark, L. A., & Carey, G. (1988). Positive and negative affectivity and their relation to anxiety and depressive disorders. *Journal of Abnormal Psychology, 97,* 346–353.

Weissman, M. M. (1985). The epidemiology of anxiety disorders: Rates, risks, and familial patterns. In H. Tuma & J. Maser (Eds.), *Anxiety and anxiety disorders* (pp. 275–296). Hillsdale, NJ: Lawrence Erlbaum.

Weissman, M. M., Bland, R. C., Canino, G. J., Greenwald, S., Hwu, H.-G., Lee, C. K., Newman, S. C., Oakley-Browne, M. A., Rubio-Stipec, M., Wickramaratne, P. J., Wittchen, H.-U., & Yeh, E.-K. (1994). The cross national epidemiology of obsessive compulsive disorder: The Cross National Collaborative Group. *Journal of Clinical Psychiatry, 55*(March Suppl.), 5–10.

Wells, A., Clark, D. M., Salkovskis, P., Ludgate, J., Hackmann, A., & Gelder, M. G. (1995). Social phobia: The role of in-situation safety behaviors in maintaining anxiety and negative beliefs. *Behavior Therapy, 26,* 153–161.

Wheeler, E., White, P., & Reed, E. (1950). Neurocirculatory asthenia (anxiety neurosis, effort, syndrome, neurasthenia): A twenty-year follow-up study of one hundred and seventy-three patients. *Journal of the American Medical Association, 142,* 878–888.

Whitehead, W. E., Robinson, A., Blackwell, B., & Stutz, R. M. (1978). Flooding treatment of phobias: Does chronic diazepam increase effectiveness? *Journal of Behaviour Therapy and Experimental Psychiatry, 9,* 219–255.

Whittal, M. L., & Goetsch, V. L. (1997). The impact of panic expectancy and social demand on agoraphobic avoidance. *Behaviour Research and Therapy, 35,* 813–821.

Wilhelm, F. H., & Roth, W. T. (1997). Acute and delayed effects of alprazolam on flight phobics during exposure. *Behaviour Research and Therapy, 35,* 831–841.

Wilks, C. G. (1993). Treatment of a dental phobic with pronounced aversion to rubber gloves by swallowing relaxation in two appointments. *British Dental Journal, 175,* 88–89.

Williams, S. L., Turner, S. M., & Peer, D. F. (1985). Guided mastery and performance desensitization treatments for severe acrophobia. *Journal of Consulting and Clinical Psychology, 53,* 237–247.

Wilson, G. T. (1996). Manual-based treatments: The clinical application of research findings. *Behaviour Research and Therapy, 34,* 295–314.

Winje, D. (1996). Long-term outcome of trauma in adults: The psychological impact of a fatal bus accident. *Journal of Consulting and Clinical Psychology, 64*(5), 1037–1043.

Winton, E. C., Clark, D. M., & Edelmann, R. J. (1995). Social anxiety, fear of negative evaluation, and detection of emotion in others. *Behaviour Research and Therapy, 33,* 193–196.

Witvliet, C. V. (1997). Traumatic intrusive imagery as an emotional memory phenomenon: A review of research and explanatory information processing theories. *Clinical Psychology Review, 17,* 509–536.

Wlazlo, Z., Schroeder-Hartwig, K., Hand, I., Kaiser, G., & Munchau, N. (1990). Exposure in vivo vs. social skills training for social phobia: Long-term outcome and differential effects. *Behaviour Research and Therapy, 28,* 181–193.

Wolfe, B. E., & Maser, J. E. (Eds.). (1994). *Treatment of panic disorder: A consensus statement.* Washington, DC: American Psychiatric Association.

Wolpe, J. (1958). *Psychotherapy by reciprocal inhibition.* Stanford, CA: Stanford University Press.

Wolpe, J., & Lazarus, A. A. (1966). *Behavior Therapy Techniques.* New York: Pergamon Press.

Woody, S. R. (1996). Effects of focus of attention on social phobics' anxiety and social performance. *Journal of Abnormal Psychology, 105,* 61–69.

Woody, S. R., & Chambless, D. L. (1989, April). *Social and personality factors predicting sex differences in fearful behavior.* Paper presented at the annual meeting of the Eastern Psychological Association, Boston, MA.

Woody, S. R., & Sanderson, W. C. (1998). Manuals for empirically supported treatments: 1998 update. *The Clinical Psychologist, 51*(1), 17–21.

Woody, S. R., Steketee, G., & Chambless, D. L. (1994). Reliability and validity of the Yale-Brown obsessive-compulsive scale. *Behaviour Research and Therapy, 33,* 597–605.

World Health Organization (1992). *The ICD-10 classification of mental and behavioral disorders: Clinical descriptions and diagnostic guidelines.* Geneva, Switzerland: World Health Organization.

World Health Organization. (1992). *International statistical classification of diseases and related health problems (ICD-10).* Geneva: Author.

Yates, B. T. (1980). *Improving effectiveness and reducing costs in mental health.* Springfield, IL: Charles C. Thomas.

Zinbarg, R. E., & Barlow, D. H. (1996). Structure of anxiety and the anxiety disorders: A hierarchical model. *Journal of Abnormal Psychology, 105,* 181–193.

Zitrin, C. M., Klein, D. F., Woerner, M. G., & Ross, D. C. (1983). Treatment of phobias: I. Comparison of imipramine hydrochloride and placebo. *Archives of General Psychiatry, 40,* 125–138.

Index